Wireless Networks

Series Editor

Xuemin Sherman Shen, University of Waterloo, Waterloo, ON, Canada

The purpose of Springer's Wireless Networks book series is to establish the state of the art and set the course for future research and development in wireless communication networks. The scope of this series includes not only all aspects of wireless networks (including cellular networks, WiFi, sensor networks, and vehicular networks), but related areas such as cloud computing and big data. The series serves as a central source of references for wireless networks research and development. It aims to publish thorough and cohesive overviews on specific topics in wireless networks, as well as works that are larger in scope than survey articles and that contain more detailed background information. The series also provides coverage of advanced and timely topics worthy of monographs, contributed volumes, textbooks and handbooks.

Chi Lin • Yu Sun • Wei Yang

Wireless Rechargeable Sensor Networks for Internet of Things

Theories and Technical Paradigms

Springer

Chi Lin
School of Software Technology
Dalian University of Technology
Dalian, Liaoning, China

Yu Sun
School of Software Technology
Dalian University of Technology
Dalian, Liaoning, China

Wei Yang
School of Software Technology
Dalian University of Technology
Dalian, Liaoning, China

ISSN 2366-1186 ISSN 2366-1445 (electronic)
Wireless Networks
ISBN 978-981-97-9542-0 ISBN 978-981-97-9543-7 (eBook)
https://doi.org/10.1007/978-981-97-9543-7

This Springer imprint is published by the registered company Springer Nature Singapore Pte Ltd.
The registered company address is: 152 Beach Road, #21-01/04 Gateway East, Singapore 189721, Singapore

To my beloved wife Mingming Yu
and daughters Xinran and Xintong.

Preface

In the era of rapid technological evolution, the emergence of Wireless Rechargeable Sensor Networks (WRSNs) marks a pivotal advancement in the realm of the Internet of Things (IoT). These networks, integral to a wide array of applications from smart home automation to industrial monitoring, and environmental conservation, represent a confluence of innovation and practicality. "Wireless Rechargeable Sensor Networks for Internet of Things" is a book conceived to address the critical challenges of energy management in these networks, particularly focusing on scenarios demanding extensive deployment and sustained operation.

This book commences with foundational principles of Wireless Sensor Networks (WSNs) and Wireless Power Transfer (WPT) technologies, shedding light on their application in vital areas such as smart homes, healthcare, industrial setups, and environmental surveillance. By delving into the technical specifics and real-world challenges of these applications, the book elucidates the significant role of WPT in propelling the growth of IoT.

Beyond discussing specific applications of wireless charging, the book ventures into advanced topics such as collaborative scheduling, priority-based scheduling, and scheduling optimization methodologies. These sections, encompassing temporal-spatial collaborative charging to three-dimensional dynamic collaborative scheduling, offer readers a comprehensive insight into the technical intricacies and practical implementations of these strategies.

Moreover, the book explores various approaches to enhance the performance of WRSNs, covering aspects such as security, promptness, robustness, and precision. These are critical elements ensuring the reliability and efficacy of network operations.

In its concluding parts, the book presents novel theories and methods in WRSNs, bringing to light innovative approaches such as integrating WPT with Fresnel zones and diffraction models, and balancing the trade-offs between charging and event monitoring. These discussions not only represent the cutting edge of current research but also serve as a wellspring of inspiration for future explorations.

"Wireless Rechargeable Sensor Networks for Internet of Things" is crafted for researchers, engineers, and technology enthusiasts. Through its clear explanations and detailed analyses of real-world case studies, the book aims to provide a comprehensive perspective on understanding and applying WPT technologies to drive innovation in IoT.

As technology continues to advance and innovate, WRSNs will undoubtedly play an increasingly significant role in the journey toward intelligent, automated, and sustainable development. We look forward to witnessing more exciting breakthroughs and applications of wireless power transfer technologies in the near future.

Dalian, China
March 2024

Chi Lin

Contents

Part I
Foundations of Wireless Sensor Networks

Chapter 1
Brief Introduction to Wireless Sensor Networks

1.1 Overview of Wireless Sensor Networks

1.1.1 Definition and Characteristics

In today's rapidly evolving IoT era, Wireless Sensor Networks (WSNs) play an indispensable role [1].WSNs are networked systems of spatially distributed autonomous sensors that are primarily used to monitor and record physical conditions in the environment, such as temperature, sound, and vibration. These networks not only sense the environment, but also process and transmit the collected data to provide real-time information for decision-making.

The design concept of WSNs highlights several key characteristics. First, they are remarkably self-organizing, meaning that sensor nodes are able to establish and maintain network connections automatically without human intervention [2]. Second, the versatility of WSNs allows each node to be not only a tool for data collection, but also for data processing and partial decision making [3]. In addition, dynamic network topology is another feature of WSNs, where the network structure can be flexibly adjusted according to environmental changes or node failures.

Designing an effective WSN system requires consideration of several aspects. The most important of them is energy efficiency, since most sensor nodes rely on limited battery power [4]. Improving energy efficiency not only extends the lifetime of the network, but also reduces maintenance costs. At the same time, the reliability and robustness of the WSN is crucial to ensure that the network can operate stably under various environmental conditions. Finally, considering the needs of different application scenarios, WSNs must be designed with good scalability and be able to support flexible expansion from small to large scale.

Although WSNs bring many benefits, they also face a series of challenges during their development. For example, data transmission and processing is a major technical challenge that requires effective management of large amounts of data and ensuring timely data transmission. In addition, the security of the network cannot

C. Lin et al., *Wireless Rechargeable Sensor Networks for Internet of Things*,
Wireless Networks, https://doi.org/10.1007/978-981-97-9543-7_1

be ignored, and protecting the network from external attacks and data leakage is an important consideration in the design of WSNs [5]. Finally, WSNs need to be seamlessly integrated with other networks and technologies, such as a wider range of IoT devices, to enable a wider range of applications [6].

In conclusion, wireless sensor networks, as a key technology for connecting the physical and digital worlds, have a promising future in IoT. From smart homes to environmental monitoring to health monitoring [7, 8], the flexibility and efficiency of WSNs show great potential in a wide range of fields. With the continuous advancement of technology, the future WSN will be more intelligent, efficient and secure, bringing more innovation and convenience to our lives.

1.1.2 Applications and Use Cases

Wireless Sensor Networks (WSNs) have become a ubiquitous component of the modern technology ecosystem with a wide range of applications and far-reaching impact. In this subsection, we present several use cases of WSNs in different domains that not only demonstrate the diversity of WSN technologies, but also highlight their great potential in solving real-world problems. Figure 1.1 illustrates the WSN application scenario.

The application of WSNs in the field of environmental monitoring is particularly important [9]. Sensor networks can be deployed in forests, rivers or urban environments to monitor environmental parameters such as air quality, water quality, temperature changes, etc. in real time. Such monitoring is particularly important for early warning systems, such as flood or forest fire warnings, and can help relevant authorities respond in a timely manner to minimize potential damage.

WSNs are also increasingly used in smart homes and building automation [7]. By deploying sensors in the home environment, intelligent monitoring of temperature, humidity, lighting and security can be realized. This not only improves living comfort, but also contributes to energy savings, e.g. by intelligently regulating heating and air conditioning systems to reduce energy consumption.

In health monitoring, WSNs offer new possibilities for telemedicine and patient monitoring [10]. Sensors can be used to monitor a patient's heart rate, blood pressure, and other vital signs, and real-time data is transmitted to medical professionals over a wireless network, enabling them to keep abreast of the patient's health status. This technology is particularly suitable for long-term health management of the elderly and chronically ill patients.

In addition, WSNs play an important role in industrial applications. In the context of smart manufacturing and Industry 4.0, sensor networks are used to monitor the performance of machines on production lines and to predict maintenance needs, thereby reducing downtime and increasing productivity [11]. Through real-time data analysis, factory managers are able to monitor and optimize production processes more effectively.

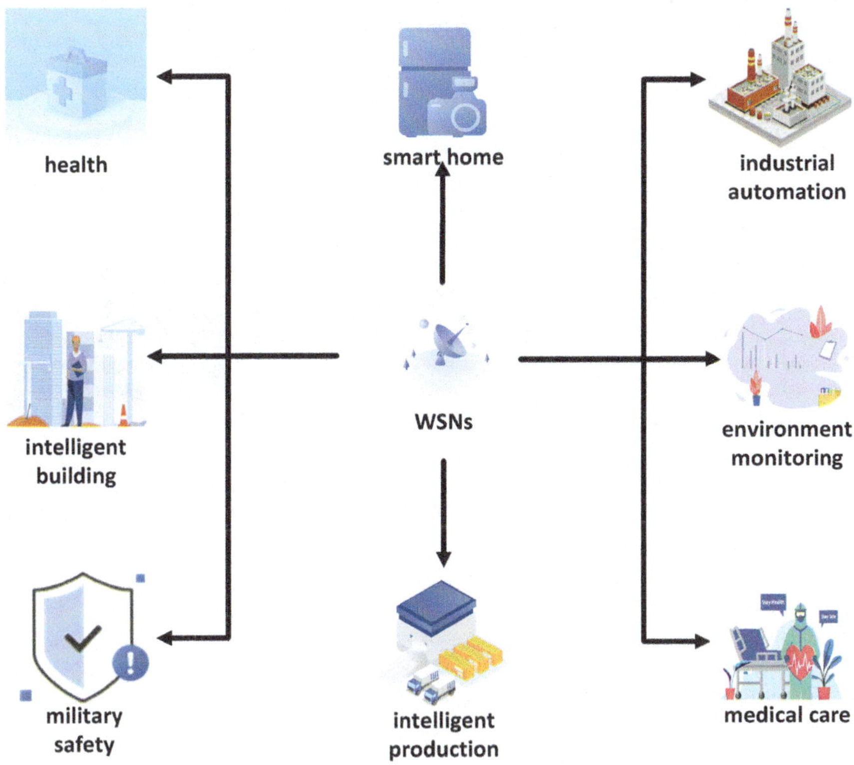

Fig. 1.1 WSNs application scenarios

WSNs play a key role in the construction of smart cities. Sensor networks can be used to monitor traffic flow, public safety, and the condition of city infrastructure, providing data support for city management and enabling more efficient and sustainable city operations.

1.1.3 Current Technologies and Trends

In this subsection, we explore the current technological developments and trends in wireless sensor networks (WSNs), which not only demonstrate the dynamics of innovations in the field of WSNs, but also foreshadow the future direction of development. Figure 1.2 illustrates the current technologies and future trends in wireless sensor networks.

Currently, WSN technology is undergoing rapid development and change. One of the notable advances is the rise of low-power wireless communication technologies. For example, low-power Bluetooth Low Energy (BLE) and low-power wide-area

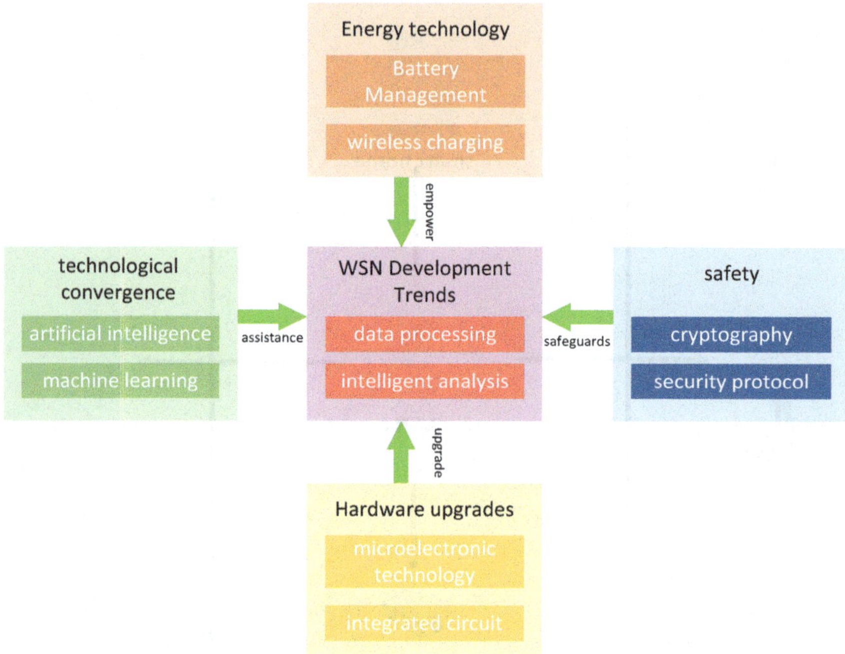

Fig. 1.2 Current technologies and future trends

network (LPWAN) technologies, such as LoRaWAN and NB-IoT, enable WSNs to communicate over long distances with very low energy consumption. This is particularly important for sensor networks that are deployed in environments that are difficult to access or require long-term operation.

Another area of interest is energy harvesting technologies such as photovoltaic cells, thermoelectric power generation and vibration energy harvesting. These technologies enable sensor nodes to be self-sustaining using ambient energy sources, significantly extending the runtime of WSNs and reducing reliance on batteries.

On the hardware side, as microelectronics advances, sensor nodes are becoming smaller and smaller while maintaining or improving their performance and energy efficiency. The trend toward miniaturization and integration not only reduces the cost of WSN systems, but also opens the door for their application in more fields.

In addition, the convergence of Artificial Intelligence (AI) and Machine Learning (ML) technologies is another important trend in the WSN field. By integrating AI and ML algorithms at the node level, smarter data processing and analysis can be achieved, improving decision-making efficiency and accuracy. This is especially important for complex application scenarios such as environmental monitoring and health monitoring.

Security is also an important aspect of WSN technology development. With the continuous evolution of network attacks, how to ensure data security and network reliability has become a hot research topic. The development of encryption technology, security protocols and intrusion detection systems are strengthening the security of WSN.

Finally, standardization and interoperability of WSNs have also received widespread attention. Standardization not only helps ensure compatibility among different manufacturers and technologies, but is also key to driving wider adoption of WSNs. For example, standards such as IEEE 802.15.4 and ZigBee [12] have been widely used in smart home and industrial automation.

In summary, current technologies and trends in the field of wireless sensor networks indicate that the field is rapidly evolving toward greater efficiency, intelligence, and security. With the continuous progress and maturity of the technology, we can expect that WSN will play a greater role in more fields in the future and make more far-reaching contributions to the development of the Internet of Things era.

1.2 Network Architecture and Design

1.2.1 Components of a Wireless Sensor Network

Wireless sensor network is mainly composed of four major parts, including nodes, sensor networks and users and base stations of these four parts. Among them, the nodes are generally covered by nodes in a certain way in a certain range, and the whole range can meet the monitoring range according to certain requirements; the sensing network is the most important part, which collects all the node information through a fixed channel, and then carries out a certain analysis and calculation of these node information, sums up the analysed results to a base station, and finally transmits them to the designated user end, thus realising the requirements of wireless sensing. Figure 1.3 illustrates the WSNs composition structure.

In a Wireless Sensor Network (WSN), the four major components—nodes, sensor networks, base stations, and users—work together to enable wireless sensing and data transmission. Let's delve into the roles of each component:

Nodes In a Wireless Sensor Network (WSN), nodes act as fundamental and crucial elements, serving as sensors and data-transmitting units. These nodes are equipped with several key components: a Data Acquisition Unit, responsible for collecting environmental data such as temperature, humidity, and light intensity; a Data Transmission Unit, handling wireless communication between nodes, enabling them to share collected data and receive data from other nodes; a Data Processing Unit, managing tasks like data routing, local analysis, and network management, and it may also take care of localization functions; and an Energy Supply Unit, providing power to the node, often using micro-batteries, to minimize the node's size and energy consumption. Figure 1.4 illustrates the sensor network node composition structure.

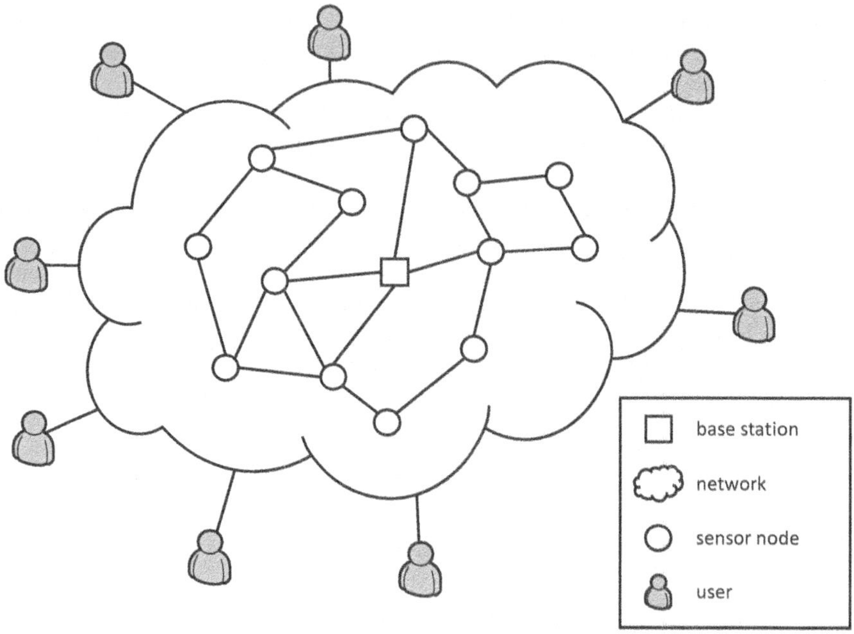

Fig. 1.3 WSNs component architecture

Fig. 1.4 Sensor network node composition

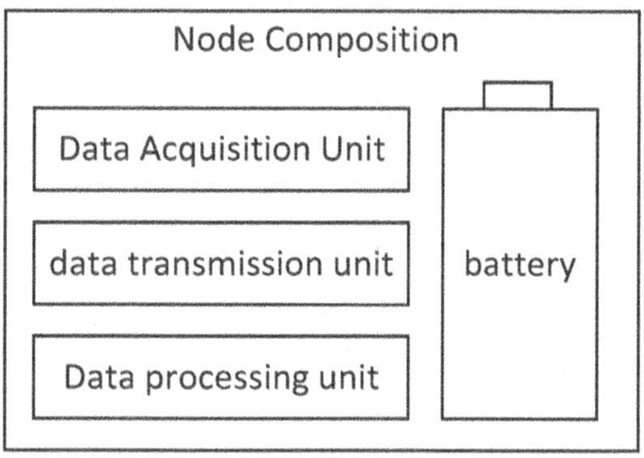

Sensor Networks Sensor networks serve as a crucial intermediary layer between nodes and users, primarily responsible for collecting, processing, and aggregating data from nodes. Their functions include collecting data from individual nodes via a fixed communication channel, which typically includes sensor readings and other relevant information. Additionally, these networks analyze and process the collected data to extract insights, identify patterns, or perform specific calculations. They also aggregate the analyzed results from multiple nodes, which helps reduce redundancy and enhance data efficiency. Finally, the aggregated data is transmitted to a central base station for further processing and distribution.

Base Stations Base stations function as the central hubs in Wireless Sensor Networks (WSN), playing several vital roles that include collecting data from sensor networks and nodes, facilitating communication with users, and overseeing the overall network operation. These roles encompass data reception from sensor networks and nodes, further processing and analyzing the received data using advanced algorithms and filtering techniques, storing historical data for future reference and analysis, transmitting the processed data to designated user endpoints, and managing network operations such as node coordination and troubleshooting.

Users In the ecosystem of Wireless Sensor Networks (WSN), users are central, engaging with the network to harness sensor data for a range of specific applications. They serve various critical functions: accessing collected and processed data to support activities such as monitoring, decision-making, or operational control. These users, be they humans or automated systems, rely on the insights provided by the WSN for informed decision-making. A practical example is in agriculture, where farmers utilize data from WSNs to optimize irrigation schedules. Beyond mere data consumption, users also play a pivotal role in providing feedback and exerting control over the WSN, adjusting its operations or managing specific devices and processes based on the sensor data they receive.

1.2.2 Network Architecture and Design

The architecture and design of WSNs are key to their effective operation [13]. In this subsection, we will take an in-depth look at the network architecture of WSNs, including their different design principles, network topologies, and key design considerations. This understanding is essential for the development and deployment of efficient and reliable wireless sensor networks. Figure 1.5 illustrates the idea of network architecture and design in re-WSNs.

The network architecture of a WSN typically consists of multiple layers, including the physical layer, data link layer, network layer, transport layer, and application layer. Each layer has its specific function, e.g., the physical layer handles the transmission of radio signals, while the network layer manages the routing of data packets through the network. This layered architecture not only helps to standardize the development process, but also makes interoperability between different network components possible.

The network topology, i.e., the physical or logical arrangement of the nodes in the network, is a central aspect in WSN design. Common topologies include star, tree, and mesh topologies. In a star topology, all nodes communicate directly with a central node, which is a simple structure but may have a single point of failure problem. Figure 1.6 illustrates a star structure in WSNs. Tree topology improves the scalability of the network by layering the nodes. Figure 1.7 illustrates a tree structure in WSNs. Whereas mesh topology provides the highest flexibility and reliability, nodes can communicate directly with each other and data can be transmitted through

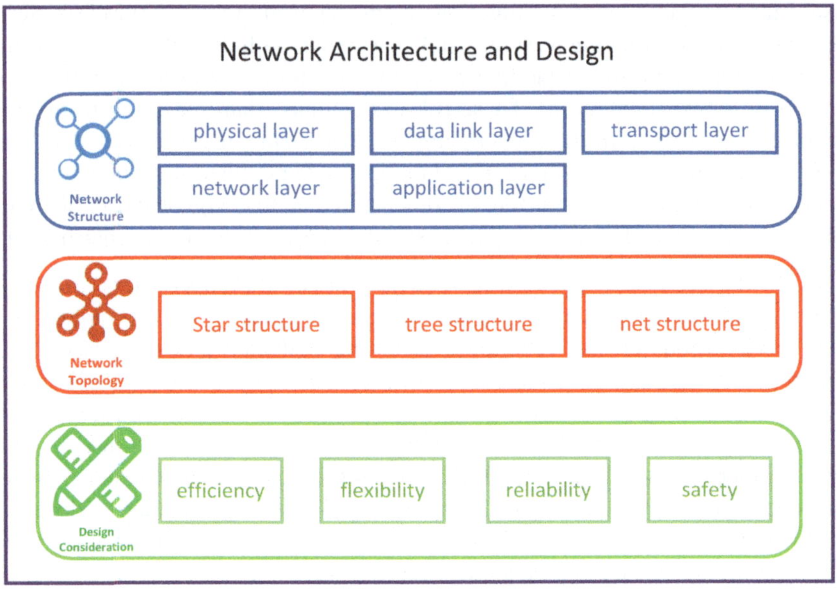

Fig. 1.5 Network architecture and design

Fig. 1.6 Star structure

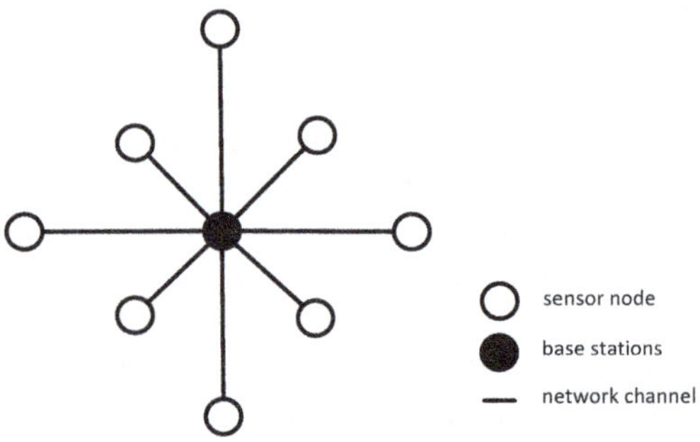

Fig. 1.7 Tree structure

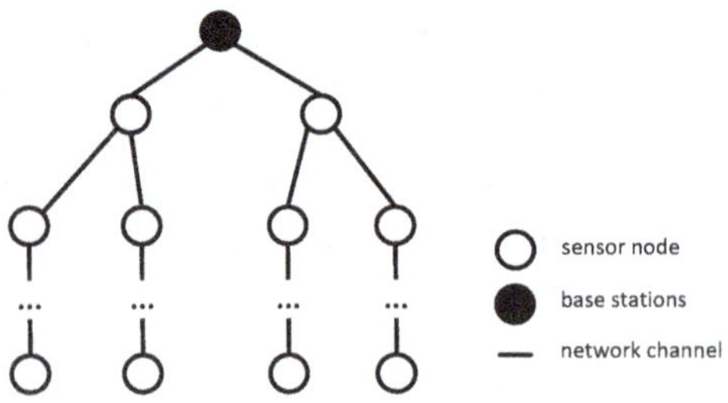

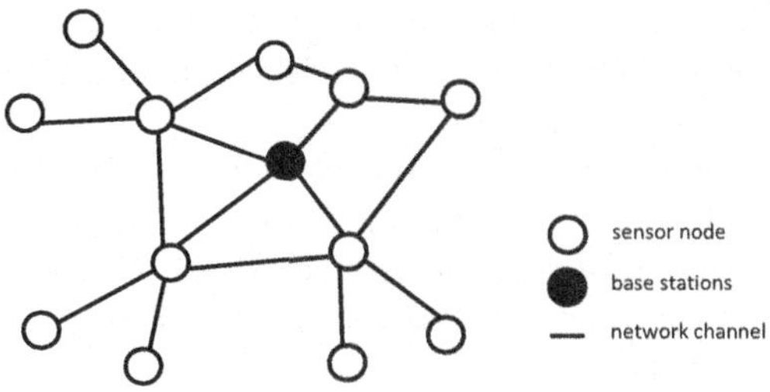

Fig. 1.8 Mesh structure

multiple paths, improving the fault tolerance of the network. Figure 1.8 illustrates a mesh structure in WSNs.

Several key factors need to be carefully considered when designing a WSN. The first is energy efficiency, which is one of the most important considerations in WSN design, as sensor nodes are usually subject to strict energy constraints. By optimizing communication protocols and data processing algorithms, energy consumption can be significantly reduced. Secondly, the reliability and robustness of the network is also crucial, especially under harsh environmental conditions or in critical applications. In addition, network scalability and flexibility are important considerations, especially in application scenarios with changing requirements.

Overall, network architecture and design for WSNs is a multifaceted consideration process that involves decisions at multiple technical and design levels. Through in-depth understanding and innovation of these key aspects, more efficient, reliable, and flexible wireless sensor networks can be designed to meet the growing demands of applications.

1.2.3 Communication Protocols

Communication protocols play a crucial role in the effective operation of Wireless Sensor Networks (WSNs). This section provides an in-depth look at the key communication protocols used in WSNs, how these protocols affect the performance of the network, and their practical use in different application scenarios. An in-depth understanding of communication protocols is essential for designing and deploying efficient and reliable WSNs.

Communication protocols for WSNs typically involve multiple network layers [14], each addressing a different aspect of network communication. At the data link layer, protocols such as IEEE 802.15.4 define the basic communication rules between nodes, how to efficiently handle data frames and error control. These protocols are designed to maintain low power consumption and high efficiency as energy management is a key consideration in WSNs.

At the network layer, protocols such as ZigBee and 6LoWPAN provide mechanisms for routing data between nodes [15, 16]. They support the self-organization and self-healing capabilities of the network, enabling the network to adapt to environmental changes and node failures. The design of these protocols focuses on optimizing data paths to reduce communication delays and increase the reliability of data transmission.

Transport layer protocols, such as TCP and UDP [17], although widely used in the traditional Internet, usually require special considerations in WSNs. For example, in order to reduce energy consumption and increase efficiency, WSNs may use lighter versions or alternative protocols that are better suited to their characteristics.

In addition to standard protocols, WSNs often use application-specific customized protocols. These protocols are designed according to the needs of a particular application; for example, a WSN used for precision agriculture may use a different protocol than a WSN used for environmental monitoring. Customized protocols allow for better optimization of network performance, such as reducing energy consumption by reducing packet size, or improving the efficiency of data transmission through specific data processing algorithms.

Security is also an important aspect of WSN communication protocol design. As network attacks become increasingly sophisticated, ensuring the security of data transmission becomes more and more important. This requires the integration of advanced encryption and authentication mechanisms in the protocol design to protect data from unauthorized access and tampering.

In summary, communication protocols for WSNs are a complex and critical component of network design. Not only do they need to be considered for energy efficiency and performance optimization, but they also need to meet the challenges of security and application-specific requirements. Through a deeper understanding and innovation of these protocols, wireless sensor networks can be built to be more efficient, reliable, and adaptable to changing application requirements.

1.2.4 Sensor Node Design

In WSNs, the design of sensor nodes is a key factor in determining the performance and efficiency of the network. This subsection explores the main elements that make up a sensor node, including hardware components, energy management strategies, and how environmental adaptability and sustainability can be considered in the design. An in-depth understanding of sensor nodes is essential for building WSNs that are efficient, reliable, and adaptable to changing environments.

Sensor nodes usually consist of several core components: sensor unit, processing unit, communication unit, and energy unit. The sensor unit is responsible for collecting environmental data such as temperature, humidity, or light intensity. The processing unit, usually a microcontroller, processes the collected data and executes the control logic of the node. The communication unit is responsible for exchanging data with other nodes or base stations in the network. The energy unit, on the other hand, provides the node with the necessary power, usually through batteries or energy harvesting technologies.

Energy management is a crucial consideration when designing sensor nodes. Since many WSN applications have nodes that are difficult to access or need to run for long periods of time, improving energy efficiency and employing energy harvesting techniques (e.g., solar, thermal, or vibration energy) becomes especially important. By optimizing algorithms and sleep patterns, the energy consumption of nodes can be significantly reduced.

In addition, sensor nodes need to be designed with environmental adaptability in mind. Nodes may need to operate stably in extreme temperatures, humidity, or other harsh environments. Therefore, the design needs to select suitable materials and protections to ensure the long-term reliability and stability of the nodes.

As IoT technology evolves, the demand for intelligence and versatility in sensor nodes increases. This includes the integration of more advanced sensing technologies, such as multiparameter sensors for detecting air quality or motion, and the use of more advanced data processing and machine learning algorithms that enable nodes to perform more sophisticated data analysis right at the source.

Security is also an important aspect of sensor node design. With the increase in cyber-attacks and data breaches, it is becoming increasingly important to ensure that data is secure and that nodes are tamper-proof. This may include integrating encryption and authentication mechanisms at both the hardware and software levels.

Overall, the design of sensor nodes is a complex and critical aspect of WSN development. It needs to consider not only energy efficiency and environmental adaptability, but also cope with security and increasing functionality requirements. By integrating and innovating these elements, sensor nodes can be designed to be smarter, more efficient, and more adaptable to different application scenarios.

1.3 Data Management in WSN

1.3.1 Data Collection Techniques

In WSNs, data collection is a critical step in obtaining valuable information. This subsection explores various data collection techniques in WSNs, including their working principles, advantages and disadvantages, and applicable scenarios. Understanding these different data collection techniques is crucial for designing efficient and effective wireless sensor networks.

First, time-driven data collection techniques are a common approach in which sensors automatically collect data at predetermined time intervals. This approach is simple and efficient for applications that require continuous monitoring, such as environmental monitoring or weather stations. However, it can lead to a waste of resources by collecting large amounts of useless data when no significant events occur.

Event-driven data collection techniques, on the other hand, are based on specific events or conditions that trigger the collection of data. For example, the sensor starts data collection and transmission only when a specific environmental change (e.g., temperature exceeding a preset threshold) is detected. This approach is superior in terms of energy efficiency, but may miss some unexpected events if the triggering conditions are not set properly.

Query-driven data collection techniques involve collecting data on demand. In this method, the central control system or the user sends a query request and the sensor then responds and provides the relevant data. This technique is suitable for applications that require on-demand data acquisition, such as user requests in smart home systems. It has the advantage that the data collection is closely related to the actual needs, but may require complex management and control mechanisms.

Adaptive data collection techniques combine the advantages of the above approaches to optimize performance and efficiency by dynamically adjusting data collection strategies. For example, sensors can adjust their data collection frequency based on environmental conditions, network status, or energy availability. This approach provides theoretically optimal efficiency, but is more complex to implement and requires advanced algorithms and strategies [18, 19].

Finally, data fusion and aggregation techniques also play an important role in data collection. By preliminary processing and fusion of data at the sensor nodes [20], the amount of data transmitted can be reduced and the overall efficiency of the network can be improved.

In conclusion, there are various data collection techniques in wireless sensor networks, each of which has its applicable scenarios and specific advantages and disadvantages. Choosing the right data collection technique is crucial for building an efficient and effective wireless sensor network. As technology develops, these data collection methods will continue to evolve to better accommodate changing application requirements.

1.3.2 Data Processing and Aggregation

Data processing and aggregation are key operations in WSNs, and they play a crucial role in improving the efficiency and scalability of the network [21]. This subsection provides an in-depth look at data processing and aggregation strategies in WSNs, including how they reduce the network burden, improve the efficiency of data transmission, and how they are implemented in different application scenarios. Understanding these concepts is essential for designing and optimizing efficient WSNs.

Data processing and aggregation play a central role in WSNs. After raw data is collected by sensor nodes, data processing involves analyzing and transforming this data for more efficient transmission and use. This may include denoising, data compression, or extracting specific features. Effective data processing reduces the amount of data to be transmitted, thereby reducing energy consumption and increasing the overall efficiency of the network.

Data aggregation is a key part of data processing in WSNs, which involves summarizing data from multiple nodes into a compressed data set. Through data aggregation, the number of data transfers in the network can be reduced, thereby reducing energy consumption and improving the scalability of the network. In practice, data aggregation is usually performed at intermediate nodes of the network or before the data reaches the base station.

The choice of data aggregation strategy depends on the requirements of a particular application. For example, in an environmental monitoring application, temperature and humidity readings from multiple sensors may be aggregated to provide a comprehensive environmental snapshot of an area. In a health monitoring application, the aggregation strategy may be more focused on anomaly detection, such as identifying potential health problems from data from multiple physiological sensors.

Data accuracy and integrity must also be considered when implementing data processing and aggregation. Data loss and errors during the aggregation process must be carefully managed to ensure that the final data still accurately reflects the true state of the monitored environment. In addition, privacy and security are important considerations, especially when dealing with sensitive information.

In summary, data processing and aggregation are essential operations in WSNs, and they are critical to maintaining the efficiency and reliability of the network. With effective data processing and aggregation strategies, network performance can be optimized and energy consumption can be reduced while maintaining data accuracy and availability. As WSN technology evolves, these strategies will continue to evolve to support a variety of applications.

1.3.3 Data Storage and Retrieval

Data storage and retrieval are key components in the application of WSNs, and they are essential to ensure data accessibility and availability. This subsection will share several strategies for data storage and retrieval in WSNs, including how to store large amounts of data efficiently and how to retrieve the required information quickly and accurately. A thorough understanding of these concepts is essential for designing efficient and reliable WSNs.

In WSNs, data storage usually faces two major challenges: space constraints and energy constraints [22]. Sensor nodes usually have limited storage space and battery power due to their miniaturized design. Therefore, data storage strategies need to be highly effective to maximize storage space and save energy. This includes the use of data compression techniques to reduce the required storage space, and intelligent data management to ensure that only critical and relevant data is stored.

Data retrieval is another key consideration. In WSNs, data may need to be retrieved from a large number of decentralized nodes. Therefore, effective retrieval mechanisms are required to ensure that the required information can be quickly retrieved from the network. This may involve the creation of an indexing system and the use of efficient query processing algorithms.

In some applications, such as environmental monitoring or health monitoring, real-time data access is critical. This requires a data storage system that is capable of not only storing historical data, but also processing and providing real-time data quickly. For this purpose, it may be necessary to implement hierarchical storage of data, where real-time and historical data are stored and managed separately.

Privacy and security are also important aspects in data storage and retrieval [23]. Ensuring data security and user privacy is crucial when handling sensitive data. This requires the integration of encryption and access control mechanisms in the system design to protect the data from unauthorized access and tampering.

In conclusion, data storage and retrieval play a key role in wireless sensor networks. With effective storage and retrieval strategies, network performance can be optimized, energy consumption can be reduced, and data security and availability can be ensured. As technology advances and application requirements grow, these strategies will continue to evolve to support a wider range of WSN applications.

1.4 Energy Management in WSNs

1.4.1 Energy Harvesting Techniques

Energy management is a key challenge in the design and operation of WSNs. Traditional battery-powered methods, although common, suffer from limited endurance and high cost of battery replacement. This subsection explores energy harvesting techniques in WSNs, i.e., how energy can be harvested from the environment to power or extend battery life [24]. An understanding of these energy harvesting technologies is essential for building sustainable and long term operating WSNs. Figure 1.9 illustrates several ways of energy harvesting in wireless sensor networks.

Energy Harvesting technologies enable WSN nodes to extract energy from their surroundings for self-sufficient energy supply [25]. These technologies include, but are not limited to, solar energy harvesting, wind energy harvesting, vibration energy harvesting, and thermal energy harvesting.

Solar energy harvesting is one of the most common energy harvesting methods [26]. By installing small solar panels on sensor nodes, sunlight can be utilized to convert to electrical energy. This method is particularly suitable for outdoor applications such as environmental monitoring or agricultural monitoring.

Wind energy harvesting [27], although not as common as solar energy harvesting, is also an effective option in certain specific environments. With a micro wind turbine, wind energy can be converted into electrical energy to power sensor nodes.

Vibration energy harvesting utilizes mechanical vibrations in the environment and converts the vibration energy into electrical energy through piezoelectric materials or electromagnetic sensors [28]. This technique is suitable for industrial

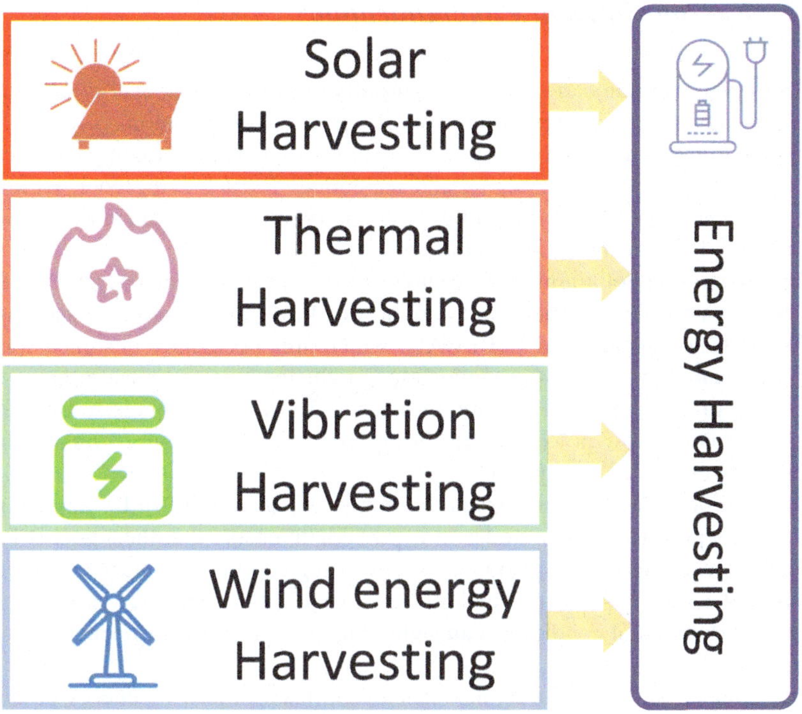

Fig. 1.9 Energy harvesting

and transportation environments where mechanical vibrations are a common source of energy.

Thermal energy harvesting generates electrical energy by utilizing the thermo-electric effect created by temperature differences [29]. This method is suitable for environments where there are temperature differences, such as heat emissions from industrial processes.

Each energy harvesting technology has its own applicable environment and limitations. When designing a WSN system, selecting the appropriate energy harvesting method needs to consider the deployment environment and energy demand of the sensor nodes. In addition, energy harvesting technologies usually need to be used in conjunction with traditional battery technologies to ensure that the network remains operational when energy harvesting is insufficient.

In summary, energy harvesting technologies provide a sustainable energy solution for wireless sensor networks, helping to extend network uptime and reduce maintenance costs. As these technologies develop and mature, they are expected to play an increasingly important role in future WSN applications.

1.4.2 Energy-Efficient Communication

In WSNs, the communication process is usually one of the most energy-consuming activities. Therefore, achieving energy-efficient communication is crucial for extending the operational life of the network and reducing maintenance costs. This subsection explores strategies and techniques for achieving energy-efficient communication in WSNs, including protocol optimization, transmission power control, and data transmission scheduling.

Optimization of communication protocols is key to improving energy efficiency. This includes the development and adoption of low-power protocols, such as the IEEE 802.15.4 standard and LoRaWAN, which are specifically designed for low data rates and long range communication, reducing energy consumption. Also important is the sleep/wake scheduling mechanism in the protocols, which allows nodes to enter a low-power mode during periods of inactivity, thus reducing unnecessary energy consumption.

Transmission power control is another important strategy [30]. By adjusting the transmission power of sensor nodes, it is possible to ensure that the signal is strong enough to reach the receiving node without wasting additional energy. Dynamically adjusting the transmission power based on the distance between nodes and the current environmental conditions can significantly improve the efficiency of energy usage.

Data transmission scheduling also has a significant impact on energy efficiency [31]. By intelligently scheduling data transmissions, conflicts and retransmissions can be reduced, thereby reducing energy consumption. This may involve performing data transfers during periods of low network congestion or aggregating data to reduce the number of transmissions.

In addition, multi-hop routing techniques are an effective way to achieve energy efficient communication. In multi-hop routing, data packets are transmitted through multiple relay nodes to reach the destination rather than directly from the source node to the base station. This method saves energy by reducing the need for long distance transmission.

Finally, communication efficiency can be further improved by utilizing advanced data processing techniques such as data compression and selective transmission. By transmitting only necessary and relevant data, the overall amount of data transmitted and the corresponding energy consumption can be significantly reduced.

Overall, energy efficient communication is a key aspect in the design of wireless sensor networks. By adopting the above strategies and techniques, the energy consumption of WSNs can be significantly reduced and their sustainability and operational efficiency can be improved. These strategies will continue to evolve as technology develops to support the future development of WSNs.

1.4.3 Battery Management and Lifetime Extension

In the design and operation of Wireless Sensor Networks (WSNs), battery management and extension of network lifetime are critical. Since sensor nodes usually rely on battery power, effective management of battery resources and extension of their lifespan are critical to ensure long-term stable operation of the network. This subsection explores battery management strategies and life extension techniques in WSNs, including energy-efficient designs, battery charging techniques, and preventive maintenance measures. An understanding of these strategies is critical to building efficient and sustainable WSNs.

First, energy-efficient design is the foundation of battery management [32]. This includes the use of low-power hardware components, such as microcontrollers and sensors, as well as optimizing software algorithms to reduce energy consumption for computation and communication. For example, the total energy consumption of a node can be significantly reduced by precisely controlling the activity cycles and sleep patterns of sensors.

Battery charging technologies, especially in applications with rechargeable batteries, are equally important. Using solar panels or other energy harvesting technologies to charge batteries not only extends their lifetime, but also reduces the frequency of battery replacement. In addition, intelligent charging strategies, such as adaptive charging based on current energy availability and network demand, can further optimize battery use.

Preventive maintenance measures are also critical to extending battery and network life [33]. This includes regular monitoring of battery status and performance, as well as measures to prevent over-discharging and charging. By monitoring the health of the battery in real time, potential problems can be identified and resolved in a timely manner, avoiding network outages caused by battery failure.

In addition, battery life extension involves optimization of data management and transmission strategies. By reducing unnecessary data transmission and adopting efficient data processing methods, the energy consumption of nodes can be reduced, thus extending battery life.

For certain WSN applications deployed over a long period of time, it may be necessary to consider more durable energy solutions such as long-life batteries or combined energy systems (combining battery and energy harvesting technologies) [34].

In summary, battery management and extended network lifetime are important aspects of WSN design. By implementing the above strategies and techniques, the energy efficiency and reliability of WSNs can be significantly improved, maintenance costs can be reduced, and long-term stable network operation can be ensured. As technology evolves, these strategies will continue to evolve to support a wider range of WSN applications.

References

1. C.S. Raghavendra, K.M. Sivalingam, T. Znati, *Wireless Sensor Networks* (Springer, Berlin, 2006)
2. B. Chen, K. Jamieson, H. Balakrishnan, R. Morris, Span: an energy-efficient coordination algorithm for topology maintenance in ad hoc wireless networks, in *Proceedings of the 7th Annual International Conference on Mobile Computing and Networking* (2001), pp. 85–96
3. F. Zhaom, L.J. Guibas, *Wireless Sensor Networks: An Information Processing Approach* (Morgan Kaufmann, Burlington, 2004)
4. T. Rault, A. Bouabdallah, Y. Challal, Energy efficiency in wireless sensor networks: a top-down survey. Comput. Netw. **67**, 104–122 (2014)
5. H. Lu, J. Li, M. Guizani, Secure and efficient data transmission for cluster-based wireless sensor networks. IEEE Trans. Parallel Distrib. Syst. **25**(3), 750–761 (2013)
6. T.M. Behera, S.K. Mohapatra, U.C. Samal, M.S. Khan, M. Daneshmand, A.H. Gandomi, Residual energy-based cluster-head selection in wsns for iot application. IEEE Internet Things J. **6**(3), 5132–5139 (2019)
7. H. Ghayvat, S. Mukhopadhyay, X. Gui, N. Suryadevara, Wsn-and iot-based smart homes and their extension to smart buildings. Sensors **15**(5), 10350–10379 (2015)
8. M. Abdulkarem, K. Samsudin, F.Z. Rokhani, M.F.A Rasid, Wireless sensor network for structural health monitoring: a contemporary review of technologies, challenges, and future direction. Struct. Health Monit. **19**(3), 693–735 (2020)
9. L.M. Oliveira, J.J. Rodrigues, Wireless sensor networks: a survey on environmental monitoring. J. Commun. **6**(2), 143–151 (2011)
10. A.B. Noel, A. Abdaoui, T. Elfouly, M.H. Ahmed, A. Badawy, M.S. Shehata, Structural health monitoring using wireless sensor networks: a comprehensive survey. IEEE Commun. Surv. Tutorials **19**(3), 1403–1423 (2017)
11. X. Li, D. Li, J. Wan, A.V. Vasilakos, C.-F. Lai, S. Wang, A review of industrial wireless networks in the context of industry 4.0. Wirel. Netw. **23**, 23–41 (2017)
12. S.C. Ergen, Zigbee/ieee 802.15. 4 summary. UC Berkeley **10**(17), 11 (2004)
13. H. Karl, A. Willig, *Protocols and Architectures for Wireless Sensor Networks* (John Wiley & Sons, Hoboken, 2007)
14. L.K. Ketshabetswe, A.M. Zungeru, M. Mangwala, J.M. Chuma, B. Sigweni, Communication protocols for wireless sensor networks: a survey and comparison. Heliyon **5**(5) (2019)
15. D. Gislason, *Zigbee Wireless Networking* (Newnes, Oxford, 2008)
16. G. Mulligan, The 6lowpan architecture, in *Proceedings of the 4th Workshop on Embedded Networked Sensors* (2007), pp. 78–82
17. B.A. Forouzan, *TCP/IP Protocol Suite* (McGraw-Hill Higher Education, New York, 2002)
18. V. Kumar, S. Jain, S. Tiwari, Energy efficient clustering algorithms in wireless sensor networks: a survey. Int. J. Comput. Sci. Issues (IJCSI) **8**(5), 259 (2011)
19. S. Jabbar, A.A. Minhas, M. Imran, S. Khalid, K. Saleem, Energy efficient strategy for throughput improvement in wireless sensor networks. Sensors **15**(2), 2473–2495 (2015)
20. D. Izadi, J.H. Abawajy, S. Ghanavati, T. Herawan, A data fusion method in wireless sensor networks. Sensors **15**(2), 2964–2979 (2015)
21. S. Randhawa, S. Jain, Data aggregation in wireless sensor networks: previous research, current status and future directions. Wirel. Personal Commun. **97**, 3355–3425 (2017)
22. A. Chamam, S. Pierre, On the planning of wireless sensor networks: energy-efficient clustering under the joint routing and coverage constraint. IEEE Trans. Mobile Comput. **8**(8), 1077–1086 (2009)
23. M. Al Ameen, J. Liu, K. Kwak, Security and privacy issues in wireless sensor networks for healthcare applications. J. Med. Syst. **36**, 93–101 (2012)
24. K.S. Adu-Manu, N. Adam, C. Tapparello, H. Ayatollahi, W. Heinzelman, Energy-harvesting wireless sensor networks (eh-wsns) a review. ACM Trans. Sensor Netw. (TOSN) **14**(2), 1–50 (2018)

25. F.K. Shaikh, S. Zeadally, Energy harvesting in wireless sensor networks: a comprehensive review. Renew. Sustain. Energy Rev. **55**, 1041–1054 (2016)
26. C. Wang, J. Li, Y. Yang, F. Ye, Combining solar energy harvesting with wireless charging for hybrid wireless sensor networks. IEEE Transa. Mobile Comput. **17**(3), 560–576 (2017)
27. A. Cammarano, C. Petrioli, D. Spenza, Pro-energy: a novel energy prediction model for solar and wind energy-harvesting wireless sensor networks, in *2012 IEEE 9th International Conference on Mobile Ad-Hoc and Sensor Systems (MASS 2012)* (IEEE, 2012), pp. 75–83
28. J. Baker, S. Roundy, P. Wright, Alternative geometries for increasing power density in vibration energy scavenging for wireless sensor networks, in *3rd International Energy Conversion Engineering Conference* (2005), p. 5617
29. Y.K. Tan, S.K. Panda, Energy harvesting from hybrid indoor ambient light and thermal energy sources for enhanced performance of wireless sensor nodes. IEEE Trans. Ind. Electron. **58**(9), 4424–4435 (2010)
30. S. He, J. Chen, F. Jiang, D.K. Yau, G. Xing, Y. Sun, Energy provisioning in wireless rechargeable sensor networks. IEEE Trans. Mobile Comput. **12**(10), 1931–1942 (2012)
31. Z. Lu, W.W. Li, M. Pan, Maximum lifetime scheduling for target coverage and data collection in wireless sensor networks. IEEE Trans. Veh. Technol. **64**(2), 714–727 (2014)
32. D.E. Tiliute, Battery management in wireless sensor networks. Elektronika ir elektrotechnika **76**(4), 9–12 (2007)
33. A.I. Vlasov, P.V. Grigoriev, A.I. Krivoshein, V.A. Shakhnov, S.S. Filin, V.S. Migalin, Smart management of technologies: predictive maintenance of industrial equipment using wireless sensor networks. Entrep. Sustain. Issues **6**(2), 489–502 (2018)
34. P. Nayak, A. Devulapalli, A fuzzy logic-based clustering algorithm for wsn to extend the network lifetime. IEEE Sensors J. **16**(1), 137–144 (2015)

Chapter 2
Brief Introduction to Wireless Power Transfer

2.1 Fundamentals of Wireless Power Transfer

2.1.1 Definition of Wireless Power Transmission

In the context of exploring wireless rechargeable sensor networks, it is crucial to understand the fundamentals of Wireless Power Transfer (WPT) [1]. This subsection provides an in-depth discussion of the underlying principles of Wireless Power Transfer, including its working mechanism, main types, and basic characteristics of the technology. This understanding provides a solid foundation for further exploration of WPT applications in wireless sensor networks.

Wireless power transfer is a technology that transmits energy wirelessly, allowing electricity to be transmitted across space without the use of traditional wire connections.The basic principles of WPT can be traced back to electromagnetic induction, one of the earliest modes of wireless power transfer, discovered by Michael Faraday in the nineteenth century [2].

In WPT, there are two main underlying transmission mechanisms: Inductive Coupling and Resonant Inductive Coupling [3, 4]. Inductive coupling relies on the interaction of the magnetic fields between two electromagnetic coils to transmit energy, and is suitable for shorter distance transmissions such as wireless charging pads and charging of some medical implantable devices. Resonant coupling, on the other hand, uses a transmitter and receiver of the same frequency to achieve more efficient energy transfer, and this method is suitable for a wider variety of applications as it can provide greater transmission distances within a certain range.

There are also far-field wireless power transmission techniques such as radio frequency (RF) energy harvesting [5]. This technique uses electromagnetic waves (e.g., radio waves or microwaves) to transmit energy, which can cover greater distances, but the transmission is relatively inefficient.RF energy harvesting is commonly used for applications with a wider range of power supply and lower energy requirements, such as certain types of remote sensors.

C. Lin et al., *Wireless Rechargeable Sensor Networks for Internet of Things*,
Wireless Networks, https://doi.org/10.1007/978-981-97-9543-7_2

Understanding the principles and characteristics of these wireless power transfer (WPT) technologies is essential for the design and implementation of wireless rechargeable sensor networks. By choosing the appropriate WPT technology, energy constraints in wireless sensor networks can be effectively addressed to achieve longer maintenance cycles and higher network stability.

In conclusion, wireless power transmission technologies bring new possibilities for wireless sensor networks, making energy supply more flexible and efficient. As these technologies continue to develop and mature, they are expected to play an increasingly important role in the design of future wireless sensor networks.

2.1.2 Principles of Wireless Power Transfer

There are three common methods of wireless energy transfer: Electromagnetic induction type, Magnetic Field Resonance and Radio Wave.

Electromagnetic Induction Type An alternating current of a certain frequency in the primary coil generates a certain current in the secondary coil through electromagnetic induction, thus transferring energy from the transmitting end to the receiving end. Electromagnetic induction is currently used in the most common charging solutions. In fact, there is not much mystery in the technical realisation of electromagnetic induction solutions, as China's homegrown BYD, which filed a patent application for a non-contact inductive charger as early as December 2005, uses electromagnetic induction technology.

Magnetic Field Resonance Consisting of an energy-transmitting device, and an energy-receiving device, when the two devices are tuned to the same frequency, or resonate at a specific frequency, they can exchange energy with each other, is a technology currently being researched, and a team of researchers led by Marin Soljacic, a professor of physics at the Massachusetts Institute of Technology (MIT), used the technology to light up a 60-watt bulb two metres away, and named it WiTricity. It was named WiTricity. the coil used in the experiment had a diameter of 50cm, which is not yet commercially available, and if the size of the coil were to be reduced, the received power would naturally fall.

Radio Wave This is a more mature technology, similar to the early use of ore radios, and consists of a microwave transmitter and microwave receiver, which captures radio wave energy bouncing back from the wall and maintains a stable DC voltage while adjusting with the load. All that is required is a transmitter mounted on a wall plug and a "mosquito" receiver that can be mounted on any low voltage product.

2.1.3 History and Evolution

Exploring the history and evolution of Wireless Power Transfer (WPT) is critical to understanding its application in modern technology, especially in wireless rechargeable sensor networks. In this subsection, the evolution of WPT technology is reviewed, from early theoretical explorations to the latest practical applications, revealing the continuous innovations and advances in this field. Figure 2.1 illustrates the evolution of WPT technology.

The concept of wireless power transfer can be traced back as far as the late nineteenth century, when scientist Nikola Tesla was a pioneer in this field. Through his experiments, Tesla demonstrated the possibilities of wireless power transmission [6], although at the time these ideas were considered too avant-garde. His construction of the Tesla coil, an early representation of wireless power

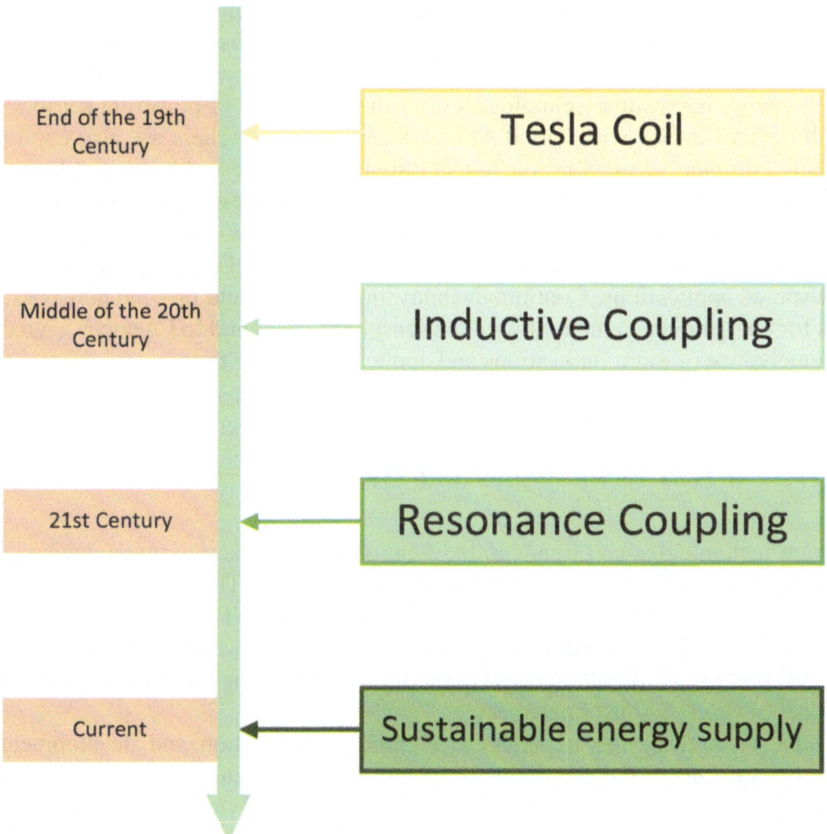

Fig. 2.1 WPT technology development

transmission technology, was capable of generating high voltage, high frequency currents, demonstrating the fundamentals of transmitting energy wirelessly.

In the mid-twentieth century, with the development of electromagnetic theory and the advancement of electronic technology, wireless power transmission technology began to make substantial progress. Particularly in inductive coupling technology, this period witnessed early applications of wireless charging technology, such as charging systems for electric toothbrushes and some medical implantable devices.

Into the twenty-first century, with the rise of smart devices and the Internet of Things (IoT), the demand for and interest in wireless power transmission increased significantly [7]. The focus of technology development shifted to improving transmission distance and efficiency, and resonant coupling technology became a research hotspot. During this period, wireless charging technology began to gain popularity in consumer electronics, such as wireless charging pads for smartphones and laptops.

Recently, the development of wireless power transmission technologies has become more diversified, including long-distance transmission solutions and attempts to integrate energy harvesting technologies [8]. For example, developments in RF energy harvesting technologies offer the possibility of powering sensors and small devices over a wider area. At the same time, researchers are also exploring ways to combine wireless power transmission technologies with renewable energy sources such as solar and wind to achieve more sustainable energy supply solutions.

In summary, wireless power transmission technology has undergone a long period of development and evolution from early theoretical explorations to modern, widespread applications. Continuous innovations in this field provide new possibilities for energy management of wireless sensor networks and IoT devices, signaling the emergence of more innovations and applications in the future.

2.1.4 Current Technologies and Trends

Current technologies and trends in the field of WPT are key to understanding and applying this technology in wireless sensor networks. This subsection explores the latest technological advances and key trends in WPT, including emerging technological solutions and their potential impact in real-world applications. These insights provide an important background for understanding the application of WPT in modern wireless sensor networks.

WPT technology has experienced significant innovation and development in recent years. One of the key trends is the move toward higher efficiency and longer transmission distances. For example, resonant coupling techniques have moved from laboratory testing to actual products that provide longer effective transmission distances than conventional inductive coupling techniques.

In addition, integrated and modular designs are becoming an important direction for WPT technologies. This design makes it easier to integrate wireless charging technology into a variety of products, from smart home devices to medical devices and even charging solutions for electric vehicles.

In terms of long-distance wireless power transmission, researchers are exploring technologies that use radio frequency (RF) waves, microwaves, and lasers as energy transmission mediums. While these technologies currently face efficiency and safety challenges, they offer the potential to wirelessly power a wider area.

Meanwhile, the combination of energy harvesting technologies and wireless power transmission is a hot trend at present. For example, by integrating solar panels and wireless charging technology, it is possible to achieve continuous power to remote sensors, which is particularly important in areas such as environmental monitoring and agricultural applications.

In addition, with the rapid development of the Internet of Things (IoT), wireless power transfer technology is increasingly being used in smart devices. This is not just limited to charging consumer electronics, but extends to solutions that provide continuous energy for a variety of sensors and devices.

Finally, security and standardization remain important aspects of wireless power transfer technology development [9]. As the technology becomes more widespread, the development of common safety standards and compatibility specifications becomes increasingly important.

In summary, current trends and developments in wireless power transmission technology bode well for a wide range of applications in this field. With the continuous progress of technology, wireless power transmission is expected to play a greater role in wireless sensor networks and IoT devices, bringing more convenience and innovation to our life and work.

2.2 Network Architecture and Design

2.2.1 System Components and Architecture

The components and architecture of a wireless power transfer (WPT) system are fundamental to its effective operation. In this subsection, we will take an in-depth look at the key components of a WPT system and its architecture, including the transmitter, receiver, control unit, etc., and how these components work together to achieve efficient energy transfer. Understanding these fundamental components and architectures is essential for designing and implementing an effective wireless charging solution. Figure 2.2 illustrates the WPT system composition structure.

A WPT system consists of three main basic components: the transmitter (or called a transmitter), the receiver, and the control unit. The transmitter is responsible for generating and transmitting electromagnetic waves, and it contains a power source, one or more transmitting coils, and associated electronic circuitry to control the emission of electromagnetic waves. The design and optimization of

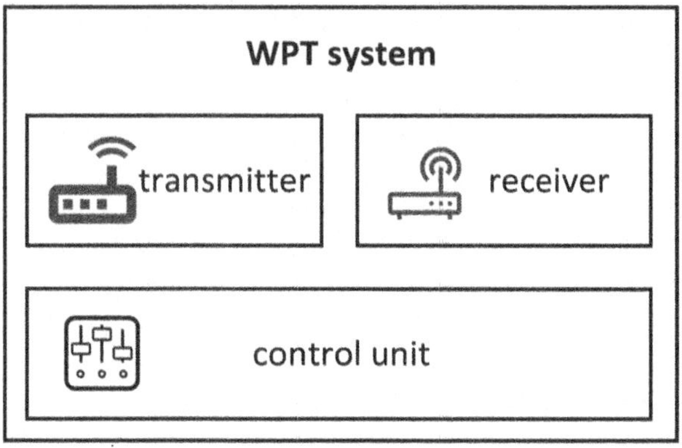

Fig. 2.2 2.2.1 WPT system components

the transmitter directly affects the energy transfer efficiency and the transmission distance of the system.

The role of the receiver is to capture energy from the emitted electromagnetic wave and convert it into electrical energy for charging the target device or battery [10]. It usually contains one or more receiver coils and electronic circuits to tune and optimize the reception and conversion of energy. The design of the receiver needs to balance efficiency, size and compatibility with the target device.

The control unit plays a central coordinating role in the WPT system. It not only controls the transmission and reception of power, but is also responsible for the overall management of the system, including power management, safety monitoring and communication functions. Advanced functions of the control unit may include adaptive adjustment of the transmitted power to cope with different environmental conditions and reception requirements.

In terms of architecture, WPT systems can be designed differently to accommodate various application requirements. For example, a point-to-point transmission architecture is suitable for single-receiver applications such as wireless charging of smartphones. The multipoint-to-multipoint architecture, on the other hand, is suitable for scenarios where multiple devices are charged at the same time, such as wireless charging stations in public places.

In addition, the architectural design of WPT systems needs to consider compatibility with existing technologies and devices, such as integration with smart home systems or industrial automation systems. This may involve standardized interfaces and communication protocols to ensure smooth interoperability between different devices and systems.

Overall, the components and architectures of a WPT system are the foundation for effective wireless power transmission. By optimizing [11] these components and architectures, the efficiency, flexibility and reliability of the system can be improved to meet the needs of various application scenarios. As technology advances, WPT systems will continue to evolve to support a wider range of applications.

2.2.2 *Efficiency and Safety Considerations*

Efficiency and safety are two critical considerations in the design and implementation of WPT systems. This subsection will provide insight into how to achieve efficient energy transfer in a WPT system while ensuring safe operation [12]. An understanding of these considerations is critical to the design and implementation of efficient, safe and reliable wireless charging solutions.

Efficiency is one of the key metrics for evaluating the performance of a WPT system. An efficient system minimizes energy loss and successfully transfers more energy to the receiver. Strategies to improve efficiency include optimizing the design of the transmitter and receiver, such as using more efficient coils or antennas, as well as improving circuit design to reduce losses in energy conversion. In addition, precise control of the transmitted power and adjustment of frequency matching can further improve the efficiency of energy transfer.

Safety is another critical aspect of WPT system design, especially when used in the vicinity of the human body. To ensure safety, it is important to consider the effects of electromagnetic fields (EMFs) and comply with relevant safety standards. This may involve limiting the transmitted power, using isolation techniques and designing the system to prevent accidental contact. Considering user and device safety at the design stage can ensure that wireless charging technology is both safe and practical in practice.

In addition, system design should also consider avoiding interference with other electronic devices.The electromagnetic interference (EMI) that may be generated by a WPT system needs to be effectively controlled so that it does not interfere with the normal operation of surrounding devices [13]. This includes the use of shielding techniques, filters and compliance with electromagnetic compatibility (EMC) standards.

In practice, the efficiency and safety of WPT systems are also affected by environmental factors. For example, metallic objects in the environment may affect the distribution of the electromagnetic field, thereby affecting efficiency and safety. Therefore, the system design needs to consider the actual application environment and adapt accordingly.

With the development of technology, the research on the efficiency and safety of WPT systems has been continuously deepened, including the exploration of new materials, technologies, and methods. These innovations are expected to further improve the performance of wireless power transmission while ensuring its safety and reliability.

In summary, efficiency and safety are two core considerations in the design of wireless power transmission systems. By emphasizing these factors in system design and implementation, it is possible to ensure that wireless charging technology is both efficient and safe for the growing number of applications.

2.2.3 Integration with WSNs

The integration of WPT technology with Wireless Sensor Networks (WSNs) is one of the important trends in current technology development. This subsection explores how to effectively integrate WPT into WSNs, including integration strategies, technical challenges, and potential application scenarios. This integration provides a new dimension to wireless sensor networks, making energy management more efficient and sustainable. Figure 2.3 shows the application of WPT technology to WSNs.

The main strategies for integrating WPTs into WSNs include utilizing wireless charging technology to extend the runtime of sensor nodes and reduce maintenance. In this setup, sensor nodes can be charged via remote charging stations or mobile charging units in the WPT system. This approach is particularly suitable for sensor networks that are difficult to access or need to operate for long periods of time.

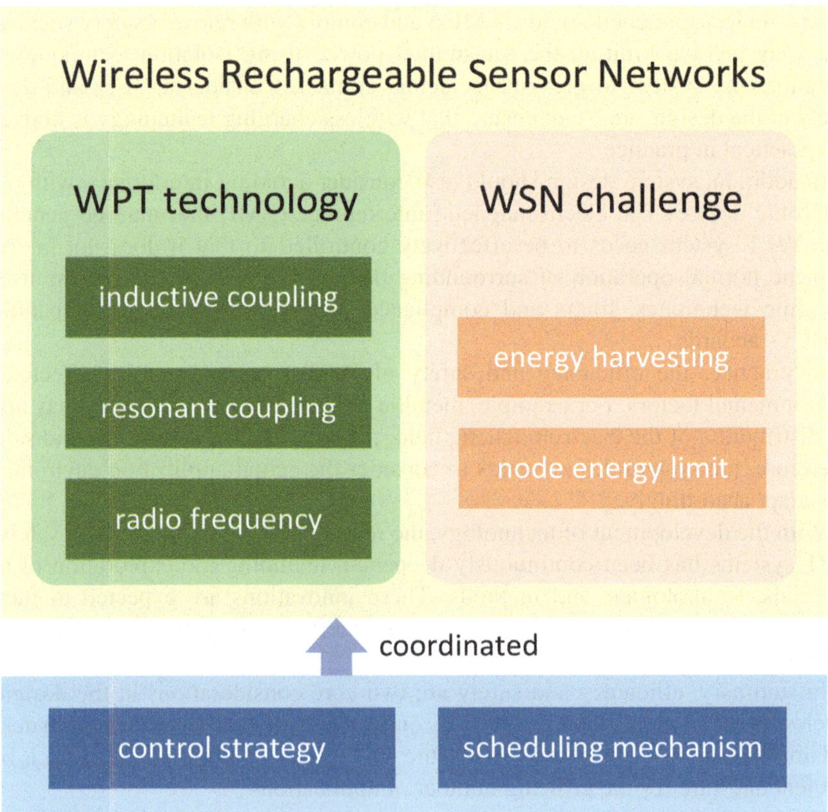

Fig. 2.3 2.2.3 WPT combined with WSNs

A key challenge in integrating WPTs with WSNs is how to effectively manage energy distribution and transmission. This requires precise control and scheduling mechanisms to ensure that all sensor nodes receive sufficient charging while optimizing the energy efficiency of the entire network. In addition, it is necessary to consider how to adaptively deploy WPT systems in different environments and application scenarios.

In practice, WSNs with integrated WPT can be widely used in various fields. For example, in environmental monitoring [14] and agricultural applications [15], this integration can enable sensor nodes to operate stably for a long time in remote or hard-to-access areas. In smart city and industrial automation scenarios, WPT can provide a more reliable and efficient way to maintain the operation of sensor networks, especially in applications that require a large number of sensor nodes.

In addition, the integration of WPT technology opens up new design and development opportunities for WSNs. For example, new sensor node designs can be developed that are specifically optimized for wireless charging, or more advanced network control algorithms can be developed to manage energy distribution and consumption.

In summary, the integration of wireless power transfer technologies into wireless sensor networks opens up new possibilities for more efficient and sustainable energy management. As technology evolves, this integration will continue to be optimized, bringing more innovation and value to various applications of wireless sensor networks.

2.3 Applications of WPT in IoT

2.3.1 Smart Homes and Buildings

Among the application areas of wireless rechargeable sensor networks, smart homes [16] and buildings [17] are highly promising areas. This subsection explores the application of wireless power transfer (WPT) technology in smart homes and buildings, including how it can be utilized to improve living and working environments, as well as to enable efficient and automated energy management in these environments. Understanding the use of WPT in smart homes and buildings is critical to driving innovation in these areas. Figure 2.4 illustrates the application scenario of WPT technology.

In smart homes and buildings, applications of WPT technology are focused on providing wireless charging solutions and enabling automated energy management. For example, wireless charging stations can be integrated into furniture to provide a convenient way to charge mobile devices and small electronic devices. In addition, wireless sensor networks can utilize WPT technology to enable continuous energy supply, which is essential for monitoring and controlling various environmental parameters (e.g., temperature, humidity, and light intensity) in buildings.

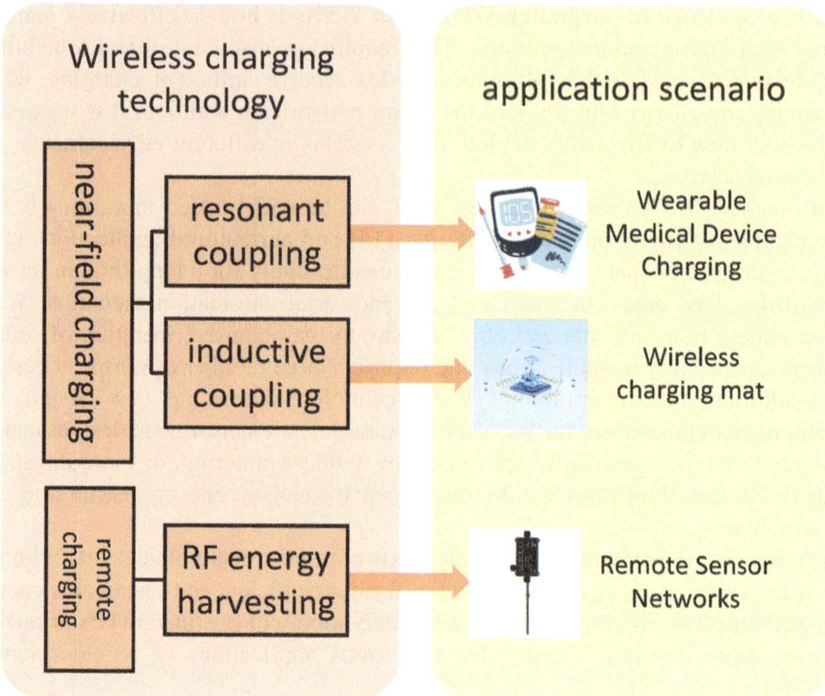

Fig. 2.4 2.2.1 WPT technology application

The application of WPT technology in smart buildings also includes integration with building automation systems [18]. Wireless power transmission allows for more flexible deployment of various sensors and controllers without having to worry about wire routing limitations. This flexibility allows buildings to respond more effectively to occupant needs, enabling more efficient energy use and a more optimized living experience.

Safety and efficiency are key considerations when applying WPT technology in smart homes and buildings. It is important to ensure that the wireless charging system does not pose a risk of electromagnetic radiation to occupants, and the system needs to be optimized to maximize energy transfer efficiency. This includes the development of intelligent energy management algorithms to ensure that energy efficiency is maximized while ensuring safety.

In addition, the application of WPT technology in smart homes and buildings faces design and aesthetic challenges. Wireless charging devices and sensors need to be integrated with interior design and architectural aesthetics to provide solutions that are both practical and aesthetically pleasing.

In short, the use of wireless power transfer technology in smart homes and buildings has revolutionized these areas. As the technology continues to evolve, we can expect WPT to play an even more important role in smart homes and buildings in the future, bringing more convenience, efficiency and comfort to the living and working environment.

2.3.2 Healthcare and Wearables

Among the application areas of wireless rechargeable sensor networks, healthcare and wearable devices are a rapidly growing and important area. This subsection explores the application of WPT technology in healthcare and wearable devices, including how WPT technology can be utilized to improve patient care and enhance the functionality of wearable devices. Understanding the application of WPT in these areas is critical to driving innovation and development in healthcare technology.

In healthcare, applications of WPT technology are focused on providing wireless charging solutions and enabling remote monitoring [19]. For example, wireless charging technology can be used to power implantable medical devices (e.g., pacemakers, insulin pumps), thereby reducing the need for battery replacement in the patient's body and the associated surgical risks. Additionally, with wireless charging technology, wearable medical devices can continuously monitor a patient's health, such as heart rate, blood pressure and blood sugar levels, providing real-time data to medical professionals.

In the field of wearable devices [20], WPT technology offers the possibility to design smaller, lighter and more powerful devices. With wireless charging, wearable devices such as fitness trackers and smartwatches can achieve more continuous use and are no longer limited by frequent charging. In addition, WPT technology allows these devices to integrate more sensors and features, enhancing the user experience.

Safety and comfort are key considerations when applying WPT technology in healthcare and wearable devices. It is important to ensure that the wireless charging system is safe and harmless to the human body and is designed with user comfort and convenience in mind. This includes the development of compact, skin-friendly wireless charging solutions, as well as optimizing the electromagnetic compatibility of the device to reduce interference with other medical devices.

In addition, the application of WPT technology in healthcare and wearable devices is challenged by battery life and charging efficiency. The system design needs to ensure sufficient charging efficiency and reliability to meet the stringent requirements of medical devices.

In conclusion, the application of wireless power transfer technology in healthcare and wearable devices brings new opportunities and challenges to these fields. With the continuous development and optimization of the technology, it is expected that WPT will play an even more important role in future healthcare and wearable devices, providing users with more efficient and convenient solutions.

2.3.3 Industrial and Environmental Monitoring

Among the application areas of wireless rechargeable sensor networks, industrial and environmental monitoring are two important and rapidly growing directions. This subsection explores the application of wireless power transfer (WPT) technology in industrial and environmental monitoring, including how this technology can be utilized to improve the efficiency and reliability of monitoring systems. Understanding the application of WPT in these areas is essential to drive innovation and development of related technologies [21].

In industrial applications [22], WPT technology can significantly improve the efficiency and reliability of sensor networks in production lines and automation systems. With wireless charging, downtime due to battery replacement or maintenance can be reduced, enhancing the continuity and stability of the production process. In addition, wireless charging allows for more flexible deployment of sensors and monitoring devices that can be installed in hard-to-wire areas or on mobile devices.

In the field of environmental monitoring, WPT technology provides a continuous supply of energy to sensors in remote and hard-to-access areas. This is critical for monitoring climate change, wildlife activity or pollution levels, for example. Wireless charging technology allows sensors to operate for long periods of time and collect critical data in areas where conventional power sources are not available.

Safety and durability are key considerations when applying WPT technology in industrial and environmental monitoring. Systems need to be designed to be rugged enough to withstand harsh environmental conditions such as extreme temperatures, humidity and chemical corrosion. In addition, the wireless charging system must ensure safe and reliable operation in these environments.

In addition, the application of WPT technology in industrial and environmental monitoring faces integration and compatibility challenges. The system needs to be seamlessly integrated with existing industrial automation and environmental monitoring systems while being compatible with a wide range of sensors and devices.

In conclusion, the application of wireless power transmission technology in industrial and environmental monitoring has brought significant benefits, especially in improving the efficiency and reliability of monitoring systems. As the technology continues to evolve, it is expected that WPT will play an even more important role in these areas, supporting the realization of more efficient and sustainable monitoring solutions.

2.4 Challenges and Future Directions

2.4.1 Technical Challenges and Research Gaps

In the development of wireless power transfer technology, it faces many technical challenges and research gaps. In this subsection, we explore the major technical challenges and future research directions currently faced by WPT technology, which are crucial for promoting the further development of wireless charging technology and wireless sensor networks. Figure 2.5 illustrates the broad application scenarios of WRSNs.

Efficiency [23] improvement remains a major challenge for WPT technology. Although WPT efficiency has been significantly improved in recent years, efficiency loss is still a key issue in long-distance transmission and high-power applications. Researchers are exploring new materials, designs and technologies, such as more

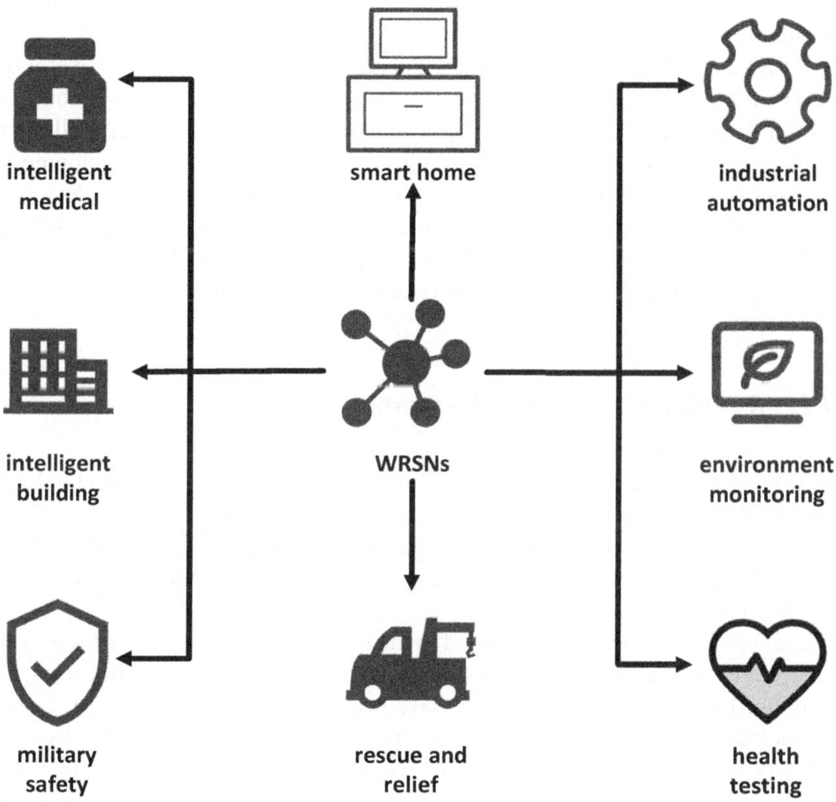

Fig. 2.5 Wireless rechargeable sensor networks

efficient converters and advanced beamforming techniques, to improve the efficiency of energy transmission.

Safety is another important consideration in the development of WPT technology [24]. Especially when used in the vicinity of the human body, it is important to ensure that WPT systems do not produce harmful electromagnetic radiation. Researchers are working on developing safer transmission methods and designing stricter safety standards to ensure that the widespread use of WPT technology will not have an impact on human health.

In addition, the scalability [25] and compatibility [26] of WPT technology is one of the current challenges. As more and more devices require wireless charging, how to ensure the compatibility of wireless charging systems between different devices and different manufacturers has become an important issue. Standardization efforts and the development of common interfaces are key to solving this problem.

In terms of environmental adaptability, the stability and efficiency of WPT systems in extreme or complex environments is also a research gap. How to ensure that WPT systems can still operate stably under harsh environmental conditions (e.g., high temperature, high humidity, strong magnetic field, etc.) is an important direction for future research.

Finally, the relationship between WPT technology and sustainable development is also an important research area. How to combine WPT technology with renewable energy sources (e.g., solar, wind) and how to improve energy efficiency while reducing environmental impact is a key direction for future research and development.

In conclusion, although significant progress has been made in wireless power transmission technology, it still faces several technical challenges and research gaps. By addressing these challenges and filling these gaps, WPT technology will play a greater role in future wireless sensor networks and IoT applications.

2.4.2 Regulatory and Standardization Issues

This subsection discusses the current status and challenges of WPT technology in terms of regulation and standardization, as well as the impact of these issues on wireless sensor networks and IoT applications. An in-depth understanding of these issues is essential to promote the healthy and sustainable development of WPT technologies.

Regulatory issues are mainly related to the impact of wireless power transmission on the environment and human health [27]. As WPT technology becomes more widely used, ways to ensure its safety have become a major concern for regulators. This includes limits on electromagnetic radiation, regulations on the frequency bands to be used, and equipment certification procedures. Different countries and regions may have different regulatory standards and requirements, which brings challenges to the design and international trade of WPT devices.

Standardization issues, on the other hand, focus on the interoperability and compatibility of devices. As the number of WPT devices developed by different vendors increases, the question of how to ensure that these devices can work together efficiently and safely becomes an important issue. Standardization organizations such as the International Electrotechnical Commission (IEC) and the Wireless Power Consortium (WPC) are working to develop uniform standards to ensure compatibility and security between different devices and systems.

In addition, standardization of WPT technology involves consistency of user experience. Providing users with a consistent experience, regardless of the brand or model of device they are using, is critical to the popularity and acceptance of the technology. This requires standardization to cover not only technical parameters, but also consistency in the user interface and operating procedures.

Rapid technological development and innovation also need to be taken into account in the standardization process. Standard-setting should be flexible enough to accommodate the emergence of new technologies and applications, while maintaining sufficient rigor to ensure safety and compatibility.

In conclusion, regulatory and standardization issues play an important role in the development of wireless power transfer technologies. By addressing these issues, it is possible to promote the healthy development of WPT technology and accelerate its application in wireless sensor networks and the Internet of Things. As these areas continue to progress, the regulatory and standardization frameworks will evolve to support the incorporation of new technologies and applications.

2.4.3 Future Perspectives and Potential Innovations

The outlook for the future in the field of WPT technology is full of potential and possibilities for innovation. This section explores future directions and potential innovations in WPT technology that are expected to drive advances in wireless sensor networks and, more broadly, IoT technology. An understanding of the future outlook and potential innovations is essential to lead technology development and capitalize on future trends.

On the one hand, future WPT technologies are expected to achieve higher transmission efficiency and longer transmission distances. This may be achieved through the development of new materials, more advanced electromagnetic wave control technologies, and smarter energy management systems. Improved efficiency and extended transmission range will enable WPT technology to be used in more areas, especially in those scenarios where conventional charging methods are difficult to implement.

On the other hand, future innovations may also include combining WPT technology with other charging or energy technologies [28]. For example, combining wireless charging with solar technology could create self-sufficient energy systems, which is especially important for remote monitoring and off-grid applications. Similarly, combining wireless charging with electric vehicle technology allows for more convenient and efficient electric vehicle charging solutions.

In terms of safety, future WPT technologies are expected to further enhance their safety features. This may be achieved through more precise EMF control, stronger interference suppression techniques, and stricter safety standards. The improved security will enhance public trust in WPT technology and promote its wider acceptance and application.

In addition, with the development of IoT technology, the application of WPT technology in smart devices will continue to grow. Wireless charging solutions will become more integrated and intelligent, providing seamless and efficient energy supply for smart homes, smart cities and industrial IoT.

Finally, researchers are also exploring the possibility of utilizing new waveforms and frequency bands for wireless power transmission. These explorations may open up new transmission bands and technological approaches to WPT technology.

In conclusion, the future of wireless power transmission technology is filled with a wide range of application prospects and innovation potential. With the continuous development and maturity of the technology, we can expect that WPT will play a more important role in the future wireless sensor networks and Internet of Things, bringing more convenience and efficiency to our life and work.

References

1. J.I. Agbinya, *Wireless Power Transfer* (CRC Press, Boca Raton, 2022)
2. S. Zhang, Z. Qian, J. Wu, F. Kong, S. Lu, Wireless charger placement and power allocation for maximizing charging quality. IEEE Trans. Mobile Comput. **17**(6), 1483–1496 (2018)
3. M.A. Hassan, A. Elzawawi, Wireless power transfer through inductive coupling. Recent Adv. Circuits 115–118 (2015)
4. A. Costanzo, M. Dionigi, F. Mastri, M. Mongiardo, G. Monti, J.A. Russer, P. Russer, L. Tarricone, Conditions for a load-independent operating regime in resonant inductive WPT. IEEE Trans. Microw. Theory Tech. **65**(4), 1066–1076 (2017)
5. X. Lu, P. Wang, D. Niyato, D.I. Kim, Z. Han, Wireless networks with RF energy harvesting: a contemporary survey. IEEE Commun. Surveys Tuts. **17**(2), 757–789 (2014)
6. W.C. Brown, The history of wireless power transmission. Solar Energy **56**(1), 3–21 (1996)
7. W. Na, J. Park, C. Lee, K. Park, J. Kim, S. Cho, Energy-efficient mobile charging for wireless power transfer in internet of things networks. IEEE Internet Things J. **5**(1), 79–92 (2017)
8. A. Massa, G. Oliveri, F. Viani, P. Rocca, Array designs for long-distance wireless power transmission: state-of-the-art and innovative solutions. Proc. IEEE **101**(6), 1464–1481 (2013)
9. Z. Zhang, K. Chau, C. Qiu, C. Liu, Energy encryption for wireless power transfer. IEEE Trans. Power Electron. **30**(9), 5237–5246 (2014)
10. A. Costanzo, M. Dionigi, D. Masotti, M. Mongiardo, G. Monti, L. Tarricone, R. Sorrentino, Electromagnetic energy harvesting and wireless power transmission: a unified approach. Proc. IEEE **102**(11), 1692–1711 (2014)
11. Y. Chen, H. Zhang, C.S. Shin, C.H. Jo, S.J. Park, D.H. Kim, An efficiency optimization-based asymmetric tuning method of double-sided LCC compensated WPT system for electric vehicles. IEEE Trans. Power Electron. **35**(11), 11475–11487 (2020)
12. L.A. Pachón, P. Brumer, Computational methodologies and physical insights into electronic energy transfer in photosynthetic light-harvesting complexes. Phys. Chem. Chem. Phys. **14**(29), 10094–10108 (2012)

13. D.M. Vilathgamuwa, J. Sampath, Wireless power transfer (WPT) for electric vehicles (Evs)—present and future trends, in *Plug in Electric Vehicles in Smart Grids: Integration Techniques* (Springer, Berlin, 2015), pp. 33–60, 2015
14. C.M. Nguyen, J. Mays, D. Plesa, S. Rao, M. Nguyen, J.C. Chiao, Wireless sensor nodes for environmental monitoring in internet of things, in *2015 IEEE MTT-S International Microwave Symposium* (IEEE, Piscataway, 2015), pp. 1–4
15. A.M. Jawad, H.M. Jawad, R. Nordin, S.K. Gharghan, N.F. Abdullah, M.J. Abu-Alshaeer, Wireless power transfer with magnetic resonator coupling and sleep/active strategy for a drone charging station in smart agriculture. IEEE Access **7**, 139839–139851 (2019)
16. M. Naz, Z. Iqbal, N. Javaid, Z.A. Khan, W. Abdul, A. Almogren, A. Alamri, Efficient power scheduling in smart homes using hybrid grey wolf differential evolution optimization technique with real time and critical peak pricing schemes. Energies **11**(2), 384 (2018)
17. A. Raciti, S.A. Rizzo, G. Susinni, Drone charging stations over the buildings based on a wireless power transfer system, in *2018 IEEE/IAS 54th Industrial and Commercial Power Systems Technical Conference (I&CPS)* (IEEE, Piscataway, 2018), pp. 1–6
18. C. Zhu, J. Yu, Y. Gu, J. Gao, H. Yang, R. Mai, Y. Li, Z. He, Analysis and design of cost-effective WPT systems with dual independently regulatable outputs for automatic guided vehicles. IEEE Trans. Power Electron. **36**(6), 6183–6187 (2020)
19. S. Yoo, J. Lee, H. Joo, S.H. Sunwoo, S. Kim, D.H. Kim, Wireless power transfer and telemetry for implantable bioelectronics. Adv. Healthcare Mater. **10**(17), 2100614 (2021)
20. Y.M. Roshan, E.J. Park, Design approach for a wireless power transfer system for wristband wearable devices. IET Power Electron. **10**(8), 931–937 (2017)
21. L. Sun, L. Wan, K. Liu, X. Wang, Cooperative-evolution-based WPT resource allocation for large-scale cognitive industrial IoT. IEEE Trans. Ind. Inf. **16**(8), 5401–5411 (2019)
22. G. Buja, M. Bertoluzzo, K.N. Mude, Design and experimentation of WPT charger for electric city car. IEEE Trans. Ind. Electron. **62**(12), 7436–7447 (2015)
23. M. Fu, H. Yin, M. Liu, C. Ma, Loading and power control for a high-efficiency class E PA-driven megahertz WPT system. IEEE Trans. Ind. Electron. **63**(11), 6867–6876 (2016)
24. T. Campi, S. Cruciani, V. De Santis, M. Feliziani, EMF safety and thermal aspects in a pacemaker equipped with a wireless power transfer system working at low frequency. IEEE Trans. Microw. Theory Tech. **64**(2), 375–382 (2016)
25. J. Song, M. Liu, C. Ma, Analysis and design of a high-efficiency 6.78-mhz wireless power transfer system with scalable number of receivers. IEEE Trans. Ind. Electron. **67**(10), 8281 8291 (2019)
26. G. Monti, D. Masotti, G. Paolini, L. Corchia, A. Costanzo, M. Dionigi, F. Mastri, M. Mongiardo, R. Sorrentino, L. Tarricone, EMC and EMI issues of WPT systems for wearable and implantable devices. IEEE Electromagnet. Compatibil. Mag. **7**(1), 67–77 (2018)
27. H. Shoki, Issues and initiatives for practical deployment of wireless power transfer technologies in Japan. Proc. IEEE **101**(6), 1312–1320 (2013)
28. L. Sun, D. Ma, H. Tang, A review of recent trends in wireless power transfer technology and its applications in electric vehicle wireless charging. Renew. Sustain. Energy Rev. **91**, 490–503 (2018)

Part II
Energy Efficient Scheduling

Chapter 3
Scheduling Optimization Methodology

3.1 Minimizing the Number of Dead Nodes

Collaborative charging schemes are effective for energy replenishment. Nonetheless, traditional collaborative charging approaches face several important challenges that are often overlooked. The lack of uniformity and dynamic decision-making in these schemes within Wireless Rechargeable Sensor Networks (WRSNs) hinders charging efficiency. To enhance charging performance, with a focus on efficiency, this section presents a game-theoretical collaborative charging scheme known as GTCharge. This approach turns the charging process into a collaborative game among wireless charging vehicles (WCVs). We investigate the roles of contribution degree, charging priority, and profits. GTCharge is thoroughly detailed, with each WCV striving to maximize its profit while carrying out charging tasks. We prove the conditions under which the charging strategies of all WCVs converge to a Nash Equilibrium. Finally, comprehensive simulations are conducted to demonstrate the proposed scheme's benefits. The simulation results affirm the advantages of the scheme regarding charging efficiency.

3.1.1 Problem Statement

This part presents the overarching framework and terminologies for the subset selection issue in Hybrld Task Scheduling with overall cost constraints (HITS). Subsequently, the HITS problem is comprehensively formulated.

C. Lin et al., *Wireless Rechargeable Sensor Networks for Internet of Things*,
Wireless Networks, https://doi.org/10.1007/978-981-97-9543-7_3

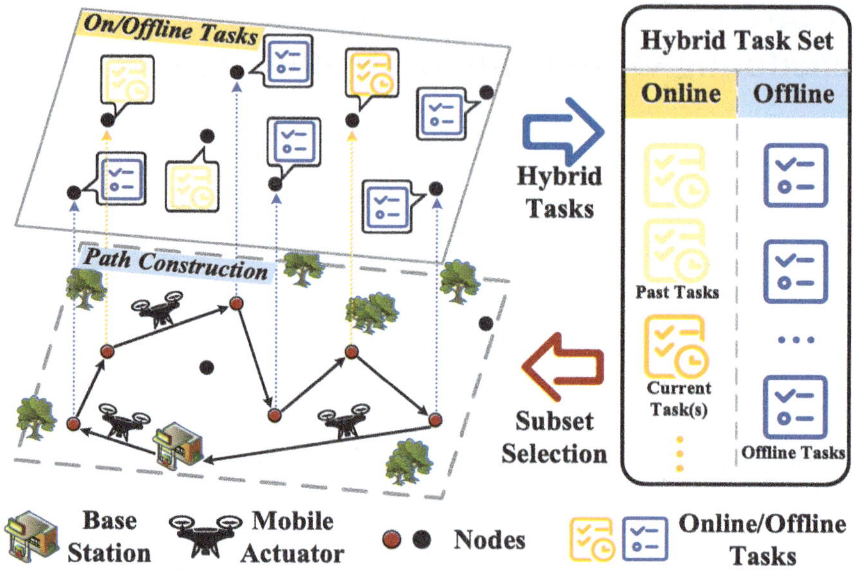

Fig. 3.1 General model

3.1.1.1 General Model

As illustrated in Fig. 3.1, the comprehensive model for hybrid task scheduling under general cost limitations includes four primary components: (1) n stationary nodes (represented as $S = \{s_1, s_2, \ldots, s_n\}$) spread randomly across a 2D plane to carry out specific sensing or monitoring operations. (2) A base station (BS) endowed with endless energy and substantial computing capabilities, tasked with data collection, processing, and managing the system. (3) A mobile actuator (MA), which can navigate freely within the zone, moving between nodes at a given pace to execute tasks in an online, offline, or mixed (both online and offline) manner, bound by a limited budget (such as time or energy). (4) The hybrid tasks, which will be further elaborated on below.

3.1.1.2 Task Model

To carry out a task, the MA needs to navigate to a designated location and conduct specific activities. For instance, the MA might approach nodes with low energy to provide wireless charging or go to a pertinent node to capture video in response to anomalous sensory data. In summary, a task necessitates the MA traveling to a specific node and executing tasks such as energy replenishment or video recording.

There are two types of tasks: online and offline. Online tasks are spontaneous and occur in real-time, making them unpredictable. In contrast, offline tasks are known in advance with specific details (such as node locations and attributes, network topology). Let $K = \{k_1, k_2, \ldots, k_m\}$ represent the set of all tasks. Each task k_i contains information about its corresponding node (location and attributes), which allows us to compute the cost (refer to Sect. 3.1.1.3) and profit. Define $K_{on} = \{k_1^{on}, k_2^{on}, k_3^{on}, \ldots\}$ as the set of online tasks, and subsequently, $K_{off} = K \backslash K_{on} = \{k_1^{off}, k_2^{off}, k_3^{off}, \ldots\}$ as the set of offline tasks. In this section, the task initiated by node s_i is referred to as k_i, and performing k_i is synonymous with serving s_i.

In online environments, tasks emerge sporadically and their occurrence is unpredictable. For every online task, it is necessary to decide whether to perform it immediately. Every online task k_i^{on} is associated with a strict deadline $t(k_i^{on})$. The MA must complete the online task prior to its deadline, otherwise, it will either provide no benefit or could lead to potentially catastrophic results.

Given the immediate necessity of online tasks, a new online task might override the ongoing task in hybrid task scheduling. The ongoing task can be either offline or online. When such a preemption happens, the MA halts its ongoing activity (whether it's traveling or executing a task) to manage the newly arrived online task.

In the offline phase, the BS computes the workload of each node using the available data (refer to Eq. (3.2)) and schedules offline tasks accordingly. Since offline tasks are not as time-sensitive as online tasks, we can forecast the future states of nodes (such as remaining energy) based on their current status, allowing us to preemptively determine potential offline tasks.

3.1.1.3 Cost Function

When executing tasks, the MA moves to the corresponding node location to carry out specific actions. The total cost includes two components: travel cost and visit cost. The travel cost is directly related to the MA's travel distance, expressed as

$$C_{tvl}(K') = \mathcal{L}(K') \cdot \alpha, \tag{3.1}$$

where K' is a subset of K and denotes the tasks to be performed by the MA. $C_{tvl}(K')$ signifies the total travel cost for the tasks in K'. $\mathcal{L}(K')$ represents the travel path length for the MA, which is a Hamiltonian path encompassing the BS and all task positions in K'. α indicates the travel cost per unit distance, and its value can vary based on the specific application (e.g., energy or time).

The cost to visit a task is determined by the *workload* needed to complete it (such as video capturing or energy recharging), which is associated with the properties of the node involved. For example, the workload represents the energy that a node requires when being recharged by the MA. Various tasks may incur different visit costs depending on their specific workloads.

$$C_{vst}(k_i) = e(k_i) \cdot \beta, \tag{3.2}$$

where $e(k_i)$ denotes the workload associated with task k_i, and η signifies the cost per unit of workload.

The overall cost for the MA is calculated by:

$$C(K') = C_{tvl}(K') + \sum_{k'_i \in K'} C_{vst}(k'_i), \tag{3.3}$$

where $C(K')$ represents the aggregate expense for completing the tasks in K', consisting of both travel and visit costs for each individual task.

Usually, the MA's activities are limited by its budget because of specific factors (e.g., restricted time or energy). Tasks cannot be performed indefinitely. In real-world scenarios, this restriction might be the MA's energy reserve or the maximum permissible duration for completing tasks. Therefore, the overall cost of accomplishing tasks in K' must not surpass a defined budget B, i.e., $C(K') \leq B$.

3.1.1.4 Profit Function

The performance of task k_i results in a certain *profit*, which is determined by the workload of k_i. A greater workload results in more profit. For instance, transmitting more energy to a node increases profit when a Mobile Agent (MA) charges a sensor node. However, in real-world scenarios, the node's capacity is limited. Therefore, the workload of task k_i must not surpass a threshold $e_{th}(k_i)$. For instance, $e_{th}(k_i)$ denotes the battery capacity of the node for wireless charging tasks. Mathematically, the profit of k_i is expressed as:

$$u(k_i) = e(k_i) \cdot \gamma, \ e(k_i) \leq e_{th}(k_i), \tag{3.4}$$

where γ represents the profit generated per workload.

3.1.1.5 Problem Statement

In this study, we explore the co-existence of online and offline tasks, where an online task can interrupt the current task (whether it's online or offline). We formally describe the subset selection problem for HybrId Task Scheduling with general cost constraints (HITS) as follows: Given a task set $K = \{k_1, k_2, \ldots, k_m\}$ consisting of both online and offline tasks, the objective is to choose a subset K^{prime} from K and determine a route for the MA to perform the tasks in K^{prime} such that the overall profit is maximized, while ensuring that the MA's cost K^{prime} does not surpass a given budget B.

3.1.2 Schematic Design

To address the HITS problem, we initially create Algorithm 1 to tackle its two subproblems: HITS-on and HITS-off. Subsequently, we balance these approaches in a combined setting and attain an overall approximated optimization for the HITS problem through Algorithm 2.

3.1.2.1 Subset Selection for Offline Task Scheduling

To begin with, we introduce the subset selection issue for offline task scheduling, which serves as a subproblem of HITS. This issue is formally akin to the HITS problem, where the task set K comprises solely of offline tasks, i.e.,

$$\textbf{(HITS} - \textbf{off)} \ \max \ U(K'_{off}) = \sum_{k'_i \in K'_{off} \subseteq K_{off}} u(k'_i), \tag{3.5}$$

$$s.t. \quad C(K'_{off}) \leq B. \tag{3.6}$$

In this context, the BS generates the offline task set K_{off} utilizing the known locations and workloads of the nodes.

To address the HITS-off problem, we choose a subset of offline tasks from K_{off} to create a result set K'_{off} that maximizes the profit. After selecting K'_{off}, we devise a travel route for the MA to accomplish all tasks in K_{off}, ensuring the total travel and visit costs remain within B.

As demonstrated in Sect. 3.1.3, the HITS-off issue is a type of the budgeted maximum coverage problem with routing limitations, classified as NP-Hard and unsolvable in polynomial time. Consequently, we introduce an efficient algorithm for hybrid task scheduling in offline environments (referred to as HITS-off) to optimize the objective function $U(\cdot)$ and achieve an approximate solution.

In order to account for both profit and expense at the same time, we introduce an alternative objective function $\mathcal{U}(\cdot)$ to substitute $U(\cdot)$, as seen in [1]. Formally, $\mathcal{U}(\cdot)$ is defined as

$$\mathcal{U}(K'_{off}) = \begin{cases} U(K'_{off}), & |K'_{off}| = 0, \\ \frac{U(K'_{off})}{1-e^{-\alpha_U C(K'_{off})/B}}, & |K'_{off}| \geq 1. \end{cases} \tag{3.7}$$

In this context, α_U represents the submodularity ratio of the function $U(\cdot)$ (refer to Definition 3.1 in Sect. 3.1.3).

The function $\mathcal{U}(\cdot)$ merges profit $U(\cdot)$ and cost $C(\cdot)$. A solution will yield a higher $\mathcal{U}$ with increased U or decreased C.

In the process of enhancing $\mathcal{U}$, a Boolean vector $\boldsymbol{K}$ is employed to denote a subset K'_{off} of K_{off}. Here, the j-th bit $\boldsymbol{K}_j = 1$ indicates that k_j^{off} is included in K'_{off}, while $\boldsymbol{K}_j = 0$ signifies that k_j^{off} is not part of K'_{off}.

During the execution of the algorithm, a set of feasible solutions Φ is maintained. These feasible solutions are categorized into $|K_{off}|$ groups according to their size l, named $\texttt{lev}(1), \texttt{lev}(2), \ldots, \texttt{lev}(|K_{off}|)$. In each iteration, a feasible solution $\boldsymbol{K}$ is chosen from Φ, and a bit-wise mutation is applied to discover another feasible solution (Lines 2–4). Once a new feasible solution $\boldsymbol{K}'$ is generated, the algorithm constructs a travel path for the mobile agent (MA) based on the tasks within it, calculating the associated cost C, profit U, and alternative profit $\mathcal{U}$ (Lines 5–7). These values are then compared with those of the solutions in $\texttt{lev}(|\boldsymbol{K}'|)$, with solutions having higher $\mathcal{U}$ and U being retained in $\texttt{lev}(|\boldsymbol{K}'|)$, denoted as $\boldsymbol{\lambda}^{|\boldsymbol{K}'|}$ and $\boldsymbol{\mu}^{|\boldsymbol{K}'|}$ (Lines 8–23). The budget constraint is consistently satisfied throughout the process. After I iterations, the solution with the highest U value is output as the result set. This algorithm helps us obtain an approximate solution with performance guarantees (refer to Theorem 3.3) to solve the HASH-off problem, which is confirmed in Sect. 7.3.4.1. This addresses the first challenge described in the Introduction Section.

3.1.2.2 Subset Selection for Online Task Scheduling

Online tasks may be introduced at any time, with their pertinent information becoming available only after their release. While scheduling, it is crucial to decide if an online task should be promptly selected according to its profit and cost, in order to maximize overall profit, even though future tasks remain uncertain.

Consider $K_{on}^i = \{k_1^{on}, k_2^{on}, \ldots, k_i^{on}\}$ as a set of tasks encompassing k_i^{on} along with all previously assigned online tasks. This problem can be formally stated as:

$$\textbf{(HITS} - \textbf{on)} \;\; \max \;\; U(K'_{on}) = \sum_{k'_i \in K'_{on} \subseteq K_{on}} u(k'_i), \tag{3.8}$$

$$s.t. \;\; C(K'_{on}) \leq B, \; and \; K_{on} \backslash K_{on}^i \; is \; unknown. \tag{3.9}$$

To tackle the unpredictability of future tasks, we initially investigate the nature of online tasks. We posit that the occurrence of online tasks adheres to an approximately periodic distribution, which is both common and reasonable in a stable and regular system, where node requests are typically generated and addressed in periodic patterns. With this premise, we forecast future scenarios using historical data and estimate: (1) the total number of online tasks, and (2) the number of tasks to be selected. This methodology allows us to create a virtual online task set K_{on} derived from historical data D_h to emulate actual online tasks. Replacing the real online task set with the virtual set K_{on}, the HITS-on problem is transformed into selecting a subset from the ground set K_{on} with the aim of

Algorithm 1 Algorithm for the HITS-on Problem (HASH-on)

Input: Online task set K_{on}, cost function $C(\cdot)$, profit function $U(\cdot)$, and budget B.
Output: Selected online task set K'_{on}.

$K^r_{on} \leftarrow K_{on}$, $B^r \leftarrow B$, $K'_{on} \leftarrow \varnothing$, and $i \leftarrow 1$;
while $B^r > 0$ and $K^r_{on} \neq \varnothing$ **do**
  Produce K_{on} based on D_h, $m \leftarrow |K_{on}|$;
  Obtain the number $|\hat{\boldsymbol{K}}|$ of tasks to select through Algorithm 1;
  Let $p \leftarrow |\hat{\boldsymbol{K}}|$, $\texttt{len} \leftarrow \lfloor \frac{m}{p} \rfloor$, $\texttt{obs} \leftarrow \lfloor \frac{\texttt{len}}{e} \rfloor$, $\epsilon_{th} \leftarrow 0$;
  while $K^r_{on} \neq \varnothing$ **do**
    Wait until online task k^{on}_i occurs;
    $K^r_{on} \leftarrow K^r_{on} \backslash \{k^{on}_i\}$;
    if $i > m$ **then**
      if $C(K'_{on} \cup \{k^{on}_i\}) \leq B$ **then**
        $K'_{on} \leftarrow K'_{on} \cup \{k^{on}_i\}$;
      end if
      Break;
    else
      Let $\texttt{seg} = \lceil \frac{i}{\texttt{len}} \rceil$;
      Compute the profit-cost ratio $\texttt{pcr} = \frac{\hat{U}(K'_{on} \cup \{k^{on}_i\}) - \hat{U}(K'_{on})}{C(K'_{on} \cup \{k^{on}_i\}) - C(K'_{on})}$;
      if $i \leq \texttt{seg} * \texttt{len} + \texttt{obs}$ **then**
        $\epsilon_{th} \leftarrow \max\{\texttt{pcr}, \epsilon_{th}\}$;
      else
        if $\texttt{pcr} \geq \epsilon_{th}$ and $C(K'_{on} \cup \{k^{on}_i\}) \leq B$ **then**
          $K'_{on} \leftarrow K'_{on} \cup \{k^{on}_i\}$;
          $i \leftarrow \texttt{seg} * \texttt{len} + 1$, $\epsilon_{th} \leftarrow 0$;
          Break;
        end if
      end if
    end if
  end while
  $K^r_{on} \leftarrow K^r_{on} \backslash K'_{on}$, $B^r \leftarrow B^r - C(K'_{on})$;
end while
return K'_{on};

maximizing a monotone objective function U under a cost constraint B. This redefined problem falls under submodular maximization with routing constraints, which can be approximately addressed using Algorithm 1. Thus, the size of the output set represents the estimated count of online tasks to be selected. With the virtual online task set K_{on} and the estimated solution $|\hat{\boldsymbol{K}}|$, we convert the HITS-on problem into a *k-secretaries problem* with a budget constraint. This is a variation of the classic *secretary problem*, which involves making irrevocable decisions to hire the best secretary from n candidates appearing sequentially with unknown future information. This scenario closely matches the online context in our model. Consequently, we consider online tasks as $|K_{on}|$ secretary candidates and select $|\hat{\boldsymbol{K}}|$ among them within a budget to maximize profit. We propose an algorithm for hybrid task scheduling in an online environment (referred to as HASH-on). The pseudocode for the HITS-on problem is detailed in Algorithm 1.

Algorithm 2 Algorithm for the HITS Problem (HASH)

Input: Task set K, including online task set K_{on} and offline task set K_{off}, cost function $C(\cdot)$, profit function $U(\cdot)$, and budget B. **Output**: Selected task set K' including online task set K'_{on} and offline task set K'_{off}.

1: **while** $K_{on} \neq \varnothing$ and $C(K'_{off} \cup K'_{on}) \leq B$ **do**
2: Create the original offline task set $\tilde{K}_{off}$;
3: Execute the tasks in $\tilde{K}_{off}$ until k_i^{on} occurs, and MA is currently at position p_m;
4: $K_{on} \leftarrow K_{on} \backslash \{k_i^{on}\}$;
5: Create $\tilde{K}'_{off}$ with starting point k_i^{on} and remained offline tasks;
6: $U^{ex} \leftarrow U_{res} - u(k_i^{on}) - U(\tilde{K}'_{off})$;
7: $C^{ex} \leftarrow d(k_i^{on}, p_m) \cdot \alpha + C_{vst}(k_i^{on})$;
8: $t^{ex} \leftarrow \frac{d(k_i^{on}, p_m)}{v}$;
9: **if** $U^{ex} \leq 0$ and $t^{ex} \leq t(k_i)$ **then**
10: Call Algorithm 1 to evaluate k_i^{on} based on U^{ex} and C^{ex} and make online selection decision;
11: Update K'_{off} and K'_{on};
12: **end if**
13: **end while**
14: $K' \leftarrow K'_{off} \cup K'_{on}$;
15: **return** K';

Let m represent the estimated number of tasks, and p represent the number of tasks to be chosen. Accordingly, we partition the online task set K_{on} into p segments, each of uniform length `len`, and strive to choose the most optimal task in each segment (Lines 3–6). When an online task k_i^{on} arrives, we compute its profit-cost ratio (Line 16). We examine the initial $\texttt{obs} = \frac{\texttt{len}}{e}$ tasks of each segment to determine a profit-cost ratio threshold ϵ_{th}, without adding them to K'_{on} (Lines 17–18). Here, ϵ_{th} indicates the highest profit-cost ratio among these tasks. For the remaining tasks in each segment, we select the first task whose profit-cost ratio surpasses ϵ_{th}, then proceed to the next segment (Lines 20–24). After an online task is selected, the residual budget B^r and task set K^r_{on} are updated, necessitating the recalibration of m and p (Line 28). If the actual number of online tasks is greater than the estimate, tasks are chosen directly within the budget limits (Lines 10–14). Ultimately, we acquire the output K'_{on} as the chosen set of online tasks, addressing the second issue stated in the Introduction Section.

3.1.2.3 Subset Selection for Hybrid Task Scheduling

In the defined HITS problem, both digital and physical tasks are considered, implying that some digital tasks will be introduced during the task scheduling process. When a digital task k_i^{on} appears, MA might be in the middle of executing a digital/physical task or traveling for the execution of a digital/physical task. Upon deciding to undertake k_i^{on}, it will halt its current action and proceed to the location of k_i^{on}. Consequently, the initial task scheduling plan may be disrupted and rendered

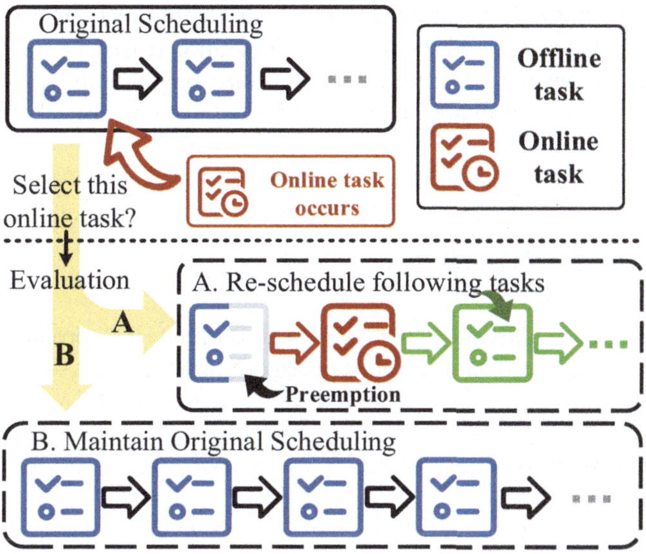

Fig. 3.2 The basic idea of Algorithm 2

impractical. To address the HITS problem, we must coordinate hybrid (both digital and physical) task scheduling to maximize their overall profit. However, the primary challenge in solving the HITS problem is the unpredictability of upcoming digital tasks.

We introduce an approximation algorithm for hybrid task scheduling (termed HASH) to address the HITS problem, utilizing Algorithm 1. As illustrated in Fig. 3.2, the core concept of this algorithm is to evaluate and choose online tasks that can enhance the total profit of all chosen online and offline tasks, considering the *extra cost* and *re-scheduling loss* prompted by the selection of this online task. Specifically, the *extra cost* is computed by $C^{ex} = d(k_i^{on}, p_m) \cdot \alpha + C_{vst}(k_i^{on})$, which signifies the added cost of completing this online task. Let U_{res} signify the profit of unexecuted tasks in $\tilde{K}_{off}$. The *re-scheduling loss* is determined by $U^{ex} = U_{res} - u(k_i^{on}) - U(\tilde{K}'_{off})$, representing the profit loss due to the disruption of the original offline task schedule. The pseudocode of the HASH algorithm is provided in Algorithm 2.

In particular, HASH initiates by choosing offline tasks to create a scheduling plan (Line 1). Next, MA leaves BS to perform offline tasks according to the predetermined route and prepares for online tasks (Line 3). The selection of online tasks adheres to the fundamental concept of The selection of online tasks follows Algorithm 1. Additionally, when an online task becomes available (Lines 4–5), it is assessed based not only on the profit-cost ratio but also on the *additional cost* and *re-scheduling loss* as described previously (Lines 7–8). Only those online tasks that have the potential to enhance the overall profit (i.e., $U^{ex} \leq 0$) will be considered, while tasks that cannot be completed before their deadlines will be disregarded (Line

10). This set of online tasks is evaluated using Algorithm 1, and the result sets K'_{off} and K'_{on} are updated at the conclusion of each iteration (Lines 11–12). Ultimately, the algorithm outputs the selected task set K', consisting of both online and offline tasks (Line 15), thus resolving the third challenge mentioned in the Introduction Section.

3.1.3 Theoretical Analysis

In this section, we initially prove the NP-Hardness of the HITS problem. Following that, we assess the approximation ratios of Algorithms 1, and 2.

3.1.3.1 NP-Hardness

Theorem 3.1 *The proposed HITS problem is NP-Hard.*

Proof As a subproblem of the HITS problem, the **HITS-off** problem entails selecting specific offline tasks to maximize total profit while keeping the overall cost within the MA's budget. This issue can be transformed into the budgeted maximum coverage problem [2], which is recognized as NP-hard. Likewise, the **HITS-on** problem, as a variant of HITS-off, is also NP-Hard. This complexity arises from the unpredictability of future tasks, which complicates scheduling from a global perspective. Moreover, performing an online task interferes with the pre-planned schedule, leading to extra costs and potentially making the original schedule unworkable. Therefore, the HITS problem, which merges two NP-hard subproblems, is also NP-hard. ■

3.1.3.2 Algorithm Analysis

Definition 3.1 (Nonnegativity, Monotonicity, and Submodularity Ratio) Given a finite ground set $\mathcal{V}$ and a real-valued set function $f : 2^{\mathcal{V}} \to R$, f is termed as *nonnegative*, *monotone (nondecreasing)*, and *submodular* if and only if it meets the following conditions, respectively:

- $f(\varnothing) = 0$ and $f(A) \geq 0$ for all $A \subseteq \mathcal{V}$ *(nonnegative)*.
- $f(A) \leq f(B)$ for all $A \subseteq B \subseteq \mathcal{V}$ or equivalently: $f(A \cup \{e\}) - f(A) > 0$ for all $A \subseteq \mathcal{V}$ and $e \in \mathcal{V} \backslash A$ *(monotone)*.
- $f(A) + f(B) \geq f(A \cup B) + f(A \cap B)$ for any $A, B \subseteq \mathcal{V}$, or equivalently: $f(A \cup \{e\}) - f(A) \geq f(B \cup \{e\}) - f(B)$ for $A \subseteq B \subseteq \mathcal{V}$ and $e \in \mathcal{V} \backslash B$ *(submodular)*.
- The *submodularity ratio* of a non-negative set function f is defined as

$$\alpha_f = \min_{X \subseteq Y,\ v \notin Y} \frac{f(X \cup \{v\}) - f(X)}{f(Y \cup \{v\}) - f(Y)}. \tag{3.10}$$

Theorem 3.2 *The utility function $U(\cdot)$ is nonnegative, monotonic, and submodular ($\alpha_U = 1$).*

Proof The proof is omitted due to space constraints. ■

Theorem 3.3 *Algorithm 1 achieves an approximation ratio of $\frac{(1-1/e)^2}{14}$ and a time complexity of $O(n^4)$.*

Proof In the context of an online scenario, due to the monotonic and submodular nature of the objective function $U(\cdot)$, Algorithm 1 attains an approximation ratio of $\frac{(1-1/e)^2}{14}$ [3, 4]. Regarding time complexity, each iteration of Algorithm 1 involves recalculating the estimated value $|\hat{\boldsymbol{K}}|$ by invoking Algorithm 1, which has a time complexity of $O(n^3)$. Considering there are at most n iterations, the overall time complexity of Algorithm 1 is $O(n^4)$. ■

Theorem 3.4 *Algorithm 2 achieves an approximation ratio of $\frac{7\xi+1}{14(\xi+1)}\left(1-\frac{1}{e}\right)^2$ with a time complexity of $O(n^5)$.*

Proof Let K_{OPT}^{off} represent the offline tasks that provide the maximum profit (i.e., the optimal solution of the HITS-off problem), and let K_{OPT}^{on} represent the optimal solution of the HITS-on problem. Accordingly, let K_{APPR}^{off} and K_{APPR}^{on} denote the approximate solutions obtained by 1, respectively. From Theorems 3.3 and 3.4, we have

$$U(K_{APPR}^{off}) \geq \frac{1}{2}\left(1-\frac{1}{e}\right) \cdot U(K_{OPT}^{off}), \tag{3.11}$$

$$U(K_{APPR}^{on}) \geq \frac{1}{14}\left(1-\frac{1}{e}\right)^2 \cdot U(K_{OPT}^{on}). \tag{3.12}$$

When integrating both offline and online scenarios, certain online tasks in K_{OPT}^{on} might be dropped due to deadlines, additional expenses, or re-scheduling penalties. Moreover, some offline tasks could be interrupted by online tasks, causing a decrease in profit. Let U_{OPT} represent the maximum profit for the HITS problem. Consequently, we have

$$U_{OPT} \leq U_{OPT}^{off} + U_{OPT}^{on}. \tag{3.13}$$

Here, $U_{OPT}^{off} = U(K_{OPT}^{off})$ and $U_{OPT}^{on} = U(K_{OPT}^{on})$. Correspondingly, let $U_{APPR}^{off} = U(K_{APPR}^{off})$, $U_{APPR}^{on} = U(K_{APPR}^{on})$, and $U_{APPR} = U_{APPR}^{off} + U(K_{APPR}^{on})$. ■

Fig. 3.3 Profit vs. budget

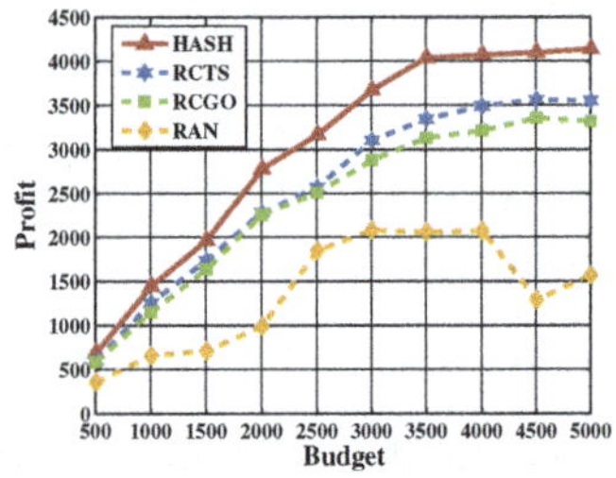

In this context, ξ denotes the ratio of offline profit to online profit in the optimal solution, that is, $\xi = \frac{U_{OPT}^{off}}{U_{OPT}^{on}}$. Therefore, we have demonstrated that Algorithm 2 achieves an approximation ratio of $\frac{7\xi+1}{14(\xi+1)}\left(1-\frac{1}{e}\right)^2$ (Fig. 3.3).

The parameter ξ varies from 0 to positive infinity, i.e., $\xi \in [0, +\infty]$, based on the ratio of online to offline tasks. A higher percentage of online tasks results in a smaller ξ, leading to a lower approximation ratio for Algorithm 2, with a minimum bound of $\frac{1}{14}\left(1-\frac{1}{e}\right)^2$. In contrast, a higher percentage of offline tasks leads to a larger ξ and consequently a higher approximation ratio, with a maximum bound of $\frac{1}{2}\left(1-\frac{1}{e}\right)^2$. This demonstrates that our proposed algorithms maintain feasibility and bounded approximation performance even when dealing exclusively with online or offline tasks. These properties of HASH are confirmed in Sect. 7.3.4.1 (see Figs. 3.6 and 3.8).

3.1.4 Simulation and Experiments

We conduct thorough simulations to assess the performance of our proposed algorithms from various viewpoints.

3.1.4.1 Simulation Setup

In the context of the HITS issue, we examine the scenario where a mobile agent is tasked with performing charging operations for sensor nodes within a wireless rechargeable sensor network. Here, tasks are specified as wireless charging activities for panic sensors. The benefit of a task is the amount of energy delivered to the sensor.

In the simulated environment, we randomly place 100 sensors within a 100×100 m square region. Each sensor comes with a rechargeable battery having a capacity of $c = 50$ kJ [5]. The workload of a sensor node with remaining energy e_r is determined by $c - e_r$. An MA navigates the network area to perform (charging) tasks using an energy budget of 2500 kJ. Our algorithm's objective is to choose certain online and offline tasks for execution in order to maximize the total profit. Based on [6], we set the energy cost per unit distance $\alpha = 0.3$, the cost per unit workload $\beta = 0.4$, and the profit per unit workload $\gamma = 0.95$.

3.1.4.2 Baseline Setup

As far as the authors are aware, no definitive method exists solely for hybrid task scheduling. In this paper, we introduce various fundamental hybrid techniques for comparison, integrating the latest online and offline methodologies:

- **RCTS:** This technique combines RC-Ratio [7] and mTS [8]. To be specific, RC-Ratio appraises offline tasks by determining their reward-to-cost ratio and employs a greedy strategy for selection. Conversely, mTS gives precedence to online tasks by considering their time and space priorities. RCTS applies RC-Ratio for scheduling offline tasks and adopts mTS for choosing online tasks.
- **RCGO:** This method combines RC-Ratio [7] with the GreedyOn algorithm. GreedyOn is an online task scheduling algorithm that consistently picks the online task with a higher profit than the preceding task until the budget is depleted.
- **RAN:** With this method, offline tasks are picked at random, and each online task is selected with a probability of $\frac{|\hat{K}|}{|K_{on}|}$.
- **GreedyRC:** It is an entirely offline algorithm that repeatedly chooses the offline task which optimizes the ratio of its profit to the distance.
- **NJNP [9]:** This is an entirely online algorithm that chooses the task nearest to the MA's position as the subsequent one to perform.

In the following discussion, we refer to Algorithms 1, and 2 as **HASH-off**, **HASH-on**, and **HASH**, respectively.

3.1.4.3 Simulation Results and Analysis

To begin, we analyze how the MA's budget affects profit. By adjusting the MA's energy budget and recording the associated profits, we derive the results depicted in Fig. 7.38. As the budget rises from 500 to 5000, the profits for HASH, RCTS, RCGO, and RAN increase sharply at first and then level off as the budget approaches 3500. This plateau effect occurs because, once the budget is sufficiently large, most high-profit nodes have already been selected, leading to minimal additional profit from further budget increments. On average, HASH surpasses RCTS and RCGO by 20.88% in profit.

Next, we evaluate the effect of varying the number of sensor nodes. By incrementing the sensor nodes from 10 to 150 while maintaining a constant network size, the numerical outcomes are depicted in Fig. 7.36. Initially, the gains of all four

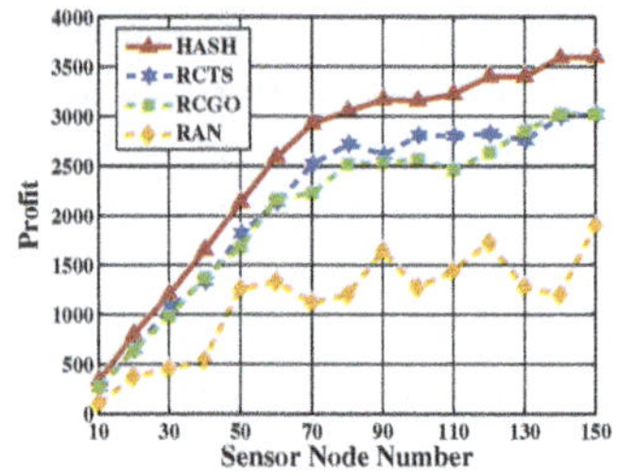

Fig. 3.4 Profit vs. sensor node number

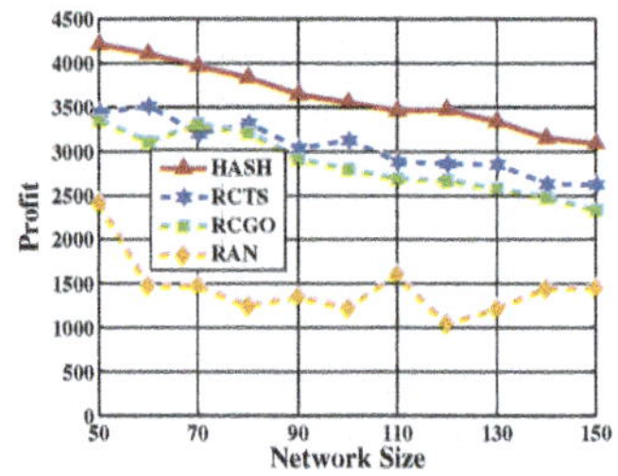

Fig. 3.5 Profit vs. network size

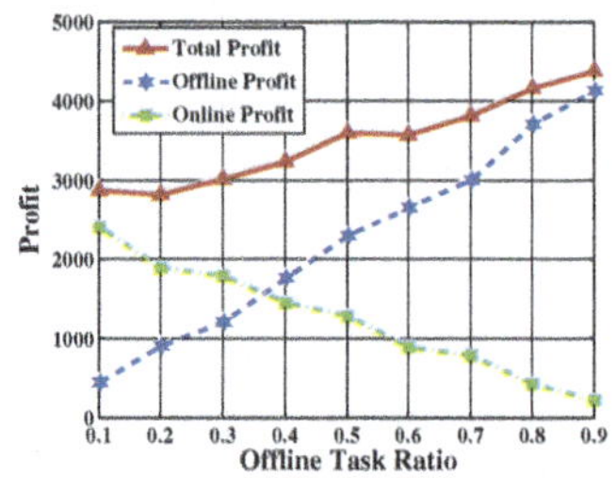

Fig. 3.6 Profit vs. offline task ratio

algorithms increase rapidly but then decelerate. With fewer sensor nodes, the MA's energy budget is sufficient to recharge nearly all sensors, resulting in a swift initial growth. However, when the number of sensor nodes surpasses the MA's charging capability, adding more nodes does not enhance overall gains. On average, HASH outperforms RCTS and RCGO by 20.82% in terms of profit (Fig. 3.4).

Third, we examine the impact of network size. By varying the side length of the square network from 50 to 150 and placing the same quantity of sensor nodes randomly within it, we obtain the results illustrated in Fig. 3.5. As the network size grows, the performance of all four algorithms diminishes due to increased distances between sensor nodes and elevated travel costs. Given that travel and task execution share the same budget, the energy allocated for task execution decreases, resulting in lower profits. On average, HASH outperforms RCTS and RCGO by 22.78% in terms of profit.

Next, we analyze how the proportion of online to offline tasks affects profit. By varying the ratio and maintaining the total number of tasks, we observe the profits of HASH under different scenarios. Figure 3.6 shows that when the offline task ratio grows from 0.1 to 0.9, HASH-off's profit increases while HASH-on's profit

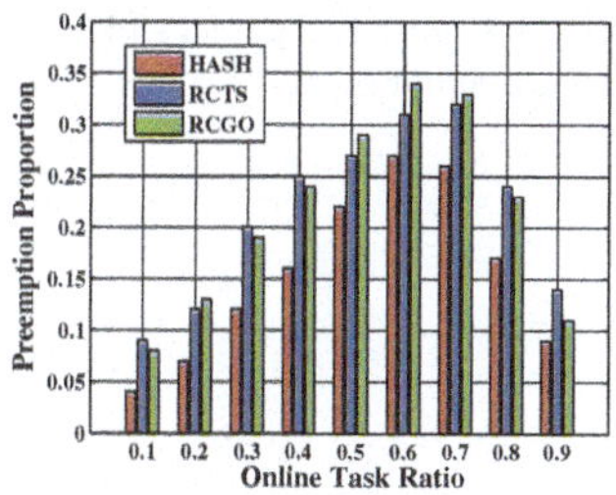

Fig. 3.7 Proportion of preempted tasks

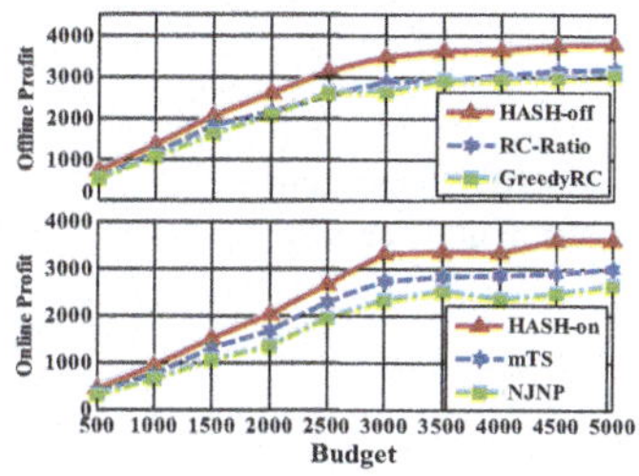

Fig. 3.8 Pure online/offline scenario

decreases. Importantly, the total profit of HASH keeps rising overall. The variability and unpredictability of online tasks generally result in lower profits than offline tasks, which means a higher share of offline tasks boosts the total profit.

In hybrid task scheduling, initiating an online task can interrupt the currently running task. We examine the preemption rate across various online task ratios. Tasks that are preempted can be either offline or online. Figure 3.7 illustrates that a lower proportion of online tasks results in fewer preemptions because most tasks are offline. Preemptions reach their maximum when the online ratio is approximately 0.6 and decline as the online ratio approaches 0.9, owing to the significant reduction in offline tasks. HASH executes fewer preemptions compared to RCTS and RCGO by assessing online tasks more globally and minimizing unnecessary interruptions.

Finally, we analyze the pure online and offline settings to assess the performance of HASH-off and HASH-on. The numerical findings are presented in Fig. 3.8. In the entirely offline scenario, where every task is offline, we benchmark HASH-off against RC-Ratio [7] and GreedyRC. The data shows that HASH-off, on average, exceeds RC-Ratio and GreedyRC by 21.08% in terms of profit. In the completely online scenario, where all tasks are online, HASH-on surpasses mTS and NJNP by 29.26% on average. To sum up, our proposed algorithms prove to be practical and profitable in online, offline, and hybrid contexts.

3.1.4.4 Test-Bed Experiments

In our test-bed experiments, we investigate the application of rechargeable wireless sensor networks by setting up our test devices in a football field. We use commercial off-the-shelf (COTS) devices to build the mobile actuator and sen-

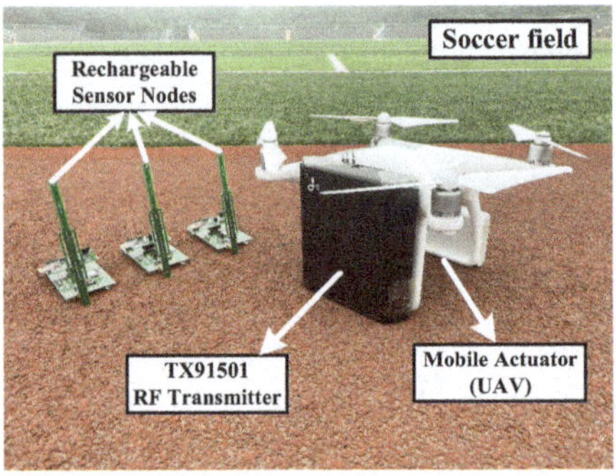

Fig. 3.9 Test-bed devices in experimental scene

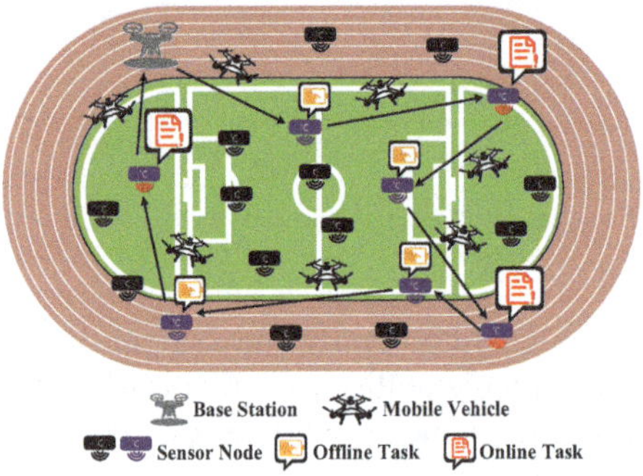

Fig. 3.10 Diagram of experimental scene

sor node testbed. Specifically, the MA is constructed by mounting a Powercast TX91501 RF transmitter (Powercast, http://www.powercastco.com) onto a DJI Phantom 4 UAV, as illustrated in Fig. 3.9, which has an energy capacity of 75.2 kJ. During the experiment, the MA approaches the rechargeable sensor nodes and activates the transmitter to emit RF signals. Each sensor node is outfitted with a Powercast P2110-EVB (Powercast P2110-EVB, https://www.powercastco.com/documentation/p2110-evb-datasheet/) for energy harvesting, converting RF signals to DC power and storing it in an onboard battery with a capacity of 2.16 kJ. The MA is also equipped with a camera module and temperature sensors.

In the experimental configuration, twenty rechargeable sensor nodes are dispersed throughout the football field to monitor the surrounding temperature. The MA navigates the field, carrying out offline recharging tasks and identifying online tasks. In particular, when a sensor's recorded temperature surpasses a set threshold [5] (29° in this instance), it triggers an emergency, thus initiating an online task. The MA then approaches the specific sensor node to investigate potential fires via images or videos, completing the online task and receiving the respective benefit. The MA adheres to the strategy explained in Algorithm 2, choosing online and offline tasks to optimize overall profit. The network arrangement is depicted in Fig. 3.10.

To validate our simulations and experiments, we juxtapose theoretical, simulation, and experimental values obtained through our algorithms, as depicted in Fig. 3.11. Keeping the experiment parameters constant, we adjusted the budget from

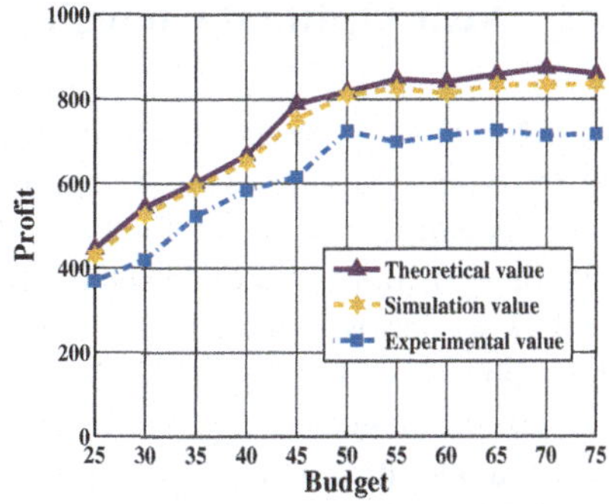

Fig. 3.11 Experiments vs. simulations vs. theoretical results

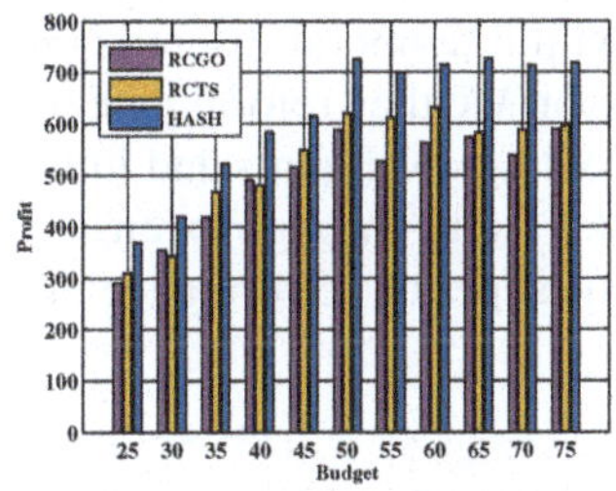

Fig. 3.12 Profit vs. budget in experiments

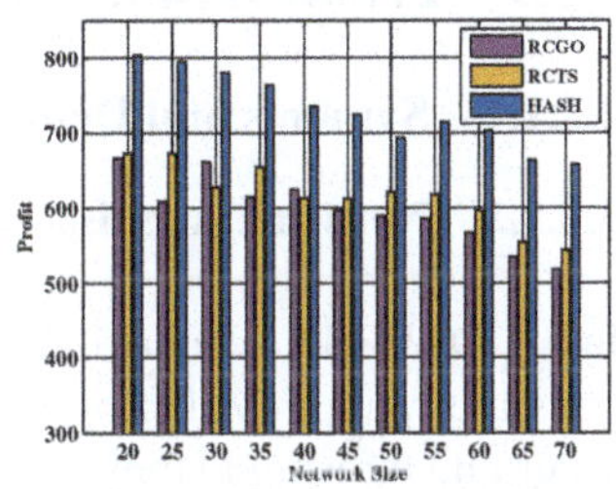

Fig. 3.13 Profit vs. network size in experiments

25 to 75 to derive the corresponding numerical outcomes. The three lines show a similar upward trend as the budget increases, signifying that our simulations and experiments are in good agreement with theoretical predictions. It is important to note a 15% performance discrepancy between simulation and experimental values, potentially attributable to environmental conditions and hardware constraints.

To evaluate the HASH algorithm's performance in practical environments, we also implemented RCTS and RCGO algorithms within our testbed for comparative purposes. Figures 3.12 and 3.13 present the numerical outcomes using HASH, RCTS, and RCGO algorithms under various budget and network setups. The profits of these methods illustrated in Figs. 3.12 and 3.13 display patterns similar to those found in the simulation context (refer to Figs. 3.3 and 3.5). HASH routinely surpasses RCTS and RCGO, yielding an average of 20.52% higher profits. These findings highlight that our HASH algorithm delivers substantial profit benefits across diverse network configurations, and experimental results further underline its applicability in real-world situations.

3.2 Near Optimal Charging Scheduling

WRSNs have emerged as a prominent research area in recent years due to advancements in wireless power transfer technology. The majority of previous work has concentrated on developing scheduling schemes for 2-D networks with mobile chargers positioned on the ground. However, few of these approaches are applicable to 3-D scenarios, which limits their practical application. This section addresses the problem of charging a 3-D WRSN using an unmanned aerial vehicle (UAV) to maximize charged energy within energy constraints.

To tackle this challenge, we propose a spatial discretization scheme to generate a finite set of feasible charging spots for the UAV in a 3-D environment, along with a temporal discretization scheme to determine the charging duration at each spot. We then reformulate the problem as a submodular maximization problem with routing constraints and introduce a cost-effective approximation algorithm to solve it. Finally, through extensive simulations and test-bed experiments, we demonstrate the superior performance of our proposed algorithm.

3.2.1 Problem Statement

3.2.1.1 Symbols and Definitions

3.2.1.2 Network Architecture

In a 3-D WRSN scenario, N sensor nodes with rechargeable batteries and receiver coils are randomly deployed. When the remaining energy of sensors drops below a certain threshold, they send charging requests to mobile chargers (UAVs) for recharging. Upon receiving these requests, UAVs with limited energy capacity travel from the base station (BS) to the sensors to replenish their energy through wireless charging. If a UAV runs out of energy, it will cease operation, necessitating a safe mechanism for UAVs to return to the BS for energy replenishment. The UAV uses electromagnetic radiation and an omnidirectional wireless charging model to provide one-to-many charging services (Fig. 3.14).

3.2.1.3 Energy Charging Model

We define R as the effective sojourn region for UAVs and express the charging spot set as S, $S = \{p|p \in R\}$. When a UAV stops at a charging spot p, the received power of sensor i is defined as:

$$\sigma_{i,p} = \frac{G_s G_r \eta}{L_p}\left(\frac{\lambda}{4\pi(d_{i,p}+\beta)}\right)\sigma, \tag{3.14}$$

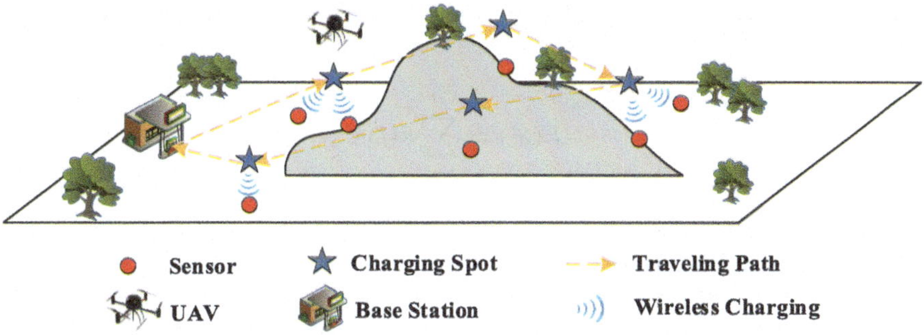

Fig. 3.14 A diagram of charging service in a 3-D WRSN

where $\sigma_{i,p}$ represents the charging power for sensor i when the transmitter is at charging spot p with source power σ. G_s and G_r are the source and receive antenna gains in WPT, respectively. L_p is the polarization loss, and λ is the electromagnetic wavelength. η denotes rectifier efficiency, and β is the distance adjustment parameter for short transmissions. $d_{i,p}$ is the Euclidean distance between sensor node i and charging spot p. In a 3-D setting, if a sensor is too far from the transmitter, its received power may be negligible. Thus, we define the minimum received power σ_{min} and redefine the charging power as:

$$\sigma_{i,p} = \begin{cases} \dfrac{\alpha}{(d_{i,p} + \beta)^2} & d_{i,p} \leq D \\ 0 & d_{i,p} > D \end{cases} \tag{3.15}$$

Here, $\alpha = \frac{G_s G_r \eta \lambda^2 \sigma}{16\pi^2 L_p}$ and $D = \sqrt{\frac{\alpha}{\sigma_{min}}} - \beta$. Due to the 3D nature of the network, points that are not feasible for UAV hovering or charging, such as those underground, underwater, or in small caves, are excluded. The total energy received by a sensor i is calculated by summing the energy from each charging station with the corresponding dwell time:

$$C_i = \sum_{p \in S} \sigma_{i,p} t_p, \tag{3.16}$$

where C_i is the total charged energy of sensor i, and t_p is the charging duration at charging spot p. Equation (3.16) indicates that a sensor can be replenished from multiple charging spots. Each sensor node has an upper bound of charged energy θ_C, so the actual charged energy for sensor i is:

$$F(i) = \min\{C_i, \theta_C\}. \tag{3.17}$$

For any selected charging spot set $S' \subseteq S$, the total energy obtained from the UAV is:

$$F(S') = \sum_{i=1}^{N} F(i). \tag{3.18}$$

3.2.1.4 Energy Cost Model

In a 3-D WRSN, each UAV has three work phases: (a) departing from the BS with full energy, (b) replenishing sensors according to the plan, and (c) returning to the BS for energy replenishment or battery replacement. The UAV incurs energy costs in three locations: (a) moving costs, (b) hovering costs, and (c) recharging costs. Assuming the moving cost is linear with the moving distance [10], and the UAV does not hover without recharging sensors, we define these energy costs. For a selected charging spot set S', the moving cost is:

$$C_{mov} = \mu \mathcal{R}(S'), \tag{3.19}$$

where C_{mov} denotes the moving cost, μ represents the cost per unit distance, and $\mathcal{R}(\cdot)$ denotes the traveling distance of a given charging spot set. For hovering costs, when the UAV stays at charging spot $p \in S'$ for duration t_p, the cost is:

$$C_{hov} = \sum_{p \in S'} \upsilon t_p, \tag{3.20}$$

where C_{hov} is the hovering cost, and υ is the hovering cost rate per unit time. While hovering at charging spot p, the UAV emits electromagnetic waves to charge sensors, with a fixed source power σ. The charging cost C_{tran} is:

$$C_{tran} = \sum_{p \in S'} \sigma t_p. \tag{3.21}$$

Due to the one-to-many charging model, the overall received energy by sensors is less than the source power at any charging spot p (i.e., $\sigma > \sum_{i=1}^{N} \sigma_{i,p}$). Energy loss during charging means C_{tran} satisfies:

$$C_{tran} > \sum_{i=1}^{N} \sum_{p \in S'} \sigma_{i,p} t_p = \sum_{i=1}^{N} C_i \geq \sum_{i=1}^{N} F(i) = F(S'). \tag{3.22}$$

Combining the three types of energy costs, the total energy cost is:

$$\begin{aligned} C_{tot} &= C_{mov} + C_{hov} + C_{tran} \\ &= \mu\mathcal{R}(S') + (\upsilon + \sigma) \sum_{p \in S'} t_p. \end{aligned} \tag{3.23}$$

With the energy supply model for sensors and energy cost models for UAVs established, we present the problem statement.

3.2.1.5 Problem

In the 3-D WRSN, a UAV with a limited energy capacity B must always return to the BS before running out of energy, otherwise, the system will fail. Therefore:

$$C_{tot} \leq B. \tag{3.24}$$

Similarly, the depletion of any sensor in a WRSN can have severe consequences, especially in real-time and safety-critical applications like forest fire detection or heart disease monitoring. Thus, it is crucial to supply as much energy as possible to keep sensors operational. Our goal is to maximize the total energy harvested by the sensors under the UAV's energy constraints in a 3-D WRSN.

The problem is to *maximize the total charged energy for sensors under the UAV's energy constraints in a 3-D WRSN*. The core of the problem is to maximize the total charged energy, directly related to the UAV's charging performance. The UAV's tasks include: (1) selecting feasible charging spots, (2) forming the shortest charging tour, and (3) staying/hovering for appropriate durations to maximize charged energy while adhering to the energy capacity constraint B. This process is formalized as a convex optimization problem:

$$max \quad F(S'), \tag{3.25}$$

$$s.t. \quad \mu\mathcal{R}(S') + (\upsilon + \sigma) \sum_{p \in S'} t_p \leq B. \tag{3.26}$$

Two critical challenges arise in solving this problem.

The first challenge is the infinite solution/search space. Since the total charged energy depends on the charging spots, which are infinite in the 3-D WRSN, determining the optimal charging spots and durations is complex. As shown in [11], this problem is NP-hard.

The second challenge is the charging schedule. Considering the energy constraints, moving costs must be accounted for, and an optimized charging tour, similar to solving an NP-hard traveling salesman problem (TSP) [12], is needed.

This problem integrates a series of NP-hard subproblems, posing a significant challenge.

3.2.2 Schematic Design

3.2.2.1 Spatial Discretization

Smallest Enclosing Space As previously mentioned, the charging spot set S is an infinite set that spans region R. To reduce the feasible charging spot region, we adopt the concept of Smallest Enclosing Space (SES) [11]. In our 3-D WRSN, SES is defined as the intersection region of the smallest sphere encompassing all sensors and the feasible positions where a UAV can sojourn and charge.

Lemma 3.1 *To maximize the total received energy of all sensors, the optimal charging spot set S' must belong to the SES C.*

Proof Suppose there exists an optimal charging spot $p \in S'$ beyond the boundary of C, and let the center of the sphere be o. We can find another charging spot q located at the intersection of the line segment $[o, p]$ and C. Consider an arbitrary sensor i located within C. For the charging spots p and q, we have $d_{i,p} > d_{i,q}$. By replacing charging spot p with q, we increase the received energy of sensor i, indicating that p is not an optimal charging spot. Thus, the optimal charging spot set S' must be within the SES C. ∎

After reducing the feasible region of charging spots from R to C using the smallest enclosing sphere, we still face the challenge of selecting finite charging spots from the infinite 3-D region C. To address this, we propose an effective discretization scheme that divides the infinite region C into a certain number of 3-D sub-regions. Each sub-region is represented by a charging spot, with different approximated received power for all sensor nodes.

In a 3-D region C (see Fig. 3.15c), we utilize a discretization scheme by implementing horizontal segmentation planes and further dividing each plane into concentric pieces with power bounds. This process is termed vertical discretization and horizontal discretization.

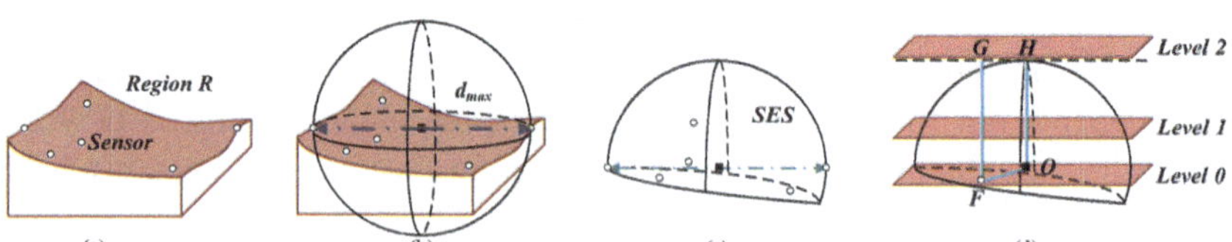

Fig. 3.15 A diagram of 3-D WRSN including: (**a**) 3-D environment of region R, (**b**) sphere with d_{max} (i.e. the maximum distance between two arbitrary sensors) radius, (**c**) smallest enclosed space (SES) for our network, and (**d**) vertical discretization for a sensor

Vertical Discretization During vertical discretization, we identify the minimum and maximum vertical distances, d_{min} and d_{max} (see Fig. 3.15b), from any sensor node i to all feasible charging spots within C. Clearly, the minimum distance is $d_{min} = 0$. Generally, a charging spot must be higher than sensor i to effectively transfer energy. Therefore, the charging spot with the maximum vertical distance is situated above the sensor i, as shown in Fig. 3.15d.

Lemma 3.2 *Given an SES C with radius r, the distance $|\mathbf{O_i}|$ between the sphere center O and sensor i, and the angle κ between the vertical line of sensor i and $\mathbf{O_i}$, the maximum vertical distance d^i_{max} of sensor i satisfies: $d^i_{max} = r + |\mathbf{O_i}| \cos \kappa$.*

Proof As shown in Fig. 3.15d, let F represent the position of sensor i. The maximum vertical distance from sensor i to the highest horizontal plane is denoted as G, and H is the highest point of C, where $\mathbf{OH}$ is parallel to $\mathbf{FG}$. We consider the plane containing points F, H, and the sphere center O. The maximum vertical distance d^i_{max} of sensor i is $|\mathbf{FG}|$, where $|\mathbf{FG}| = |\mathbf{OH}| + |\mathbf{OF}| \cos \angle OFG$. Therefore, we have $d^i_{max} = r + |\mathbf{O_i}| \cos \kappa$ accordingly. ■

With the minimum and maximum vertical distances identified and using Eq. (3.15), we can determine the range of charging power for sensor i as follows:

$$\sigma^i_{max} = \frac{\alpha}{\beta^2}, \tag{3.27}$$

$$\sigma^i_{min} = min\{\frac{\alpha}{(d^i_{max} + \beta)^2}, \sigma_{min}\}. \tag{3.28}$$

To make vertical discretization, we divide C into horizontal subregions by drawing V_i horizontal planes for sensor i.

Theorem 3.5 *Given a sensor i, its the maximum vertical distance d^i_{max}, its charging power range $[\sigma^i_{min}, \sigma^i_{max}]$, and error rate ϵ of charging power where $0 < \epsilon < 1$, the number V_i of discretized horizontal subregions satisfies:*

$$V_i = max\{\lceil \frac{2ln(1 + \frac{d^i_{max}}{\beta})}{ln(1 + \epsilon)} \rceil, \lceil \frac{ln\frac{\alpha}{\sigma_{min}\beta^2}}{ln(1 + \epsilon)} \rceil\}.$$

Proof Since the vertical distance between adjacent planes is determined by bounding the variance ratio of adjacent region within a coefficient ϵ. Therefore, the discretized charging power σ^i_v of the vth plane is represented as:

$$\sigma^i_v = \sigma^i_{max}(1 + \epsilon)^{-v} \quad 1 \le v \le V_i.$$

Furthermore, we define the vertical distance from sensor i to its discretized plane v as d_v^i, which is computed as:

$$d_v^i = \sqrt{\frac{\alpha}{\sigma_v^i}} - \beta \quad 1 \le v \le V_i.$$

The number of horizontal planes V_i is related to the minimum charging power above which the sensor i cannot be effectively charged. Thus, V_i can be considered as the smallest integer that satisfies this condition:

$$\sigma_{V_i}^i = \sigma_{max}^i (1+\epsilon)^{-V_i} \le \sigma_{min}^i.$$

Then we can compute V_i as:

$$V_i = \lceil \frac{ln(\frac{\sigma_{max}^i}{\sigma_{min}^i})}{ln(1+\epsilon)} \rceil = max\{\lceil \frac{2ln(1+\frac{d_{max}^i}{\beta})}{ln(1+\epsilon)} \rceil, \lceil \frac{ln\frac{\alpha}{\sigma_{min}\beta^2}}{ln(1+\epsilon)} \rceil\}.$$

Therefore, we can obtain the number of subregions after the vertical discretization scheme. ■

Horizontal Discretization After executing vertical discretization scheme, the 3-D region C is replaced by $\sum_{i=1}^{N} V_i$ horizontal planes. In each plane, we further implement horizontal discretization (i.e. 2-D discretization) by concentric circles as shown in Fig. 3.16a. We define the center O_v^i as the projection of sensor i on its vth plane. Then in each plane, we define the maximum distance from O_v^i within C as B_v^i, which is easy to compute. Afterwards, we can obtain the maximum distance of M_v^i between sensor i and its vth plane as follows.

$$M_v^i = \sqrt{{d_v^i}^2 + {B_v^i}^2}. \tag{3.29}$$

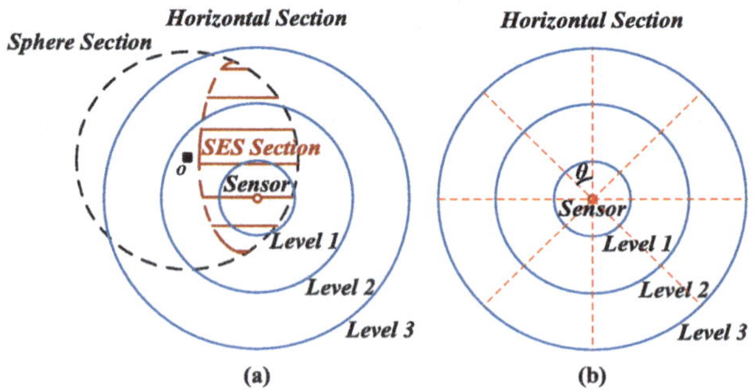

Fig. 3.16 A diagram of horizontal discretization scheme after vertical discretization

Obviously, the maximum charging power in plane v is σ_v^i according to vertical discretization scheme. Similar to Eq. (3.28), we calculate the minimum charging power in plane v for sensor i as:

$$\sigma_{min}^i(v) = min\{\frac{\alpha}{(M_v^i + \beta)^2}, \sigma_{min}\}. \tag{3.30}$$

We still use the variance ratio ϵ to achieve horizontal discretization and the uth concentric circle of plane v for sensor i is expressed as:

$$\sigma_v^i(u) = \sigma_v^i(1+\epsilon)^{-u} = \sigma_{max}^i(1+\epsilon)^{-(u+v)}, \tag{3.31}$$

where $1 \le u \le U_v^i$ and $1 \le v \le V_i$. U_v^i is denoted as the number of concentric circles in plane v for sensor i, which is also the smallest integer that satisfies $\sigma_v^i(1+\epsilon)^{-U_v^i} \le \sigma_{min}^i(v)$.

In particular, if we take a concentric circle as a charge point in horizontal discretisation, the practical charge point will be difficult to determine because the maximum distance between two charge points in a concentric circle may be large, which cannot be ignored. Here we adopt an angular discretisation coefficient θ to further segment each concentric circle into $\frac{2\pi}{\theta}$ sectors. Thus, the entire region C is divided into finite discretised subregions. The total number of candidate charge points after spatial discretisation is defined as P_s. In particular, if no concentric circle is covered by obstacles, as shown in Fig. 3.16b, P_s can be calculated as:

$$P_s = \sum_{i=1}^{N}\sum_{v=1}^{V_i}\frac{2\pi U_v^i}{\theta}. \tag{3.32}$$

Thus, the first challenge mentioned in Sect. 3.2.1.5 is solved.

3.2.2.2 Temporal Discretization

Determining the charging time is challenging because calculating the exact charged energy for each sensor at each charging point is difficult. Therefore, based on spatial discretization, we consider a fixed charged energy at each charging spot by dividing the total time into equivalent time slots. This transforms the problem from infinite charging spots and uncertain durations into a specific solution space.

To perform temporal discretization for each discretized charging point, we determine the maximum charging time T_{max} as follows:

$$T_{max} = \frac{\theta_C}{\sigma_{min}}. \tag{3.33}$$

Charging a sensor with the minimum power σ_{min} to its maximum energy θ_C results in the maximum charging duration. The minimum charging duration at each charging spot is defined as t_{min}, which satisfies $t_{min} << \frac{\theta_C}{\sigma_{max}}$. For each discretized charging spot, we replace it with $Q = \frac{T_{max}}{t_{min}}$ virtual spots, each with the minimum charging duration t_{min}.

After spatial and temporal discretization, the infinite charging spots are reduced to $P_s Q$ virtual charging spots, forming the solution space X (i.e., $|X| = P_s Q$) in the 3-D WRSN. For any $p \in X$, the charged energy for sensor i is redefined as:

$$C_i = \begin{cases} \sum\limits_{p\in X} \frac{\alpha q t_{min}}{(d_{i,p}+\beta)^2} & d_{i,p} \le D \\ 0 & d_{i,p} > D \end{cases}, \tag{3.34}$$

where qt_{min} denotes the charging duration of charging spot p and $1 \le q \le Q$.

Next, we consider the UAV's travel costs. We use the longest distance between two discrete load spot regions as the travel path. The distance between any two charging spots within the same region is approximated to zero, minimizing performance loss due to spatial discretization. We denote the optimal trajectory for the UAV as $R(X')$.

We reformulate the problem as:

$$max \quad F(X') = \sum_{i=1}^{N} \min\{C_i, \theta_C\}, \tag{3.35}$$

$$s.t. \quad \mu R(X') + (\upsilon + \sigma) \sum_{p\in X'} qt_{min} \le B. \tag{3.36}$$

The problem of maximizing the charged energy for sensors in a 3D WRSN is thus transformed into a submodular maximization problem with routing constraints. We address this by proposing an approximation algorithm.

Theorem 3.6 *The reformulated problem is NP-hard.*

Proof Consider a special case: if only one-to-one charging is applied, and each sensor requires one unit of energy, the UAV must compute the shortest path through these sensors within energy constraints, which is a variant of the NP-hard traveling salesman problem [12]. Hence, the reformulated problem is NP-hard. ■

3.2.2.3 Approximation Algorithm

To solve the submodular function maximization problem, we develop a greedy approximation algorithm that provides provable approximation guarantees. The core idea is to find the most cost-effective virtual loading point during each iteration, satisfying:

$$p^* = \arg\max_{p \in X \setminus X'} \frac{F(X' \cup \{p\}) - F(X')}{\hat{C}_{tot}(X' \cup \{p\}) - \hat{C}_{tot}(X')}, \tag{3.37}$$

where $\hat{C}_{tot}$ denotes an approximate cost function computable in polynomial time since the optimal cost function may not be computable.

Algorithm 3 Cost-Efficient Algorithm (CEA)

Require: The number of sensor nodes N, the SES C, transmitting coefficients α and β, the energy consumption parameters μ and υ, source charging power σ, upper bound of sensor energy θ_C, and energy capacity B of a UAV.
Ensure: The selected virtual charging spot set $X' \subseteq X$ and total charged energy for sensors.

```
Execute spatial discretization for the 3-D region and form P_s subregions with a variance ratio ϵ.
Execute temporal discretization for each subregion with Q virtual charging spots.
Form solution space X where X = P_s Q.
Set 𝓑 ← arg max{F(p)|p ∈ X, Ĉ_tot(p) ≤ B}
X' ← ∅, Ĉ_tot(X') ← 0.
while X ≠ ∅ do
    for each p ∈ X do
        Calculate marginal charged energy Δ_F^p ← F(X' ∪ {p}) − F(X').
        Calculate marginal energy cost Δ_{Ĉ_tot}^p ← Ĉ_tot(X' ∪ {p}) − Ĉ_tot(X') using the Nearest Neighbor (NN) algorithm [13].
    end for
    p* ← arg max{Δ_F^p / Δ_{Ĉ_tot}^p | p ∈ X}.
    if Ĉ_tot(X' ∪ {p*}) ≤ B then
        Set X' ← X' ∪ {p*}
    end if
end while
X' ← arg max_{X' ∈ {𝓑, X'}} F(X').
return X', F(X')
```

We summarize the low-cost approximation algorithm (i.e., Algorithm 1). First, we perform spatial discretization from the vertical and horizontal perspectives, dividing infinite regions into P_s subregions with effective energy boundaries between adjacent regions. Next, we implement the temporal discretization scheme to divide each sub-region into Q virtual charge durations, forming the candidate charge point set X ($|X| = P_s Q$). To find the set X' with maximum charging energy, we calculate the marginal charged energy Δ_F^p when inserting a virtual charging spot p into set X'. We address the marginal energy cost $\Delta_{\hat{C}_{tot}}^p$ using an approximation algorithm: Nearest Neighbor [13], which has a $log(P_s Q)$-approximation ratio. The virtual charging spot with the maximum value of $\Delta_F^p / \Delta_{\hat{C}_{tot}}^p$ and satisfying energy cost constraints is selected to form the set X'. Finally, we choose the maximum result between $F(X')$ and $F(\mathcal{B})$, obtaining the corresponding set X' as the charging spots for the UAV.

Hence, the second challenge mentioned in Sect. 3.2.1.5 is addressed.

3.2.3 Theoretical Analysis

In this work, we aim to maximize the charged energy within the fixed energy budget of the UAV. However, in practical applications, this budget may be dynamic.

The previous work has focused on a static budget constraint; however, the UAV's energy budget may change dynamically in many real-world applications. Considering that the energy capacity of lithium batteries varies after charging and discharging cycles [14], we introduce a real-world dynamic budget scenario using UAVs equipped with lithium batteries. We extend our research to this dynamic budget scenario to achieve our goal.

3.2.3.1 The Dynamic Budget Problem

Due to the complexity of the dynamic budget scenario, we use the approximation ratio obtained in the previous fixed budget scenario and extend the charging schedule problem to accommodate a changing budget. The dynamic budget problem is defined as follows:

The Dynamic Budget Problem *Let X be a ϕ-approximation solution for Eq. (3.35) under a static budget. For a current budget B, changes in the budget are defined as $B^* = B + d$, where $d \leq -B$. Our goal is to obtain a ϕ-approximation X' for each changed B^*.*

As the budget changes over time, any fixed budget scenario can be treated as a static budget problem, and the cost-efficient algorithm can be re-executed for the newly given budget. To solve the dynamic budget problem, we focus on developing an algorithm that can adapt to the constraint bound.

3.2.3.2 Adaptive Cost-Efficient Algorithm (ACEA)

In this section, we propose an Adaptive Cost-Efficient Algorithm (ACEA) to handle the dynamic budget problem. Applying the CEA in Sect. 3.2.2.3 provides a solution for a fixed budget. However, running the CEA for a new budget involves redundant computations, and adapting the current solution may be more efficient. We will illustrate the need for CEA at the end of this section.

ACEA is modified from CEA to address the variable budget problem. Assume that S is the solution under budget B. The core idea of our algorithm involves two aspects based on changes in budget B. When the budget decreases (i.e., $B^* < B$), some charging spots will be excluded from S until a feasible solution is obtained. Conversely, if the budget increases, more charging spots will be added to S, similar to CEA.

Algorithm 4 Adaptive Cost-Efficient Algorithm (ACEA)

Require: Initial solution X, solution space P, budget B, and new budget B^*
if $B^* < B$ **then**
  while $\hat{C}_{tot}(X) > B^*$ **do**
    $p^* \leftarrow \arg\min_{p \in X} \frac{F(X)-F(X \backslash \{p\})}{\hat{C}_{tot}(X)-\hat{C}_{tot}(X \backslash \{p\})}$
    $X \leftarrow X \backslash \{p^*\}$
  end while
else if $B^* > B$ **then**
  $P' \leftarrow P \backslash X$
  while $P' \neq \emptyset$ **do**
    $p^* \leftarrow \arg\max_{p \in P'} \frac{F(X \cup p)-F(X)}{\hat{C}_{tot}(X \cup p)-\hat{C}_{tot}(X)}$
    if $\hat{C}_{tot}(X \cup p^*) \leq B^*$ **then**
      $X \leftarrow X \cup p^*$
    end if
    $P' \leftarrow P' \backslash \{p^*\}$
  end while
end if
$p^* \leftarrow \arg\max_{p \in P, \hat{C}_{tot}(p) \leq B^*} F(p)$
return $\arg\max_{S \in \{X, p^*\}} F(S)$

ACEA operates as follows. Given an initial solution X computed by the Cost-Efficient Algorithm under budget B, we seek a new solution under a modified budget of B^*. First, if the budget B^* is less than B, the charging point with the lowest charged energy ratio for sensors is removed from the initial set X until the total energy cost is within the constraint B^*. Second, if the budget B^* has grown positively from B, the charging spot with the largest percentage of increased charged energy for the sensor to the increased energy cost is added. Finally, the updated solution is obtained for the new budget of B^*.

The complexity of ACEA is similar to CEA in one iteration, i.e., $O(P_s^2 Q^2)$. When applying CEA to the dynamic budget problem, the complexity will be $O(T P_s^2 Q^2)$, where T is the number of dynamic budget changes. Thus, ACEA is more efficient than CEA for dynamic energy budget problems.

However, the proposed adaptive low-cost algorithm may not effectively handle dynamic changes due to potential deterioration in the approximation ratio after dynamic changes. Therefore, we consider a scenario with increasing budgets. We simplify our problem to a basic dynamic problem where the objective and the cost function are linear.

Given $n + 1$ charging spots $p_i = (c_i, f_i)$ where c_i is the energy cost and f_i is the charged energy for sensors, assume $n > 4$ where spatial discretization forms at least 4 charging spots, and temporal discretization can be ignored. We divide these charging spots into three types: (a) $p_i = (1, \frac{2}{n})$ for $1 \leq i \leq \frac{n}{2}$, (b) $p_i = (2, 1)$ for

$1 + \frac{n}{2} \leq i \leq n$, (c) $p_{n+1} = (1, 3)$. The objective and cost functions are $f(X) = \sum_{p_i \in X} f_i$ and $c(X) = \sum_{p_i \in X} c_i$, respectively.

Theorem 3.7 *Given the base dynamic problem* $(f(X), c(X))$*, the dynamic budget set is* $\{1, 2, \ldots, 1 + \frac{n}{2}\}$ *and the initial budget* $B = 1$*. The approximation ratio obtained by the adaptive cost-efficient algorithm is* $O(\frac{1}{n})$.

Proof When $B = 1$, the optimal solution is $X = \{p_{n+1}\}$. Due to the increment between two dynamic budgets being 1, the adaptive cost-efficient algorithm can only select charging spots of type a) to satisfy budget constraints during each change. When the budget changes to $B = 1 + \frac{n}{2}$, the solution is $X = \{p_{n+1}, p_1, \ldots, p_{\frac{n}{2}}\}$, resulting in charged energy $f(X) = 4$ with cost $c(X) = 1 + \frac{n}{2}$. However, the optimal solution is $X^* = \{p_{n+1}, p_{1+\frac{n}{2}}, \ldots, p_{\frac{3n}{4}}\}$ with $f(X^*) = 3 + \frac{n}{4}$. Thus, the approximation ratio is $f(X)/f(X^*) = O(\frac{1}{n})$. ■

To further verify ACEA's local optima problem, we conducted a brief experiment as shown in Fig. 3.17. ACEA always updates the solution set based on the previous budget, which may lose a global view when dealing with the dynamic budget problem.

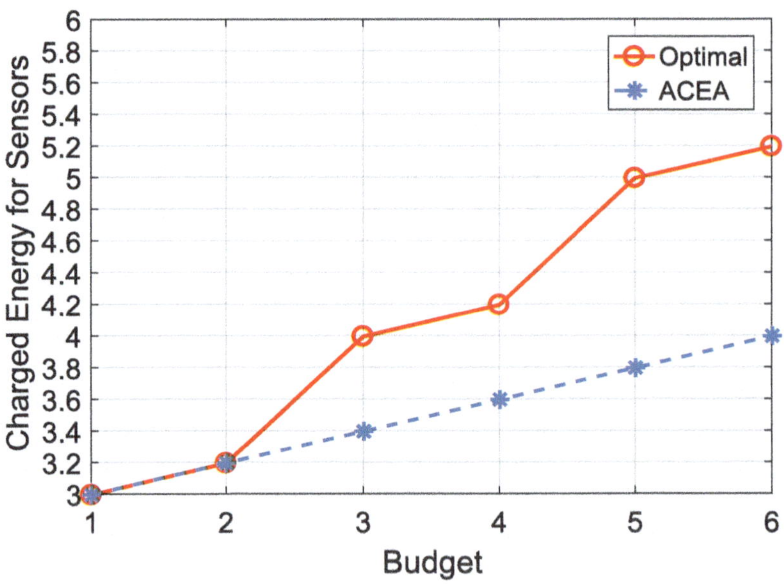

Fig. 3.17 Local optima problem of ACEA

3.2.3.3 Pareto Optimization

In this section, to solve the local optima problem of ACEA, we use a multi-objective optimization approach based on Pareto optimization for solving a monotonic function maximization problem with a monotonic cost constraint, called POMC. We formulate our problem as a bi-objective problem as follows:

$$\arg\max X \in \{0, 1\}^n (F_1(X), F_2(X)) \tag{3.38}$$

and the function F_1 and F_2 is given below:

$$F_1(X) = \begin{cases} -\infty & \hat{C}_{tot}(X) > B + 1 \\ F(X) & \text{otherwise} \end{cases}, \tag{3.39}$$

Here, our objective is to maximize the charged energy function F and minimize energy cost function $\hat{C}_{tot}$ simultaneously. When $\hat{C}_{tot}(X) > B+1$, we set F_1 to $-\infty$ to exclude the corresponding infeasible solutions.

In the multi-objective problem, we have to compare two solutions X_1 and X_2, which are obtained from two objective individually. We use the concept of *dominance* to evaluate the solutions. When $F_1(X_1) \geq F_1(X_2) \wedge F_2(X_1) \geq F_2(X_2)$, then X_1 is better than X_2 (i.e. X_1 weakly dominates X_2), denoted as $X_1 \succeq X_2$. When $X_1 \succeq X_2$ and either $F_1(X_1) > F_1(X_2)$ or $F_2(X_1) > F_2(X_2)$, then X_1 is strictly better (i.e. X_1 dominates X_2), denoted as $X_1 \succ X_2$. Moreover, two solutions are incomparable when each solution is not better than the other.

Algorithm 5 POMC Algorithm

Require: Budget B, and the iteration number T
Ensure: A solution X with $\hat{C}_{tot} \leq B$
Let $X \leftarrow \{0\}^{P_s Q}$, $P \leftarrow \{X\}$ and $t \leftarrow 0$
while $t < T$ **do**
    Select X from P uniformly at random
    $X' \leftarrow$ flip each bit of X with probability $\frac{1}{P_s Q}$
    Calculate $(F_1(X'), F_2(X'))$
    if $\nexists x \in P$ such that $z \succ X'$ **then**
        $P = (P \backslash \{z \in P | X' \succeq z\}) \cup \{X'\})$
    end if
    $t \leftarrow t + 1$
end while
return $\arg\max_{X \in P : \hat{C}_{tot}(X) \leq B} F(X)$

The process of Algorithm 5 is described below. An empty set is given where no charging spot is chosen, and POMC tries to improve the quality of solutions. During each iteration, solution X' is obtained by randomly flipping bits of the solution X

selected from P. When the new solution X' is not dominated by previous solutions, it will be added to P. Moreover, solutions worse than X' will be excluded from P.

POMC takes each charge point as a bit for further calculation. 0-bit means that the corresponding charge point is not selected in the solution and 1-bit means that the charge point can be added to the current solution set.

Theorem 3.8 *POMC performs better than ACEA in dealing with local optima.*

Proof POMC can escape local optima in two ways. Then the first way is backward search where a bit value can be flipped from 1 to 0. The second way is a multi-bit search where more than one 0-bits are simultaneously flipped to 1-bits. According to theoretical proof in [15], POMC owns advantages in dealing with the local optima. ■

Thus, POMC has a better performance than the adaptive cost-efficient algorithm in dealing with the dynamic budget problem. Then, according to Theorem 5 and Theorem 6 in subset selection optimization [16] we prove that POMC can solve the dynamic budget problem with a ϕ-approximation. The corollary of POMC on the dynamic budget problem is given below.

Corollary 3.1 *In the dynamic budget problem with initial budget constraint B. Assume that population in POMC contains a ϕ-approximation for each $b \in [0, B]$. With budget B changes to B^*, POMC can obtain a ϕ-approximation solution within time $T = cP_s^2Q^2max\{d, log P_s Q\}$ with probability $1 - o(1)$ for each $b \in [0, B^*]$ where $c \geq 8e + 1$ and $d = |B^* - B|$.*

Due to the bit flipping and iteration times during POMC, the complexity of POMC is $O(P_s QT)$. Here, P_s indicates the number of subregions, Q is the number of virtual charging spots, and T is the iteration time of POMC.

3.2.4 Simulation and Experiments

3.2.4.1 Simulation Setup

In our simulation, the network region is a $100 \times 100 \times 100$ m cube area where 100 sensor nodes are randomly deployed. The upper bound of sensor capacity is set as 10 KJ while the energy capacity of the UAV (i.e., budget B) is 250 KJ. In the spatial and temporal discretization scheme, the error rate of charging power ϵ and minimum charging duration t_{min} are set as 0.5 and 10 s, respectively. Detailed configurations of the simulations are listed in Table 3.1.

Table 3.1 Simulation setup

Parameters	Values
Network area	$100 \times 100 \times 100$ m
Number of nodes	100
Upper bound of sensor capacity	10 KJ
Energy capacity of the UAV (budget)	250 KJ
Minimum charging duration	10 s
Error rate of charging power	0.5
Source power	200 J/s
Moving cost rate	10 J/m
Hovering cost rate	20 J/s
Charging scheme	CEA, ACEA, POMC, FC, MEP

3.2.4.2 Performance Comparison

We mainly compare our algorithm with FC and MEP in terms of the error rate of the spatial discretisation scheme, the energy capacity of the UAV (i.e., the budget B), the upper bound of the sensor capacity and the minimum charging time. With the result of the simulations, the objective of our reformulated problem is finally achieved.

3.2.4.3 Impact of Error Rate ϵ

We investigate the impact of the error rate on the charged energy of sensors, where the error rate reflects the degree of spatial discretization. We set the error rate for 3-D network spatial discretization from 0.2 to 0.6 as shown in Fig. 3.18a. All algorithms exhibit a diminishing trend as the error rate increases, with our algorithm achieving the highest charged energy compared to others. Furthermore, the charged energy decreases rapidly as the error rate rises. This is because a larger error rate ϵ increases the energy difference between adjacent subregions and causes longer distances between discretized subregions, leading to a proportional decline in energy. We can conclude that a lower error rate will result in more energy gained by sensors.

3.2.4.4 Impact of Budget B

The maximum energy capacity of the UAV is 250 KJ, as shown in Table 3.1. We set the energy budget from 120 to 220 KJ for comparison. As shown in Fig. 3.18b, our algorithm outperforms FC and MEP by at least 2.3 and 12.8%, respectively. The total charged energy of the sensors increases as the budget B increases in all three cases. This is because if the UAV has enough energy to charge, move, and hover,

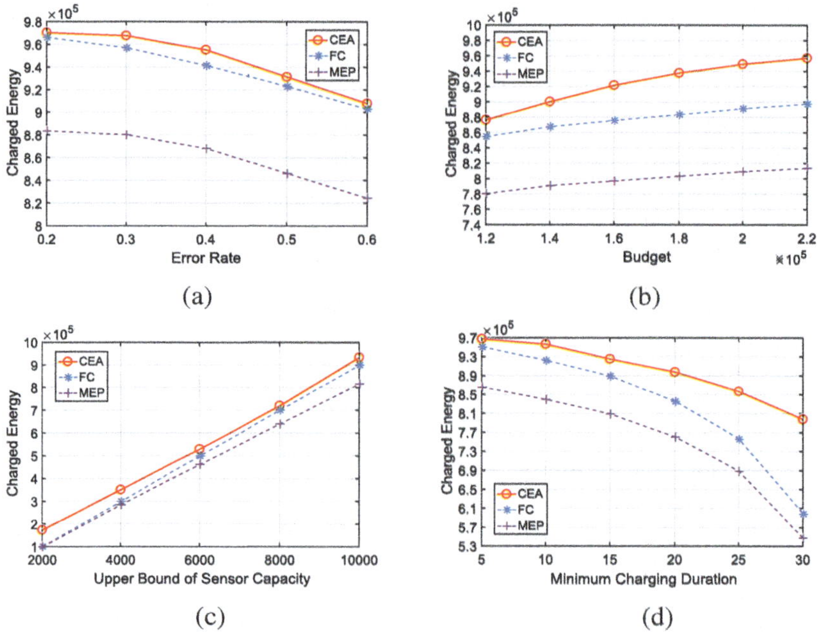

Fig. 3.18 Performance comparison among CEA, FC, and MEP in terms of charged energy. (**a**) Charged energy vs. Error rate ϵ. (**b**) Charged energy vs. budget B. (**c**) Charged energy vs. upper bound of sensor capacity. (**d**) Charged energy vs. minimum charging duration

it will serve more sensor nodes before it runs out of energy. Thus, the sensors can eventually receive more energy.

The simulations for each budget B are independent, which is different from the dynamic budget scenario. The cost-efficient algorithm calculates the charged energy of sensors for each single budget, leading us to conclude that a larger energy budget brings more energy supplements for sensors.

3.2.4.5 Impact of Upper Bound of Sensor Capacity θ_C

As shown in Fig. 3.18c, our algorithm increases the total charged energy by 4.7 times as the upper bound of sensor capacity ranges from 2 to 10 KJ. Our proposed algorithm outperforms MEP by approximately 50% when $\theta_C = 2$ KJ. This is because our algorithm selects the charging spot with the maximum p^* in Eq. (3.37), while MEP charges the sensor with the minimum energy, which may incur significant moving costs. Thus, enhancing the capacity of sensors will improve the performance of the charging schedule.

3.2.4.6 Impact of Minimum Charging Duration t_{min}

The minimum charging duration t_{min} in the temporal discretization scheme is crucial for algorithm performance. In FC and MEP, we set the total charging duration at each charging spot as an integer multiple of t_{min}. As shown in Fig. 3.18d, when t_{min} ranges from 5 to 30, the total charged energy in all three algorithms decreases sharply. This is because if the minimum time is set too long, the UAV will spend extra time in one place after it has finished recharging, causing more hovering and recharging costs, which will result in less total energy being recharged.

3.2.4.7 Dynamic Budget

In this section, we compare ACEA and POMC in dealing with dynamic budget charging schedule problems. We simplify the discretization procedure and provide 50 charging points for dynamic budget experiments.

3.2.4.8 Performance under Dynamic Budget

We initialize the energy budget at 1 KJ and set $B^* = B + 1$ to stabilize the dynamic change. According to the simulation results in Fig. 3.19a, POMC excels others by

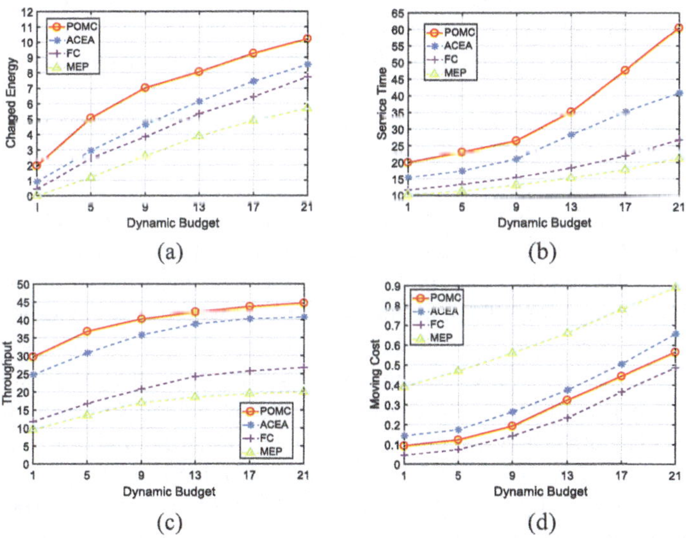

Fig. 3.19 Impact of dynamic budget among ACEA, POMC, FC, and MEP on charged energy, service time, throughput and moving cost. (**a**) Charged energy vs. dynamic budget. (**b**) Charged energy vs. dynamic budget (**c**) Service time vs. dynamic budget. (**d**) Throughput vs. dynamic budget. (**e**) Moving cost vs. dynamic budget

40% in charged energy on average. This is because ACEA greedily calculates the optimal charging point for each budget increment. A higher energy budget may result in the charging point with the highest charging efficiency and relatively high cost being included in the solutions. However, ACEA tends to form a local solution with suboptimal performance. POMC is able to find and update a better solution for each budget, and the characteristics of the dynamic budget pose minimal difficulty unless time is a critical factor.

We define the duration of charging sensors as service time, which reflects the advantages of charging strategies. As shown in Fig. 3.19b, POMC has the shortest service time than others, the reason is that a near-optimal charging spot set causes the highest charging efficiency, which means the charging process takes less time to charge a certain amount of energy. The service time in FC is the longest because each sensor should be charged to its full capacity, and remote sensors with low charging efficiency take a long time to service in the one-to-many charging model.

Then, we define throughput as the number of charged sensors during the whole charging process, which can directly judge the service quality of the network. As shown in Fig. 3.19c, POMC serves the most sensors than others, and as the budget increases, the throughput gradually decreases. The reason for this is that in the beginning the charging point with the higher charging power is selected, which means that the throughput is high in the first phase.

Another characteristic is the moving cost, which is a critical type of energy cost in charging schedule. As shown in Fig. 3.19d, FC has the least moving cost all the time. The reason for this is that the UAV always charges the sensors to full capacity without considering the charging power, which can waste a lot of energy on a few sensors and result in lower moving cost. POMC and ACEA have relatively low moving costs while having the most charged energy of the sensors.

3.2.4.9 Comparison of Run Time

After proving that POMC can obtain an optimal solution for the dynamic budget problem in Sect. 3.2.4.8, we focus on analyzing the running time of the ACEA and POMC. Here, the running time is defined as the iteration time of algorithms. We compare the running time of calculating the solution where $B = 20$ KJ. The number of charging spots is $n = 50$ and we use iteration times $T = 10eBn^2$ [15]. As shown in Fig. 3.20, ACEA is extremely fast for searching for the solution. Hence, the running time is presented as a horizontal line. POMC achieves the optimal solution at $0.46Bn^2$, and the whole running time is about $29.5Bn^2$ when T iterations are completed. The result shows that POMC can quickly achieve a better solution.

Through simulation for the dynamic budget problem, we can experimentally prove that POMC can cost some running time to reach a better solution than the adaptive cost-efficient algorithm and avoid falling into local solutions.

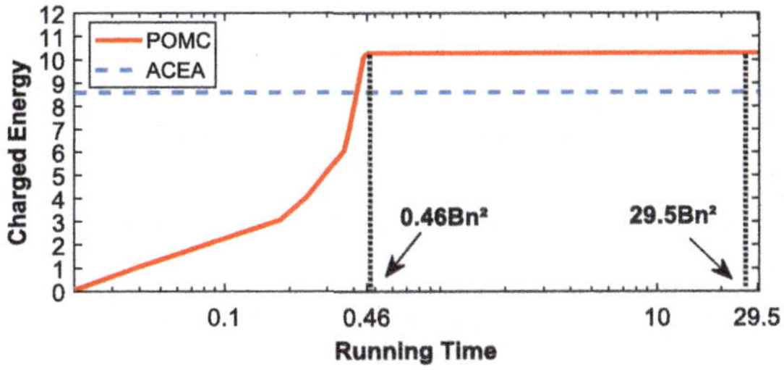

Fig. 3.20 Running time in Bn^2 between ACEA and POMC ($B = 20$)

References

1. C. Bian, C. Feng, C. Qian, Y. Yu, An efficient evolutionary algorithm for subset selection with general cost constraints, in *AAAI* (2020), pp. 3267–3274
2. S. Khuller, A. Moss, J. Naor, The budgeted maximum coverage problem. Inf. Process. Lett. **70**(1), 39–45 (1999)
3. M. Bateni, M.T. Hajiaghayi, M. Zadimoghaddam, Submodular secretary problem and extensions. ACM Trans. Algorithms **9**(4), 32:1–32:23 (2013)
4. W. Liu, Y. Yang, E. Wang, J. Wu, Dynamic user recruitment with truthful pricing for mobile crowdsensing, in *IEEE INFOCOM* (2020), pp. 1113–1122
5. Y. Sun, C. Lin, H. Dai, Q. Lin, L. Wang, G. Wu, Trading off charging and sensing for stochastic events monitoring in WRSNs, in *IEEE ICNP* (2020), pp. 1–11
6. W. Xu, Z. Xu, J. Peng, W. Liang, T. Liu, X. Jia, S.K. Das, Approximation algorithms for the team orienteering problem, in *IEEE INFOCOM* (2020), pp. 1389–1398
7. T. Wu, P. Yang, H. Dai, W. Xu, M. Xu, Collaborated tasks-driven mobile charging and scheduling: A near optimal result, in *IEEE INFOCOM* (2019), pp. 1810–1818
8. C. Lin, Z. Wang, J. Deng, L. Wang, J. Ren, G. Wu, mTS: temporal-and spatial-collaborative charging for wireless rechargeable sensor networks with multiple vehicles, in *IEEE INFOCOM* (2018), pp. 99–107
9. L. He, L. Kong, Y. Gu, J. Pan, T. Zhu, Evaluating the on-demand mobile charging in wireless sensor networks. IEEE Trans. Mobile Comput. **14**(9), 1861–1875 (2014)
10. C. Lin, Z. Wang, J. Deng, L. Wang, J. Ren, G. Wu, mTS: temporal-and spatial-collaborative charging for wireless rechargeable sensor networks with multiple vehicles, in *IEEE INFOCOM* (2018), pp. 99–107
11. L. Fu, P. Cheng, Y. Gu, J. Chen, T. He, Optimal charging in wireless rechargeable sensor networks. IEEE Trans. Veh. Technol. **65**(1), 278–291 (2016)
12. D. Feillet, P. Dejax, M. Gendreau, Traveling salesman problems with profits. Transp. Sci. **39**(2), 188–205 (2005)
13. D.J. Rosenkrantz, R.E. Stearns, P.M. Lewis, II, An analysis of several heuristics for the traveling salesman problem. SIAM J. Comput. **6**(3), 563–581 (1977)
14. N. Kim, J. Ahn, D. Kim, B. Lee, Adaptive loss reduction charging strategy considering variation of internal impedance of lithium-ion polymer batteries in electric vehicle charging systems, in *2016 IEEE Applied Power Electronics Conference and Exposition (APEC)* (2016), pp. 1273–1279
15. C. Qian, J.-C. Shi, Y. Yu, K. Tang, On subset selection with general cost constraints. Int. J. Comput. Artif. Intell. **17**, 2613–2619 (2017)
16. V. Roostapour, A. Neumann, F. Neumann, T. Friedrich, Pareto optimization for subset selection with dynamic cost constraints. Proc. AAAI Conf. Artif. Intell. **33**, 2354–2361 (2019)

Chapter 4
Priority-Based Scheduling

4.1 Temporal and Distantial Priority-Based Scheduling

In the preceding section, we introduced a preemptive scheduling strategy utilizing dual thresholds. Here, we present a Temporal and Distantial Priority (TADP) charging scheduling algorithm, which considers both the separation between nodes and the mobile charger as well as the arrival times of charging requests. TADP systematically assigns weights to these two factors, creating a mixed priority queue that guides the mobile charger in recharging the nodes. We conduct extensive simulations to validate the advantages of TADP. The results reveal that TADP enhances scheduling performance by ensuring the success of high-priority task scheduling and boosting the system's overall stability.

4.1.1 Problem Statement

Figure 4.1 illustrates the structure of the on-demand charging system. Nodes with identical battery capacities and energy consumption rates V_d are positioned within a square region of side length L. Post-deployment, each node's location can be identified through certain localization techniques, like those presented in [1]. When a node's power level drops below a specific threshold ϕ, it promptly sends a real-time charge request to the WCV utilizing advanced protocols [2] for tracking and communicating with the mobile charger. To simplify comparisons, this study assumes the request delivery time to be negligible [3] relative to the WCV's travel time. Consistent with the assumptions made in [4], sensor nodes can quickly determine the WCV's position.

In this section, we utilize an omnidirectional model for wireless charging. We assume that the charging power received by various nodes is influenced by the

C. Lin et al., *Wireless Rechargeable Sensor Networks for Internet of Things*,
Wireless Networks, https://doi.org/10.1007/978-981-97-9543-7_4

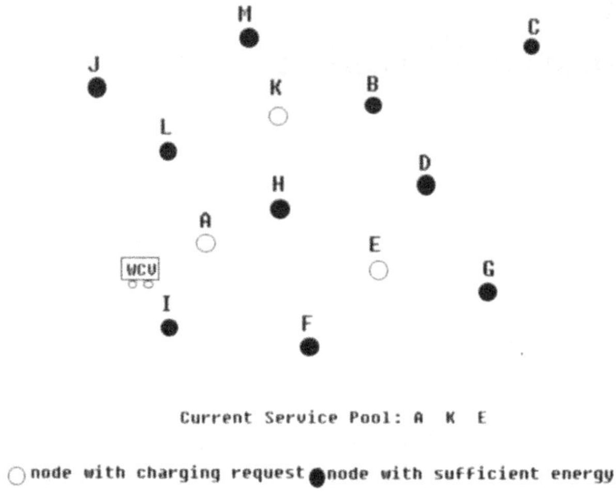

Fig. 4.1 On-demand charging architecture

distance from the charger and the power transmitted by the charger [5]. Specifically, the wireless charging model is represented by the following equation:

$$P_{rx}(d) = \frac{\tau}{(d+\xi)^2} \tag{4.1}$$

where $\tau = \frac{G_{tx}G_{rx}\eta}{L_p}\left(\frac{\lambda_0}{4\pi}\right)^2 P_{tx}$ is a constant defined by the WCV and sensor nodes. Here, P_{tx} represents the source power from the WCV. G_{tx} and G_{rx} are the gains of the source and receiver antennas, respectively. λ_0 denotes the wavelength. L_p stands for the polarization loss. η indicates the rectifier efficiency. d is the distance between the WCV and the sensor node being charged. The parameter ξ is set to 0.2316 as detailed in [6].

We presume that there is a single WCV operating within the WRSN. This WCV gathers all charging requests and logs them into the service pool. Figure 4.1 illustrates that the service pool maintains the location details of Node A, Node K, and Node E. Given that the charging requests are time-sensitive, scheduling them can be treated as a real-time task scheduling issue. The requests need to be ordered in a queue based on immediacy and importance. When a request is picked as a high-priority task, the WCV will promptly proceed to charge the node. Consequently, the sequence in the task queue directly influences the WCV's travel route to the node. Under the context of on-demand charging, the WCV maintains a constant speed. Consistent with [6], we disregard the charging duration's impact.

In an on-demand charging framework, a node initiates an immediate charging request to the WCV whenever its remaining energy drops below a specified threshold ϕ. During the scheduling phase in this on-demand system, charging requests are modeled using a Poisson distribution, implying that their inter-arrival

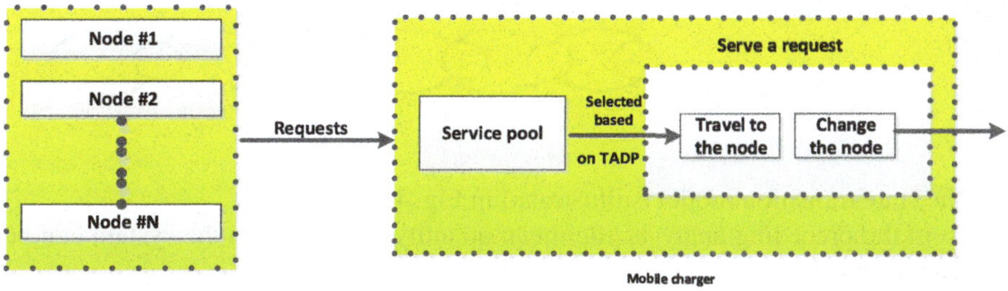

Fig. 4.2 Formalized queuing model

times follow an exponential distribution [4]. Additionally, the service duration for each request adheres to a negative exponential distribution.

As illustrated in Fig. 4.1, three nodes (A, K, and E) have submitted charging requests to WCV, which are then placed in a waiting queue based on their order of arrival. Using certain scheduling algorithms, WCV picks a request, designates the sender of the request as the target node, and moves towards it. Consequently, the task scheduling issue in an on-demand architecture applying the TADP scheduling algorithm can be represented as an M/M/1/∞/N/TADP queuing model (refer to Sect. 4.1.2), depicted in Fig. 4.2.

4.1.2 TADP Queuing Model

In this portion, we delve into the traits of the suggested M/M/1/∞/N/TADP framework ($N = 100$), offering essential insights for the development of the charging algorithm and the execution of simulations.

In the M/M/1/∞/N/TADP queue model, packets arrive according to a Poisson distribution characterized by the parameter λ. The service times are distributed exponentially with a mean of $\frac{1}{\mu}$. The arrival and service processes are independent of each other. In the WRSN, there is one WCV, indicating there is a single server. The system's capacity is infinite, denoted by ∞. Given that the network comprises 100 nodes ($N = 100$), the number of customer sources is 100. This study adopts the TADP service policy. We represent the number of packets in the system at any time t by $\{N(t) = j, t \geq 0\}$, and the state space is $\psi = \{0, 1, 2, \cdots, j, \cdots\}$.

The state transition probability of $N_j = N(t = j\sigma)$ is:

The likelihood of receiving one charging request is given by $\lambda\sigma + o(\sigma)$. Conversely, the likelihood of receiving no requests is $1 - \lambda\sigma + o(\sigma)$. In this context, $o(\sigma)$ denotes the higher-order infinitesimal of σ.

If a WCV is handling a request, the likelihood that a data request is completely fulfilled is given by $\mu\sigma + o(\sigma)$. In contrast, the likelihood of it not being fully served is $1 - \mu\sigma + o(\sigma)$.

The likelihood of multiple data requests coming or going is $o(\sigma)$.

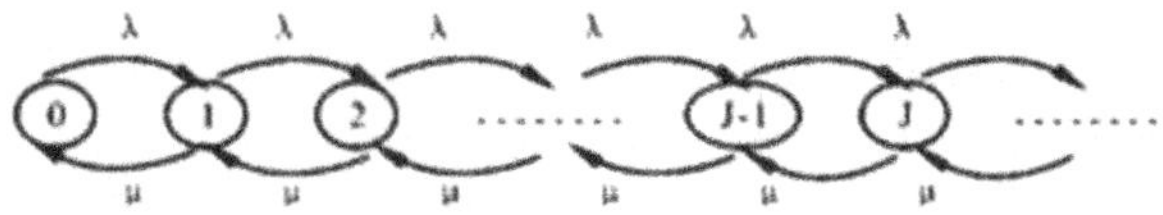

Fig. 4.3 State transition model

The state transition model is illustrated in Fig. 4.3.

From the preceding analysis, the mean quantity of packets in the system can be determined by:

$$L_s = \sum_{k=0}^{\infty} kp_k = \rho(1-\rho)\sum_{k=0}^{\infty} k\rho^{k-1} = \frac{\rho}{1-\rho} = \frac{\lambda}{\mu - \lambda} \tag{4.2}$$

where ρ represents the service intensity of the system, computed as $\rho = \frac{\lambda}{\mu}$. The system remains stable if $\rho < 1$.

Theorem 4.1 *Suppose that the charging requests arrive according to a Poisson process with an average rate of λ, and the service time for the WCV adheres to a negative exponential distribution with an average service rate of μ. Then:*

$$L_s = \lambda W_s \tag{4.3}$$

$$L_q = \lambda W_q \tag{4.4}$$

In this context, L_s represents the average count of requests in sojourn, while L_q denotes the average count of groups waiting within the queue system.

Proof The sojourning time for requests within the time interval T is denoted as $t_1, t_2, \cdots$. The expected number of arriving requests over this time period is λT. Consequently, the average number of requests sojourning in the system can be determined as:

$$L_s = \frac{\sum_i t_i}{T} \tag{4.5}$$

The average time for a request to sojourn in the service pool is:

$$W_s = \frac{\sum_i t_i}{\lambda T} \tag{4.6}$$

Hence, we have Eqs. (4.3) and (4.4). ∎

Based on Theorem 4.1, the mean waiting time for a charge request to be fulfilled is determined by:

$$W_s = \frac{L_s}{\lambda} = \frac{1}{\mu - \lambda} \tag{4.7}$$

The typical count of groups waiting in line within the queuing system is:

$$L_q = L_s - \rho = \frac{\lambda^2}{\mu(\mu - \lambda)} \tag{4.8}$$

Finally, we express the average waiting time for the requests to be responded to as:

$$W_q = \frac{L_q}{\lambda} = \frac{\lambda}{\mu(\mu - \lambda)} \tag{4.9}$$

In WRSNs, the scheduling algorithm needs to address both the time-related and location-based features of loading tasks. In our proposed method, we integrate the temporal and spatial priorities of a task into a unified priority. Consequently, this unified priority governs the charging actions of the WCV.

We establish ϕ as the threshold for minimum residual energy warning. That is, whenever a node's residual energy drops below ϕ, it will promptly request recharging by sending its coordinates and energy level to the WCV. We denote $t_w(A)$ as the time it takes for the WCV to reach the node.

The scheduling of on-demand tasks must satisfy several criteria, including temporal and spatial independence, preemptive capabilities, priority adjustment, among others. Thus, we will now discuss the method to fulfill these criteria.

4.1.3 Schematic Design

4.1.3.1 Determination of Warning Threshold

The warning threshold ϕ is an essential variable in the process of request ordering. This section will outline the procedure to determine this threshold. Assume L is the side length of the area and V_m is the walking speed of the WCV. The variable T indicates the maximum time needed for the WCV to move from one location to another within the square area. This relationship is described in Eq. (4.10):

$$T = \frac{\sqrt{2} * L}{V_m} \tag{4.10}$$

In order to keep all nodes functioning, a node's remaining lifetime when requesting a charge should be no less than T, ensuring it gets charged prior to running out of power. Moreover, since not every charging request is attended to right away, the size of the charging queue L_q needs to be taken into account. Therefore, the threshold for the remaining power ϕ can be calculated using Eq. (4.11):

$$\phi = T * V_d * L_q \tag{4.11}$$

4.1.3.2 Adjustment of Temporal Priority

This section describes the method for modifying the priorities of charging requests in the queue.

In a WRSN, certain nodes might run out of energy after an extended wait for recharging. Hence, prioritizing based only on the warning threshold is inadequate. A more efficient approach is to enhance the temporal priority of nodes when their waiting time t_w meets a threshold t_0. Identifying t_0 is essential. We define P_{cur} as the current residual energy of a node.

$$P_{cur} = \phi - V_d * t_w \tag{4.12}$$

When the node's energy reaches a critical point, T_{cur} represents the remaining lifetime of the node, which is determined as follows:

$$T_{cur} = \frac{P_{cur}}{V_d} \tag{4.13}$$

Therefore, we can determine the value of t_0 as:

$$t_0 = T - T_{ma} \tag{4.14}$$

in which T_{ma} represents the mean of the maximum service times for all charging demands within the service pool.

4.1.3.3 Preemption

As nodes have differing amounts of remaining energy and the waiting durations for charging requests fluctuate, with additional requests potentially entering the service queue at any time, a preemptive strategy is required to reorganize the WCV's charging sequence and improve charging efficiency.

As stated earlier, when t_w equals t_0, the time-based priority of a charging request will rise.

Even though nodes may reach their critical energy level or the t_w value may hit t_0 at different moments, it is essential to keep each charging request's t_w value below t_0. The specific timing is not important. This method modifies the temporal priority to guarantee that there is always a node where t_w reaches t_0. Therefore, the preemption interval should be established as t_0.

4.1.3.4 TADP Scheduling Algorithm

In this subsection, we provide a detailed explanation of how to compare the priorities of two charging requests. In our study, two main factors define the priority of a charging request: the first factor is the *temporal factor*, which is essentially the charging deadline of a request. It also indicates the time at which a charging request is made. The shorter the charging deadline, the higher the *temporal priority*. The second factor is the *distantial factor*, which refers to the distance between the node in need of charging and the WCV. The closer they are, the higher the *distantial priority*.

If multiple requests are received by the WCV, it must prioritize these requests. Initially, we assess the temporal priorities of two charging requests, as described in Algorithm 6:

Algorithm 6 Temporal Priority Comparison

Require: $T(A), T(B)$
Ensure: Comparison of $Pt(A)$ and $Pt(B)$
if $T(A) < T(B)$ **then**
    $Pt(A) > Pt(B)$;
else
    $Pt(A) \leq Pt(B)$;
end if

As described by Algorithm 6, among two requests A and B, it is possible to identify a charging request that has a greater temporal priority by comparing their deadlines. Following this, we arrange the requests into a queue according to their temporal priorities. The request with the highest priority is positioned at the beginning of the queue. The temporal priority of each request is then converted into an integer value that reflects its position within the temporal priority queue.

We analogously evaluate the distance-based priorities of two charging requests, as demonstrated in Algorithm 7:

Algorithm 7 Distantial Priority Comparison

Require: $D(A), D(B)$
Ensure: Comparison of $Pd(A)$ and $Pd(B)$
if $D(A) < D(B)$ **then**
    $Pd(A) > Pd(B)$;
else
    $Pd(A) \leq Pd(B)$;
end if

As specified in Algorithm 7, the distantial priority of two requests is compared. Likewise, the distantial priority is transformed into an integer.

Based on Algorithms 6 and 7, two priority queues are obtained in the service pool. As previously discussed, temporal priority and spatial priority are denoted by two integers.

We then merge temporal and distantial priorities to form a combined priority. As referenced in [7], the combined priority of a request can be obtained by consulting

Fig. 4.4 Temporal and distantial priority table

The location of the charging request in deadline queue

The location of the charging request in distance queue

2	3	4	5	6	7	8	9	10
3	4	5	6	7	8	9	10	11
4	5	6	7	8	9	10	11	12
5	6	7	8	9	10	11	12	13
6	7	8	9	10	11	12	13	14
7	8	9	10	11	12	13	14	15
8	9	10	11	12	13	14	15	16
9	10	11	12	13	14	15	16	17
10	11	12	13	14	15	16	17	18

the table in Fig. 4.4. Each charging request is assigned a combined priority $P(A)$, which dictates the preliminary charging sequence for the WCV. In this context, $Pt(A)$ and $Pd(A)$ represent the temporal and distantial priorities of a request A, respectively. The combined priority $P(A)$ can be determined by using Eq. (4.15).

$$P(A) = \alpha Pt(A) + \beta Pd(A) \tag{4.15}$$

In this context, α and β represent the proportions of temporal and spatial priorities, respectively. Let $\vartheta = \frac{\alpha}{\beta}$ be the ratio between α and β. As ϑ approaches infinity ($\vartheta \to +\infty$), our algorithm transitions into the EDF scheduling algorithm [8, 9]. Conversely, as ϑ approaches zero ($\vartheta \to 0$), it transforms into the NJNP scheduling algorithm [4, 10]. For our purposes, we set ϑ to 1 and design Algorithm 8 to evaluate the mixed priorities of charging requests A and B.

Algorithm 8 Mixed Priority Comparison Algorithm

Require: $Pt(A), Pt(B), Pd(A), Pd(B)$
Ensure: Comparison of $P(A)$ and $P(B)$
1: **if** $\alpha Pt(A) + \beta Pd(A) < \alpha Pt(B) + \beta Pd(B)$ **then**
2: $P(A) < P(B)$;
3: **else if** $\alpha Pt(A) + \beta Pd(A) = \alpha Pt(B) + \beta Pd(B)$ **then**
4: $P(A) = P(B)$;
5: **else**
6: $P(A) > P(B)$;
7: **end if**

Algorithm 8 can be utilized to assess the mixed priorities between two nodes. A scenario that must also be considered is that two different charging requests might have identical mixed priorities after executing Algorithm 8. For instance, the mixed priorities of two nodes might align on the same diagonal line, as illustrated in Fig. 4.4. The WCV cannot serve both nodes simultaneously in such a case.

Consequently, we devise additional comparisons to address the issue of priority equivalence.

We presented the notion of distantial density, symbolized by $De(A)$. A lower distantial density leads to a greater mixed priority. According to [7], distantial density is computed as shown in Eq. (4.16).

$$De(A) = D(A) * T(A) \tag{4.16}$$

Next, we present Algorithm 9 for additional comparisons based on distantial density.

Algorithm 9 Further priority comparison based on distantial density

Require: $D(A), T(A), D(B), T(B)$
Ensure: Comparison of $De(A)$ and $De(B)$
1: **if** $D(A) * T(A) < D(B) * T(B)$ **then**
2: $De(A) < De(B)$;
3: **else**
4: $De(A) > De(B)$;
5: **end if**

Based on Algorithm 9, the charging requests in the service pool are arranged according to their spatial density, which assists in directing the charging movements of the WCV.

Prior to executing the charging actions, it is necessary to verify the success of such actions. The value V is calculated as shown in Eq. (4.17).

$$V = \frac{D(A)}{T(A)} \tag{4.17}$$

If $V \leq V_m$, it signifies that the WCV is able to charge the node prior to its power depletion. Consequently, the WCV will proceed to charge the node without delay. Conversely, if this condition is not met, it implies that the node will run out of power before it can be charged. In such a case, the WCV will remove the charge request from the service pool.

Thus, a critical situation where a WCV opts to charge a node that would fail to survive (e.g., a node whose request is unfulfillable due to temporal or spatial limitations) will be avoided. Additionally, this will further ensure that the overall scheduling process remains unaffected.

4.1.3.5 Case Study

To clearly illustrate the benefits of the proposed scheme, a straightforward example is provided below. We execute TADP and NJNP to exhibit the charging behavior of the WCV and highlight the advantages of TADP.

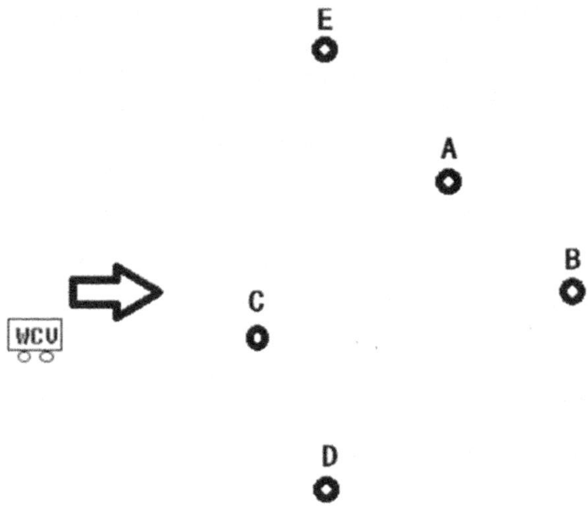

Fig. 4.5 Deployment of rechargeable sensor nodes

Table 4.1 Distances among nodes and WCV in the beginning

Distances(m)	WCV	Node E	Node D	Node C	Node B	Node A
Node A	40	20	32	30	15	–
Node B	50	34	35	35	–	–
Node C	20	45	20	–	–	–
Node D	30	50	–	–	–	–
Node E	45	–	–	–	–	–
WCV	–	–	–	–	–	–

As shown in Fig. 4.5, five nodes (A, B, C, D, and E) are randomly placed in the WRSN. The distances between the nodes and the WCV are given in Table 4.1. Note that the data in the lower part of the table is identical to the upper part, so these cells are omitted to avoid duplication. The five nodes send their charging requests to the WCV at 12:00:00, 12:01:00, 12:01:30, 12:01:45, and 12:02:30, respectively. For simplicity, we assume $\phi = 30\%$, the energy consumption rate is $0.1\%/s$ and the nodes all have an energy capacity of 30J. The distances between the WCV and nodes A, B, C, D, and E are 40, 50, 20, 30, and 45 m, respectively. At 12:04:00, the WCV completes other charging tasks and prepares to decide on the charging path for these five requests.

We then use TADP to plan the charging route. First, charging requests are arranged by their start times to create a temporal priority queue. Next, Algorithm 7 is employed to determine a spatial priority for the five nodes. With two priority queues available, Algorithm 8 calculates the combined priority for each charging request. Considering the arrival times and distances between the nodes and the WCV, the sequence is $T(A) < T(B) < T(C) < T(D) < T(E)$ and $D(C) < D(D) < D(A) < D(E) < D(B)$. Consequently, the priorities are $Pt(A) = 1$, $Pt(B) = 2$, $Pt(C) = 3$, $Pt(D) = 4$, $Pt(E) = 5$ and $Pd(A) = 3$, $Pd(B) = 5$,

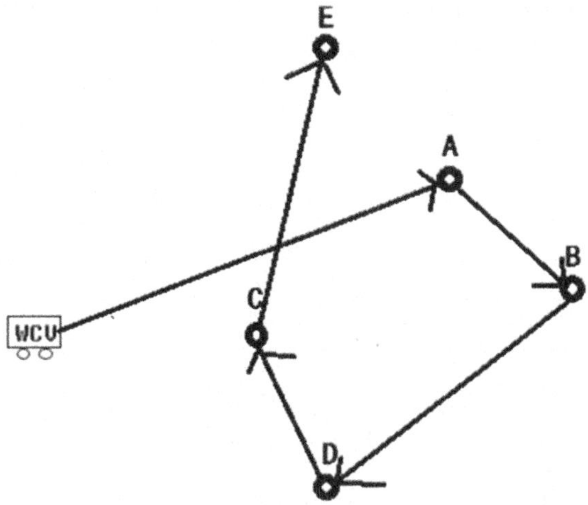

Fig. 4.6 Charging path of TADP

$Pd(C) = 1$, $Pd(D) = 2$, $Pd(E) = 4$. Using Eq. (4.15), we get $P(A) = 4$, $P(B) = 7$, $P(C) = 4$, $P(D) = 6$, and $P(E) = 9$. Thus, the charging order is $A = C > D > B > E$. Since nodes A and C have the same mixed priority, Algorithm 9 is applied for further comparison. With a warning threshold $\phi = 30\%$ and an energy consumption rate of $0.1\%/\text{s}$, an emergency node can last 300 s after requesting a charge. At 12:04:00, the remaining lifetimes of nodes A and C are $T(A) = 60$ and $T(C) = 150$, respectively. Given distances $D(A) = 40$ and $D(C) = 20$, the distantial densities are $De(A) = D(A) * T(A) = 2400$ and $De(C) = D(C) * T(C) = 3000$. Hence, node A has a higher priority than node C, organizing the service pool sequence as A, C, D, B, E. The WCV will charge node A first and then recalculate the next node based on its current position at node A. Repeating this procedure four times, the final charging route for the WCV is $A \to B \to D \to C \to E$, as shown in Fig. 4.6.

By comparing NJNP with TADP, it is evident that TADP provides a more concise charging path and reduced latency. Additional simulations will be performed to thoroughly evaluate the advantages of TADP.

4.1.4 Simulation and Experiments

4.1.4.1 Simulation Setup

As shown in Table 4.2, the simulation entails the random deployment of 100 nodes in a 100×100 m area. The energy consumption rate for wireless sensor nodes is designated as $V_d = 0.002$ kJ/s, and the WCV travels at a speed of 4 m/s. The alert threshold ϕ is defined at 30%, causing sensor nodes to issue a charging request to

Table 4.2 Simulation parameters

Parameters	Values
Charging algorithm	TADP, NJNP, EDF
Network size(m^2)	100 × 100
Number of nodes	100
Energy consumption rate(kJ/s)	0.002
Warning threshold	30%
Initial energy (kJ)	100
WCV speed(m/s)	4

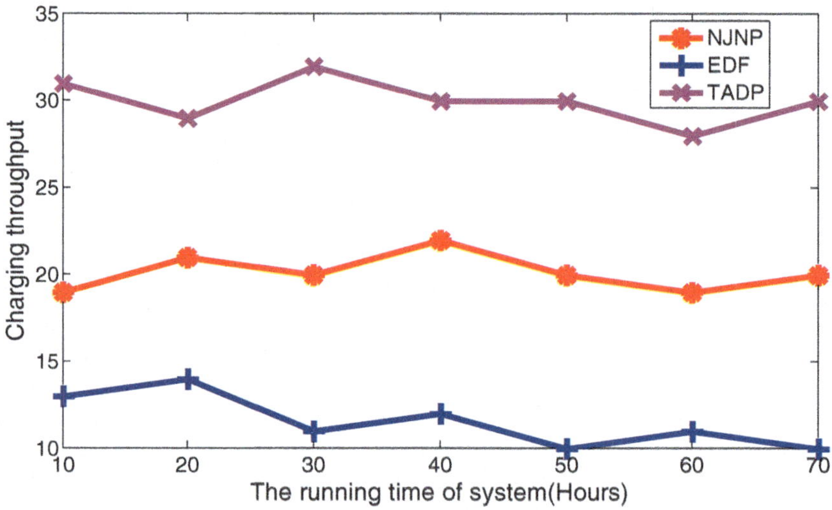

Fig. 4.7 Charging throughput comparison

the WCV. The WCV ranks the charging requests based on a combined priority and decides which node to charge.

4.1.4.2 Throughput of Charging Requests

In an on-demand charging system, the throughput rate of charging requests is an essential measure for assessing the charging scheduling algorithm. This rate represents the quantity of charging requests effectively completed within a given timeframe, indicating the performance of the WCV's movement and charging activities.

As depicted in Fig. 4.7, the throughput capacity of the TADP scheduling algorithm grows over time, whereas the NJNP scheduling algorithm displays instability. Furthermore, TADP's throughput capacity considerably exceeds that of both NJNP and EDF. Statistically, the throughput capacity of NJNP is merely half of TADP's,

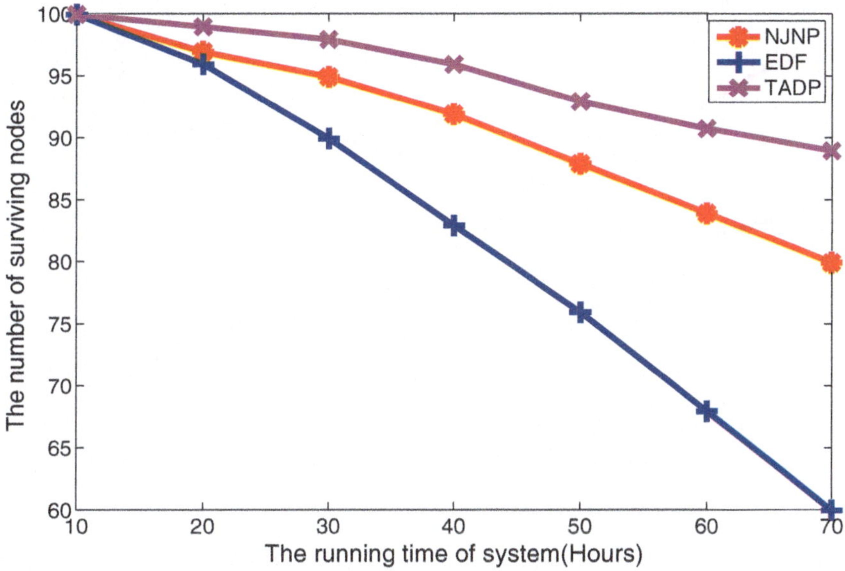

Fig. 4.8 Survival nodes number comparison

underscoring TADP's significant enhancement in recharging throughput and its proficiency in charging more nodes before they deplete their power.

4.1.4.3 Survival Node Number

This simulation evaluates the count of surviving nodes for TADP, NJNP, and EDF. As shown in Fig. 4.8, there is a gradual decline in the number of nodes over time in all three algorithms due to restricted charging capacities and time limitations, which hinder the timely charging of all nodes.

The findings indicate that TADP preserves a larger quantity of active nodes in comparison to NJNP and EDF, suggesting a more effective charging rate for TADP.

4.1.4.4 Average Response Time

This simulation assesses the mean response time, also known as charging latency, defined as the duration from when a node sends a charging request to when it successfully receives a charge. This measure indicates the WCV's responsiveness and the effectiveness of the charging algorithm.

As illustrated in Fig. 4.9, the average response time of TADP diminishes steadily, whereas NJNP shows a swift decline. This rapid decrease in NJNP is attributed to its low throughput, leading to delays in charging certain nodes. NJNP's average

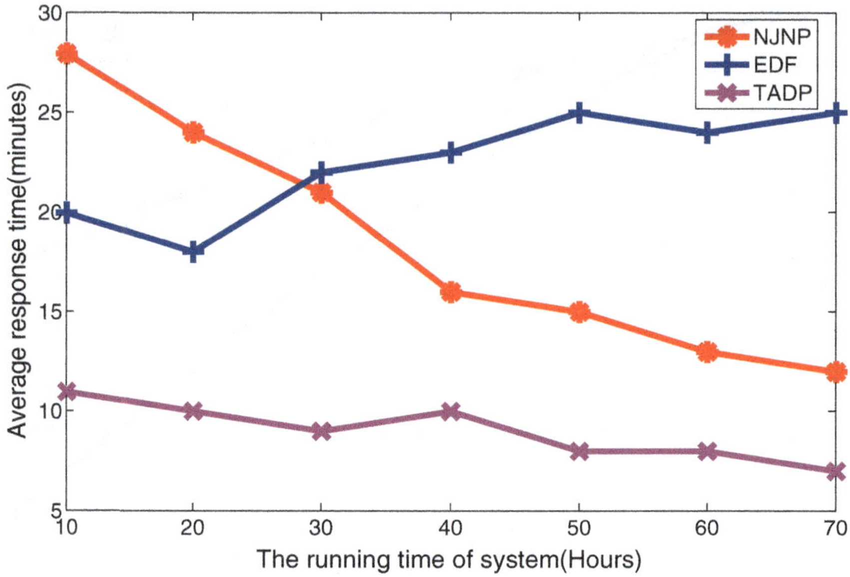

Fig. 4.9 Average response time comparison

response time exceeds TADP's by 5 minutes. A reduced average response time correlates with a higher rate of successful charges. The average response time for EDF rises gradually, highlighting the superior effectiveness of TADP.

4.1.4.5 Average Length of Waiting Queue

The mean length of the waiting queue, which signifies the quantity of charging requests in the service pool, serves as a crucial metric of the WCV's operational status. A reduced queue length signifies fewer outstanding charging requests, indicating enhanced charging efficiency.

As shown in Fig. 4.10, the TADP algorithm consistently achieves an average queue length of four, whereas the NJNP and EDF algorithms result in significantly longer queues. The shorter queue length in TADP indicates quicker completion of charging tasks and improved charging efficiency.

4.1.4.6 Successful Charging Rate

Figure 4.11 illustrates a comparison of the success rates for TADP, NJNP, and EDF. As time progresses, NJNP and EDF show increasing success rates, whereas TADP maintains a consistent 100% success rate. This demonstrates that TADP efficiently

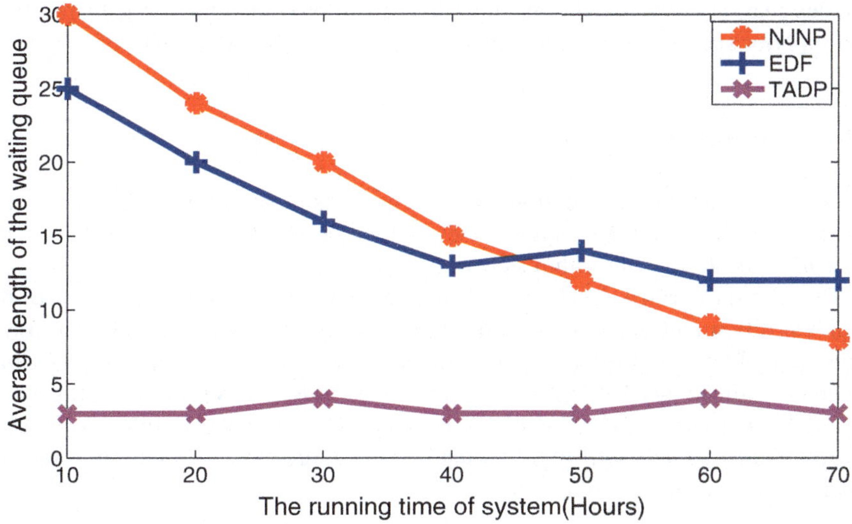

Fig. 4.10 Average length of waiting queue comparison

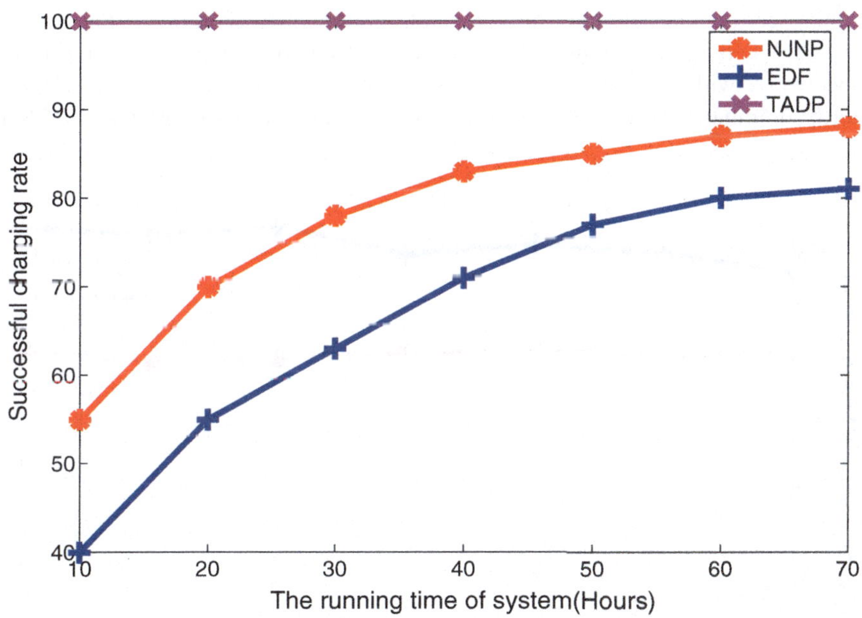

Fig. 4.11 Successful charging rate comparison

handles charging requests, despite the WCV's restricted charging capacity, resulting in a superior successful charging rate in comparison to NJNP and EDF.

4.1.4.7 Average Service Time

Finally, the mean service duration, which represents the mean time required by the WCV to fulfill a charging request, is evaluated among the three algorithms. This measure indicates the algorithm's charging performance.

The average service duration encompasses both the WCV's travel time to the node's position and the charging time for the node. According to [11], the travel time is notably more prolonged than the charging duration, making it negligible. Figure 4.12 illustrates that NJNP's average service duration is four to five times that of TADP. On average, NJNP and EDF need an extra 3 minutes to fulfill a charging request compared to TADP, highlighting TADP's more efficient charging route and greater responsiveness to requests.

4.1.4.8 Other Characteristics Analysis

In this section, we explore how α and β influence charging efficiency. In Sect. 4.1.3.4, α and β signify the importance of temporal and spatial priority, respectively, with ϑ as their ratio. As per Eq. (4.17), when $\vartheta > 1$, temporal priority dominates over spatial priority. Consider two scenarios with $\alpha = 2$ and

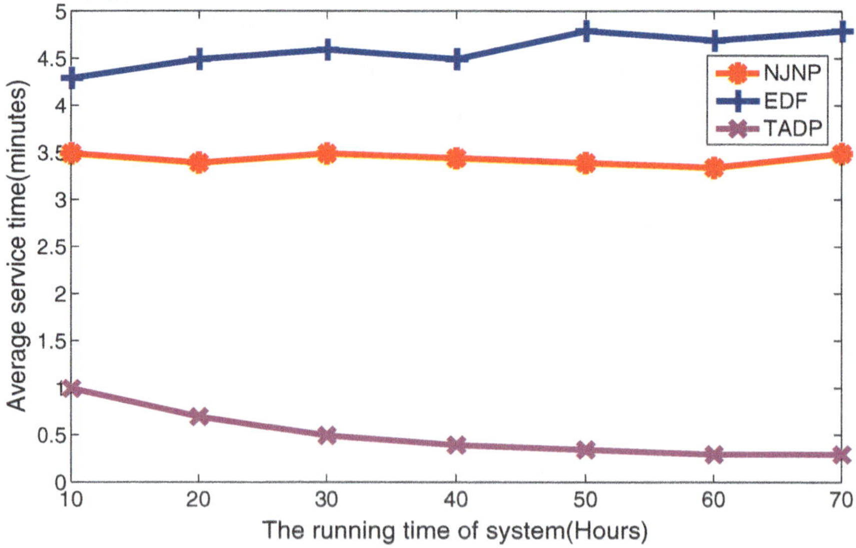

Fig. 4.12 Average service time comparison

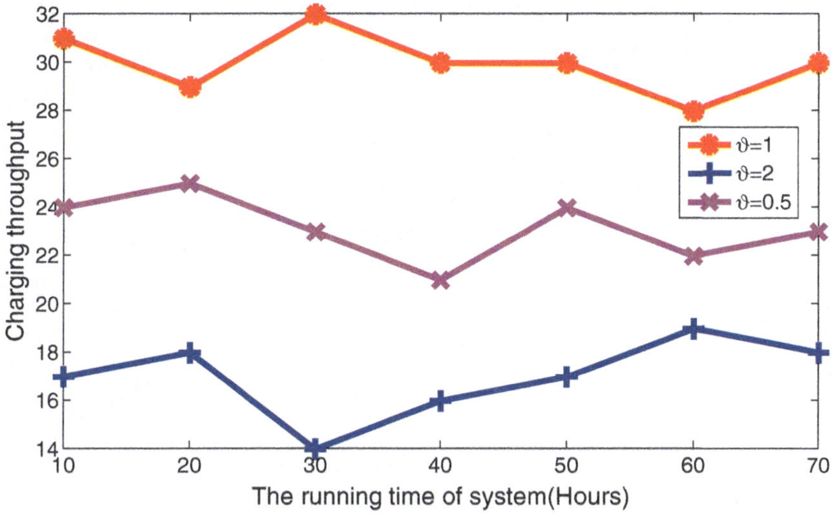

Fig. 4.13 Influence of ϑ on charging throughput

$\beta = 1$, yielding $\vartheta = 2$. For nodes A and B with temporal and spatial priorities of $(1, 2)$ and $(2, 1)$, respectively, if $\vartheta = 1$, their combined priorities are equal, $P(A) = P(B) = 3$, necessitating further comparison through Algorithm 9, which consumes computation time. Conversely, with $\vartheta = 2$, $P(A) = 4$ and $P(B) = 5$, hence the node with higher temporal priority is charged first.

Examining nodes C and D with priority pairs $(4, 2)$ and $(3, 4)$ respectively, when $\vartheta = 1$, $P(A) < P(B)$, prioritizing the node with the lesser temporal priority. When $\vartheta = 2$, both $P(A)$ and $P(B)$ are set to 10, requiring Algorithm 9 to assess the distantial densities, which may result in prioritizing the node with the greater temporal priority first (Fig. 4.13).

In terms of surviving nodes, there is little variation across different ϑ values. Figure 4.14 illustrates that around 98 nodes persist for the initial 20 hours in every scenario. Nevertheless, after 70 hours, the number of nodes diminishes more rapidly with $\vartheta = 2$ and $\vartheta = 0.5$ than with $\vartheta = 1$, indicating that $\vartheta = 1$ results in a higher count of surviving nodes and a prolonged system lifetime.

4.2 Real-Time Charging Scheduling

In the previous section, we proposed a scheduling strategy based on spatio-temporal prioritization. This section elaborates on the construction of a spatio-temporal charging scheduling algorithm, named TSCA, designed for the on-demand charging architecture. The aim is to reduce the number of dead nodes while enhancing energy efficiency, thereby extending the network's lifespan. Initially, after gathering

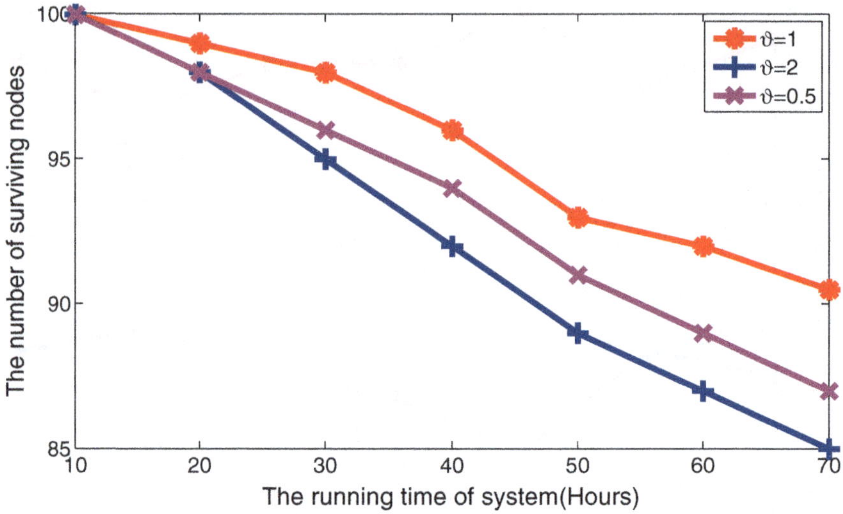

Fig. 4.14 Influence of ϑ on surviving nodes

the charging requests, a WCV devises a viable motion plan. Following this, a basic path planning algorithm is introduced to rearrange the charging sequence for better efficiency. Additionally, global-level optimizations are performed. A node deletion algorithm is then devised to eliminate low-efficiency charging nodes. Lastly, a node insertion algorithm is applied to avert the death of abandoned nodes. Comprehensive simulations reveal that, compared to leading charging scheduling algorithms, our approach can achieve notable improvements in charging throughput, charging efficiency, and various other performance metrics.

4.2.1 Problem Statement

4.2.1.1 One Prominent Problem

A major problem in this area of research is the common belief that the shortest Hamiltonian cycle is the best solution for almost all scheduling methods [12, 13]. These methods focus mainly on reducing travel expenses, which are directly related to the duration of the charging cycle. Therefore, the shortest Hamiltonian cycle is generally regarded as the most effective and efficient movement strategy.

Nonetheless, an in-depth analysis of the spatial and temporal aspects of charging tasks shows that although the shortest Hamiltonian cycle typically ensures minimal energy usage, it might be impractical under extreme conditions. Surprisingly, an option that does not yield the shortest route or the least energy expenditure can

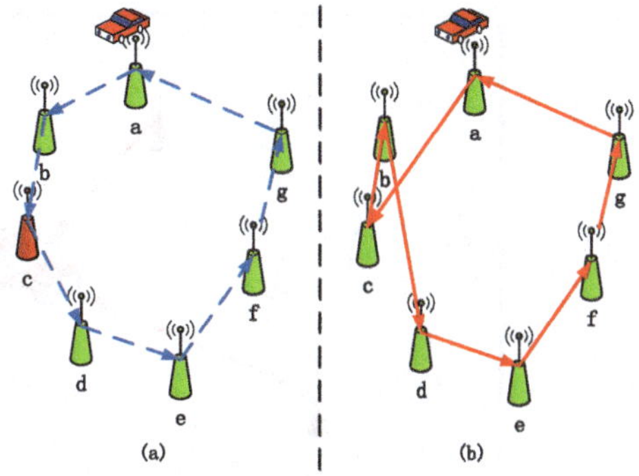

Fig. 4.15 Comparison of charging strategies: (**a**) the shortest Hamiltonian cycle which is not feasible and (**b**) a feasible solution which is not the shortest

occasionally be the most practical and efficient choice for a WCV, as depicted in Fig. 4.15.

As shown in Fig. 4.15, the charging request from node *c* is the most crucial and demands immediate action. The route depicted in Fig. 4.15a (a–b–c–d–e–f–g–a) is obtained from the shortest Hamiltonian cycle, providing the least travel distance and cost. On the other hand, the cycle in Fig. 4.15b (a–c–b–d–e–f–g–a) represents a more standard solution. Following the shortest Hamiltonian cycle, node *c* cannot be recharged before its deadline, resulting in failure despite the optimal path. However, even though the sequence (a–c–b–d–e–f–g–a) involves extended travel and increased charging expenses, it meets the temporal, spatial, and energy requirements of node *c*, making it a viable or even the optimal choice. In future research, we intend to (a) identify viable solutions for charging schedules and (b) enhance these solutions.

4.2.1.2 Problem Statement

We foresee a situation in which a WRSN has several homogeneous sensor nodes scattered randomly within an open area depicted in Fig. 4.16. A single WCV is in charge of recharging all the sensors. When the energy level of a node falls below a certain point, it promptly sends a recharge request to the WCV, which then schedules the recharging.

We describe the schedulable region as a rectangular area where WCV can receive charging requests at any time and from any location. In the scheduling process within the on-demand framework, each request's arrival time adheres to a Poisson distribution, while the service time follows a general distribution [14]. As illustrated in Fig. 4.16, four nodes have sent their charging requests to WCV. Subsequently, WCV queues these requests according to their arrival times (refer to Fig. 4.17). By applying specific scheduling algorithms, WCV selects and proceeds to serve a request.

While responding to requests, as noted by [4, 14], the delay in charging is deemed inconsequential relative to the travel time. For the sake of simplicity, we presume the

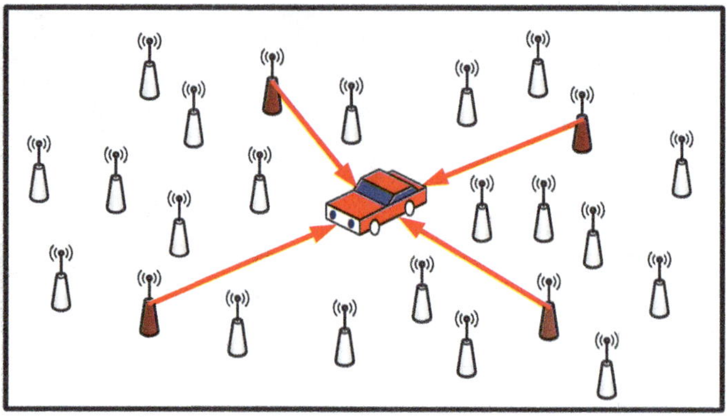

Fig. 4.16 An overview of on-demand charging architecture

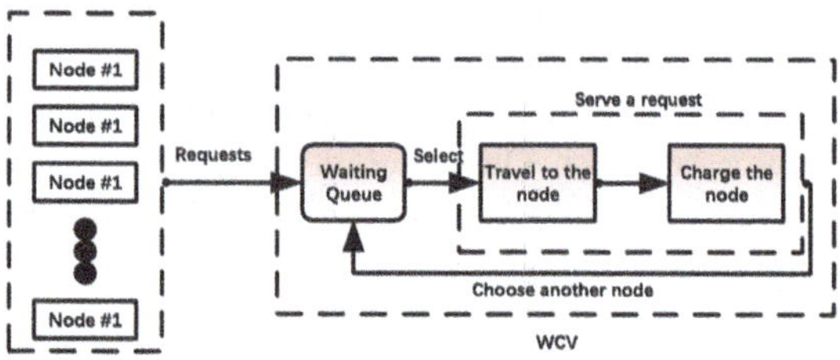

Fig. 4.17 Queueing model for on-demand charging architecture

WCV moves at a consistent speed v and maintains a uniform energy consumption rate. A node can be charged only when the WCV arrives at its site. Each node functions continuously, and if its power depletes to zero, it ceases to operate, which leads to irrevocable damage to system performance.

To counteract such impacts, it is vital to optimize charging efficiency. Nonetheless, as highlighted in [15], concentrating only on efficiency may be inadequate for sustaining monitoring performance and operational functionality. Given that unforeseen incidents can arise anywhere in the network at any moment, the depletion of any node could lead to event detection failure, which is particularly undesirable in safety-critical scenarios. We describe this charging scheduling challenge as a *multi-objective optimization problem*, where the *primary goal* is to keep the maximum number of sensors operational or to minimize the count of non-functional nodes. Furthermore, our secondary aim is to enhance energy efficiency. Below, we outline the related notations to tackle this issue.

Let $S_N(i)$ represent the status of a node. A sensor can be in one of two states: active ($S_N(i) = 1$) or inactive ($S_N(i) = 0$), summarized as:

$$S_N(i) = \begin{cases} 0 & T \leq T_D(i) \\ 1 & T > T_D(i) \end{cases}. \tag{4.18}$$

T represents the present moment, while $T_D(i)$ denotes the deadline for node i. The aim of our approach is to minimize the count of dead nodes $\mathcal{N}_D$ and to enhance the energy efficiency η of WCV throughout the sensor network's lifespan, which can be articulated as follows.

$$\min \quad \mathcal{N}_D = \sum_{i=0}^{N} S_N(i) , \tag{4.19}$$

$$\max \quad \eta = \frac{E_e}{E_e + V_D \sum_{j=1}^{N_{task}} \sum_{k=0}^{|Q_{optimized}(j)|-1} D_{n_k,n_k+1}(j)} . \tag{4.20}$$

Subject to:

$$t_{i+1} = t_i + \frac{D_{i,i+1}}{v} \quad 0 \le i \le \epsilon \tag{4.21}$$

$$T_R(i) = T_D(i) - T \tag{4.22}$$

$$T_R(i) = \frac{E_C(i)}{V_M(i)} \tag{4.23}$$

$$E_e = \sum_{i=0}^{N} (V_M(i)T(1 - S_N(i)) + V_M(i)T_D(i)S_N(i)) \tag{4.24}$$

Equation (4.21) outlines the charging process between two neighboring nodes, where t_i represents the arrival time of the WCV at node i, and $D_{i,i+1}$ is the distance between nodes i and $i + 1$, with v being the speed of the WCV. The remaining time for node i is influenced by its remaining energy $E_C(i)$ and the energy consumption rate $V_M(i)$. It can also be determined through the dead time $T_D(i)$ and the current time T, as shown in Eqs. (4.22) and (4.23). The effective energy of the WCV, E_e, which is the energy that is ultimately received by the nodes, is defined by Eq. (4.24). If node i is operational (i.e., $S_N(i) = 0$), it receives $V_M(i)T(1 - S_N(i))$ energy; otherwise, $E_e = V_M(i)T_D(i)S_N(i)$.

4.2.2 *Schematic Design*

4.2.2.1 Model Description

We assume a network consisting of several identical rechargeable sensor nodes. Each node i is equipped with the same energy capacity P_M and energy consumption rate $V_M(i)$.

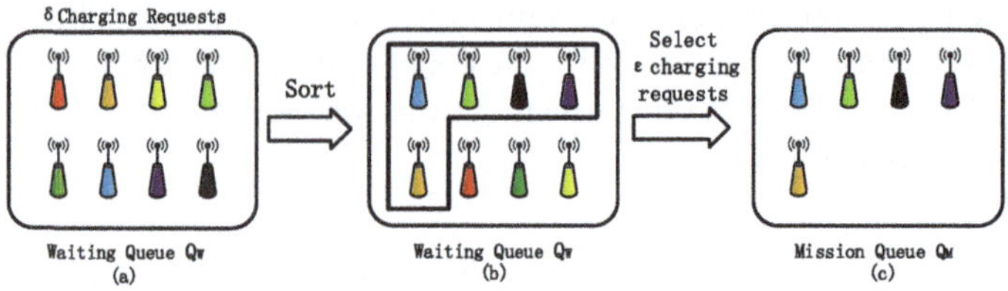

Fig. 4.18 An example of setting up Q_W and Q_M

The work process of a WCV is modeled as the repeated performance of loading tasks. A task involves charging several nodes. Upon receiving a charging request, it is initially placed in a waiting queue Q_W. Subsequently, a charging task j comprising the most recent ϵ requests is generated. Each task j has a mission queue $Q_M(j)$ that logs the previous ϵ requests from Q_W.

For clarity, we provide an example to demonstrate the setting of Q_W and $Q_M(j)$ in a WCV. Illustrated in Fig. 4.18, at a certain point, the WCV has received $\delta = 8$ charging requests ($\delta > \epsilon$) (refer to Fig. 4.18a). The WCV logs these requests in Q_W and sorts them by their deadlines in ascending order (see Fig. 4.18b). Subsequently, the WCV selects the first $\epsilon = 5$ requests to form task j and places them in $Q_M(j)$ to build a charging route (illustrated in Fig. 4.18c). In theory, Q_W should be sufficiently large to store all charging requests. However, in our model, $|Q_W|$ is relatively small (see findings in Sect. 4.2.4).

After a comprehensive analysis, the principles and requirements listed below should be considered when developing a charge scheduling algorithm.

1. Global path planning and optimizations (refer to Algorithms 10, 11, and 13). The travel path should be created from a global perspective using path planning. This should be done offline, as opposed to prioritizing and selecting the first item from the queue as the charging target.
2. A short charging queue (refer to the definition of $Q_M(j)$). Owing to the NP-hard characteristics of path planning [16], constructing a charging path each time with fewer nodes in the queue will yield a more precise solution. In other words, having fewer nodes allows the path planning to be executed more swiftly, accurately, and with reduced computational and storage requirements.
3. Avoiding and discarding low-efficient nodes (refer to Algorithm 12). In this study, nodes that significantly escalate travel costs are defined as *low-efficient nodes*, which greatly diminish charging efficiency. Therefore, the proposed strategy must alleviate such impacts. For instance, if a node cannot be charged promptly or results in high travel costs, it should be preemptively removed.
4. Minimizing dead nodes (refer to Algorithms 10, 11, 12, and 13). Enhancing the robustness and stability of the network requires ensuring the survival of most sensors. The fundamental approach focuses on reducing the number of dead nodes while improving charging efficiency.

In order to meet the goals outlined in Sect. 4.2.1.2 and adhere to the aforementioned criteria, we establish conventions for Eq. (4.20).

Suppose that in task j, a mission queue $Q_M(j)$ is created, consisting of $|Q_M(j)|$ requests. Next, we aim to determine an optimized queue $Q_{optimized}(j)$ (i.e. an optimal charging route) to guide charging movements. Consequently, the number of dead nodes can be represented as:

$$N_D = \sum_{j=1}^{N_{task}} |Q_M(j)| - |Q_{optimized}(j)| \,, \tag{4.25}$$

where $|Q_M(j)|$ represents the size of $Q_M(j)$, confirmed to be small in Sect. 4.2.3. The size of the optimized queue, $|Q_{optimized}(j)|$, will be determined in Sect. 4.2.4. Hence, our primary goal (see Eq. (4.19)) is to minimize N_D by maximizing the length of the charging path $|Q_{optimized}(j)|$ for each task.

Next, our attention shifts to the secondary goal, which is to maximize energy efficiency. As stated in Eq. (4.20), the goal is to maximize η by minimizing the value of $\sum_{k=0}^{|Q_{optimized}(j)|-1} D_{n_k,n_k+1}(j)$. Hence, by reducing the travel distance, we can accomplish our secondary objective.

Drawing on these results, we create the temporal spatial charging algorithm (TSCA) to meet our goals, consisting of four distinct algorithms.

4.2.2.2 Basic Path Planning Algorithm

Initially, we introduce a fundamental path planning algorithm designed to offer a viable charging schedule that largely adheres to the time and location constraints of charging demands. The detailed methodology is presented in Algorithm 10.

Algorithm 10 functions as described below. First, we choose the initial ϵ charging requests from Q_W and add them to $Q_M(j)$. Each request r_i is given a temporal priority, $P_T(i)$, which is based on its deadline $T_D(i)$. Requests with shorter deadlines receive higher temporal priority. These requests are then ordered in descending order according to $P_T(i)$. We construct a charging route $\Pi = (\pi_{1,2}, \pi_{2,3}, ...\pi_{\epsilon-1,\epsilon}, \pi_{\epsilon,1})$ for a trip cycle, where $\pi_{i,j}$ denotes the path from node i to node j, and D_{n_i,n_j} represents the distance between nodes i and j. Finally, we assess whether Π fulfills the spatial and temporal requirements.

If there is a dead node, denoted as i, which means node i cannot be charged prior to its deadline, we aim to adjust the charging order to preserve the maximum number of nodes that are at risk of dying.

A node n_a that cannot be recharged in a timely manner needs to be moved to an earlier position in $Q_{optimized}(j)$. Each preceding slot is checked to determine the best position for n_a. When the following conditions are satisfied: a) n_a remains operational after recharging another node n_b; and b) placing n_a immediately after n_b does not cause failures in other nodes, n_a is inserted after n_b. If rearranging a single node in $Q_B(j)$ to find a solution is not feasible, Algorithm 11 is used to optimize

Algorithm 10 Construct a basic path through best effort

1: **Input**: A mission queue $Q_M(j)$ and a queue Q_P for recording nodes to be dropped;
2: **Output**: A feasible path $Q_B(j)$;
3: **while** $Q_M(j) \neq \emptyset$ **do**
4:   Select the first node n_a from $Q_M(j)$;
5:   $Q_B(j) \leftarrow Q_B(j) \cup \{n_a\}$;
6:   **if** $t_{n_a} < T_D(n_a)$ **then**
7:     $S_N(n_a) \leftarrow 0$;
8:   **else**
9:     **for** Each node $n_b \in Q_B(j)$ **do**
10:       Insert n_a next to n_b;
11:       **if** Nodes in $Q_B(j)$ are all alive **then**
12:         $S_N(n_a) \leftarrow 0$;
13:       **else**
14:         Call Algorithm 11 for optimizing $Q_B(j)$;
15:         **if** $Q_B(j)$ is the optimized path **then**
16:           $Q_P \leftarrow Q_P \cup \{n_a\}$;
17:         **else**
18:           Try to insert n_a into the optimized $Q_B(j)$;
19:         **end if**
20:       **end if**
21:     **end for**
22:   **end if**
23: **end while**

$Q_B(j)$. If $Q_B(j)$ is already optimal and no appropriate position for n_a is found, n_a is moved to Q_P. As a result, the Wireless Charging Vehicle (WCV) will temporarily disregard the charge request from n_a.

4.2.2.3 Charging Path Optimizations

As shown in line 14 of Algorithm 10, we employ Algorithm 11 to enhance the achieved charging path with the aim of further increasing the minimum remaining time. Our intention is to save more time for future scheduling, thereby guaranteeing that the remaining time of each sub-path is maximized. In this context, a sub-path refers to a section of a charging path. Our goal is formulated as follows:

$$\max \quad M_A(\Pi) = min(T_R(i)) \quad i \in \Pi \,, \tag{4.26}$$

where $T_R(i)$ represents the time left for node i, and Π is the particular path we are trying to optimize. Upon obtaining the current path $Q_B(j)$ from Algorithm 10, the first step is to determine the node i that has the least remaining time $T_R(i)$. Next, the goal is to maximize the minimum remaining time of the current path $Q_B(j)$, thus ensuring that $M_A(\Pi)$ equals $T_R(i)$.

It is clear that advancing node i is the only way to increase the minimum remaining time of the path. To modify the position of node i, characterized by the minimum remaining time in the present path, we utilize the increased time $T_C(i)$ from inserting node n_i to identify an effective strategy:

$$T_C(i) = \frac{D_{x,i} + D_{i,y} - D_{x,y}}{v} \quad i, x, y \in \Pi \,, \tag{4.27}$$

where the positions of nodes x and y are in front of node i.

To position i forward, our goal is to reduce the remaining path time by minimizing $T_C(i)$. If the current path already achieves the minimum remaining time $M_A(Q_B(j))$, the insertion action will eventually be undone. Additionally, minimizing $T_C(i)$ leads to shortening the current path's travel distance, implying any other node insertion will result in an additional travel cost as indicated by Eq. (4.27). Therefore, by reducing travel distance, we enhance energy efficiency, meeting the objectives outlined in Sect. 4.2.1.2.

The optimization of the current path is given in Algorithm 11.

Algorithm 11 Convert the current path to the optimized path

Input: $Q_B(j)$;
Output: An optimized path $Q_B(j)$;
Find the node n_c with $M_A(Q_B(j)) = T_R(n_c)$;
for Each two adjacent nodes x and y ahead of n_c **do**
  $T_C(n_c) \leftarrow \frac{D_{x,n_c} + D_{n_c,y} - D_{x,y}}{v}$;
  Form a strategy Q_O by minimizing $T_C(n_c)$;
end for
while $M_A(Q_O) < M_A(Q_B(j))$ **do**
  Adjust strategy Q_O by increasing $T_C(n_c)$;
end while
$Q_B(j) \leftarrow Q_O$;
if n_c is in the last sub-path **then**
  return $Q_B(j)$;
else
  Call Algorithm 11 again to optimize sub-path of $Q_R(j)$;
end if

The steps of Algorithm 11 are as follows. Initially, a node, labeled n_c, with the shortest remaining time is chosen from $Q_B(j)$. This node n_c is then re-inserted between every pair of consecutive nodes in the path. The additional time caused by n_c's insertion is recorded, and eventually, the charging strategy (i.e., a charging path Q_O) that results in the least increased time $T_C(n_c)$ is selected using Eq. (4.27). If the shortest remaining time exceeds that of the current path $Q_B(j)$, then $Q_B(j)$ is updated to the new charging strategy Q_O. The optimization process is executed recursively within the remaining sections of the path until the node with the shortest remaining time is found in the final sub-path.

4.2.2.4 Low Efficient Nodes Avoiding

A detailed analysis reveals that certain nodes within the charging paths are less efficient. These nodes negatively impact network performance and elevate the count of non-functioning nodes. To counter these consequences, we have designed the Algorithm 12.

The objective of the Algorithm 12 is to ensure node survivability and minimize the loading path propagation time through adjustments in loading sequences. This approach aims to decrease the amount of dead nodes by removing the less efficient ones as extensively as feasible.

To determine if a node i is considered low efficiency, we suggest the following criteria. A node is identified as low efficient if all criteria are met.

1. $D_{i,i+1} > D_{i-1,i+1}$ or $D_{i-1,i} > D_{i-1,i+1}$.
2. The angle between two adjacent nodes in the charging queue is lower than 90°.

To simplify our explanation, we present a straightforward example. As illustrated in Fig. 4.19, it is clear that the following three conditions hold concurrently: (a) $\angle aec < 90°$, (b) $D_{a,e} > D_{a,c}$, and (c) $D_{e,c} > D_{a,c}$; hence, node e is identified as a low-efficiency node.

Upon completing Algorithms 10 and 11, an optimized path $Q_B(j)$ and a collection of dropped nodes Q_P are obtained. In what follows, we create Algorithm 12 to remove nodes with low efficiency in $Q_B(j)$, aiming to further improve the charging performance.

Algorithm 12 operates as described. We select every three consecutive nodes a, b, and c to determine if the middle node b is inefficient according to the specified criteria. If b is found to be inefficient, it is added to Q_P, and a new edge connecting a directly to c is established. As detailed in Sect. 4.2.4, the impact of removing inefficient nodes will be confirmed through simulations, highlighting the importance of this procedure.

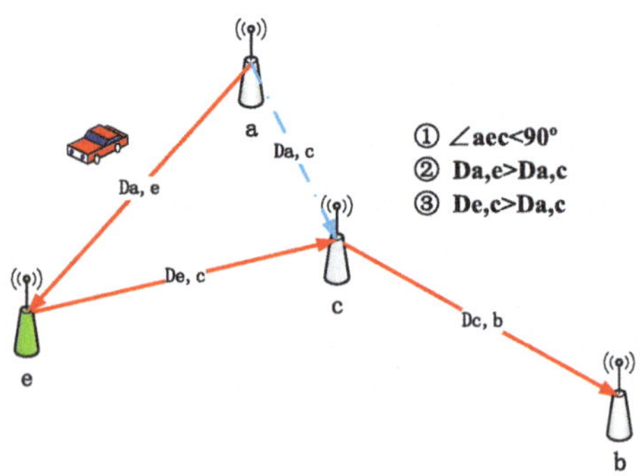

Fig. 4.19 An example of judging a low efficient node(i.e. node e)

Algorithm 12 Delete low efficient nodes

Input: $Q_B(j)$ and Q_P;
Output: An optimized path $Q_H(j)$;
for Any three adjacent nodes a, b and c **do**
  if b is a high efficient node **then**
    continue;
  else
    $Q_P \leftarrow Q_P \cup \{b\}$ (i.e. Delete node b);
    Connect a and c;
  end if
end for

4.2.2.5 Global Path Optimizations

After identifying and removing low-efficiency sensor nodes, an efficient charging path $Q_H(j)$ is established. Finishing this path will result in a high ratio of successful charges, as the path closely resembles a circle, yielding shorter travel distances. Moreover, the nodes along this route will receive charges well ahead of their request deadlines, providing ample redundant time. Nevertheless, some less efficient nodes will be left uncharged, and dead nodes will appear, which goes against our goals. Hence, it is vital to balance the load throughput during scheduling to make the most of the available redundant time. Our approach involves reinserting certain nodes from Q_P into the charging path to reduce $\mathcal{N}_D$, as highlighted in the problem statement.

Within Q_P, there are two categories of nodes: (I) nodes eliminated by Algorithm 10 and (II) nodes with low efficiency. Furthermore, nodes of type (I) come before type (II) nodes in Q_P, and type (II) nodes have a negative influence on the spatial aspect of the charging process. By running Algorithm 13, some of the closest sensor nodes will be chosen and included in $Q_{optimized}(j)$. Additionally, the influence of dying nodes can be prevented. If a sensor node fails to meet the conditions, its index will be adjusted and it will be re-eliminated in Q_P.

To achieve minimal travel distance for charging, we execute the insertion process by reducing T_C as outlined in Algorithm 11. By accomplishing the insertion with the least travel cost, we ultimately fulfill the goal of maximizing charging efficiency.

The following section presents Algorithm 13 in detail for better understanding.

Algorithm 13 operates as follows. First, we extract the initial node i from Q_P and place it in the optimal position, where the increase in time $T_C(i)$ is minimal within Q_O. Next, we try to adjust the insertion point of i if there are dead nodes in the previous path. If re-inserting i is not possible, it will be directly added to the set of dead nodes $\mathcal{N}_D$. Finally, the outcomes of the algorithm will be $Q_{optimized}(j)$ and $\mathcal{N}_D$.

In order to confirm that the proposed scheme can generate feasible solutions under extreme cases, we refer to Fig. 4.15 in Sect. 4.2.1.1 as an example. Ultimately, we obtain a traveling cycle a–c–b–d–e–f–g–a, which demonstrates the validity and effectiveness of TSCA.

Algorithm 13 Re-insert nodes from Q_P to $Q_{optimized}(j)$

Input: $Q_H(j)$ and Q_P;
Output: An optimized path $Q_{optimized}(j)$ and the set of dead nodes $\mathcal{N}_D$;
$Q_{optimized}(j) \leftarrow Q_H(j)$;
while $Q_P \neq \emptyset$ **do**
  Fetch the first node i from Q_P;
  for Each two adjacent nodes x and y in $Q_{optimized}(j)$ **do**
    $T_C(i) \leftarrow \frac{D_{x,i}+D_{i,y}-D_{x,y}}{v}$;
    Form a strategy Q_O by minimizing $T_C(i)$;
  end for
  while A dead node exists in Q_O **do**
    if n_i is on the edge of the path **then**
      $\mathcal{N}_D \leftarrow \mathcal{N}_D \cup \{i\}$;
    else
      Adjust Q_O by changing the insertion index of i;
    end if
  end while
  $Q_{optimized}(j) \leftarrow Q_O$;
  $Q_P \leftarrow Q_P \setminus \{i\}$;
end while

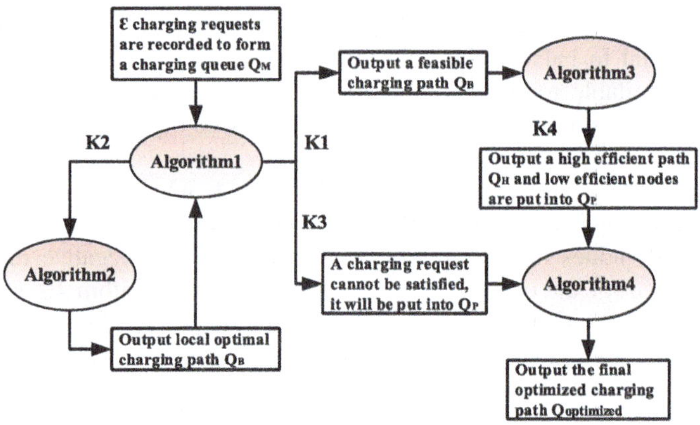

Fig. 4.20 Relations and converting conditions between algorithms

4.2.2.6 Relations of Algorithms

Then we draw a paradigm (see Fig. 4.20) to show the relationship between algorithms in TSCA for making our idea more clear.

The definitions of the conditions (i.e. K1,K2,..) are defined in Table 4.3.

Figure 4.20 illustrates the relations between the algorithms proposed in this section more clearly. Initially, Algorithm 10 is invoked with two charging queues $Q_M(j)$ and Q_P as arguments. This yields a feasible charging queue $Q_B(j)$, which serves as a basic path for further optimization. Meanwhile, Algorithm 11 is employed to maximize the number of $Q_B(j)$, thereby minimizing $\mathcal{N}_D$ and

Table 4.3 Conditions and Definitions

Symbol	Definition
$K1$	The scheduling of all nodes are finished.
$K2$	If node n_a can not be inserted into a front position, Algorithm 11 will be called. The optimized charging path $Q_B(j)$ will be input into Algorithm 10 for local optimization.
$K3$	After executing Algorithm 10, nodes will be resorted. If a dropped node still exists, which means the charging path is not scheduable, it will be put into Q_P temporarily.
$K4$	Low efficient nodes will be put into Q_P after executing Algorithm 12, moreover, a path $Q_H(j)$ will also be output.

improving charging throughput in subsequent optimizations. However, if that node is still dropped, it indicates that its request cannot be fulfilled, so we move on to another request. After completing these tasks and achieving a feasible charging schedule, Algorithm 12 is executed to remove inefficient sensors, forming a high-efficiency path. Finally, Algorithm 13 is applied to minimize N_D by reinserting nodes in Q_P and maximizing $Q_{optimized}(j)$ to enhance the throughput of WCV for task j while maintaining network stability.

4.2.3 *Theoretical Analysis*

4.2.3.1 Determining Size of Task Set

This part utilizes an M/G/1/∞/N/TSCA queueing model [14] to perform a characteristic analysis of TSCA based on queueing theory.

Within our framework, the WCV functions as a service counter while charging requests are treated as customers. The service duration for each request is defined from the moment the WCV chooses a destination node until it arrives at that node. Additionally, the arrival times of requests adhere to a negative exponential distribution characterized by parameter λ, and the service times are distributed according to a general exponential distribution. The queue can accommodate an unlimited number of requests, denoted by the capacity N. In this setup, nodes may experience starvation, meaning a charging request cannot be fulfilled promptly.

Let $a_j = P(Y_n = j) > 0$ represent the probability distribution for the number of new requests during the service time of node $n + 1$. Consequently, $\{X_n\}$ can form a Markov chain, often referred to as an embedded Markov chain.

Denote $p_{ij} = P(X_{n+1} = j|X_n = i)$. Then we have:

$$p_{ij} = P(Y_n = j + 1 - X_n|X_n = i) = \begin{cases} 0 & i > j \\ a_{j+1-i} & i \leq j + 1 \end{cases}. \tag{4.28}$$

The service times $\{T_n, n \geq 1\}$ are a series of independent and identically distributed random variables. Let $G(t) = P(T_n \leq t)$ represent the cumulative distribution function of T_n. Consequently, we obtain the following.

$$a_j = P(Y_n = j) = \int_0^{\infty} P(Y_n = j|T_n = t)dG(t) \,, \tag{4.29}$$

$P(Y_n = j|T_n = t)$ denotes the likelihood of j new requests occurring during the service time of node $n+1$. In the M/G/1/∞/N/TSCA queueing model, the request arrival times are modeled by a Poisson distribution. Consequently, we obtain:

$$P(Y_n = j|T_n = t) = \frac{(\lambda t)^j}{j!}e^{-\lambda t} \,. \tag{4.30}$$

Thus, $\rho = \frac{\lambda}{\mu}$ is used to represent service intensity. It must remain below 1; otherwise, the queue length would become infinite. If the Markov chain is ergodic, the distribution of $\{P_j, j \geq 0\}$ can stabilize. Additionally, $\{p_j\}$ must fulfill:

$$p_j = \sum_{i=0}^{\infty} p_i p_{ij} \quad j \geq 0 \,. \tag{4.31}$$

Clearly, since $a_0 = P_{00} > 0$ and the states of the Markov chain are linked, we can infer that the Markov chain is both aperiodic and irreducible. Additionally, we can readily determine that $E(Y_n) = \rho$ and $E(Y_n^2) = \rho + \rho^2 + \lambda^2 D(T_n)$. This leads us to the following.

$$D(Y_n) = E(Y_n^2) - [E(Y_n)]^2 = \rho + \lambda^2 D(T_n) \,. \tag{4.32}$$

Let $P(x) = \sum_{j=0}^{\infty} p_j x^j$ and $A(x) = \sum_{j=0}^{\infty} a_j x^j$ represent the generating functions used to determine p_j. Based on Eq. (4.31) and the Markov chain state transitions, we obtain the following:

$$\begin{aligned} x^0 p_0 &= (p_0 a_0 + p_1 a_0)x^0 \\ x P_1 &= (p_0 a_1 + p_1 a_1 + p_2 a_0)x \\ &\vdots \\ x^n p_n &= (p_0 a_n + p_1 a_n + p_2 a_{n-1} + \ldots + p_{n+1} a_0)x^n \\ &\vdots \end{aligned} \tag{4.33}$$

Then we have:

$$P(x) = \frac{(1-x)p_0 A(x)}{A(x)-x} \, . \tag{4.34}$$

The stationary distribution for the embedded Markov chain matches that of the M/G/1/∞/N/TSCA queueing model, as confirmed theoretically. Subsequently, we derive the generating function for the queue length distribution in the steady state of the M/G/1/∞/N/TSCA queueing model:

$$P(x) = \frac{(1-\rho)(1-x)A(x)}{A(x)-x} \, . \tag{4.35}$$

4.2.3.2 Other Characteristics Analysis

To comprehensively examine the attributes of the proposed system, we offer the subsequent analysis of its features.

Within our framework, the times at which charging requests arrive adhere to a Poisson distribution characterized by an average rate of λ. Consequently, the time intervals between consecutive arrivals are modeled by a negative exponential distribution. The charging durations for the WCV conform to a standard exponential distribution, with the mean charging rate μ defined as $\frac{1}{E(T_n)}$.

Within a WRSN, the WCV is tasked with recharging all the sensors. The replenishment requests from nodes about to lose power follow a Poisson distribution with rate parameter λ; upon receiving a replenishment request, the WCV places it into the queue for subsequent scheduling.

To determine the average count of nodes queuing for charging L_s, we begin by deriving the equation from Eq. (4.32) and $A'(1) = \rho$:

$$A''(1) - \rho^2 + \lambda^2 D(T_n) \, . \tag{4.36}$$

Thus, based on Eqs. (4.35) and (4.36), we can determine the average number of nodes awaiting charging, L_s. The derivation process is as follows:

$$\begin{aligned} L_s = E(X_n) = P'(1) &= \left[\frac{(1-p)(1-x)A(x)}{A(x)-x} \right]' \Bigg|_{x=1} \\ &= (1-\rho)\frac{-2[A'(1)]^2 + 2A'(1) + A''(1)}{2[A'(1)-1]^2} \\ &= \rho + \frac{\lambda^2 D(T_n) + \rho^2}{2(1-\rho)} \\ &= \rho + \frac{\lambda^2\sigma^2 + \rho^2}{2(1-\rho)} \, . \end{aligned} \tag{4.37}$$

The average sojourning time of a charging request W_s is:

$$W_s = \frac{L_s}{\lambda} = \frac{1}{\mu} + \frac{\rho^2 + \lambda^2\sigma^2}{2\lambda(1-\rho)}. \tag{4.38}$$

The average number of nodes that wait in the charging queue L_q can be computed as:

$$L_q = L_s - \rho = \frac{\rho^2 + \lambda^2\sigma^2}{2(1-\rho)}. \tag{4.39}$$

The average queueing time for a node to get charged is:

$$W_q = \frac{L_Q}{\lambda} = \frac{\rho^2 + \lambda^2\sigma^2}{2\lambda(1-\rho)}. \tag{4.40}$$

The aforementioned outcomes serve as a crucial foundation for subsequent parameter adjustments in simulations. Additionally, the theoretical value of L_S has been corroborated by the simulation results, thereby confirming the accuracy of our model; corresponding validation will be presented in Sect. 4.2.4.

4.2.3.3 Algorithm Complexity

Because charging scheduling is NP-hard [14], obtaining a global optimal solution could be unachievable. Nevertheless, our approach makes it potentially possible to discover such a global optimum. Initially, we evaluate the complexity of TSCA.

The complexity of our scheme has been analyzed by categorizing the proposed algorithms into three distinct components: (a) Formulating a basic path with best effort (Algorithm 10) and transforming the current path into the optimized path (Algorithm 11), (b) Removing low-efficiency nodes (Algorithm 12), (c) Re-inserting nodes from Q_P back into $Q_{optimized}$ (Algorithm 13). An analysis of the complexity for each algorithm is given below.

Algorithms 10 and 11 Complexity Upon receiving requests, the WCV stores them in Q_W, and subsequently, ϵ requests are moved to $Q_M(j)$. The primary objective of these algorithms is to build a foundational path $Q_B(j)$ with optimal effort. Each node is initially added to $Q_B(j)$ ensuring none of the nodes deplete their energy. Following this, if adding a node is unfeasible, Algorithm 11 is applied to rearrange the charging sequence. The overall time complexity for this process is $O(n^3)$.

Algorithm 12 Complexity Analysis Following the establishment of a basic path by best effort, low-performing nodes are removed to boost network efficiency. The importance of Algorithm 12 is confirmed in Sect. 4.2.4. Low-efficiency nodes are detected and eliminated by examining each set of three consecutive nodes, and the complexity of Algorithm 12 is O(n).

Algorithm 13 Complexity Analysis To globally optimize the path, nodes from Q_P are reinserted into $Q_{optimized}(j)$. For each node in Q_P, we must first assess whether it can be inserted into a position without causing other nodes to fail. If it is possible, the optimal insertion strategy that minimizes $T_C(i)$ is chosen. Therefore, the complexity of Algorithm 13 is $O(n^2)$.

In the worst-case scenario, the total complexity is $O(n^3)$. Nonetheless, as indicated by the results in Sect. 4.2.4, the average queue length is approximately 10, ensuring that the computational load is still feasible. In addition, Sect. 4.2.4.2 will show that because of its simplicity, TSCA is capable of identifying the globally optimal charging solution in the majority of situations.

4.2.4 *Simulation and Experiments*

To highlight the benefits of the proposed approach, comprehensive simulations have been performed. Our method is compared against two cutting-edge charging scheduling algorithms, NJNP [14] and DWDP [17], within the on-demand charging framework to demonstrate our features. Additionally, characteristic validation and property analysis are included to gain a deeper understanding of our schemes.

4.2.4.1 Simulation Setup

As shown in Table 4.4, our simulations involve the random deployment of 100 nodes within a 1000×1000 m area. Each sensor has an energy consumption rate of 0.02 J/s and a maximum energy capacity of 100J. If a sensor's remaining energy drops below 30%, it promptly sends a charging request to the WCV, which moves at a velocity of 5 m/s. Other simulation parameters match those of NJNP [14]. Upon receiving multiple charging requests, our algorithm creates a charging path to direct the WCV's charging activities. During the simulations, we sample the energy status of the nodes every 3500 seconds.

Table 4.4 Simulation Setup

Parameters	Values
Network size	1000×1000 m
Number of nodes	100
Energy consumption rate of nodes	0.02 J/s
Velocity of the WCV	5 m/s
Maximum energy capacity of nodes	100 J
Energy threshold for sending a request	30%
Sampling interval	3500 s
Sampling times	11
Charging scheme	TSCA, DWDP, NJNP

Table 4.5 Comparison between theoretical value and simulation value of average length of charging queue with different numbers of nodes

Numbers of node	100	150	200	250	300
Theoretical value	6.455	8.148	11.21	8.081	10.91
Simulation value	3.667	6.5	5.889	4	5.5

Initially, we confirm the accuracy of our analysis as presented in Sect. 4.2.3. Within the proposed M/G/1/∞/TSCA queueing model, because the value L_S in Eq. (4.37) can be determined through simulation, we compare the theoretical outcomes with the simulation results of L_S to authenticate our model's validity.

As illustrated in Table 4.5, the theoretical average length of the charging queue is approximately 10 based on Eq. (4.37), while the simulated value is around 5. This suggests that the queue length for recording requests is relatively small compared to the number of nodes. In the simulation, a queue with 10 rooms is more than adequate. Additionally, determining the global optimal charging path with such a small queue is straightforward, without concerns about computational overhead or accuracy of the results, fulfilling the requirements specified in Sect. 4.2.2.1. These findings provide a valuable foundation for parameter selection in future simulations.

We primarily compare our approaches with NJNP [14] and DWDP [17] across eight characteristics, which provide a comprehensive measure of the entire network's performance. The simulation results help us achieve the goal of our problem statement, allowing for a more thorough analysis of the proposed methods' performance in various facets.

4.2.4.2 Average Length of the Charging Queue

Initially, we examine the mean length of the charging queue as stored in the WCV's memory.

Within our simulation, illustrated in Fig. 4.21a, no more than 10 rooms are needed to document charging requests, confirming the theoretical findings discussed in Sect. 4.2.4.1.

In Fig. 4.21a, the lengths of the three algorithms reach steady values. It is evident that the queue length for TSCA is significantly shorter compared to DWDP and NJNP. On average, DWDP has a queue length of 30, implying that nearly 30% of requests are delayed and cannot be promptly addressed. For TSCA, the average queue length is around 5, suggesting a shorter waiting line for requests and a quicker response time.

4.2.4.3 Charging Throughput

Charging throughput refers to the number of nodes that get successfully charged within a unit of time. As illustrated in Fig. 4.21b, the load throughput of the three

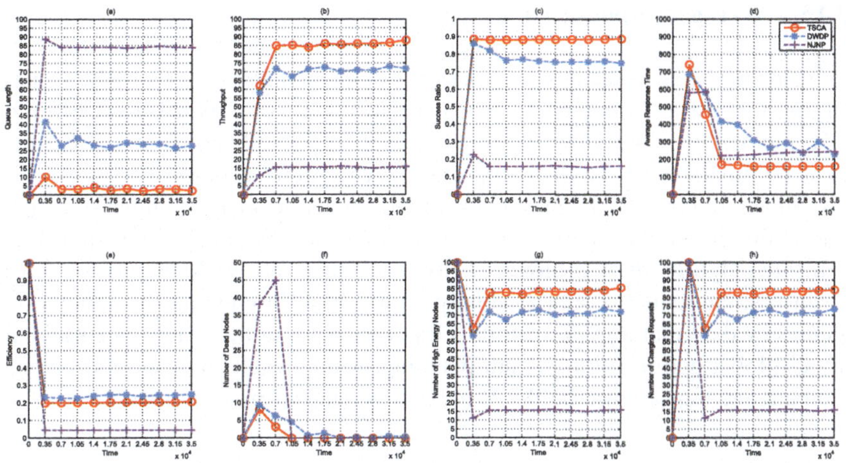

Fig. 4.21 Performance comparison between TSCA, NJNP [14] and DWDP [17] in terms of (**a**) queue length, (**b**) throughput, (**c**) successful charging ratio, (**d**) average response time, (**e**) charging efficiency, (**f**) number of dead nodes, (**g**) number of high energy nodes and (**h**) number of charging requests

algorithms exhibits a rapid increase with runtime and then plateaus. Statistically, TSCA's throughput is five times that of NJNP and 10% higher than DWDP. Our approach, in comparison to NJNP and DWDP, meets more charging requests. Additionally, WCV shows a greater capacity to replenish energy for nodes in need, ensuring the network's normal function. Moreover, fulfilling more charging requests means reduced traveling time, highlighting the proposed scheme's higher charging efficiency.

4.2.4.4 Successful Charging Ratio

The successful charging ratio represents the proportion of charge requests that the WCV responds to promptly and effectively.

As illustrated in Fig. 4.21c, it is observed that the successful charging rates of the three techniques eventually become steady at particular levels. TSCA exceeds DWDP by approximately 10%, suggesting it can fulfill over 10 more charging requests compared to DWDP. This observation implies a greater energy retention capability of WCV.

The TSCA achieves a successful loading rate of approximately 90%. This is primarily because TSCA focuses on minimizing dead nodes through schedulability optimizations, and additionally, it works on lowering the energy consumption of travel and reorganizing the task sequence to enhance energy efficiency. As a result, nearly all load requests are fulfilled, ensuring smooth network operation.

4.2.4.5 Average Response Time

The response time indicates the period commencing when the WCV gets a charging request and concluding when it reaches the designated node. It reflects the promptness in addressing charging inquiries. As already noted, the TSCA travel time is minimal; hence, TSCA will promptly respond to requests.

As shown in Fig. 4.21d, the sensors initially generate a large number of charging requests due to similar energy consumption. At the beginning, the response time of all three algorithms is prolonged. However, once the WCV begins to recharge the sensors, the request count gradually diminishes. Throughout the simulation, it becomes evident that TSCA exhibits a quicker response time. This is attributed to TSCA's global optimization in path planning, which results in a shorter replenishment path and thus allows the WCV to address requests more swiftly.

4.2.4.6 Charging Efficiency

Charging efficiency is defined as the percentage of energy obtained by sensor nodes.

In Fig. 4.21e, it is evident that the charging efficiency across all algorithms remains fairly constant. The loading efficiency of TSCA and DWDP is nearly equivalent. A clear reason behind this is that TSCA prioritizes throughput over efficiency to strike a balance between the two. On the other hand, NJNP and DWDP aim to reduce travel expenses, leading to optimal loading efficiency. Consequently, we infer that TSCA demonstrates commendable energy loading efficiency.

4.2.4.7 Density of Dead Nodes

The density of dead nodes means the number of exhausted nodes during a time unit.

As illustrated in Fig. 4.21f, initially, the density of dead nodes for the three algorithms is fairly high. Over time, this density decreases to 0 for all algorithms. The density for TSCA remains consistently lower than that for DWDP and NJNP. The peak densities observed for DWDP and TSCA are 10% and 8%, respectively. Additionally, it is evident that the densities for TSCA and NJNP stabilize at 10,500 seconds, while DWDP's density stabilizes at 21,000 seconds. Thus, we can infer that TSCA results in fewer dead nodes, promoting the long-term stable functioning of the network and fulfilling our goal.

4.2.4.8 Density of High Efficient Nodes

This simulation measures the concentration of nodes with high energy levels. In this context, a high-energy level node is defined as one that possesses energy above a specified threshold.

As illustrated in Fig. 4.21g, the densities of the three approaches initially decline as execution continues. Subsequently, after the initiation of the first round of recharge requests, the WCV begins to restore energy to all nodes. Thanks to the exceptional performance of the charging task scheduling, the density of nodes with high energy levels begins to stabilize over time. It is observed that the average density of DWDP is 70, while TSCA exhibits approximately a 10% improvement in performance. Consequently, there are more nodes with high energy levels in TSCA, indicating that the WCV can effectively sustain energy charging for the network, ensuring that it continues to function properly for an extended period.

4.2.4.9 Charging Request Density

We evaluate charging request density, defined by counting the number of requests within a specific time frame. This metric indicates the demand for energy recharging and indirectly measures the WCV's capacity to supply energy.

As illustrated in Fig. 4.21h, it is clear that the charging request density of TSCA and DWDP surpasses that of NJNP significantly. The density for TSCA stands at approximately 80, about 10% higher compared to DWDP. Hence, we infer that TSCA has a lower number of dead nodes than DWDP, implying a superior capacity to sustain the network, thereby ensuring its connectivity and stability.

4.2.4.10 Impact of Low Efficient Nodes

As discussed in Sect. 4.2.2.1, nodes with low efficiency reduce the overall charging effectiveness. To mitigate these effects, this paper utilizes Algorithm 12. We conduct an experiment to demonstrate its impact, focusing on comparing the performance concerning dead nodes when TSCA is executed with and without the inclusion of Algorithm 12.

As illustrated in Fig. 4.22, executing the TSCA scheme without incorporating Algorithm 12 results in a significant increase in the number of dead nodes. This outcome highlights that the impact of low-efficiency nodes on the count of

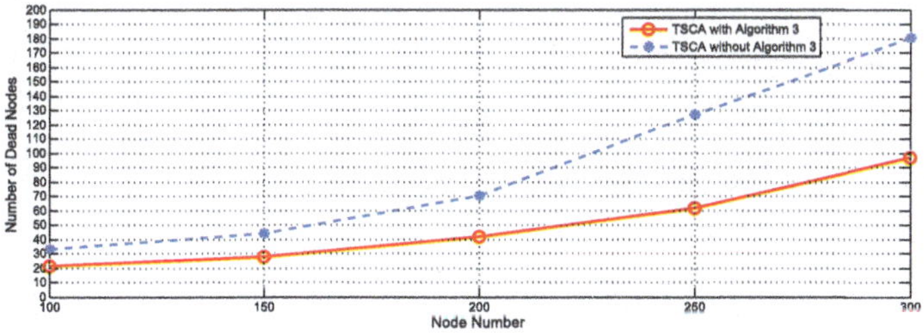

Fig. 4.22 Effectiveness of Algorithm 12 in deleting low-efficiency nodes

dead nodes is considerable, thereby causing a substantial rise in traveling costs. Consequently, it is important to focus on mitigating such effects. By implementing Algorithm 12 within the TSCA scheme, the number of dead nodes is almost halved, which significantly improves charging efficiency.

4.2.4.11 Performance of Objectives

As mentioned in Sect. 4.2.1.2, our approach targets addressing a multi-objective issue, focusing on reducing the number of dead nodes and enhancing charging efficiency. In this study, we evaluate the objectives' performance through experiments that compare practical results with theoretical values of our dual objectives.

Figure 4.23 demonstrates that the simulation closely matches the theoretical count of dead nodes, validating that the aim to minimize dead nodes is largely accomplished.

Figure 4.24 demonstrates that the simulated loading efficiency closely matches the theoretical value, suggesting the secondary objective is ultimately accomplished. Hence, our multi-objective problem is effectively addressed by TSCA.

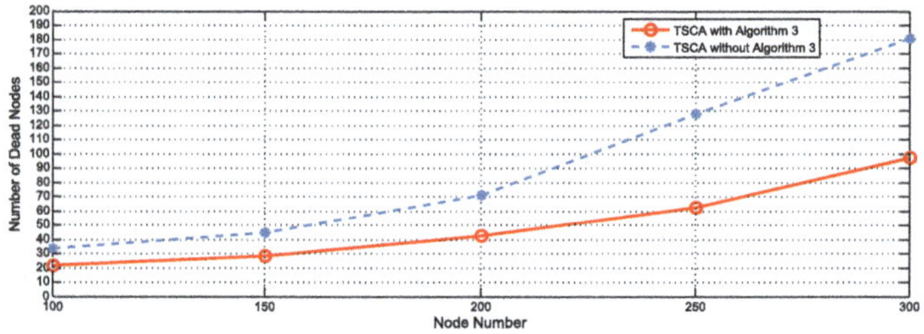

Fig. 4.23 Comparison of theoretical value and simulation value of objective with Eq. (4.19)

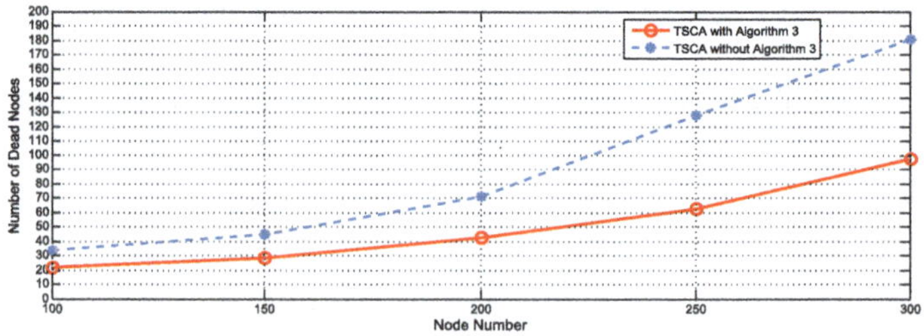

Fig. 4.24 Comparison of theoretical value and simulation value of objective

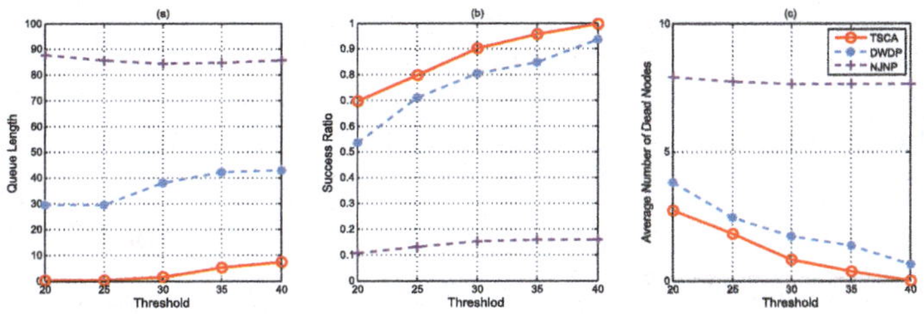

Fig. 4.25 Performance comparison between TSCA, NJNP and DWDP with different thresholds in terms of (**a**) average length of charging queue, (**b**) successful charging ratio and (**c**) number of dead nodes

4.2.4.12 Properties Analysis

The ensuing sections delve into the network's behavior under varying configurations, including parameters like charge threshold, node count, and energy usage rate. The corresponding simulation parameters are consistent with those presented in Table 4.4.

Impact of Charging Threshold In this study, we focus on examining the impact of the charging thresholds. The threshold specifies the duration a sensor needs to wait before being recharged. It plays a crucial role in showcasing the network's stability, persistence, and efficiency.

In this study, the trigger points for initiating a charging request are set to $\{20, 25, 30, 35, 40\}$. A comparative analysis of TSCA, NJNP, and DWDP is provided in Fig. 4.25.

Figure 4.25a illustrates that the queue length for TSCA is shorter compared to those for NJNP and DWDP. This is due to the fact that the WCV selects ϵ charging requests each time in TSCA, indicating that the charging queue length will never exceed ϵ.

As shown in Fig. 4.25b, the successful charging ratio of the three algorithms progressively rises with the increase in charging threshold. TSCA shows a higher ratio compared to DWDP and NJNP. This observation suggests that increasing the charging threshold decreases the urgency of charging requests, enabling WCV to fulfill more of them.

In Fig. 4.25c, we evaluate the performance of the three algorithms based on the number of dead nodes. We notice that as the charging threshold increases, the values $|\mathcal{N}_D|$ for the three algorithms gradually decrease. Quantitatively, the number of dead nodes in TSCA is almost below 5, which is fewer compared to NJNP and DWDP.

Impact of Node Number Next, we investigate how varying the number of nodes affects the three algorithms. We assess the performance with $\{100, 150, 200, 250, 300\}$ nodes deployed. The findings are presented in Fig. 4.26.

As illustrated in Fig. 4.26a, the queue length for TSCA is significantly shorter compared to NJNP and DWDP. This is because, with our approach, only ϵ requests

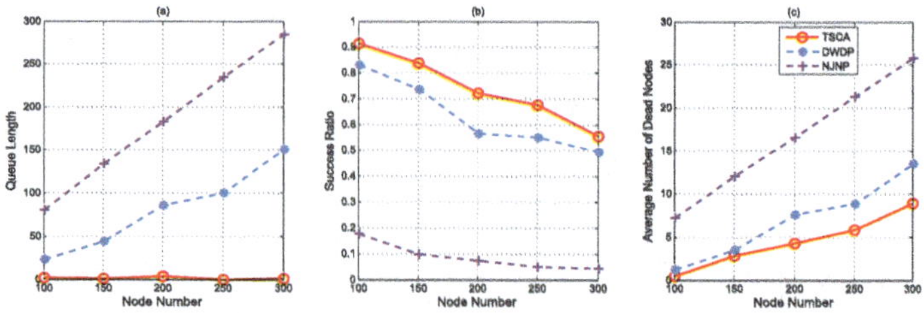

Fig. 4.26 Performance comparison between TSCA, NJNP and DWDP with different node numbers in terms of (**a**) average length of charging queue, (**b**) successful charging ratio and (**c**) number of dead nodes

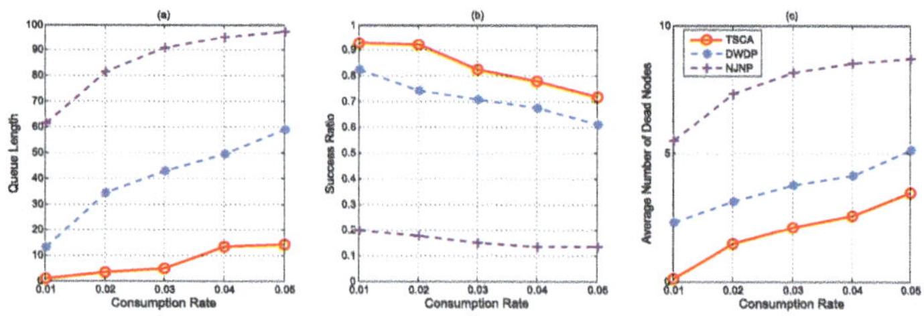

Fig. 4.27 Performance comparison between TSCA, NJNP and DWDP with different energy consumption rates in terms of (**a**) average length of charging queue, (**b**) successful charging ratio and (**c**) number of dead nodes

are placed in the load queue simultaneously. Additionally, as demonstrated in the preceding sections, a shorter queue length does not negatively impact loading performance, thereby guaranteeing the optimal performance of TSCA.

As illustrated in Fig. 4.26b, an increase in the number of nodes results in a gradual decline in the successful load ratios for all three algorithms. This drop is attributed to the surge in charging requests caused by the additional nodes, which adds to the WCV's burden in performing the charging tasks. Consequently, there are more nodes that become exhausted. Additionally, Fig. 4.26b shows that the TSCA ratio is consistently higher compared to NJNP and DWDP.

As illustrated in Fig. 4.26c, as the number of nodes rises, so does the count of dead nodes. This occurs because the WCV's charging capacity is finite; thus, an increase in charging requests leads to an inability to fulfill all of them, causing more requests to go unaddressed. Figure 4.26c demonstrates that TSCA has fewer dead nodes compared to DWDP and NJNP.

Effect of Energy Usage Rate In this study, we primarily examine how the energy usage rate of nodes influences outcomes. An elevated energy usage rate results in nodes depleting their energy faster, which in turn increases the frequency of charging requests. The comparative outcomes are illustrated in Fig. 4.27.

Regarding the comparison of queue lengths illustrated in Fig. 4.27a, akin to the findings from prior sections, the queue length for TSCA is significantly shorter than those for DWDP and NJNP.

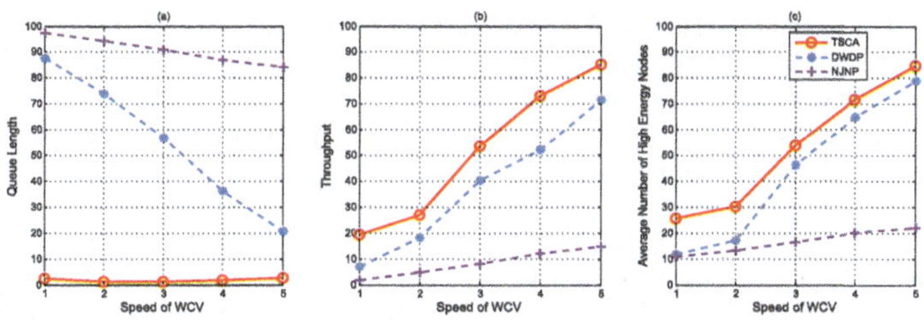

Fig. 4.28 Performance comparison between TSCA, NJNP and DWDP with different speeds of the WCV in terms of (**a**) average length of charging queue, (**b**) throughput and (**c**) average number of high energy nodes

Regarding the successful charging ratio, Fig. 4.27b demonstrates that TSCA has the highest ratio. It is noted that some nodes fail to sustain themselves before being serviced, resulting in a reduction in the success rate.

Figure 4.27c demonstrates that the number of dead nodes in all three algorithms rises as the energy consumption rate increases. This occurs because faster energy consumption leads to more frequent recharge requests. Consequently, a WCV cannot fulfill all the charging demands, causing some nodes to deplete their energy eventually due to unmet requests. It is important to note that the number of dead nodes remains under 10 for all three algorithms, with TSCA exhibiting the lowest count.

Impact of Speed of WCV We examine how charging performance is affected when the WCV moves at speeds of $\{1, 2, 3, 4, 5\}$ meters per second. The comparative outcomes are illustrated in Fig. 4.28.

As depicted in Fig. 4.28, TSCA outperforms the other two algorithms in three key aspects. In Fig. 4.28a, TSCA has the shortest load queue. In Fig. 4.28b, it achieves the highest load throughput. At a WCV travel speed of 5 m/s, the throughput reaches 85%, surpassing both DWDP and NJNP. Analyzing the proportion of high energy nodes, we see in Fig. 4.28c that TSCA has a larger fraction than DWDP and NJNP. At a travel speed of 5 m/s, this fraction is approximately 86%.

References

1. Y. Shu, P. Cheng, Y. Gu, J. Chen, T. He, Toc: Localizing wireless rechargeable sensors with time of charge. ACM Trans. Sen. Netw. **11**, 1–22 (2015)
2. V. Kulathumani, A. Arora, M. Sridharan, M. Demirbas, Trail: a distance-sensitive sensor network service for distributed object tracking. ACM Trans. Sensor Netw. (TOSN) **5**(2), 1–40 (2009)
3. G. Xing, T. Wang, W. Jia, M. Li, Rendezvous design algorithms for wireless sensor networks with a mobile base station, in *Proceedings of the 9th ACM International Symposium on Mobile ad hoc Networking and Computing* (ACM, 2008), pp. 231–240

4. L. He, Y. Gu, J. Pan, T. Zhu, On-demand charging in wireless sensor networks: Theories and applications, in *IEEE 10th International Conference on Mobile Ad-Hoc and Sensor Systems (MASS 2013)* (IEEE, 2013), pp. 28–36
5. Y. Shu, H. Yousefi, P. Cheng, J. Chen, Y. Gu, T. He, K. Shin, Optimal velocity control for time-bounded mobile charging in wireless rechargeable sensor networks. IEEE Trans. Mobile Comput. (2016, to appear)
6. S. He, J. Chen, F. Jiang, D.K. Yau, G. Xing, Y. Sun, Energy provisioning in wireless rechargeable sensor networks. IEEE Trans. Mobile Comput. **12**(10), 1931–1942 (2013)
7. Y.-Y. Wang, Q. Wang, H.-A. Wang, H. Jin, G.-Z. Dai, A real-time scheduling algorithm based on priority table and its implementation. J. Softw. **3**, 005 (2004)
8. A. Thekkilakattil, S. Baruah, R. Dobrin, S. Punnekkat, The global limited preemptive earliest deadline first feasibility of sporadic real-time tasks, in *2014 26th Euromicro Conference on Real-Time Systems (ECRTS)* (IEEE, 2014), pp. 301–310
9. M. Spuri, G.C. Buttazzo, Efficient aperiodic service under earliest deadline scheduling, in *Real-Time Systems Symposium, 1994. Proceedings* (IEEE, 1994), pp. 2–11
10. L. He, L. Kong, Y. Gu, J. Pan, T. Zhu, Evaluating the on-demand mobile charging in wireless sensor networks. IEEE Trans. Mobile Comput. **14**, 1861–1875 (2015)
11. M. Zhao, J. Li, Y. Yang, A framework of joint mobile energy replenishment and data gathering in wireless rechargeable sensor networks. IEEE Trans. Mobile Comput. **13**, 2689–2705 (2014)
12. L. Xie, Y. Shi, Y.T. Hou, A. Lou, Wireless power transfer and applications to sensor networks. Wirel. Commun. IEEE **20**(4), 140–145 (2013)
13. C. Hu, Y. Wang, Schedulability decision of charging missions in wireless rechargeable sensor networks, in *2014 Eleventh Annual IEEE International Conference on Sensing, Communication, and Networking (SECON)* (IEEE, 2014), pp. 450–458
14. L. He, L. Kong, Y. Gu, J. Pan, T. Zhu, Evaluating the on-demand mobile charging in wireless sensor networks. IEEE Trans. Mobile Comput. **14**(9), 1861–1875 (2014)
15. W. Liang, W. Xu, X. Ren, X. Jia, X. Lin, Maintaining large-scale rechargeable sensor networks perpetually via multiple mobile charging vehicles. ACM Trans. Sensor Netw. **PP**(99), 1–1 (2016)
16. L. Xie, Y. Shi, Y.T. Hou, H.D. Sherali, Making sensor networks immortal: An energy-renewal approach with wireless power transfer. IEEE/ACM Trans. Netw. **20**(6), 1748–1761 (2012)
17. C. Lin, B. Xue, Z. Wang, D. Han, J. Deng, G. Wu, Dwdp: a double warning thresholds with double preemptive scheduling scheme for wireless rechargeable sensor networks, in *IEEE International Conference on High Performance Computing and Communications* (2015) , pp. 503–508

Chapter 5
Collaborative Scheduling

5.1 Temporal and Spatial-Collaborative Charging with Multiple Vehicles

The utilization of charging unmanned aerial vehicles (CUAVs) for wireless power transfer offers a promising approach to prolonging the lifespan of wireless rechargeable sensor networks (WRSNs). Nonetheless, optimizing the positioning of CUAVs to boost charging efficiency presents a significant challenge. This section introduces a CUAV deployment optimization problem (CUAVDOP), which focuses on concurrently increasing the number of sensor nodes within CUAVs' charging ranges, enhancing the minimum charging efficiency across the network, and minimizing the motion energy consumption of the CUAVs. Additionally, we examine and establish that the formulated CUAVDOP is NP-hard. Following this, we introduce an enhanced firefly algorithm (IFA) designed to tackle the formulated CUAVDOP. The IFA incorporates three key improvements: an opposition-based learning model, an attraction model, and an adaptive step size factor, all aimed at boosting the effectiveness of the conventional firefly algorithm, thereby making it more adept at addressing the CUAVDOP. Simulation results indicate that the proposed algorithm efficiently solves the joint optimization problem. Moreover, the superiority of IFA has been substantiated through various tests.

5.1.1 Problem Statement

As illustrated in Fig. 5.1, we examine a WRSN set up with an on-demand real-time charging system. It includes numerous stationary sensor nodes, several WCVs, and a base station (BS). Both WCVs and sensors come with GPS modules and batteries with limited capacity. The nodes use a standard protocol for communication. The WCVs can accurately locate the sensors to carry out replenishment tasks. The main

C. Lin et al., *Wireless Rechargeable Sensor Networks for Internet of Things*,
Wireless Networks, https://doi.org/10.1007/978-981-97-9543-7_5

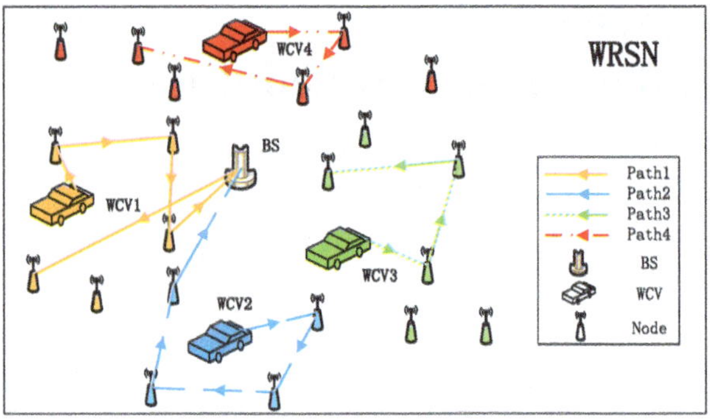

Fig. 5.1 System architecture of a WRSN with multiple WCVs

function of the sensor nodes is to monitor, collect, and transmit data from the environment. The BS is in charge of aggregating and fusing data to forecast events for the entire monitored region. The BS is assumed to have an unlimited energy supply.

As the network functions, nodes use battery power. When a node's energy drops below a certain level, it sends a recharge request to neighboring WCVs. This request contains the node ID, its GPS coordinates, its current energy level, and its energy consumption rate. Upon receiving this request, it is added to the service queues for later handling. If the node is not recharged promptly, it will drain its energy and cease to function, thereby providing no service to the network. In WRSNs with stringent real-time requirements, unexpected events can happen anywhere and at any moment in the network. The depletion of any node could result in event detection failures, which is strictly forbidden. Hence, in this research, we focus closely on these real-time scheduling challenges.

All immediate charging requests (within the specified region, refer to Sect. 5.1.2.2) are added to the service queue and ordered. The WCV then moves to the location of the sensor at the front of the queue to commence charging. After completing the charging, it chooses the next sensor from the top of the queue. This process continues until the WCV notices its battery level dropping below a critical level, prompting it to go to the BS for recharging.

In WRSN, the survival rates of nodes and the efficiency of energy use are likely the most crucial elements. The latter reflects the amount of energy that sensors collect from the WCVs.

$$\varepsilon = \frac{q_r}{q_c}, \tag{5.1}$$

where q_c represents the rate of energy provided to the network by the base station (via WCVs) and q_r indicates the rate of energy effectively received by the sensor nodes.

Problem Statement *In a WRSN with a BS, multiple WCVs, and numerous sensor nodes, how can the WCVs both consider the temporal and spatial dependencies* *of the recharging tasks and choose a node for recharging based on the sequence of recharging requests to optimize energy efficiency η and maintain the highest number of active sensor nodes?*

Prime Objective To address this challenge, we frame it as a dual-objective problem, aiming to both maximise energy efficiency η and enhance the survival rate δ concurrently. The energy efficiency η is defined as the proportion of energy acquired by nodes and can be computed as:

$$\begin{aligned}\max \eta =& \frac{E_{node}}{E_{charge} + E_{move} + E_{WCV}} \\ =& \frac{t \sum q_i + \sum e_n^i}{\frac{(t \sum q_i + \sum e_n^i) q_c}{q_r} + q_m (t - \frac{t \sum q_i + \sum e_n^i}{q_c}) + \sum e_w^j}.\end{aligned} \tag{5.2}$$

Subject to

$$0 < q_i, q_c, q_r, q_m,$$
$$0 < e_n^i \le E_n,$$
$$0 < e_w^j \le E_w.$$

The survival rate η can be calculated as:

$$\max \delta = \frac{|N|_a}{|N|}. \tag{5.3}$$

Subject to

$$0 < |N|_a \le |N|.$$

Here, $|N|$ is the number of nodes and $|N|_a$ is the number of alive nodes which are working normally.

Next, we introduce mTS solve this problems.

5.1.2 Schematic Design

In this subsection, we provide a detailed description of mTS. As illustrated in Fig. 5.2, each WCV, denoted as W_j, in mTS has a service queue Ψ_j which is arranged according to a metric derived from distance and charging deadlines.

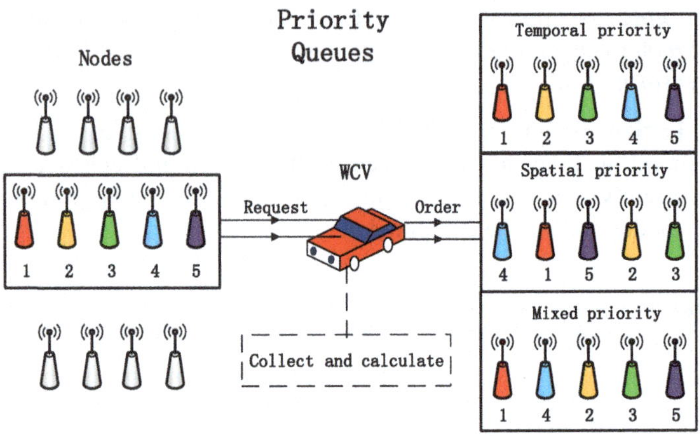

Fig. 5.2 An example of queueing process in mTS

The deadline for charging is determined by the remaining energy and the rate of energy consumption:

$$t_i = \frac{e_n^i}{q_i}, \tag{5.4}$$

where e_n^i represents the remaining energy and q_i signifies the rate of energy usage of N_i. In the present task queue, the arrival time of the first task is denoted by t_{min} and that of the final task by t_{max}. A temporal priority is subsequently defined as: Alternative allocations can be considered, such as a function t_i, $f(t_i)$; however, we defer the examination of these alternatives to future research.

$$\begin{aligned} \lambda_j^{(t)}(i) &= \lceil \frac{t_i - t_{min}}{\frac{t_{max} - t_{min}}{|N|}} \rceil \\ &= \lceil \frac{(t_i - t_{min})|N|}{t_{max} - t_{min}} \rceil. \end{aligned} \tag{5.5}$$

In a similar manner, let d_i^j represent the distance from node N_i to WCV W_j. We denote the closest node's distance as d_{min}^j and the farthest one's distance as d_{max}^j. Thus, the spatial priority $\lambda_j^{(d)}(i)$ can be determined by:

$$\begin{aligned} \lambda_j^{(d)}(i) &= \lceil \frac{d_i^j - d_{min}^j}{\frac{d_{max}^j - d_{min}^j}{|N|}} \rceil \\ &= \lceil \frac{(d_i^j - d_{min}^j)|N|}{d_{max}^j - d_{min}^j} \rceil. \end{aligned} \tag{5.6}$$

A mixed priority $\lambda_j^{(m)}(i)$ is obtained by combining spatial and temporal priorities:

$$\lambda_j^{(m)}(i) = \alpha\lambda_j^{(t)}(i) + \beta\lambda_j^{(d)}(i) + \lg(\lambda_j^{(t)}(i)\lambda_j^{(d)}(i) + 1), \tag{5.7}$$

where α and β stand for the weights of temporal and spatial priorities. We discuss the actual assigned values of these in Sect. 6.2.4.

Generally, nodes with smaller values of mixed priority, $\lambda_j^{(m)}(i)$, are given higher priority to be served first.

5.1.2.1 Algorithm Overview

Algorithms 14 and 15 illustrate the procedures of the mTS scheme. Initially, the network is segmented into several subdomains using a modified K-means algorithm, as demonstrated in Algorithm 14. Subsequently, in Algorithm 15, nodes send charging requests to their assigned WCVs when energy replenishment is required, and these requests are fulfilled by the corresponding WCVs. In cases where a request cannot be met, the assigned WCV will pass it on to a neighboring WCV for support. The scheduling methodology is depicted in Fig. 5.3, ranging from the network initialization (Fig. 5.3a) to the final loop scheduling (Fig. 5.3h).

In this context, we utilize the K-means clustering algorithm to divide the network into subregions $\{\Omega_k\}$, $k \in [1, |W|]$. Each Ω_k is assigned a WCV, which is mainly tasked with recharging the sensors situated within the corresponding subregion.

In our approach, we develop the shortest Hamiltonian cycle for the centroids formed by the K-means clustering method, employing Eq. (5.8):

$$\min V = \sum_{i=1}^{k} \sum_{N_j \in S_i} (x_i - \bar{x}_i)(y_i - \bar{y}_i), \tag{5.8}$$

In this context, V represents the optimal object of the K-means algorithm, S_i denotes the node set of the i-th cluster, and k indicates the number of clusters. The coordinates (x_i, y_i) specify the position of N_j, while $(\bar{x}_i, \bar{y}_i)$ denote the center of the i-th cluster.

According to Algorithm 14, each time a node $N_i'(x_i', y_i')$ (where N_i' represents the index within its respective domain, distinct from the value of N_i) is included in a domain Ω_k, the cluster center $P_k(\bar{x}_k, \bar{y}_k)$ will be updated using Eqs. (5.9) and (5.10).

$$\begin{aligned} \bar{x}_k' &= \frac{\sum_{i=1}^{|\Psi_k|} x_i}{|\Psi_k|} \\ &= \frac{\bar{x}_k(|\Psi_k| - 1) + x_i'}{|\Psi_k|}; \end{aligned} \tag{5.9}$$

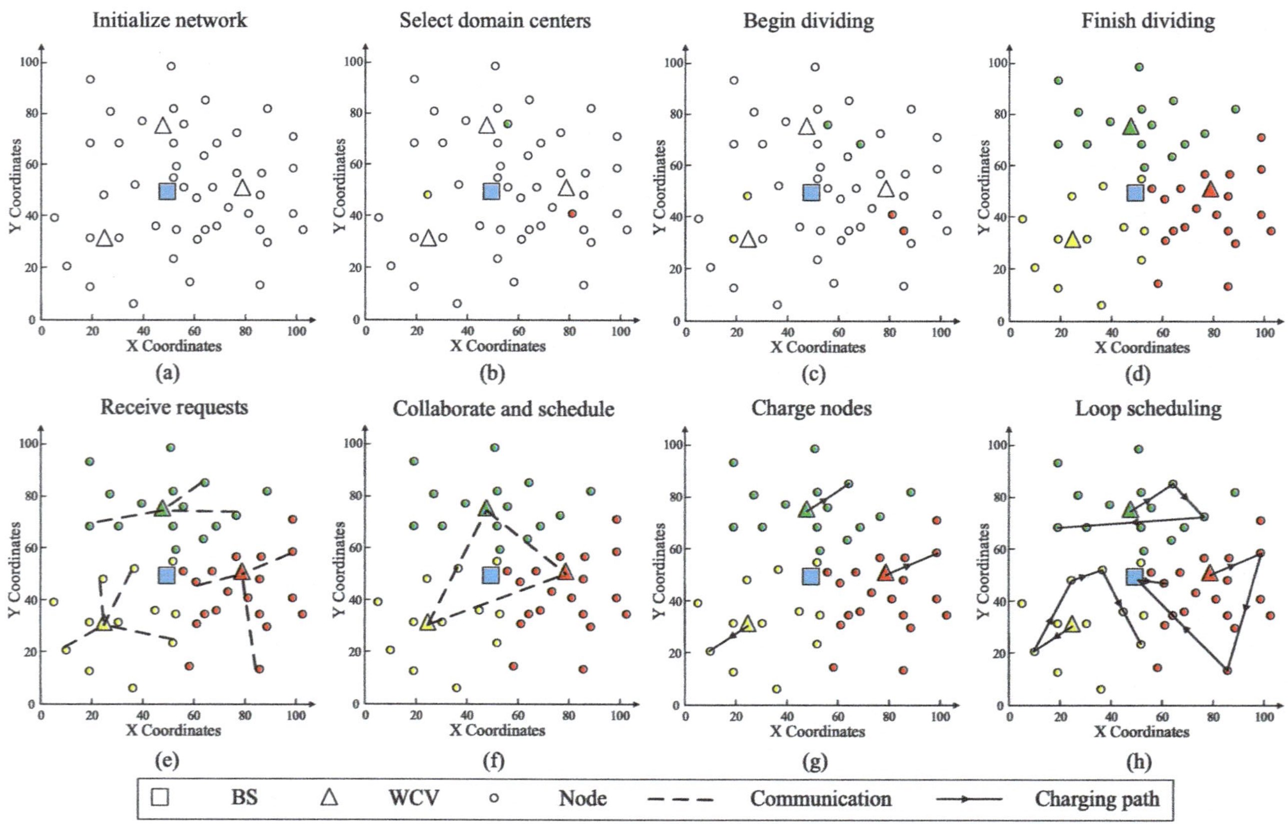

Fig. 5.3 The work process of a network with mTS algorithm (**a**) Initialize network, (**b**) Select domain centers, (**c**) Begin dividing, (**d**) Finish dividing, (**e**) Receive requests, (**f**) Collaborate and schedule, (**g**) Charge nodes and (**h**) Loop scheduling

Algorithm 14 Adjusted K-means algorithm

Require: Node set N,WCV set W
Ensure: All subdomains Ω_k

Ensure the number of WCVs $|W|$ as the number of clusters K in K-means;
Define $P_k(\bar{x}_k, \bar{y}_k)$ as the clusters center of Ω_k;
Initialize P_k;
for $i \leftarrow 1$ to K **do**
  Randomly select a node $N_j(x_j, y_j)$ as $N_i'(x_i, y_i)$;
  if $N_i' \neq N_{i-1}'$ to N_1' **then**
    $\bar{x}_i \leftarrow x_i$;
    $\bar{y}_i \leftarrow y_i$;
  else
    Reselect a node as N_i';
    $i \leftarrow i - 1$;
  end if
end for
ChangeFlag $\leftarrow 1$;
while ChangeFlag $== 1$ **do**
  ChangeFlag $\leftarrow 0$;
  for $i \leftarrow 1$ to K **do**
    $P_i' \leftarrow P_i$;
  end for
  for $i \leftarrow 1$ to $|N|$ **do**
    Calculate distances between N_i to all P_k;
    Choose the nearest one as P_j;
    Add N_i to Ω_j;
    Refresh P_j by Eqs. (5.9) and (5.10);
  end for
  for $i \leftarrow 1$ to K **do**
    if $P_i' \neq P_i$ **then**
      ChangeFlag $\leftarrow 1$;
    end if
  end for
end while
return All Ω_k;

$$\begin{aligned} \bar{y}_k' &= \frac{\sum_{i=1}^{|\Psi_k|} y_i}{|\Psi_k|} \\ &= \frac{\bar{y}_k(|\Psi_k| - 1) + y_i'}{|\Psi_k|}. \end{aligned} \tag{5.10}$$

In addition, the quantity of clusters is set as $|W|$ when partitioning the clusters. In certain extreme scenarios, if a WCV cannot manage the load from a certain number of nodes, some of these nodes will be redirected to adjacent WCVs following specific forwarding guidelines. We define adjacent WCVs as follows: if the separation between two cluster centers is less than a certain radius r, the WCVs

Algorithm 15 mTS scheduling algorithm

Require: Domains Ω_k, WCV set W
Ensure: Target charging nodes N_i
Initialize parameters: α; β;
Initialize WCVs;
$K \leftarrow |W|$;
for $i \leftarrow 1$ to K **do**
  Add W_i to Ω_i;
end for
for $j \leftarrow 1$ to K **do**
  Get current task queue Ψ_j;
  for $i \leftarrow 1$ to $|\Psi_j|$ **do**
    Sort $\Psi_j^{(t)}$ by t_i according to Eq. (5.4);
    Sort $\Psi_j^{(d)}$ by $d_{i,j}$;
    Get $\lambda_j^{(t)}(i)$ and $\lambda_j^{(d)}(i)$ according to Eqs. (5.5) and (5.6);
  end for
  for $i \leftarrow 1$ to $|\Psi_j|$ **do**
    Calculate $\lambda_j^{(m)}(i)$ according to Eq. (5.7);
  end for
  Sort $\Psi_j^{(m)}$ by $\lambda_j^{(m)}(i)$;
  Get top of the sorted queue, N_i;
  Test whether a node is reachable by Eq. (5.13);
  if Reachable **then**
    return Target N_i;
  else
    Send request of N_i to neighbor WCV;
    Neighbor WCV adds the request to its priority queue;
    Reselect node N_i by priority in $\Psi_j^{(m)}$;
  end if
end for

are considered adjacent, and r can be computed using Eq. (5.11):

$$r = \frac{\sum_{k=1}^{|W|} L_k}{|W|}. \tag{5.11}$$

In this context, L_k denotes the length of the kth segment of the Hamiltonian path, which is formed according to the cluster centers.

A notable scenario involving neighboring WCVs arises when a WCV goes back to the BS for recharging, at which point a nearby WCV may be called upon for assistance. This topic is elaborated in Sect. 5.1.2.2.

5.1.2.2 Scheme Analysis

In an on-demand charging system, WCVs handle charging requests from sensor nodes and establish a charging order. A nuanced issue is that despite the WCV's best efforts, some charging requests might remain unfulfilled. These requests should either be removed from the queue or directed to a WCV in a neighboring region for support. A related, yet distinct, scenario occurs when the active WCV depletes its power and must recharge at the BS. In such cases, most, if not all, charging requests will require assistance from neighboring WCVs.

Timely Arrival Verification Upon receiving a recharge request, the WCV must determine the soonest possible arrival time at the node and evaluate it against the recharge deadline. Should the WCV be unable to arrive at the sensor before the specified deadline, the recharge request needs to be either dismissed or relayed to adjacent WCVs for help.

In this context, let H_i denote the length of the ith segment of the Hamiltonian path, which is constructed from the nodes in Ψ_j and includes the position of W_j. The distance between N_m and N_n is represented as l_m^n, and H_i is determined:

$$H_i = \begin{cases} d_{s_2}^j, & i = 1 \\ l_{s_i}^{v_i}, & 1 < i \leq |\Psi_j|. \end{cases} \tag{5.12}$$

In this context, s_i denotes the starting node of the ith path, while v_i represents the terminal node.

This decision can be calculated by Eq. (5.13) as well:

$$\text{Reachable-In-Time Test} = \begin{cases} \text{serve}, & t_i \geq \frac{\sum_{k=1}^{i} H_k}{v} \\ \text{remove}, & t_i < \frac{\sum_{k=1}^{i} H_k}{v}. \end{cases} \tag{5.13}$$

Residual Energy Test Upon choosing a target node N_i, a WCV will assess in advance whether its remaining energy is adequate to return to the BS after completing the replenishment. If the energy is sufficient, it will head to node N_i; otherwise, it will head straight to the BS after relaying any requests to nearby WCVs.

$$\text{Residual Energy Test} = \begin{cases} \text{BS}, & \frac{e_w^j - \frac{E_n - e_n^i}{\epsilon}}{q_m} < \frac{d_i^j + d_i^{BS}}{v} \\ N_i, & \frac{e_w^j - \frac{E_n - e_n^i}{\epsilon}}{q_m} \geq \frac{d_i^j + d_i^{BS}}{v}. \end{cases} \tag{5.14}$$

In this context, e_w^j represents the residual energy of W_j, E_n denotes the energy capacity of a sensor node, and q_m indicates the energy consumption rate of WCVs.

5.1.3 Theoretical Analysis

In this section, we apply queueing theory to analyze mTS. Within the network, sensor nodes and WCVs are deployed randomly. Each WCV functions as a service

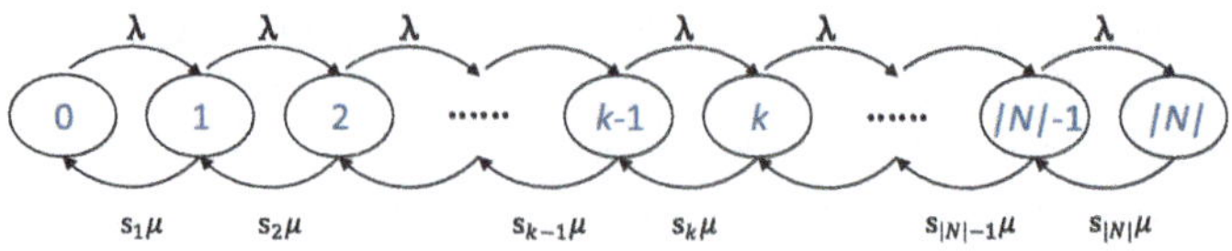

Fig. 5.4 State flow-chart

window and they operate cooperatively. Requests arrive following a Poisson distribution with rate parameter λ, and the service times follow a negative exponential distribution with rate μ. Thus, the system can be described as an $M/G/n/mTS$ queueing model. The system achieves a stable state when $\frac{\lambda}{n\mu} < 1$, as shown in Fig. 5.4. In this context, state values represent the number of current requests, and s_k denotes the number of active WCVs in state k.

We represent the value of the current state by the count of charging requests a WCV possesses (denoted as k), and the associated probability by p_k, which can be determined using Eq. (5.15):

$$p_k = \frac{\rho_1^k}{\prod_{i=1}^{k} s_i} p_0. \tag{5.15}$$

Here, $\rho_1 = \frac{\lambda}{\mu}$ and $\rho = \frac{\lambda}{n\mu}$. Since

$$\sum_{k=0}^{|N|} p_k = 1 \tag{5.16}$$

We can get:

$$p_0 = (\sum_{k=0}^{|N|} \frac{\rho_1^k}{\prod_{i=1}^{k} s_i})^{-1}. \tag{5.17}$$

Then some features of the system can deduced. The average length of the waiting queue L_q can be computed as Eq. (5.18):

$$L_q = \sum_{k=0}^{|N|} k p_k. \tag{5.18}$$

Then the service time T_s^k of a single WCV can be formalized as:

$$T_s^k = \begin{cases} \frac{d_1^j}{v} + \frac{E_n - e_n^1}{q_r}, & k = 0 \\ \frac{l_{k-1}^k}{v} + \frac{E_n - e_n^1}{q_r}, & k > 0. \end{cases} \tag{5.19}$$

Here, l_{k-1}^{k} is the distance between N_{k-1} and N_k.
The average service time of all WCVs is:

$$\overline{T_s} = \sum_{k=0}^{|N|} T_s^k p_k. \tag{5.20}$$

The response time of a charging request T_w^k can be computed as:

$$T_w^k = \sum_{l=1}^{k} T_s l. \tag{5.21}$$

The corresponding average response time $\overline{T_w}$ can be obtained as Eq. (5.22):

$$\overline{T_w} = \sum_{k=0}^{|N|} T_w^k p_k. \tag{5.22}$$

5.1.4 Simulation and Experiments

We assess the mTS algorithm by benchmarking it against two cutting-edge collaborative charging scheduling algorithms: Pushwait [1] and Hierarchical [2], showcasing its benefits. The simulation parameters used are outlined in Table 5.1.

In a 1000 × 1000 m^2 area, we randomly deployed $N = 50$ sensor nodes that can be recharged. $M = 5$ WCVs are used to power these nodes, with a charging

Table 5.1 Parameters of simulation

Parameters	Values
Network size (m^2)	1000 × 1000
Number of nodes	50
Number of WCVs	5
Consumption rate of node (mAh/s)	0.02 – 0.03
WCVs' traveling consumption rate (mAh/s)	10
WCVs' charging consumption rate (mAh/s)	500
Charging efficiency	0.90
Emergency level	0.30
Initial energy of node (mAh)	900
Initial energy of WCV (mAh)	50000
Speed of WCVs (m/s)	5.0
Weight of time α	1.0
Weight of distance β	1.0

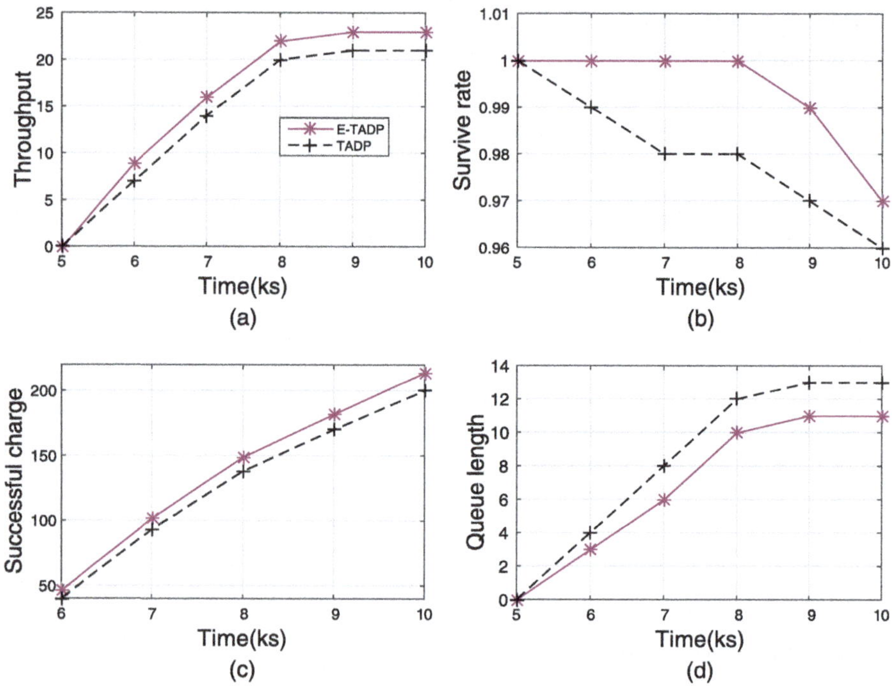

Fig. 5.5 Comparison between mTS and TADP in terms of (**a**) throughput, (**b**) survival rate, (**c**) request number and (**d**) queue length

efficiency of 0.9, as referenced in iNPOFi [3]. The alert threshold for the on-demand charging system is set at 30%.

Given that mTS is an enhancement of TADP, we start by assessing the improvements made by mTS. Figure 5.5 illustrates that mTS boosts TADP's performance across all metrics by a minimum of 10%. This improvement is due to TADP converting priority values into integers, which fails to capture the interdependence between spatial and temporal features accurately. In contrast, mTS uses the ratios of deadlines to distances as priorities, resulting in more precise prioritization and improved outcomes.

We compare the performance of mTS against Pushwait and Hierarchical in terms of queue length, successful charges, survival rate, and throughput, as illustrated in Fig. 5.6. Figure 5.6a indicates that the survival rate of nodes in mTS is the highest. In terms of successful charges, mTS consistently achieves a success rate that is 5% to 10% higher than the others (see Fig. 5.6b). Figure 5.6c presents the comparison of queue lengths, showing that mTS is 29% shorter on average. According to our simulations, the queue length is 11, which is approximately equal to the 12 predicted by Eq. (5.18), confirming our theoretical analysis. Additionally, Fig. 5.6d demonstrates that mTS achieves the highest throughput compared to the other two schemes.

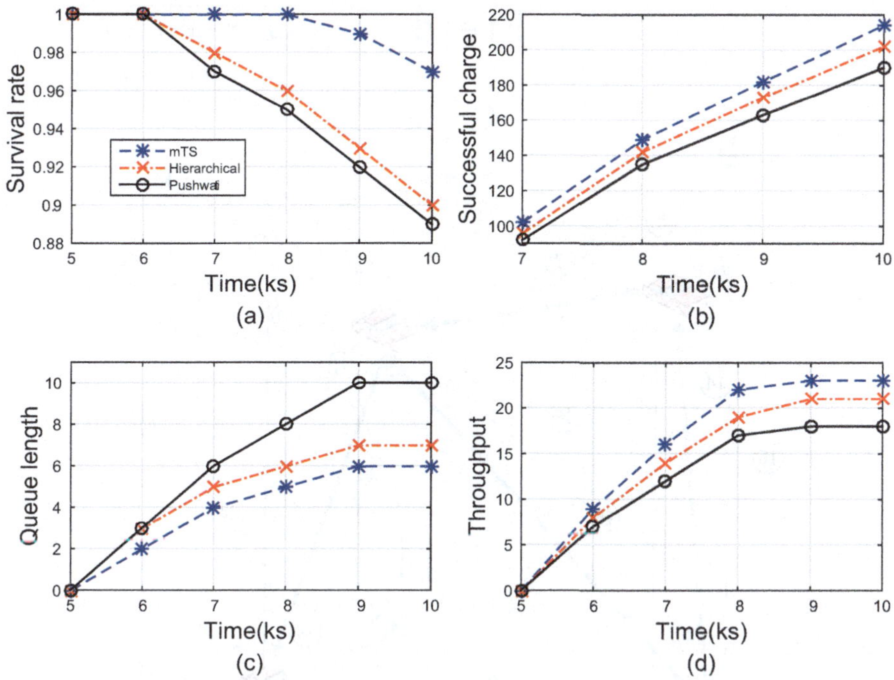

Fig. 5.6 Comparison between mTS, Pushwait and Hierarchical in terms of (**a**) survival rate, (**b**) successful charging rate, (**c**) queue length and (**d**) throughput

5.1.4.1 Experiment Configurations

In this section, we perform experiments to demonstrate the benefits of mTS. We have chosen two settings for the experiments, a field and an artificial lake, which are illustrated in Figs. 5.7 and 5.8. The detailed experimental setups are provided in Table 5.2.

The dimensions of the rechargeable sensor nodes are 50 $\times$ 70 mm. Each node features a receiving coil to harvest energy. We utilize different hardware components for three distinct charging standards: WiTricity [4], Qi [5], and iNPOFi [3] in our implementation of rechargeable sensors. Each standard necessitates relatively compact coil sizes: iNPOFi (17.5 $\times$ 74 mm), WiTricity (31 $\times$ 47.5 mm), and Qi (34 $\times$ 45.5 mm), as depicted in Fig. 5.10.

Our study first determines the optimal ratio for balancing temporal and spatial priorities, represented by α and β. As shown in Fig. 5.9a, there's a noticeable shift in node survival rate around $\frac{\alpha}{\beta} = 1$. This shift might stem from an imbalance in prioritizing these two factors. If temporal priority is too dominant, distant nodes may deplete their energy. Conversely, if spatial priority is overemphasized, nearby nodes in need of immediate recharging might be neglected. Consequently, for maximizing recharging efficiency, we set $\frac{\alpha}{\beta} = 1$ in subsequent experiments.

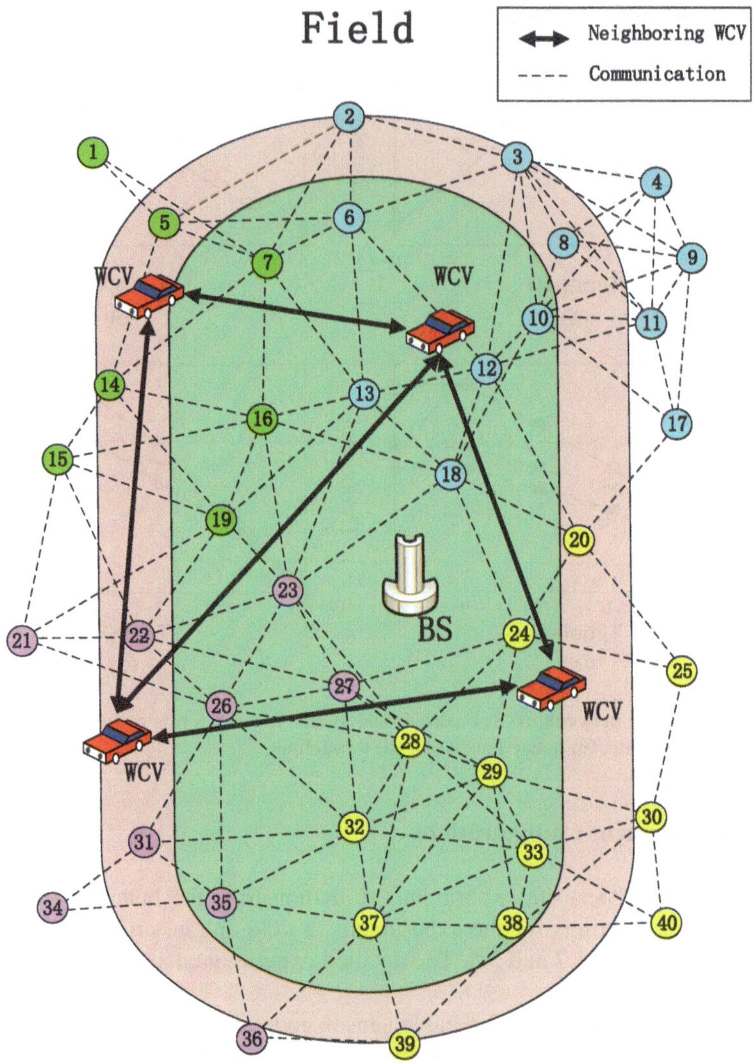

Fig. 5.7 Soccer field experiment

Next, we evaluate how coil distance affects energy efficiency. As illustrated in Fig. 5.9b, charging efficiency diminishes as the distance increases. Thus, the highest efficiency is attained when the coils are in contact. In contrast to previous studies that utilized mobile vehicles [6–8], our experiment leverages robotic arms with GPS and camera modules for precise localization and contact charging. Additionally,

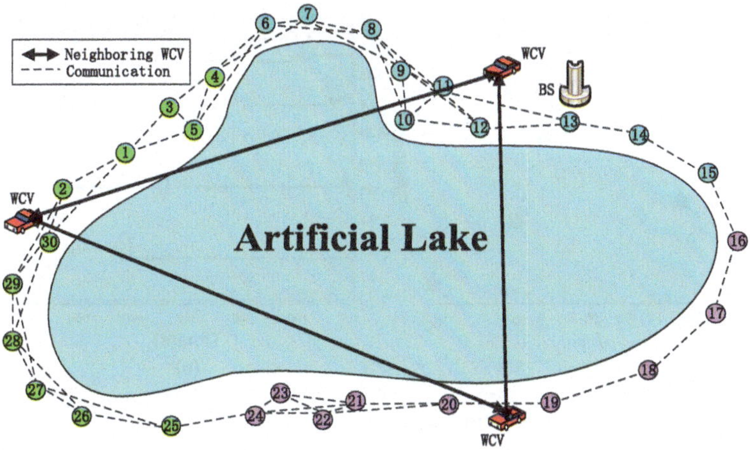

Fig. 5.8 Artificial lake experiment

Table 5.2 Parameters of experiments

Parameter	Field	Lake
Network size (m^2)	300×150	100×100
Number of nodes	40	30
Number of WCVs	4	3
Consumption of nodes (mAh/s)	$0.02 - 0.03$	$0.02 - 0.03$
WCVs' moving consumption (mAh/s)	10	10
WCVs' charging consumption (mAh/s)	500	500
Charging efficiency	0.90	0.90
Emergency level	0.30	0.30
Initial energy of nodes(mAh)	900	900
Initial energy of WCVs(mAh)	50000	50000
Speed of WCVs(m/s)	5.0	5.0
Weight of time	1.0	1.0
Weight of distance	1.0	1.0

these robotic arms support both contactless (WiTricity and Qi) and contact charging standards (iNPOFi). Throughout all experiments, the robot arms ensure that the charging and receiving coils of the three standards are perfectly aligned and in contact to optimize charging efficiency (Fig. 5.10).

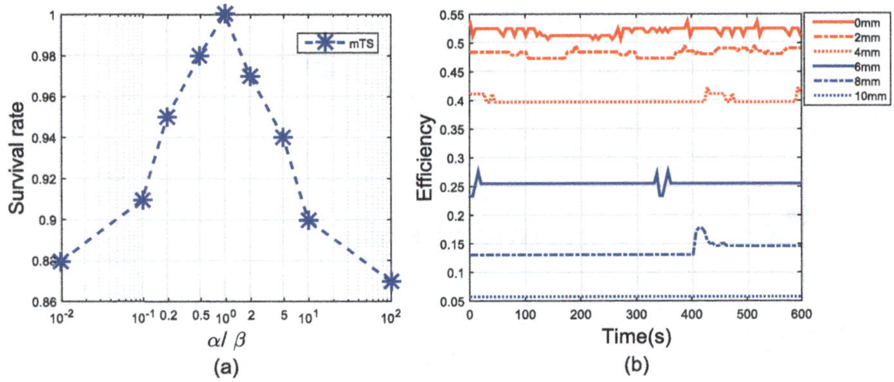

Fig. 5.9 Determining the values of (**a**) $\frac{\alpha}{\beta}$ and (**b**) ε

Fig. 5.10 Test-bed: mobile robot arm and three types of rechargeable sensors

5.2 Three-Dimensional Dynamic Collaborative Scheduling Scheme

In the prior segment, we discussed the issue of charging scheduling within a multi-vehicle setting. This section explores 3-D networks, where Unmanned Aerial Vehicles (UAVs) integrate with Wireless Charging Vehicles (WCVs). To extend the network's operational duration, we analyze device sleep durations and energy use, introducing a 3-D Dynamic Collaborative Scheduling (3DCS) approach. We derive theoretical values for energy thresholds and partition numbers to delegate charging tasks to chargers. Subsequently, we develop scheduling algorithms encompassing target selection, infeasibility assessments, and target updates. Furthermore, a collaborative method is devised to redistribute charging responsibilities from overburdened chargers to neighboring units, enhancing charging efficiency. Empirical trials and comprehensive simulations reveal that our strategy excels in terms of

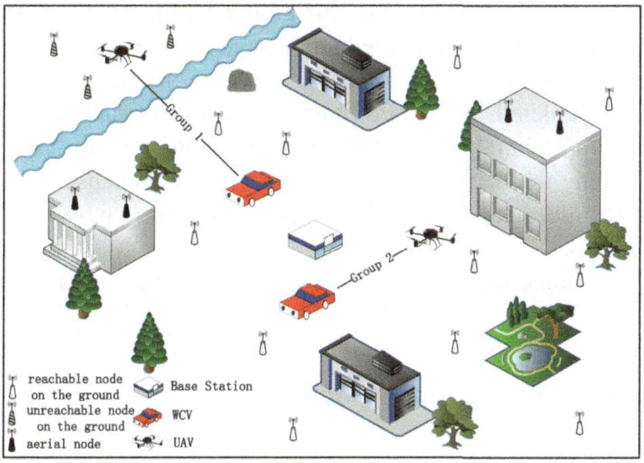

Fig. 5.11 A diagram of network model with 3-D environment

charging throughput, energy conservation, and other metrics when compared to various renowned scheduling methods.

5.2.1 Problem Statement

5.2.1.1 Network Model

In a 3-D WRSN, sensors are deployed uniformly, but their locations categorize them into three types: (a) accessible nodes on the ground, (b) inaccessible nodes on the ground (e.g., obstructed by obstacles), and (c) airborne nodes (e.g., on table surfaces, roofs, trees, etc.). Figure 5.11 presents a diagram of the WRSN in a 3D setting. When sensor energy levels drop beneath a critical threshold, recharge requests are sent. Subsequently, WCVs and UAVs are deployed and scheduled to reach the requesting node's location and recharge it together. We establish a rectangular region with a square base as the area for charging scheduling and collaboration, where various groups of WCVs and UAVs are deployed. In our scenario, WCVs handle nodes of type a), while UAVs, owing to their unique flexibility, can service all types of nodes. This work concentrates on collaborative scheduling challenges.

5.2.1.2 Problem Statement

In the specified 3-dimensional network, we consider both UAVs and WCVs to act as chargers. An effective strategy here involves first partitioning the entire network into multiple sub-regions and then assigning MCs to each one to deliver energy.

As a result, the scheduling protocol is carried out within each sub-region, while a cooperative mechanism is implemented among the chargers.

In our model, the sensor node remains active (i.e., monitoring and transmitting) until its energy is depleted. Afterward, it enters a dormant state until it is recharged and reactivated. Unpredictable events can happen at any moment and in any part of the network, making the depletion of any node a potential cause for missed events, which we aim to minimize. Consequently, we focus on maximizing the so-called active time of sensors.

In order to determine the total lifetime, we describe the deadline au_i^k for node i as:

$$\tau_i^k = T_{pre}^i + \frac{E_s}{\delta_i} \,. \tag{5.23}$$

Upon receiving requests from sensors, a charging route is established and dynamically adjusted. We refer to the kth charging cycle as T_{cycle}^k, during which no node will be charged more than once. Furthermore, T_{cycle}^k represents the maximum value that satisfies the corresponding definition. We denote t_i^k as the arrival time when a mobile charger reaches node i during cycle k. Consequently, we define the sleep status of node i during cycle k as:

$$\xi_i^k = \begin{cases} 0 & t_i^k \leq \tau_i^k \\ 1 & t_i^k > \tau_i^k \end{cases} , \tag{5.24}$$

where $\xi_i^k = 1$ means that node i will enter sleep mode and 0 otherwise.

The primary challenge is *to maintain network performance by reducing the overall sleep duration of sensors.* We define this charging scheduling issue as the **Minimum Total Sleep Time Problem (MTSTP)** in the following manner:

$$min \quad \sum_{k=1}^{M} \sum_{i=0}^{N} \xi_i^k (t_i^k - \tau_i^k) \,, \tag{5.25}$$

Subject to:

$$t_b^k = t_a^k + C_a^k + \Gamma_{a,b} \,, \tag{5.26}$$

$$\Gamma_{a,b} = \frac{\ell_{a,b}}{\upsilon_u} \,, \tag{5.27}$$

$$\Gamma_{a,b} = \frac{\ell_{a,b}}{\upsilon_w} \,, \tag{5.28}$$

$$E_v^m > \omega \ell_{P_M^m, P_B} , \tag{5.29}$$

$$E_c + \omega_u D_u + \omega_w D_w < E_v . \tag{5.30}$$

Equation (5.25) illustrates the cumulative sleep time for N sensors across M charging cycles, where $\sum_{i=0}^{N} \xi_i^k (t_i^k - \tau_i^k)$ represents the total sleep duration of the sensors for cycle k. Equation (5.26) explains the full servicing process between two contiguous nodes, with C_a indicating the time required to recharge node a, and the real distance between two nodes being represented as $\ell_{a,b}$. The traversal time $\Gamma_{a,b}$ for UAVs and WCVs is determined as in Eqs. (5.27) and (5.28), where v_u and v_w signify the respective moving speeds of the chargers.

Equation (5.29) ensures that the energy of charger m is sufficient for its return to the base station (BS), where P_M^m represents the position of charger m and P_B represents the position of the BS. Equation (5.30) asserts that the energy provided by the chargers is lesser than the total energy E_v transported by the MCs. E_c refers to the effective output energy of chargers, and $\omega_u D_u$ represents the movement cost of UAVs, where D_u signifies their overall moving distance during the charging operation and ω_u is the energy usage rate per unit distance for them. Likewise, the movement cost for WCVs is denoted as $\omega_w D_w$.

5.2.2 *Schematic Design*

The 3DCS scheme involves the following steps: (1) assigning chargers; (2) managing the charging schedule within each partition. We will detail each of these steps below, and afterwards, we will discuss our method for calculating the number of partitions and the energy limit.

5.2.2.1 Charging Scheduling Scheme

After dividing the regions, two MCs (a UAV and a WCV) are allocated to each area for energy refueling. Both MCs utilize a comparable scheduling scheme for recharging, which differentiates only the distances across various dimensions. We propose three algorithms for the replenishment scheduling process: target selection, infeasibility check, and target update.

Target Selection When a request is received, the charger will initially register the details of the requested node, such as the deadline, remaining energy, and additional fundamental parameters, and place each request into a waiting queue Q_W according to the deadline. Typically, the request at the front of the queue is served as the next charging target. However, certain exceptions necessitate a dynamic decision mechanism. For instance, servicing a distant node might consume considerable time, potentially causing other requested nodes to deplete their battery power. We introduce an algorithm to identify the most urgent and viable charging target in Algorithm 16.

Algorithm 16 Target selection

Input: A waiting queue Q_W and a mission queue Q_M;
Output: The target node n_{target};
Sort Q_W in ascending order based on deadline $\tau_{n_i}^k$ of node n_i;
for $\forall\, n_i \in Q_W$ **do**
  Execute Algorithm 17 to judge feasibility of n_i;
  if n_i is an infeasible isolated node **then**
    Change another node;
  else
    $n_{target} \leftarrow n_i$;
    return n_{target};
  end if
end for
Pick the head node n_0 from Q_W;
$n_{target} \leftarrow n_0$;
return n_{target};

Algorithm 16 operates as follows. Initially, to make sure the most critical node survives, we arrange Q_W based on the nodes' deadlines. Next, we assess the feasibility of the chosen most urgent node by running Algorithm 17 to further optimize our target node. If no feasible node is found, the head node is directly chosen as the current target node. Lastly, the loading target is appended to Q_M for further optimization.

Infeasibility Test Distant nodes can have a severe negative impact on the normal operation of WRSNs, as it can be extremely costly to recharge them. We hereby develop an infeasibility test algorithm, shown in Algorithm 17.

Algorithm 17 Infeasibility test

Input: Node n_i, position P of charger and center S_c of region;
Output: Feasibility of node n_i;
Calculate average distance Ω of all nodes;
if $\ell_{n_i,S_c} > \Omega$ and $\ell_{n_i,P} > \ell_{S_c,P}$ **then**
  n_i is a feasible node;
else
  n_i is an infeasible node;
end if

Algorithm 17 begins with the input of several crucial details, such as the average node distance, the charger's position, and the region's center, to identify an infeasible node. Additionally, two criteria are introduced to determine an infeasible node (refer to Fig. 5.12):

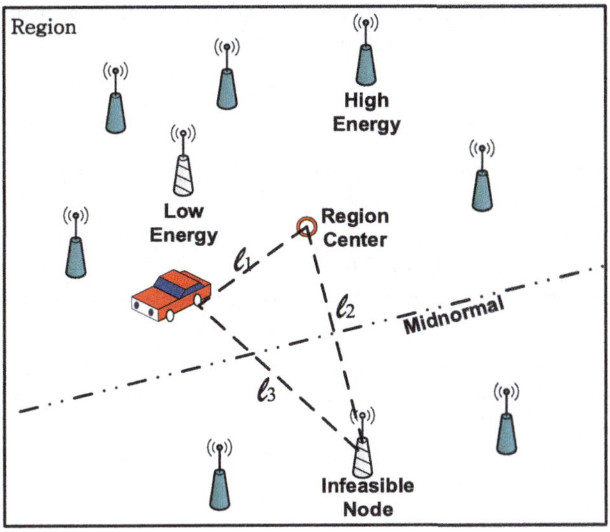

Fig. 5.12 An example of judging an infeasible node

1. $\ell_2 > \Omega$ The distance between the region center and the node is larger than the average distance of all nodes.
2. $\ell_3 > \ell_1$ The distance between the node and the charger is larger than the distance between the region center and the charger.

The initial criterion, $\ell_2 > \Omega$, signifies that the assessed node is fairly secluded within the specified area. In contrast, the subsequent criterion, $\ell_3 > \ell_1$, guarantees that the charger is not positioned adjacent to the assessed node. It is only when both criteria are met concurrently that the node can be considered infeasible.

After presenting two algorithms, it is important to mention two additional points. Firstly, following the second condition of the infeasibility test, the infeasibility characteristic of sensor nodes evolves dynamically as the charger moves. Secondly, if Algorithm 17 determines that all nodes are infeasible, the charging service will still proceed according to the sequence of Q_W.

Target Update To enhance the efficiency of the charging path, the chosen target node can be adjusted locally. Considering the overall task, charging the chosen target node directly while neglecting other nodes might lead to the failure of a nearby requested node. Hence, we propose target updating, incorporating some intermediary nodes on the route to the target node.

Adding a node in front of the target node will lengthen the response time for the following nodes. To ensure the total sleep time is minimized during this insertion, we need to dynamically assess the additional time to evaluate its effect on the current path. Consequently, we calculate the additional time ΔT_m when placing node m between nodes i and j, as illustrated in UAV scheduling:

$$\Delta T_m = (\ell_{i,m} + \ell_{m,j} - \ell_{i,j})\upsilon_u + C_m^k\,, \tag{5.31}$$

in which the additional time ΔT_m includes both travel and charging durations, with C_m^k representing the time allocated to charging node m during the kth cycle. Notably, the endurance of the current target node is used as the insertion criterion to guarantee a global optimization in Algorithm 16.

We present the detailed updating and inserting process in Algorithm 18 for better comprehension.

Algorithm 18 Target update

Input: A waiting queue Q_W, a mission queue Q_M, position P_M of charger and current time T;
Output: Target node n_{target};
if $Q_M = \varnothing$ **then**
  $Q_M \leftarrow n_{target}$;
end if
while n_{target} has changed **do**
  Construct a sphere S with diameter $\ell_{P,n_{target}}$;
  for $\forall\, n_i \in Q_W$ **do**
    if $T + \Delta T_{n_i} \leqslant \tau_{n^k_{target}}$ **then**
      Find $\min\limits_{n_i \in S}\{\Delta T_{n_i}\}$;
      Insert n_i in the head of Q_M and $n_{target} \leftarrow n_i$;
      return n_{target};
    end if
  end for
end while

The steps for Algorithm 18 are outlined below. Initially, the target node is updated only after the current charging task is finished. If the mission queue Q_M is empty, the node chosen by Algorithm 16 is placed at the head of Q_M. Next, a sphere is created with a diameter equivalent to the distance between the charger's position and the target node. Within this sphere, nodes that do not cause the target node to sleep are identified as potential insertable nodes. Among these, the node that adds the least extra time is chosen as the suitable insertable node. This node is then inserted and replaces the current target. This process is repeated until no more suitable nodes can be found.

5.2.2.2 Collaboration Mechanism

As previously indicated, the entire network is first segmented into multiple regions, and our optimized scheduling algorithms are deployed in each region for every charger. However, this method decreases the flexibility of the charging process. Allocating tasks in a fixed manner restricts the mobility of the chargers, potentially leading to a significant increase in the total sleep time of all nodes. Therefore, we have devised a cooperative mechanism that permits chargers to traverse their own regions to support others.

Owing to the inefficient energy transfer and the limited capacity of chargers, direct transfer or sharing of energy between chargers is excluded [9]. In this study, we exclusively focus on collaboration between chargers and nodes across different regions. Additionally, the primary objective of the collaboration mechanism is to minimize sleep time.

Algorithm 19 Collaboration among chargers

Input: H waiting queues $Q_W^1, Q_W^2, \ldots, Q_W^H$ and mission queues $Q_M^1, Q_M^2, \ldots, Q_M^H$;
Output: Mission queues $Q_M^1, Q_M^2, \ldots, Q_M^H$;
Find a set of sleep nodes S_D in Q_W^H;
for $\forall\, n_i \in S_D$ **do**
    Find an idle charger and insert n_i into its Q_M^H;
    if No request emerges during service time of n_i in its region **then**
        Update mission queue Q_M^H;
        return $Q_M^1, Q_M^2, \ldots, Q_M^H$;
    else
        Change other idle chargers;
    end if
end for

Algorithm 19 operates as follows. Initially, we identify all sleep nodes in Q_W of each region, and subsequently, potential collaborative chargers are identified. It is important to note that nodes in Q_M are excluded from consideration as Q_M has already established a locally optimized path. Following this, all idle chargers are selected for collaboration, and if no request arises during the collaborative charging service period, cross-region collaboration is permitted.

5.2.2.3 Network Region Partition

Network region partitioning is performed as follows: initially, K partition centers are chosen, and nodes are subsequently grouped into K regions based on their distances. The method for selecting K will be described later in this subsection. Without loss of generality, it is assumed that the height of airborne sensors is restricted by their transmission ranges and that the network has a flat structure. Consequently, partitioning is applied solely to ground sensors, with the resulting regions being extendable into the third dimension for additional planning.

To determine the optimal number of partitions K, we employ two criteria: (i) each region must be plannable, and (ii) the total number of loaders must be minimized. To develop an appropriate allocation solution, we utilize a modified distance-based K-means partitioning algorithm [10]. A major drawback of the traditional K-means clustering algorithm is the determination of the number of clusters K. Based on our analysis of criteria (i) and (ii), K can be ascertained as follows.

To meet our main goal, the smallest partition number K must ensure that all sensors remain operational. The wait time for the final sensor is represented by $\frac{E_s}{\delta_i}$, assuming that the energy E_s is constant and that δ_i is the peak consumption rate δ_{max}. Therefore, we obtain the following.

$$\frac{E_s}{\delta_{max}} > \frac{\frac{N}{K}\Omega}{\upsilon_w} + \frac{N}{K}\frac{E_s}{\chi} . \tag{5.32}$$

Equation (5.32) shows that within the response time of the last sensor, the charger in any area must finish all other tasks. This implies that the total of travel time and charging time needs to be restricted by $\frac{E_s}{\delta_{max}}$. Therefore, we derive K as follows:

$$K > N\delta_{max}(\frac{1}{\chi} + \frac{\Omega}{E_s \upsilon_w}) . \tag{5.33}$$

To better ascertain K, it is necessary to precisely forecast the mean distance Ω between any two random sensors. Within a randomly distributed network, the squared sum of the distance between sensors (x_i, y_i) and (x_j, y_j) can be determined as:

$$\begin{aligned}\sum_{i>j} \ell_{i,j}^2 &= \sum_{i>j}(x_i - x_j)^2 + \sum_{i>j}(y_i - y_j)^2 \\ &= N\sum_i(x_i - \overline{x})^2 + N\sum_i(y_i - \overline{y})^2\end{aligned} . \tag{5.34}$$

We can derive the expected value of the squared distance between any two sensors:

$$E(\Omega^2) = E(\ell_{i,j}^2) = 2(\sigma_x^2 + \sigma_y^2) , \tag{5.35}$$

where σ_x^2 and σ_y^2 denote the variance of sensor's coordinates. We define node density β as $\frac{XY}{(N-1)^2}$, where X and Y denote the side length of area. Then σ_x^2 and σ_y^2 can respectively be represented as:

$$\begin{aligned}\sigma_x^2 &= \frac{2\Sigma_{i=0}^{\frac{X}{2\beta}-1}(i\beta - \frac{X}{2})^2}{N} \\ \sigma_y^2 &= \frac{2\Sigma_{i=0}^{\frac{Y}{2\beta}-1}(i\beta - \frac{Y}{2})^2}{N}\end{aligned} . \tag{5.36}$$

From Eqs. (5.35) and (5.36), we deduce that node density β significantly influences Ω, which is crucial for determining K. Therefore, K can be theoretically ascertained.

Given that the number of partitions is predetermined, K groups of MCs, consisting of a UAV and a WCV, are allocated to serve each region. In each region, the two chargers employ the planned scheduling and collaboration strategy to find the MTSTP solution.

5.2.2.4 Determine Threshold θ

Choosing the energy threshold, θ, is crucial for WRSNs functioning. If θ is set too low, sensors might drain their batteries before recharging. On the other hand, setting θ too high causes sensors to request charging prematurely, leading to network congestion and difficult charging scheduling. We analyze the minimum and maximum limits of θ that network systems should use for smooth operations.

To establish the minimum threshold $heta$, we envision a situation where the final node in an exhaustive task list is recharged precisely as its energy depletes. In this scenario, all other nodes remain active without entering sleep mode. The overall duration of the entire task list, using a WCV scheduling procedure as an instance, is:

$$(\epsilon - 1)\Omega = (\tau_i^k - C)\upsilon_w \ , \tag{5.37}$$

where Ω represents the average distance between all nodes, and ϵ signifies the task number. υ_w indicates the velocity of the WCVs, while C denotes the total charging time for the nodes, adhering to the following inequality:

$$C > \frac{E_s - \theta}{\chi}(\epsilon - 1) \ . \tag{5.38}$$

In this context, E_s represents the total energy of the nodes, and χ signifies the charging rate of the nodes. Requests are triggered when the nodes' energy reaches θ, so by the time a charger arrives at target node i, its energy will be below θ. Consequently, we can determine the lower bound of the energy threshold by combining Eqs. (5.37) and (5.38), assuming $T_{pre}^i = 0$:

$$\theta > E_s(1 - \frac{\chi}{\delta_i(\epsilon - 1)}) + \frac{\chi\Omega}{\upsilon_w} \ . \tag{5.39}$$

To ensure system stability (preventing any nodes from entering sleep mode), we identify the time period in which each node is attended to exactly once. When the charger loops back to the initial node on the list, all other nodes should have been attended to once, thus enabling us to set the upper limit as:

$$\frac{E_s - \theta}{\delta_i} = \frac{\Omega(\frac{N}{K} - 1)}{\upsilon_w} + C\,, \tag{5.40}$$

where $racNK$ represents the mean number of sensors within a single region (this mean value has been used in place of the specific count). Subsequently, following Eq. (5.38), the upper limit is determined as:

$$\theta < E_s - \frac{\Omega\delta_i\chi(\frac{N}{K} - 1)}{\upsilon_w\chi - \upsilon_w\delta_i(\frac{N}{K} - 1)}, \tag{5.41}$$

where the ratio of the energy consumption rate to the charging rate for node i must meet the condition $\frac{\chi}{\delta_i} > \frac{N}{K} - 1$. If this condition is not met, the maximum threshold is limited by the total energy E_s of the nodes. Finally, we have:

$$\begin{aligned} E_s(1 - \frac{\chi}{\delta_i(\epsilon - 1)}) + \frac{\chi\Omega}{\upsilon_w} < \\ \theta < E_s - \frac{\Omega\delta_i\chi(\frac{N}{K} - 1)}{\upsilon_w\chi - \upsilon_w\delta_i(\frac{N}{K} - 1)}\,. \end{aligned} \tag{5.42}$$

5.2.3 *Theoretical Analysis*

5.2.3.1 Average Queue Length

In our framework, chargers function as charging servers while clients are nodes that have initiated their requests. Given that each MC is accountable for a segment of the network, the $M/G/1/\infty/N/3DCS$ queueing model [11] is employed. For each charging process, the service time for a client is defined as the period from the charger's arrival to the client's complete charge. Additionally, request arrivals follow a Poisson distribution with rate λ, and the service times for chargers are governed by a General distribution, with the queue length constrained to N [12].

Let T_n represent the service duration for node n. Define $\mathcal{A}_n$ as the occurrence where A_n nodes are in the server's waiting queue when node n is fully charged. Additionally, define $\mathcal{B}_n$ as the occurrence of B_n requests being sent to the server during T_n, the service time for node $n + 1$.

Denote transition probability as $p_{ij} = P(A_{n+1} = j|A_n = i)$. We have:

$$\begin{aligned} p_{ij} &= P(B_n = j + 1 - A_n|A_n = i) \\ &= \begin{cases} 0 & i > j \\ r_{j+1-i} & i \leq j + 1 \end{cases}, \end{aligned} \tag{5.43}$$

where $r_k(t) = P(B_n = k|(T_n = t))$ is simply:

$$r_k(t) = \frac{(\lambda t)^j}{j!} e^{-\lambda t} , \quad (5.44)$$

due to the Poisson arrival assumption.

Let $\rho = \frac{\lambda}{\mu}$ represent the service capacity. The steady-state probability distribution ζ_j can be determined as:

$$\zeta_j = \sum_{i=0}^{\infty} \zeta_i p_{ij} \quad j \geq 0 . \quad (5.45)$$

Clearly, every state in the Markov chain is linked, and $r_0 = P_{00} > 0$. Consequently, we obtain:

$$D(B_n) = E(B_n^2) - [E(B_n)]^2 = \rho + \lambda^2 D(T_n) . \quad (5.46)$$

Let $Z(x) = \sum_{j=0}^{\infty} \zeta_j x^j$ and $R(x) = \sum_{j=0}^{\infty} r_j x^j$ represent the generating functions for ζ_j and r_j, respectively. Based on Eq. (5.45) and the Markov chain's transition process, we obtain:

$$\begin{aligned} x^0 \zeta_0 &= (\zeta_0 r_0 + \zeta_1 r_0) x^0 \\ x^1 \zeta_1 &= (\zeta_0 r_1 + \zeta_1 r_1 + \zeta_2 r_0) x^1 \\ &\vdots \\ x^n \zeta_n &= (\zeta_0 r_n + \zeta_1 r_n + \zeta_2 r_{n-1} + \ldots + \zeta_{n+1} r_0) x^n \\ &\vdots \end{aligned} \quad (5.47)$$

The generating function for the queue length distribution in a stable queuing model is determined as follows:

$$Z(x) = \frac{(1-\rho)(1-x)R(x)}{R(x) - x} . \quad (5.48)$$

With $R'(1) = \rho$, the average length of queue is formulated as:

$$L_s = \rho + \frac{\lambda^2 \sigma^2 + \rho^2}{2(1-\rho)} . \quad (5.49)$$

We validate our theoretical analysis in Sect. 5.2.4.

5.2.3.2 Scheme Complexity

To understand the complexity of our approach, we can break it down into three segments: selecting an initial target node, revising the target node, and facilitating collaboration among regions. We will explore each of these segments in depth.

Complexity of Algorithms 16 and 17: Identifying an initial target node involves an infeasibility test for nodes that has linear complexity, with the majority of computational time devoted to sorting the waiting queue Q_W for each charger. When integrating the partition results, the overall complexity for this operation is $O(N \log \frac{N}{K})$, where N represents the total number of sensors in the network and K denotes the partition number.

Complexity of Algorithm 18: While updating the target node, eligible nodes may be added one by one into the mission queue Q_M. Therefore, to achieve local optimization of the scheduling, an $O(N^2)$ complexity is necessary.

Complexity of Algorithm 19: During the collaboration phase, the idle chargers will sequentially be assigned to the sleeping nodes in each region, while also ensuring the schedulability within their respective regions. Therefore, the complexity of collaboration is $O(KN)$, where K represents the number of regions and $K < N$.

To sum up, the overall complexity of our scheme is $O(N^2)$ in the worst case.

5.2.4 Simulation and Experiments

As an experimental setup, we created a test-bed Wireless Rechargeable Sensor Network (WRSN) in our laboratory, featuring one Wireless Charging Vehicle (WCV), one Unmanned Aerial Vehicle (UAV), and multiple sensors. The sensors were constructed using Powercast [13] and charged via RF energy (radio frequency waves). The P2110 Powerharvester Receiver wireless sensor board transforms RF energy into direct current (DC) power. The charging units, which consist of both a UAV and a WCV, are fitted with TX91501 transmitters that continuously emit RF signals at a frequency of 915 MHz. Although the charging range can reach up to 12 m (approximately 40 ft), we configured it to around 2 m to enhance energy efficiency.

As illustrated in Figs. 5.13 and 5.14, a total of 8 sensors were utilized, including 3 accessible, 2 inaccessible on land, and 3 airborne nodes. The experiment was conducted over a duration of 30 days, during which we evaluated the total sleep time, energy efficiency, and average service time across different energy thresholds θ of the sensors. It is worth mentioning that all charging requests were completed before their deadlines, leading to a total sleep time of zero.

We compare the theoretical, simulation, and experimental outcomes on service time as depicted in Fig. 5.15. The theoretical assessment did not include travel time, which accounts for the 15–20% discrepancy between theoretical and simulation/experimental results. The simulation outcomes align well with the experimental findings. Generally, service time reduces as the energy threshold rises due to shorter

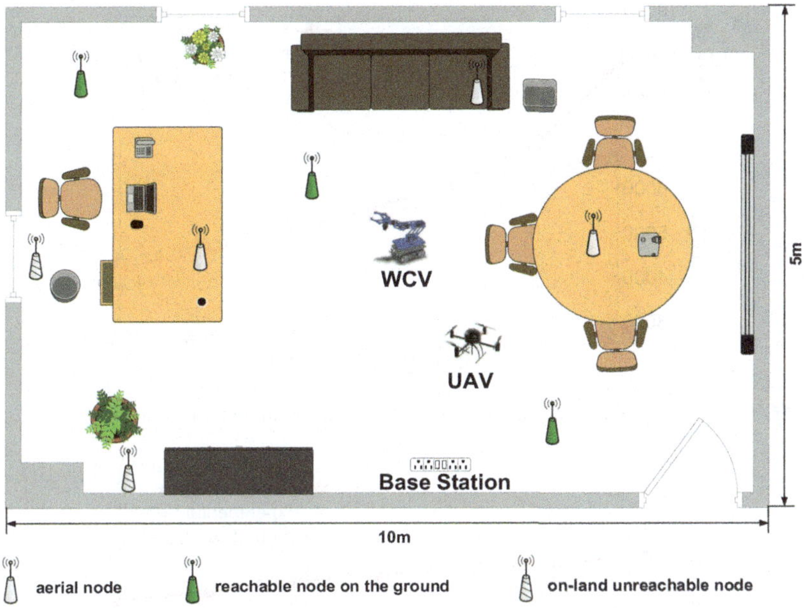

Fig. 5.13 A diagram of our lab

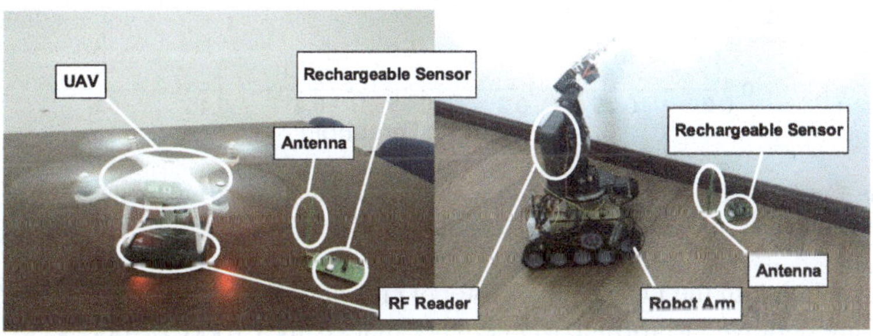

Fig. 5.14 Practical charging process served by one WCV and one UAV

charging times. Figure 5.16 shows that similar disparities in energy efficiency are noted between theoretical and simulation/experimental outcomes. With an increasing threshold, there are shorter charges, leading to more travel for the chargers and a drop in energy efficiency. Nonetheless, the efficiency stays above 70%.

5.2.4.1 Simulation Setup

As shown in Table 5.3, the network setup includes 500 nodes, consisting of 350 reachable nodes, 20 on-land unreachable nodes, and 130 aerial nodes. These nodes

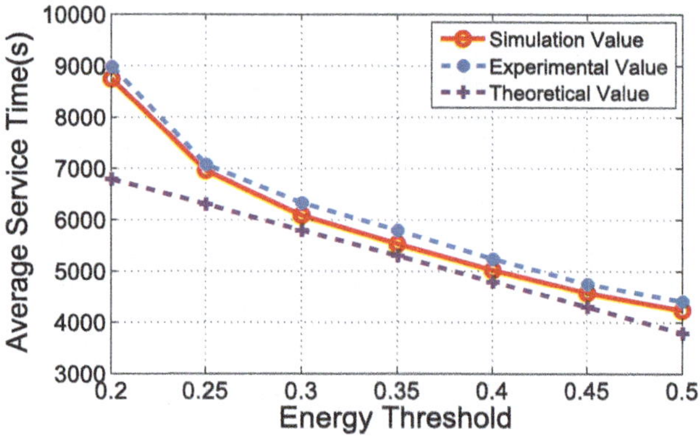

Fig. 5.15 Comparison of average service time in experiment, simulation, and analysis

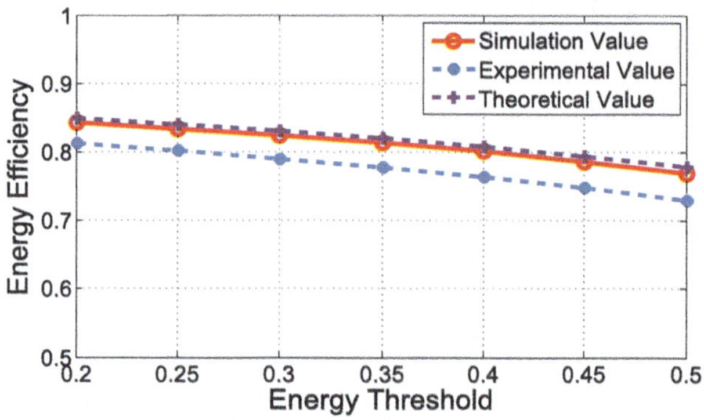

Fig. 5.16 Comparison of energy efficiency in experiment, simulation, and analysis

are configured with the DD routing protocol [14] and the S-MAC protocol [15]. The sensors are deployed to form a 3-D network that spans a $1000 \times 1000 \times 50$ m area. The proportion of reachable and unreachable sensors, 70 and 30% respectively, is maintained for different node counts, such as 1000. Node energy consumption varies between 5 and 9 mJ/s, with each node capable of storing up to 12 KJ of energy. The energy capacities of the WCV and UAV are 120 and 40 KJ, respectively. The energy threshold is set at 30%, aligning with the range defined in Eq. (5.42). The average travel velocities for WCVs and UAVs are 2 and 3 m/s, respectively. The energy consumption rate during travel is 8 J/m for all chargers, and the node energy charging rate is 2 J/s, in agreement with our test-bed experiments. The simulation is conducted for a duration of 12 months.

As prior studies have not addressed 3-D WRSNs utilizing heterogeneous chargers, we choose several established methods from a 2-D context for comparison: FCFS, EDF, and NJNP [12]. FCFS and EDF handle requests by first-come-first-served and earliest-deadline-first criteria, respectively, whereas NJNP replenishes nodes according to proximity.

Table 5.3 Simulation setup

Parameters	Values
Network area	1000 × 1000 × 500 m
Number of nodes	500–1000
Energy consumption rate of nodes	5 − 9 mJ/s
Average velocity of the WCV	2 m/s
Average velocity of the UAV	3 m/s
Energy consumption rate in traveling	8 J/m
Energy charging rate for sensors	2 J/s
Total energy capacity of nodes	12 KJ
Total energy of WCV	120 KJ
Total energy of UAV	40 KJ
Energy threshold	30%
Simulation time	12 months
Sampling interval	1 month
Charging scheme	3DCS, NJNP, EDF, FCFS

5.2.4.2 Partition Number *K*

In Sect. 5.2.2.3, we provide a theoretical explanation for determining the parameter K, which represents the number of charger groups required in a network. Our goal is to identify the optimal number of partitions considering various system parameters.

In Fig. 5.17a, the results for $K = 2, 3, \ldots, 7$ are depicted. When K is 4 or less, certain nodes are obliged to enter sleep mode (denoted as sleep time). However, once K attains a value of 5, this sleep time vanishes, which is consistent with the theoretical prediction as per Eq. (5.34).

5.2.4.3 Collaborations vs. Without Collaborations

The unique feature of 3DCS is the collaboration among chargers from various regions, as depicted in Algorithm 19. Figure 5.17b illustrates a comparison of the total sleep time for 3DCS both in scenarios involving collaboration and those without. A notable difference is seen between 3DCS with and without collaboration. This is because an idle charger aids in charging sleeping sensors located in other regions, thereby decreasing the total sleep time.

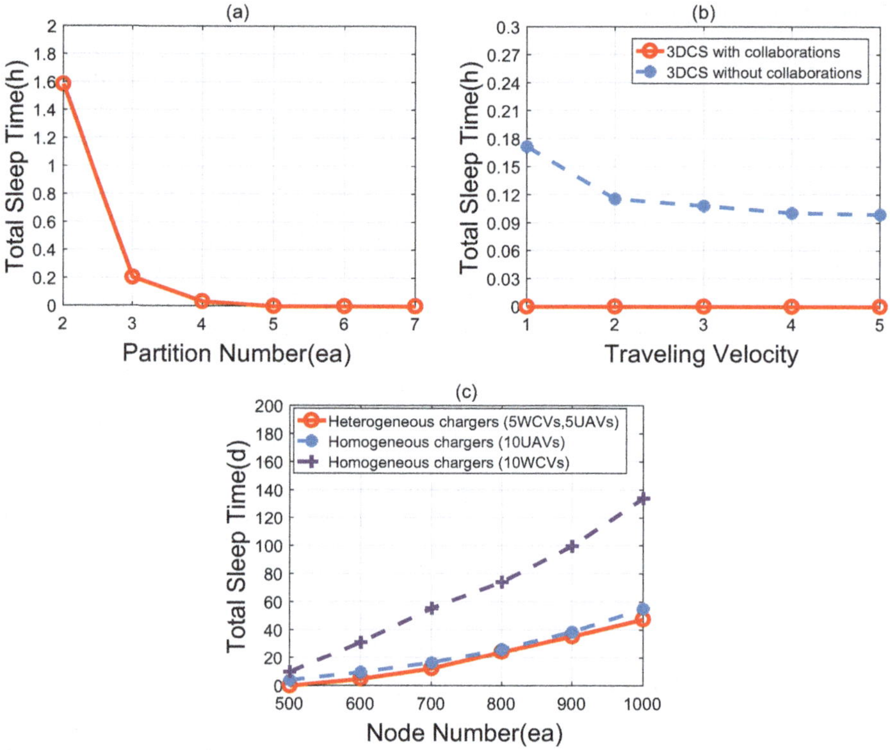

Fig. 5.17 Verifications including (**a**) determination of partition number of networks, (**b**) total sleep time of sensors with collaboration and without collaboration, and (**c**) total sleep time between three charging scenarios: heterogeneous chargers (5 WCVs and 5 UAVs), homogeneous chargers (10 WCVs), and homogeneous chargers (10 UAVs)

5.2.4.4 Heterogeneous Chargers vs. Homogeneous Chargers

To highlight the advantages of using heterogeneous chargers, we assess the network performance between homogeneous chargers (i.e., all UAV chargers) and heterogeneous chargers (i.e., UAVs and WCVs).

As stated in Eq. (5.34), the predicted partition number K for a 2-D network is 5. Subsequently, the overall count of chargers, which totals 10 (comprising 5 WCVs and 5 UAVs), can be rearranged into various heterogeneous and homogeneous groups to investigate their properties further.

As illustrated in Fig. 5.17c, the total sleep duration in the heterogeneous scenario (5 WCVs and 5 UAVs) is the least when compared to the homogeneous cases (10 WCVs) and (10 UAVs). Evidently, a 3D network serviced solely by WCVs will result in permanent sensor failures, leading to extensive sleep times. Using only 10 UAVs has a sleep time that is approximately 20% higher than in the heterogeneous setup. This is because, despite UAVs' higher speed, their smaller energy capacity necessitates more frequent returns to the BS, leading to an increased number of sleep nodes. Thus, employing heterogeneous chargers proves to be more beneficial.

References

1. S. Zhang, J. Wu, S. Lu, Collaborative mobile charging. IEEE Trans. Comput. **64**(3), 654–667 (2015)
2. A. Madhja, S. Nikoletseas, T.P. Raptis, Hierarchical, collaborative wireless energy transfer in sensor networks with multiple mobile chargers. Comput. Netw. **97**, 98–112 (2016)
3. http://www.inpofi.com/
4. http://witricity.com/.
5. https://en.wikipedia.org/.
6. C. Lin, Z. Wang, D. Han, Y. Wu, C.W. Yu, G. Wu, TADP: enabling temporal and distantial priority scheduling for on-demand charging architecture in wireless rechargeable sensor networks. J. Syst. Architect. **70**, 26–38 (2016)
7. C. Lin, D. Han, J. Deng, G. Wu, P^2S: a primary and passer-by scheduling algorithm for on-demand charging architecture in wireless rechargeable sensor networks. IEEE Trans. Veh. Technol. **66**(9), 8047–8058 (2017). https://doi.org/10.1109/TVT.2017.2683493
8. C. Wang, J. Li, F. Ye, Y. Yang, A mobile data gathering framework for wireless rechargeable sensor networks with vehicle movement costs and capacity constraints. IEEE Trans. Comput. **65**(8), 2411–2427 (2016)
9. W. Liang, W. Xu, X. Ren, X. Jia, X. Lin, Maintaining large-scale rechargeable sensor networks perpetually via multiple mobile charging vehicles. ACM Trans. Sens. Netw. **12**(2) (Association for Computing Machinery, NY, 2016)
10. J.A. Hartigan, M.A. Wong, Algorithm AS 136: a k-means clustering algorithm. J. R. Stat. Soc. C **28**(1), 100–108 (1979)
11. D. Gross, *Fundamentals of Queueing Theory* (Wiley, Hoboken, 2008)
12. L. He, L. Kong, Y. Gu, J. Pan, T. Zhu, Evaluating the on-demand mobile charging in wireless sensor networks. IEEE Trans. Mobile Comput. **14**(9), 1861–1875 (2014)
13. Powercast. http://www.powercastco.com
14. C. Intanagonwiwat, R. Govindan, D. Estrin, Directed diffusion: a scalable and robust communication paradigm for sensor networks, in *Proceedings of the 6th Annual International Conference on Mobile Computing and Networking* (ACM, New York, 2000), pp. 56–67
15. W. Ye, J. Heidemann, D. Estrin, An energy-efficient MAC protocol for wireless sensor networks, in *INFOCOM 2002. Twenty-First Annual Joint Conference of the IEEE Computer and Communications Societies. Proceedings. IEEE*, vol. 3 (IEEE, Piscataway, 2002), pp. 1567–1576

Part III
Advanced Topics and Interdisciplinary Insights

Chapter 6
Advanced Charging Models in WRSNs

6.1 Directional Charging Model

The advent of Wireless Power Transfer (WPT) technologies enhances the convenience and reliability of charging. Numerous studies have concentrated on addressing the energy utility maximization issue, often disregarding the different users' sensitivity to charging delays. In response to this, we focus on the minimal charging delay (MAD) problem in this section to reduce charging delays. It is observed that the sensor's received energy depends not only on the distance but also on the angle between the sensor and the charger's orientation in a directional WPT. Consequently, we develop a practical energy transfer model, substantiated by experimental validation. To find the optimal solution, we cast the problem as a linear programming task. Additionally, we propose a technique for discretizing the charge power, which considerably limits the search space. A merging approach is also presented for more realistic application scenarios. Lastly, we show through simulations and experiments that our methods exceed the performance of the Set Cover baseline method by an average of 34.2%.

6.1.1 Problem Statement

6.1.1.1 Network Model

As depicted in Fig. 6.1, a WRSN network comprises N wireless rechargeable sensors and M mobile chargers (MCs). Each node n_j within the network can be localized using techniques such as a range-free localization scheme with mobile anchor points [1], and the position is denoted as $\mathbf{n_i} = (x_i, y_i)$. Due to the rapid decay of the MC's radiated energy over distance, only the sensors situated within a circle C_e of radius D can receive significant energy. Consequently, the MC moves

C. Lin et al., *Wireless Rechargeable Sensor Networks for Internet of Things*,
Wireless Networks, https://doi.org/10.1007/978-981-97-9543-7_6

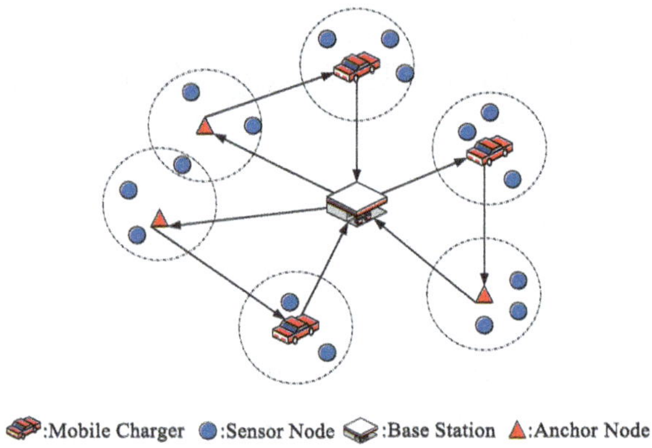

Fig. 6.1 Overview of the network model

and halts at several predetermined points to wirelessly recharge the surrounding sensors. When the MC stops at position L_l and charges at the j-th orientation angle, its orientation o_k^ρ can range from 0 to 2π, thereby charging only the nodes within the coverage area. After recharging all nodes, the MC returns to the base station (BS) for a quick battery replacement.

6.1.1.2 Charging Model

To explain the energy charged during directional charging, we investigate the relationship between an MC's position and a sensor's position. An MC v_i is used to charge a sensor s_j located at $\mathbf{n_j} = (x_j, y_j)$. The orientation angle vector for charging is denoted as $\mathbf{o_k}$, the charging range of the MC is D, and the effective charging orientation angle is γ. For a sensor node to receive non-zero energy, it should be positioned within the effective charging zone of the MC, which means $d_{ij} = \|m_i n_j\| \leq D$ and $\cos\gamma \leq \frac{\mathbf{n_j o_k}}{|\mathbf{n_j o_k}|}$.

Thus, the MC's effective charging region is a sector with a radius of D and an angle of 2γ, where sensor nodes are capable of receiving the energy being transmitted by the MC.

As illustrated in Fig. 6.2, sensor nodes n_i and n_k fall within an effective directional region defined by the vector of the MC's orientation angle $\mathbf{o_k}$. These nodes will receive varying degrees of energy depending on different orientation angles α_i and α_k, as well as different distances d_i and d_j. However, if the MC's orientation shifts to $\mathbf{o_l}$, the energy cannot be received by the two sensor nodes. Therefore, in a directional charging system, the received energy is influenced by both distance and orientation angle. The energy transfer model can be represented as $P_r = f(d_{ij}, \alpha)$.

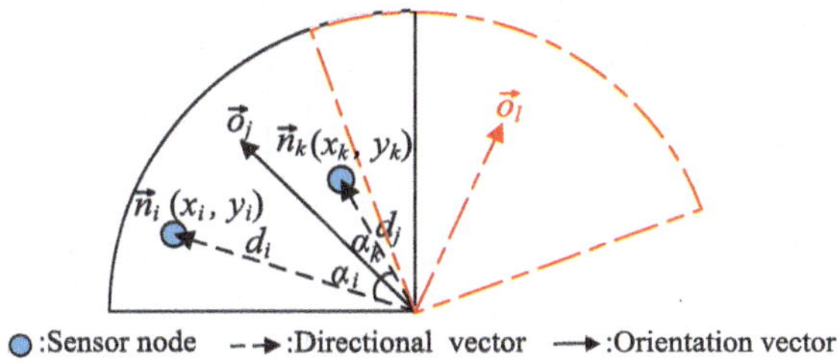

Fig. 6.2 Directional charging model

To develop the model for energy transfer, we begin by presenting Friis's free space equation:

$$P_r = G_s G_r \left(\frac{\lambda}{4\pi d}\right)^2 P_0, \tag{6.1}$$

which indicates the power received P_r at a distance d from a transmitter with initial power P_0. In Eq. (6.1), G_s and G_r represent the gains of the transmitting and receiving antennas, respectively. Following this, He et al. [2] suggested an empirical model for wireless recharging in WRSNs as described:

$$P_r = \frac{G_s G_r \eta}{L_p} \left(\frac{\lambda}{4\pi(d+\beta)}\right)^2 P_0, \tag{6.2}$$

where η represents the rectifier efficiency, L_p indicates the polarization loss, and β is a parameter used to modify Friis's free-space equation for short-range communication. According to antenna theory [3], Eq. (6.1) can be expressed through the notion of effective area:

$$P_r = A_{er} \cdot S_r = \frac{P_0 G_t A_{er}}{4\pi d^2}, \tag{6.3}$$

where A_{er} represents the effective area of the receiving antenna, and S_r denotes the power density at the receiving antenna. Additionally, the gain of the source antenna G_t can be described as

$$G_t = \frac{4\pi A_{et}}{\lambda^2}. \tag{6.4}$$

As illustrated in Fig. 6.3, in this context, A_{er} represents the effective receiving area of a sensor node, while A_{et} denotes the effective transmitting area of the MC. When the MC directly faces the sensor node (i.e., the angle between the sensor and MC is zero), the effective transmitting area A_{et} reaches its maximum, denoted as A_{et}^{max}. For an angle α between the MC and the sensor, the effective transmitting area becomes $A_{et} = A_{et}^{max} \cos\beta$. It can be easily demonstrated that $\alpha = \beta$, leading to the expression $A_{et} = A_{et}^{max} \cos\alpha$.

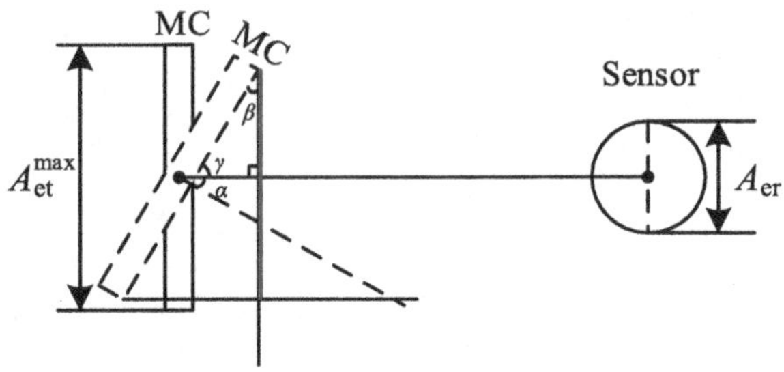

Fig. 6.3 Directional charging schematic

Now we can derive an energy transfer model by combining the above equations, taking into account the rectification efficiency and the planned loss.

$$P_r = \frac{G_t G_r \eta}{L_p}\left(\frac{\lambda}{4\pi(d+\beta)}\right)^2 P_0 = \frac{\eta A_{er} A_{et}^{max} cos\alpha}{L_p \lambda^2 (d+\beta)^2} P_0. \tag{6.5}$$

Next, we present an experimental model for energy transfer:

$$P_r = \frac{\eta A_{er} A_{et}^{max}(cos\alpha + c)}{L_p \lambda^2 (d+\beta)^2} P_0, \tag{6.6}$$

where c serves as an adjustment parameter for the equation under vertical conditions, specifically when $\alpha = \pm\frac{\pi}{2}$. To streamline the forthcoming design discussion, we represent the experimental energy transfer model as:

$$P_r = \mu \frac{cos\alpha + c}{(d+\beta)^2}, \tag{6.7}$$

The constants c, μ, and β are defined by the experimental conditions and the MCs hardware specifications [2].

We conduct experiments to validate the energy transfer model. In our laboratory, we utilize a commercial TX91501 Powercaster wireless transmitter and Powercast wireless rechargeable sensor nodes. Initially, we use Eq. (6.7) to fit the experimental data, with the fit results displayed in Fig. 6.4, demonstrating that Eq. (6.5) is applicable in our experimental settings. Next, we fix the orientation angle of the transmitter relative to the line connecting the transmitter and the sensor node, and vary the distance between the charger and the sensor node from 0.4 meters to 1.1 meters. Finally, we adjust the charger's orientation angle from $-\pi$ to π at different distances. The experimental outcomes are presented in Figs. 6.5 and 6.6. Figure 6.5 confirms the anisotropic energy reception characteristic of rechargeable sensors.

The experimental findings provide two key points: Firstly, the sensor node receives significant energy only when the orientation angle falls between $-\frac{\pi}{2}$ and $\frac{\pi}{2}$, denoted as $\alpha \in [-\frac{\pi}{2}, \frac{\pi}{2}]$. Secondly, the energy harvested by the sensor node is minimal when the distance exceeds 1 m. Consequently, the effective charging

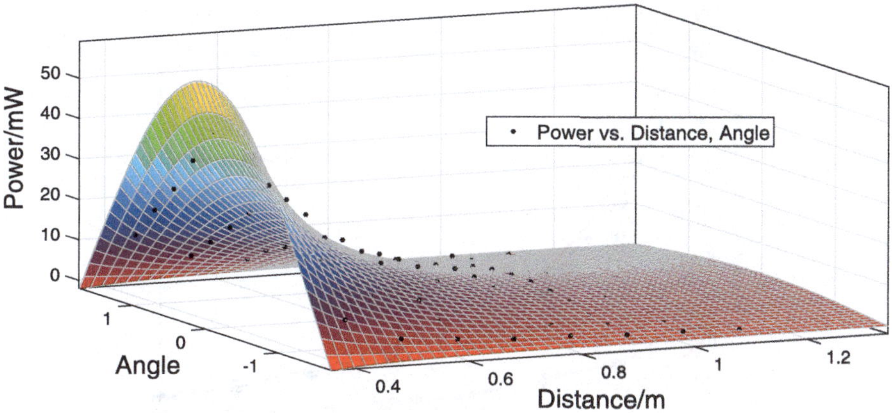

Fig. 6.4 Receiving power vs. distance and angle

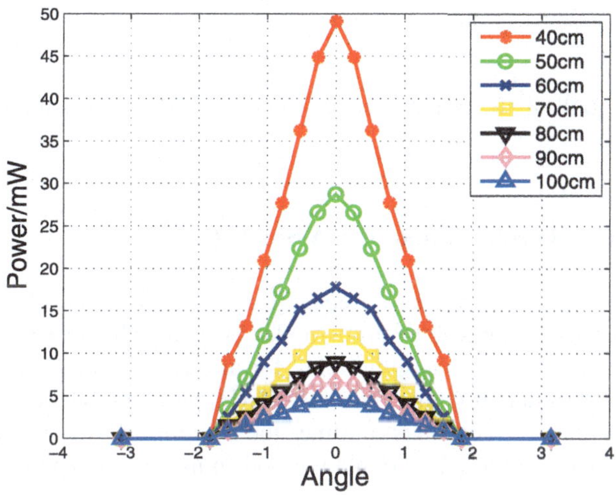

Fig. 6.5 Receiving power vs. angle

distance D of the MC is set to 1 m, with the effective charging area C_e defined by the circle of radius D.

Based on our experimental findings and Eq. (6.7), the power delivered from the MC m_i to the sensor node n_j can be described as follows.

$$P_r(d,\alpha) = \begin{cases} \mu\frac{cos\alpha + c}{(d+\beta)^2}, & 0 \le d \le D, \frac{-\pi}{2} \le \alpha \le \frac{\pi}{2} \\ 0, & \text{otherwise.} \end{cases}$$

$$d = \|m_i n_j\|, \alpha = arccos\frac{\mathbf{n_j o_k}}{|\mathbf{n_j o_k}|}, \tag{6.8}$$

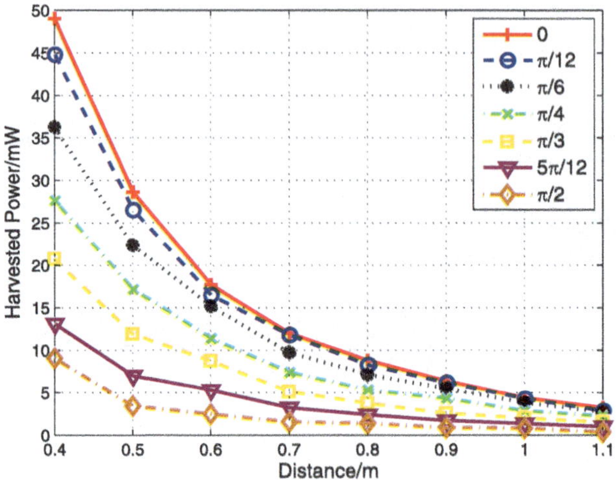

Fig. 6.6 Receiving power vs. distance

where d refers to the distance between m_i and n_j, α is denoted as the angle between $\mathbf{o_j}$ and $\mathbf{n_j}$.

6.1.1.3 Problem Formalization with A Single Charger

This issue deals with a Wireless Rechargeable Sensor Network (WRSN) that includes numerous rechargeable sensor nodes and one Mobile Charger (MC). In order to reduce the overall charging delay for all sensor nodes, we introduce the Single charger Minimal chArging Delay (S-MAD) problem. Section 6.1.1.1 covers the placement of sensor nodes and outlines the charging model. We aim to deploy the charger to achieve the best orientation and minimize the charging delay. The S-MAD problem is defined as follows.

$$\text{S-MAD: } \min T = \sum_{l=1}^{L} \sum_{j=1}^{A} t_j^l, \tag{6.9}$$

Subject to:

$$\sum_{l=1}^{L} \sum_{j=1}^{A} P_{ij}^l t_j^l \geq \delta_i E_s, \ \forall i \in N, \tag{6.10}$$

$$P_{ij}^l = P_r(d_{il}, \alpha_{ij}). \tag{6.11}$$

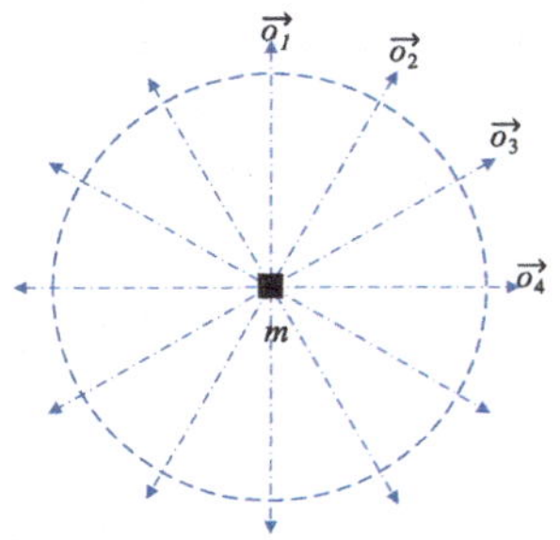

Fig. 6.7 Illustration of orientation angles

In Eq. (6.9), t_j^l represents the charging delay when the MC halts at the l-th position with orientation angle j. Equation (6.10) indicates that the MC must meet the threshold constraint $\delta_i E_s$ for each sensor node to function properly. P_{ij}^l in this context denotes the charging power of sensor node j during the charging delay t_j^l.

6.1.2 Schematic Design

Given that the S-MAD problem is represented as a linear programming (LP) problem, a brute-force approach could be used to evaluate all possible orientation angles in order to determine the best strategy by employing an LP solver [4]. Nevertheless, the orientation angles span from 0 to 2π (refer to Fig. 6.7), and the energy absorption varies with different distances, making this method computationally intensive and impractical for real-world use.

To lower the computational expense, we present a discretization of the charging power along with a merging algorithm. Initially, we identify the optimal orientation angle for charging in each region. For simplicity, we denote the solution of the S-MAD problem as Optimal Directional Charging with a Single charger (S-ODC).

A key benefit of the S-ODC approach is its ability to determine the charging orientation angle and charging power for each MC when addressing the energy distribution issue, greatly cutting down on computational load. Additionally, as demonstrated in Sect. 6.1.3, the S-ODC solution effectively limits the performance discrepancy from the optimal solution.

6.1.2.1 Charging Power Discretization

Inspired by the method of discretizing charging power based on distance, we apply a similar approach to discretize charging power according to angles. When the MC halts at a location l, only the nodes within the effective charging region C_e can receive significant energy. Moreover, a node n_j will gain varying power depending on the angle and distance between itself and the MC (refer to Figs. 6.6 and 6.5). Since a node can only receive a substantial amount of energy when the angle lies within the interval from $-\frac{\pi}{2}$ to $\frac{\pi}{2}$, the minimum and maximum angles between a node n_j and the MC are $\alpha_i^{min} = 0$ and $\alpha_i^{max} = \frac{\pi}{2}$, respectively. By combining this angle interval with Eq. (6.7), we can ascertain the corresponding range of charging power:

$$P_j^{max} = \mu \frac{cos0 + c}{(d_{ij} + \beta)^2} = \frac{\mu(1 + c)}{(d_{ij} + \beta)^2}, \tag{6.12}$$

$$P_j^{min} = \mu \frac{cos\frac{\pi}{2} + c}{(d_{ij} + \beta)^2} = \frac{\mu c}{(d_{ij} + \beta)^2}. \tag{6.13}$$

To discretize the charging power at node n_j, we use V_i vectors that start from the stop location of the MC and denote the charging power at the v-th vectors as P_j^v.

We partition the region into V sectors using the threshold factor ϵ, designating them as $\{V_0, V_1, \ldots, V_{v-1}\}$. In particular, the charging power variation between adjacent vectors is constrained to be less than the threshold factor ϵ $(0 < \epsilon < 1)$, meaning that the ratio of charging power in neighboring sectors is consistently $(1 + \epsilon)$.

$$P_j^v = (1 + \epsilon) P_j^{v+1}, \tag{6.14}$$

where P_j^v can be calculated as below:

$$P_j^v = P_j^0 (1 + \epsilon)^{-v} = P_j^{max} (1 + \epsilon)^{-v}, \; 1 \le v \le V_i. \tag{6.15}$$

After combining Eqs. (6.12) and (6.13), we have

$$P_j^{min} = \frac{c}{1 + c} P_j^{max}. \tag{6.16}$$

Given that the V_i-th charging power vector adheres to the condition $P_j^{V_i} \le P_j^{min}$, the determination of the total number of vectors V_i is based on the last power vector exceeding P_j^{min}, the two extreme orientations (i.e., $-\frac{\pi}{2}, \frac{\pi}{2}$), and an orientation where the MC is directed towards n_j. Additionally, the charging power exhibits symmetry with respect to angles. Thus, V_i can be derived using the following equation:

$$V_i = 2\lfloor \frac{ln(\frac{P_j^{max}}{P_j^{min}})}{ln(1 + \epsilon)} + 1 \rfloor + 1 = 2\lfloor \frac{ln(\frac{1}{c} + 1)}{ln(1 + \epsilon)} + 1 \rfloor + 1. \tag{6.17}$$

We provide an illustration of the discretization of power for n_1 in Fig. 6.8. The charging power in the direction of $\mathbf{o_1^0}$ is at its peak, which means $P_1^0 = P_1^{max}$ and $V_1 = 9$.

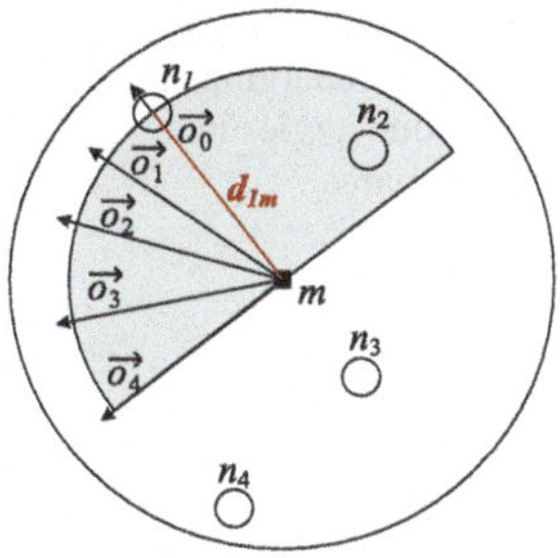

Fig. 6.8 Discretize charging power for node n_1

Algorithm 20 Charging Power Discretization (CPD)

Require: The location of sensor node N and mobile charger (MC) M.
Ensure: The number of sector charging area V after discretization, the collection of charging power P when charging orientation angles in these areas.

Initial: $P \leftarrow \varnothing$;
Calculate the distance d between N and M;
Calculate the max charging power $P_{max} \leftarrow \mu(1+c)/(d+\beta)^2$;
$P_{min} \leftarrow \mu c/(1+\beta)^2$;
$V \leftarrow 2\lfloor ln(P_{max}/P_{min})/ln(1+\epsilon)+1\rfloor + 1$;
for all $i \leftarrow [0, V-1]$ **do**
    $P_i \leftarrow P_{max}(1+\epsilon)^{-1}$;
    $P_i \leftarrow P \cup P_i$;
end for
return V, P.

A charging power discretization (CPD) algorithm is introduced in Algorithm 20. Initially, we determine the distance between the sensor node N and the respective mobile charger M. Subsequently, using Eq. (6.8), we calculate both the maximum and minimum power when the orientation angle ranges from 0° to 90°. Based on the computed values and the threshold parameter ϵ, we derive the number V of sector areas. Then, we compute the charging power of each sector area post-discretization. Consequently, we obtain the number of sector areas V and the set P representing the possible charging power for the sensor node N.

First, we break down the charging power for each sensor node when the MC halts at a specific point. After this division, the charging area C_e can be segmented into several sectors, referred to as S_g. Each sector S_g is formed by orientation angle vectors, and we denote $v_i^{S_g}$ as the highest vector's sequence number (i.e., the energy level received by the sector) near S_g for sensor n_j. Additionally, we represent the charging power within the sector by its minimum value. Here, C remains a constant influenced by device specifications and environmental conditions, while the count of sector regions is decided by the threshold factor ϵ, which impacts the approximation ratio to the ideal solution.

In Fig. 6.9, an illustrative example is provided for enhanced understanding. The sector S_g is defined by $\mathbf{o}_1^0$ and $\mathbf{o}_1^1$ of n_1, and S_g lies within the sector outlined by $\mathbf{o}_2^3$ and $\mathbf{o}_2^4$ of n_2. For sensor nodes n_1 and n_2, we have $v_1^{S_g} = 1$, $v_2^{S_g} = 4$ because

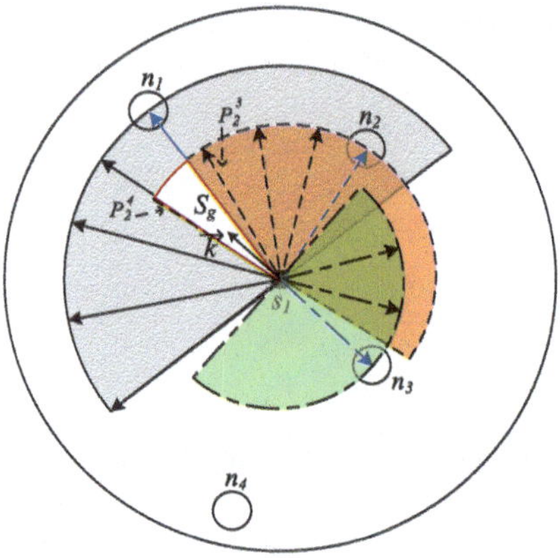

Fig. 6.9 An example of discretized charging orientation angles in a charging area

node n_1 receives the highest charging power and node n_2 receives the fourth highest charging power. Furthermore, due to the properties of directional charging, n_3 will not receive substantial energy when the MC's orientation angles fall within S_g, and we denote the sequence number as a negative value in such cases, i.e., $v_3^{S_g} < 0$.

For every orientation angle vector $\mathbf{k}$ within sector S_g, the charging power for sensor node n_j varies. However, the charging power for any orientation angle vector $\mathbf{k}$ in sector S_g meets the condition

$$P_i^{v_i^{S_g}} \leq P_i^k \leq P_i^{v_i^{S_g}-1}. \tag{6.18}$$

For the charging power P_i^k, it has a tight lower and upper bounds since

$$\frac{P_i^{v_i^{S_g}}}{P_i^{v_i^{S_g}-1}} = \frac{1}{1+\epsilon}, \tag{6.19}$$

we adopt the lower bound as the charging power for sensor node n_j, meaning $P_i^k = P_i^{v_i^{S_g}}$. If $v_i^{S_g} < 0$ holds true, indicating that the received energy of n_j is negligible, we assign $P_i^k = 0$.

At present, the charging power of all sensor nodes under any orientation angle vector within any sector S_g can be defined and constrained as: $\mathbf{P_{S_g}} = [P_1^{v_1^{S_g}}, P_2^{v_2^{S_g}}, \ldots, P_N^{v_N^{S_g}}]$. Ultimately, the objective problem (see Eq. (6.9)) is solvable by the LP solver with a finite set of alternative orientation angles. The optimal charging delay determined by the LP solver after discretization maintains an approximation ratio of $\frac{1}{1-\epsilon^2}$ to the optimal solution. Detailed proof is given in Sect. 6.1.3. Additionally, we will confirm the validity of the approximated ratio through extensive simulations in Sect. 6.1.4, considering a more general scenario where the MC halts multiple times and selects multiple orientation angles during the charging process.

6.1.2.2 Orientation Angle Merging (OAM)

Even after discretisation, numerous orientation angle options remain. In certain application scenarios, however, the MC might not rotate to as many angles because of device restrictions, or users might choose to compromise performance in favor of lower computational complexity. Hence, we propose a method for merging orientation angles to further limit the search space.

To combine the orientation angles, we introduce an Orientation Angle Merging (OAM) method that utilizes the well-established K-means clustering algorithm [5]. Initially, the K-means algorithm partitions the input points (i.e., the discretized representation of the sensor nodes' locations) into *K* initial groups. We then choose *K* candidate solutions to serve as the centers of the *K* clusters based on the distances between these solutions and the other cluster centers. Given that sensor nodes cannot receive power when they are outside the effective directional area, we initialize *K* points within each effective directional area of the sensor nodes to ensure that every sensor node gets charged at least once.

Subsequently, these points are allocated to the closest cluster centers, and the cluster centers are iteratively refined. This procedure continues until the cluster centers stabilize.

The aforementioned specifics (i.e., OAM algorithm) are outlined in Algorithm 21. As depicted in Fig. 6.10, n_3 is unable to receive energy when the MC rotates to $\mathbf{o_1}$. Subsequently, the proposed OAM algorithm allocates points to the nearest cluster based on the centroid of each cluster. The distance is formulated as follows:

$$d = ||\mathbf{d_{ij}}||_2 = ||\frac{\mathbf{o_i}}{|\mathbf{o_i}|} - \frac{\mathbf{o_j}}{|\mathbf{o_j}|}||_2. \tag{6.20}$$

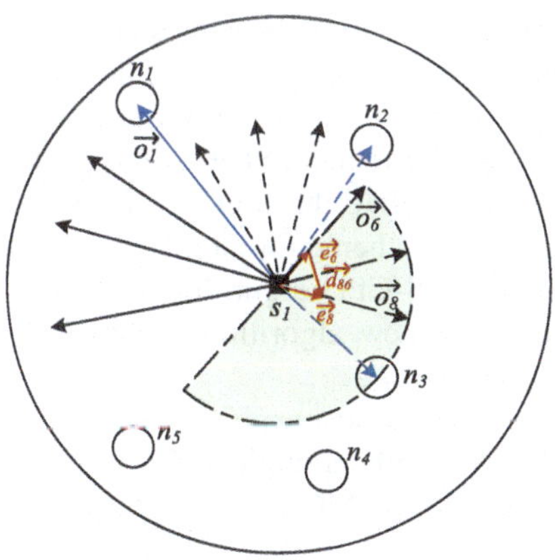

Fig. 6.10 Illustration for calculating *d* in K-means

Algorithm 21 Orientation Angles Merging by K-means Clustering Algorithm (OAM)

```
Require: The collection of orientation angles O, the number of clusters K.
Ensure: K clusters of orientation angles C = {c_1, c_2, ..., c_k}.
for all i ∈ [1, K] do
    Choose an orientation angle o_i stochastically c_i ← o_i;
    O ← O − o_i;
    Calculate the center t_i;
end for
for all o ∈ O do
    for all i ∈ [1, K] do
        Calculate the distance d_i between o and the center t_i;
    end for
    Choose the minimal d_i corresponding c_i do;
    c_i ← c_i ∪ {o};
    Recalculate the center t_i;
end for
return C.
```

As illustrated in Fig. 6.10, $d = ||\frac{\mathbf{o_8}}{|\mathbf{o_8}|} - \frac{\mathbf{o_6}}{|\mathbf{o_6}|}||_2 = ||\mathbf{e_8} - \mathbf{e_6}||_2$. Subsequently, the OAM algorithm will recompute the cluster centers and adjust the cluster positions until all centers converge, meaning their positions remain unchanged.

In a scenario with a single MC (Master Controller), our scheme is quite appropriate. Nevertheless, with the deployment of a substantial number of sensor nodes within the network, the scenario involving multiple MCs seems more advantageous. Therefore, we investigate ways to expand our scheme to accommodate multiple MCs.

6.1.2.3 Problem Analysis

As mentioned in Sect. 6.2.2, our method to reduce charging latency using a single MC is detailed. However, this approach is insufficient for extensive networks since one MC cannot manage a large quantity of sensor nodes. Therefore, utilizing several MCs collaboratively emerges as a feasible strategy for real-world scenarios. To solve the S-MAD issue with multiple MCs (M-MAD), we introduce an Optimal Direction Charge with Multiple chargers (M-ODC) method inspired by the S-ODC solution.

Similar to the S-ODC solution, the M-ODC solution can be derived using the LP solver. Unlike the S-ODC, the M-ODC solution focuses on quickly developing a charging scheme for large networks. Hence, we persist in using the OAM algorithm and the S-CPD algorithm for each MC individually. Simultaneously, we aim to create a new algorithm to simplify the computations necessary for the M-ODC solution.

After careful analysis, we found that addressing the challenge of managing a WRSN with multiple MCs (e.g., M MCs) can be seen as a collaborative effort among these MCs, with each MC handling charging tasks as detailed in Sect. 6.2.2

(i.e., each MC tackles the S-MAD problem). This requires attention to two main issues: 1) dividing the network region into M subareas (given M MCs), and 2) modifying the S-MAD solution to suit the context of multiple MCs. A key concern is the potential overlap in sensor coverage areas by different MCs, which may result in sensors being serviced by more than one MC.

As stated in [6], the energy received by a sensor node s_j can be linearly added, with the total charged power being the sum of the power provided by each charger serving the sensor node, i.e.,

$$P_j = \sum_{i=1}^{M} P(m_i, n_j), \tag{6.21}$$

When a sensor node draws power from multiple MCs, it receives a cumulative amount of energy equivalent to the sum provided by each MC. For example, if a sensor is located at the convergence of two MCs, the first MC may deliver 40% of its energy needs, while the second MC contributes the remaining 60%. Consequently, the sensor attains full charge (note that for simplicity, we do not consider the sensor's energy consumption in this scenario).

However, the sensor nodes within these overlapping regions may occasionally be supplied with excess energy, resulting in potential energy loss. To put it differently, the total energy delivered by the MCs to a sensor node must not exceed C_j. Therefore, a maximum energy threshold is enforced:

$$\sum_{i=1}^{M} Q_j^i \leq C_j. \tag{6.22}$$

6.1.2.4 Problem Re-Formulation

Upon resolving the issue of sensor nodes positioned in the intersection area, we expand the S-MAD problem to a large-scale network employing multiple MCs for energy replenishment. Our emphasis is on the charging delay of sensor nodes within the intersection area. The total charging delay is presented as follows:

$$T = \sum_{i=1}^{M} \sum_{l=1}^{L} \sum_{k=1}^{A} t_{l,k}^i. \tag{6.23}$$

To efficiently reduce the overall charging delay in a large-scale network, we transform the original S-MAD problem into a Minimal chArging Delay with Multiple chargers (M-MAD) problem. This newly defined problem aims to find the optimal orientation and the associated charging delay in scenarios involving multiple MCs. We define the M-MAD problem as follows.

$$\text{M-MAD: } \min T = \sum_{i=1}^{M} \sum_{l=1}^{L} \sum_{k=1}^{A} t_{l,k}^{i}, \tag{6.24}$$

Subject to:

$$\sum_{i=1}^{M} \sum_{l=1}^{L} \sum_{k=1}^{A} P_{l,k}^{i,j} t_{l,k}^{i} \geq E_j, \ \forall j \in N, \tag{6.25}$$

$$P_{l,k}^{i,j} = P_r(d_{ij}, \alpha_{lk}). \tag{6.26}$$

In Eqs. (6.23) and (6.24), $t_{l,k}^{i}$ signifies the charging delay when MC m_i halts at the l-th location with the k-th orientation angle. Equation (6.25) demonstrates that every sensor node demands energy replenishment exceeding the threshold E_j by the MC to operate effectively. $P_{l,k}^{i,j}$ represents the transmission power of MC m_i during the charging of sensor node n_j at the l-th location with the k-th orientation angle. Equation (6.26) describes the computation method for the constraint $P_{l,k}^{i,j}$.

In order to address the issue of reducing the charging delay for multiple MCs, given that the charging delay cannot be negative and the constraints' variables (refer to Eq. (6.37)) are linear, we can consequently express the objective function as a linear programming problem (refer to Eq. (6.23)) with the goal of minimizing the charging delay.

The key distinction between S-MAD and M-MAD is the count of MCs involved. To tackle the M-MAD problem, the same charging model based on distance and orientation angle used in S-MAD is adopted, and M-MAD is structured as a linear programming problem. Nonetheless, this approach might lead to significant computational burden when deploying several MCs. Therefore, we suggest a novel algorithm to segment the whole network into multiple subareas, enabling the S-ODC solution to function effectively.

The main distinction between S-MAD and M-MAD pertains to their methods of charging sensor nodes in overlapping regions. Consequently, it is sufficient to regulate the charging thresholds of these sensor nodes and address it via an LP solver.

After determining the orientation angle, the power $p_k^{i,j}$ of the mobile charger m_i to charge the sensor nodes n_j at the k-th charging direction angle can be calculated, along with the charging duration t_k^i for that orientation angle. Assuming there are I mobile chargers $\{m_1, m_2, ..., m_I\}$ and J sensor nodes $\{n_1, n_2, ..., n_J\}$, and each location L_l has O charging orientation angles, we can define the charging duration at each position as $\{t_1^1, t_2^1, ..., t_O^1, t_1^2, ..., t_O^I\}$ and the corresponding charging power as $\left\{p_1^{1,1}, p_2^{1,1}, ..., p_O^{I,J}\right\}$. For simplicity, we represent the charging delay matrix as

$\tau = \left[t_1^1, t_2^1, ..., t_O^I\right]$ and the lower energy threshold matrix of the sensor nodes as $\kappa = \left[E_1, E_2, ..., E_j\right]$.

Additionally, the matrix for charging power is displayed as follows:

$$\rho = \begin{bmatrix} p_1^{1,1} & p_1^{1,2} & ... & p_1^{1,J} \\ p_2^{1,1} & p_2^{1,2} & ... & p_2^{1,J} \\ ... & ... & & ... \\ p_O^{I,1} & p_O^{I,2} & ... & p_O^{I,J} \end{bmatrix}. \tag{6.27}$$

Therefore, the linear programming problem aimed at reducing charging delay can be expressed as:

$$\min\ T = \sum_{k=1}^{O}\sum_{i=1}^{I} t_k^i, \tag{6.28}$$

Subject to:

$$\tau \times \rho \geq \kappa, \tag{6.29}$$

$$t_o^i > 0,\ \forall o \in O, i \in I. \tag{6.30}$$

In Eqs. (6.28), (6.29), and (6.30), the variables are non-negative. Therefore, we apply the dual simplex method to solve this problem.

Initially, we transform the problem into its standard form:

$$\max\ -T = -\sum_{k=1}^{O}\sum_{i=1}^{I} t_k^i, \tag{6.31}$$

Subject to:

$$\tau \times \rho + \chi = \kappa, \tag{6.32}$$

$$t_o^i > 0, \forall o \in O, i \in I. \tag{6.33}$$

To convert the constraints into a form that can be solved using the general linear programming algorithm, we define the matrix of residual variables as $\chi = \left[X_1, X_2, ..., X_{IO}\right]$. In the subsequent sections, we will present an efficient solution approach for this problem.

When dealing with the M-MAD problem in a WRSN, a frequent challenge is the large number of sensor nodes, which leads to considerable computational overhead. In practical scenarios, users may prefer to minimize computational complexity over achieving optimal results. To address this, we propose the Quick Solution (QS) algorithm, which eases the charging constraint. We introduce an upper energy limit

C_j for a sensor node n_j and establish the charging threshold δ for sensor nodes situated in the intersection area. The energy received by the sensor node is restricted by this threshold.

Suppose there are J sensor nodes within a charging area L, with K of these nodes located in the overlapping region catered to by multiple MCs. The set of these sensor nodes can be denoted as $\{n_1, n_2, \ldots, n_K, n_{K+1}, \ldots, n_J\}$, and we arrive at

$$\begin{cases} n_j \in L_p \cap (\cup_{q=1}^{L} L_q), \ q \neq p, 1 \leq j \leq K, \\ n_j \in L_p \cap (\cup_{q=1}^{L} L_q), \ q \neq p, K+1 \leq j \leq J. \end{cases} \tag{6.34}$$

If sensor nodes fulfill $\{n_j, 0 \leq j \leq K\}$, it signifies that they are outside the intersection area. Therefore, we must guarantee that the charged energy does not surpass the lower energy threshold E_j. Thus, we obtain

$$\sum_{k=1}^{O} P_k^j \cdot t_k \geq E_j, \ \forall j \in [K+1, J]. \tag{6.35}$$

For sensor nodes located at an intersection (i.e. , $\{n_j, K+1 \leq j \leq J\}$), a charging threshold δ is established. The MC is responsible for charging only a portion of the energy (i.e. partial charge [7]) needed by the sensor. The remaining energy will be supplied by other MCs, thus we have

$$\sum_{k=1}^{O} P_k^j \cdot t_k \geq \delta \cdot E_j, \lambda \leq \delta < 1, \ \forall j \in [0, K]. \tag{6.36}$$

Within this charging scheme, a sensor node might accumulate energy exceeding its capacity, leading to wastage. To avoid this, a maximum energy limit of C_j is applied.

$$\sum_{i=1}^{M} Q_j^i = C_j. \tag{6.37}$$

Once sensor node n_j has gathered sufficient energy to exceed its maximum threshold, it will stop receiving additional energy. The MC will notify the base station of this event. As a result, other MCs dispatched by the base station will avoid recharging sensor node n_j until it requires energy again. Therefore, it is crucial to carefully plan the energy distribution for each charging session, especially when the sensor nodes to be served are in overlapping areas.

In this study, we introduce a quick solution (RS) for energy distribution to accommodate a large-scale WRSN with many MCs. More details can be found in Algorithm 22.

The QS algorithm (i.e., Algorithm 22) functions in the following manner. First, the charging power for each sensor node of the MCs is calculated at each angle

Algorithm 22 Quick Solution for Energy Distribution (QS)

Require: The collection of orientation angles O in charging location L, the collection of sensor node N in the charging area of L, their receiving power P, and their energy threshold E, the charging threshold of the sensor nodes in the intersections δ.

Ensure: The collection of charging delay T.

Initial: $T \leftarrow \varnothing$.
for all $o_i \in O$ **do**
  for all n_j that can receive energy when charging orientation angle is o_i **do**
    if n_j in an intersection **then**
      $t_j \leftarrow \delta \cdot e_j/p_j$;
    else
      $t_j \leftarrow e_j/p_j$;
    end if
    $T \leftarrow T \cup \max t_j$;
  end for
end for
return T.

within the charging region. Following this, the charging delay is determined based on the energy threshold of each sensor node. The maximum charging delay at each angle is selected as the charging delay and is then used as the charging scheme. As noted in Sect. 6.1.3, the optimal charging delay obtained by the LP solver after discretization offers a $\frac{1}{1-\epsilon^2}$ approximation ratio to the ideal solution.

6.1.3 Theoretical Analysis

In this context, we provide a related theoretical analysis.

6.1.3.1 Approximation Ratio Proof

To assess the approximation ratio of the suggested solution, we first examine its behavior when the mobile component stops once and selects an orientation angle at that moment.

Theorem 6.1 *Given an orientation angle vector* $\mathbf{k}$ *within the sensor nodes' effective directional area, the associated charging power vector is* P_r^*, *and the optimal minimum charging delay is* T^*. *The discretized sector* S_g, *which includes* $\mathbf{k}$, *is defined by a threshold* ϵ *where* $0 < \epsilon < 1$. *The charging power for sector* S_g *is* P_{S_g}, *and the corresponding minimum charging delay,* T_g, *adheres to the condition* $T_g \leq \frac{T^*}{1-\epsilon^2}$.

Proof Initially, we employ a non-optimal charging vector P_{sub} to denote the charging power of S_g, with the associated minimum charging delay being T_{sub}, where $T_g \leq T_{sub}$. Subsequently, our goal is to demonstrate that T_{sub} complies with

$T_{sub} \leq \frac{T^*}{1-\epsilon^2}$. Based on the constraints of the objective (Eq. (6.25)), we have

$$P_i \cdot \frac{T^*}{1-\epsilon^2} > P_i \cdot T^* \geq \delta \cdot E_s. \tag{6.38}$$

Thus, the minimum charging delay T_{sub} is at most $\frac{T^*}{1-\epsilon^2}$. In conclusion, we have proved that $T_g \leq \frac{T^*}{1-\epsilon^2}$. ■

Subsequently, the theoretical optimal orientation angle vector is denoted by $\mathbf{o_{opt}}$, with its associated charging delay represented by T_{opt}. The optimal charging vector and its corresponding charging delay, as derived from charging power discretization, are represented as P_r and T, respectively. The following theorem is presented.

Theorem 6.2 *In the context of the S-MAD problem, after discretization, the optimal charging delay T determined by the LP solver is within a factor of $\frac{1}{1-\epsilon^2}$ of the optimal delay T_{opt}.*

Proof Consider a special case of *Theorem 1*, where $\mathbf{k}$ is exactly the optimal orientation angle vector $\mathbf{o_{opt}}$, and the corresponding charging delay is T_{opt}. We can obtain $T \leq \hat{T}_{sub}$, where $\hat{T}_{sub}$ is a suboptimal charging delay when the MC charges nodes with a suboptimal charging vector. Moreover, we have $\hat{T}_{sub} \leq \frac{T_{opt}}{1-\epsilon^2}$. Hence, $T \leq \frac{T_{opt}}{1-\epsilon^2}$ is established. ■

Theorem 6.3 *In the M-MAD problem, the optimal charging delay T obtained by LP solver after discretization also has a $\frac{1}{1-\epsilon^2}$ approximation ratio to the optimal delay T_{opt}.*

Proof Consider the case where Theorem 6.1 is applied with multiple MCs. We divide the whole network region into L subareas, each with a corresponding charging delay T_l, where T_l satisfies $T_l \geq \frac{T^*}{1-\epsilon^2}$. For all subareas, the total delay still holds, and we have the following equation:

$$\sum_{l=1}^{L} T_l \geq \frac{1}{1-\epsilon^2} \sum_{l=1}^{L} T_l^*. \tag{6.39}$$

Thus, in a large-scale network with multiple MCs, the approximation ratio of the charging delay T obtained by LP solver is still $\frac{1}{1-\epsilon^2}$. ■

6.1.3.2 Computational Complexity

To tackle the MAD problem, we propose a method that includes two main steps: discretization and merging. During the discretization step, alternative orientation angles are discretized, and an LP solver is used to determine the approximate optimal angles. The complexity of this procedure can be expressed as:

$$O(N \cdot V_i) = O(N \cdot (2\lfloor \frac{ln(\frac{1}{c}+1)}{ln(1+\epsilon)} + 1 \rfloor + 1)) = O(\frac{N}{\epsilon}), \tag{6.40}$$

which is defined by the total number of sectors. During the merging phase, K centers are combined within the effective directional area of each sensor node, leading to a complexity of $O(N \cdot K \cdot V_i) = O(K \cdot \frac{N}{\epsilon})$.

Introducing the charging threshold addresses the energy distribution issue of sensor nodes at the intersection without impacting the overall computational complexity. This is because the threshold modification merely alters the charging requirements of the nodes at the intersection. Essentially, the energy required by a sensor node changes from E_j to δE_j. This allows us to simultaneously determine the optimal orientation angle and energy distribution plan. Therefore, for a single charging area, the algorithm's time complexity remains $O(N \cdot K \cdot V_i) = O(K \cdot \frac{N}{\epsilon})$.

If there are L charging zones throughout the whole wireless sensor network, the total time complexity of the algorithm becomes:

$$O(N \cdot V_i \cdot K \cdot L) = O(K \cdot L \cdot \frac{N}{\epsilon}). \tag{6.41}$$

We will next perform testbed experiments within a small-scale network and conduct extensive simulations in a large-scale WRSN to evaluate the performance of the proposed schemes.

6.1.4 *Simulation and Experiments*

6.1.4.1 Simulation Setup

Within the scope of our simulations, sensor nodes are placed at random within a 100-meter by 100-meter two-dimensional square space.

Assuming the sensor remains chargeable at an orientation angle of $\pi/2$, we incorporate the constant C into the charging model. Considering the rectification efficiency, the variable β is introduced in Eq. (6.5) to denote a minimal distance between the MC and the sensor.

The parameter μ in the simplified Eq. (6.8) is influenced by experimental conditions and hardware characteristics, while D represents the charging radius or the effective range of the MCs. The parameters of the charging model (i.e., Eq. (6.7)) are defined as: $\beta = 0.1$, $\mu = 3.893$, and $c = 0.1161$, which are derived from fitting our experimental data. Additionally, we assign the effective transfer distance as $D = 1m$ and set $\alpha \in [-\frac{\pi}{2}, \frac{\pi}{2}]$ according to our experimental findings.

During the simulation, we primarily examine the influence of the following factors on charging performance: the discretized charging power threshold factor ϵ, the count of K-means clustering algorithms with charging orientation angle K, the sensor nodes' charging threshold δ at the intersection, the quantity of MCs M, and the sensor nodes' number N.

In the simulation settings, a sensor node has a total energy of 350 J, represented as $E_s = 350$ J. The minimum energy threshold for the sensor node is specified as 340 J. This means the sensor node will operate normally when the energy level is at least 340 J.

6.1.4.2 Performance Comparison

In this section, we assess our design's performance by benchmarking it against baseline algorithms under various charging discretization thresholds ϵ, cluster merging values K, charging thresholds δ, number of MCs M, and the number of sensor nodes in the network N.

Impact of Charging Power Discretization Threshold ϵ As mentioned before, the discretization threshold ϵ affects both the computational complexity of the discretization approach and the charging delay gap concerning the optimal solution (see Sects. 6.1.3.2 and 6.1.2.1). We begin by investigating the influence of the charging power discretization threshold ϵ with a network size of $N = 50$. As shown in Fig. 6.11, we assess the number of discretized charging orientations at

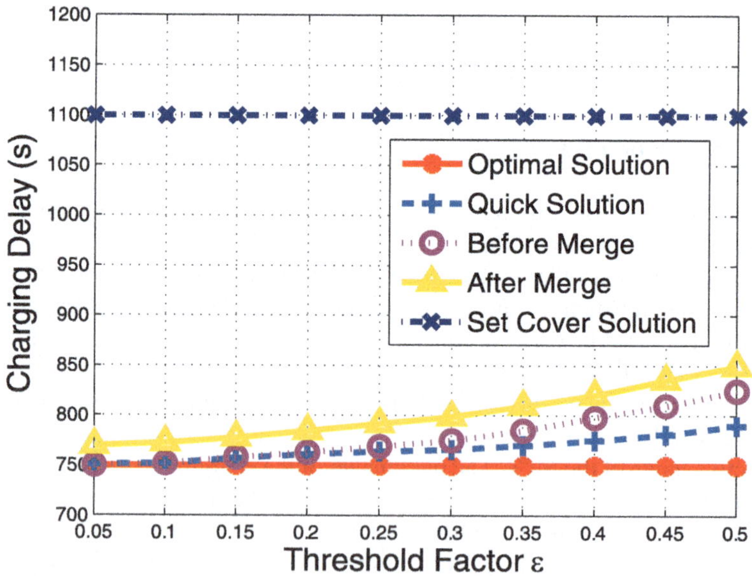

Fig. 6.11 Number of discretized charging orientations with varying discretization threshold ϵ

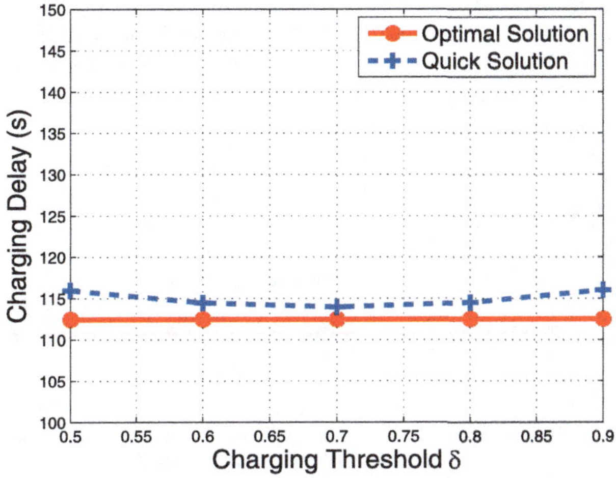

Fig. 6.12 Charging delay of different solutions with varying discretization threshold ϵ

a single point. Initially, as the charging power discretization threshold increases, the number of discretized charging orientations drops sharply, followed by a more gradual reduction.

Next, we examine how charging delay varies with increasing values of the charging power discretization threshold ϵ. As illustrated in Fig. 6.12, the charging delay with both the optimal and the Set Cover solutions remains consistent across different discretization thresholds. Conversely, the charging delay for the discretization and merging solutions shows a gradual increase as the discretization threshold ϵ becomes larger. This is due to the fact that a higher discretization threshold ϵ results in a less strict energy threshold, leading to a longer charging delay. Additionally, we can determine the upper bound of the charging delay when $\epsilon = 0.2$: $\frac{1}{1-0.2^2} \times 409{,}544\,\text{s} = 426{,}609.25\,\text{s}$, with the simulated charging delay for the discretization solution being 409,577.46 s, which is within the anticipated performance range.

Furthermore, the charging delay in the merging solution is greater than that in the discretization solution because of its lower precision. Even with the upward trend in charging delay, it still outperforms the Set Cover baseline. The loading delay in the merging solution is about 32% less.

As illustrated in Figs. 6.11 and 6.12, there is a slight increase in charging delay when the discretization threshold ϵ is adjusted from 0.05 to 0.2. Nonetheless, the number of discretized charging orientations drops substantially. Hence, selecting an optimal discretization threshold can help balance computational overhead with charging delay needs. This outcome corroborates our findings in Sect. 6.1.2.1.

Impact of Orientation Clusters Number K We investigate the impact of orientation clusters K in the merging solution.

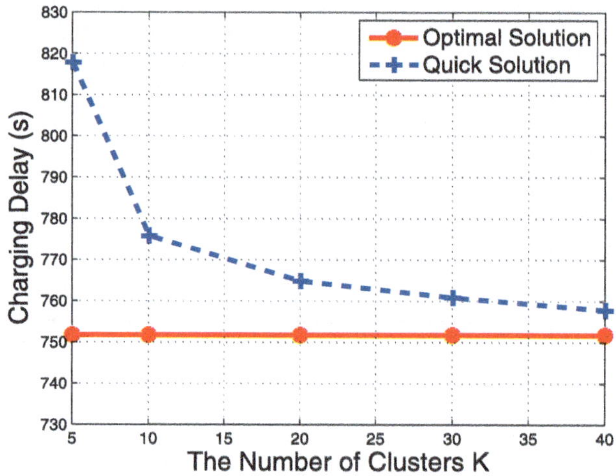

Fig. 6.13 Charging delay with different number of orientation clusters K

We aim to analyze how the number of clusters K impacts the overall charging delay once the charging orientation angles are combined through the OAM algorithm after discretizing the charging power. We contrast the outcomes before and after employing the OAM algorithm for merging the charging orientation angles. The cluster number K plays a crucial role in decreasing computational expense and enhancing the approximation accuracy toward the optimal solution.

As presented in Fig. 6.13, the loading delay exhibits a downward trend. Additionally, it drops steeply when the number of clusters changes from $K = 2$ to approximately $K = 40$, after which it reduces more slowly. This is due to the fact that an increase in the number of clusters brings the result nearer to the discretization solution.

Overall, the OAM algorithm can drastically decrease computational expenses by combining numerous candidate solutions into a specified number of clusters post-discretization. When K equals 20, the deviation between the outcomes before and after applying the OAM algorithm is under 2%. This finding corresponds with our assertions in Sect. 6.1.2.2, confirming the accuracy of our theoretical examination.

Impact of Charging Threshold δ In this section, we explore how the charging threshold δ for sensor nodes positioned at the intersection affects the total charging delay. By executing the CPD and OAM algorithms, we can determine a set of optimal charging orientation angles for each charging location. Consequently, the received power for each sensor node can be computed from this outcome.

Figure 6.14 illustrates the effect of the charging threshold δ on overall delay. By selecting an optimal value, the QS algorithm can achieve near-optimal performance when assessing each algorithm's efficiency. In comparison to the set covering method, this approach decreases the charging delay by a minimum of 32%.

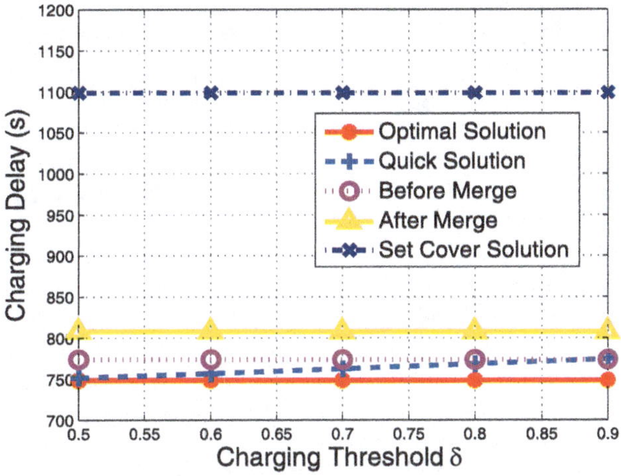

Fig. 6.14 Charging delay with different number of charging threshold δ

We thus conclude that the QS algorithm can considerably decrease loading delay relative to other techniques, with outcomes nearly matching the optimal solution. Additionally, the computational expense of employing the QS algorithm is much lower than utilizing a linear programming solver for the optimal solution. In practical scenarios, the gap between the quick solution and the optimal solution can be minimized by choosing an appropriate charging threshold δ. This finding is consistent with our conclusions in Sect. 6.1.2.4, confirming the validity of our theoretical analysis.

Impact of Number of MC M We explore the influence of the quantity of MCs M on the total charging delay. Employing multiple MCs enhances charging efficiency, significantly reducing the network's overall charging delay through cooperative MC scheduling compared to using a single MC. We fix the number of sensor nodes at $N = 50$, the threshold factor at $\epsilon = 0.2$, and vary the charging threshold δ from 50%. As illustrated in Fig. 6.15, the overall charging delay diminishes with an increase in the number of MCs.

In Fig. 6.15, increasing the number of MCs M from 7 to 8 leads to a significant reduction in the overall charging delay. However, adding more MCs to a large WRSN results in only a minor decrease in delay. Thus, it is crucial to determine the optimal location of the MCs to effectively schedule them and minimize the charging delay.

We further examine how each algorithm performs with varying counts of MCs. Figure 6.15 illustrates that while a higher number of MCs M lowers the total charging delay, the reduction impact gradually lessens as the MCs in the network grow.

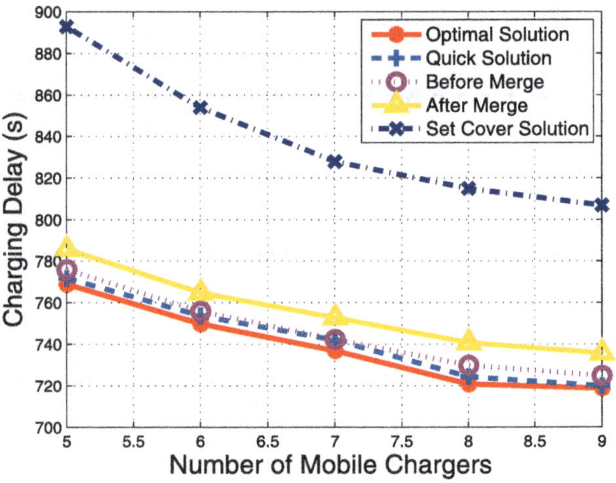

Fig. 6.15 Charging delay of different solutions with different numbers of MC M

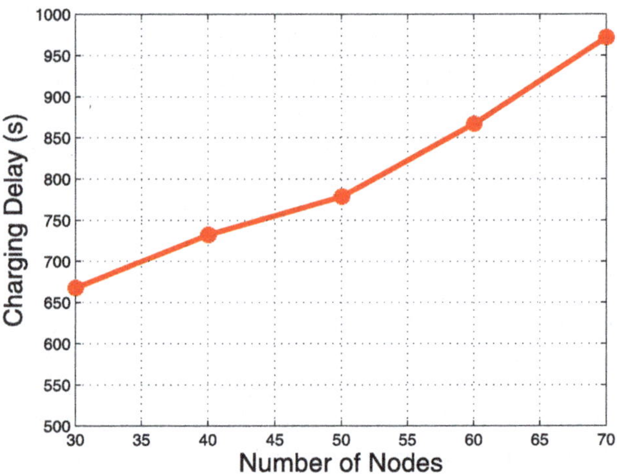

Fig. 6.16 Charging delay with different number of sensor nodes N

Impact of Nodes Number N In this section, we examine the total charging delay for varying quantities of sensor nodes N with a charging power discretization threshold of $\epsilon = 0.2$.

Given the dynamic nature of network topology, it is common in practical scenarios for new sensor nodes to be continuously incorporated into the network during the operation of the WRSN. This addition affects the overall network charging delay. Consequently, the simulation experiment needs to examine how varying the number of sensor nodes N impacts the overall network charging delay.

Figure 6.16 illustrates that the number of nodes N affects the charging delay. As the count of sensor nodes N, or node density, increases, the charging delay pro-

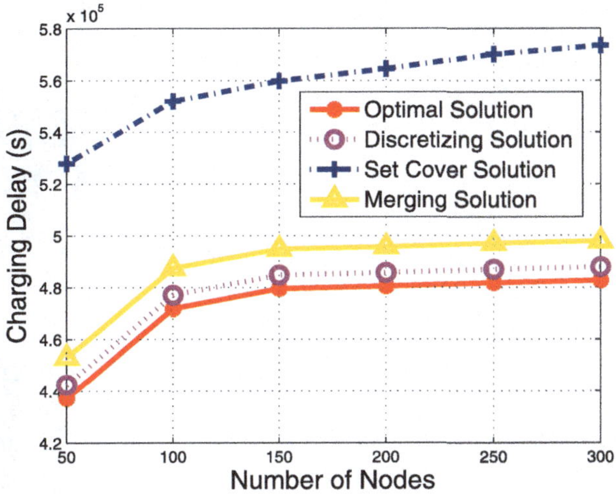

Fig. 6.17 Charging delay of different solutions with different numbers of sensors N

gressively heightens across all solutions. Since multiple sensor nodes can undergo charging multiple times, unlike a scheme where each sensor node is charged only once, the increase in charging delay follows a more gradual trend rather than a linear one. When the sensor population is large, the trend becomes even smoother. Nevertheless, the charging delays for the discretization solution and the merging solution are more favorable compared to the set-cover solution. Additionally, the charging delay for the discretization solution ranges from 442,614.65 s to 487,837.99 s, whereas the upper limit varies between $\frac{1}{1-0.2^2} \times 437{,}401.64\,\text{s} = 455{,}626.71\,\text{s}$ and $\frac{1}{1-0.2^2} \times 482{,}627.1\,\text{s} = 502{,}736.56\,\text{s}$, maintaining compliance with the approximation ratio $\frac{1}{1-\epsilon^2}$ discussed in Sect. 6.1.3 (Fig. 6.17).

An increase in the number of sensor nodes within a wireless sensor network leads to a rise in overall charging delay. Furthermore, the unpredictability in the deployment of new sensor nodes makes it challenging to foresee the extent of this rise. When the sensor node count hits a certain threshold, the pace of increase begins to slow down. This observation corroborates our findings in Sect. 6.1.2, confirming the accuracy of our theoretical analysis.

6.1.4.3 Experiment Setup

As illustrated in Fig. 6.18, the experiments are carried out using the TX91501 Powercast wireless charger along with wireless rechargeable sensor nodes. For the purpose of making the charger mobile and capable of rotation, a robot arm with a rotator is utilized as a mobile charger (refer to Fig. 6.19). Additionally, it is equipped with GPS and a camera for positioning and recording.

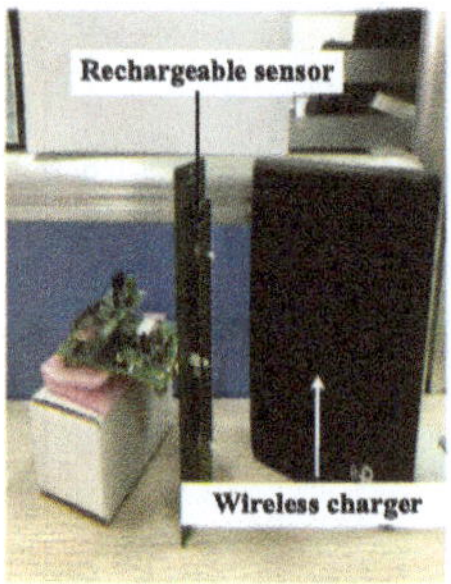

Fig. 6.18 TX91501 Powercast wireless charger and wireless rechargeable sensor node

Fig. 6.19 A rotatable mobile robot arm

In our test-bed experiment, a single MC is utilized to attend to five rechargeable sensors. These sensors are placed within a 100×100 cm region, and their respective coordinates are $(65, 56)$, $(-34, 43)$, $(40, 84)$, $(37, 62)$, and $(70, 23)$. Each sensor node requires an energy threshold of 2 J to function normally. Additionally, the charging power discretization threshold ranges from $\epsilon = 0.1$ to $\epsilon = 0.5$, and the merging clusters value is set to $K = 5$.

6.1.4.4 Baseline Setup

Currently, there are no techniques to reduce the charging delay for directional charging in WRSN. Hence, we evaluate the performance of various methods.

- Optimal Solution: The theoretically optimal outcome is determined through a detailed exhaustive search using an LP solver.
- Before Merging: Prior to the application of the OAM algorithm, the solution exhibits a greater approximation ratio to the optimal outcome and encounters increased computational expense.
- After Merging: Following the application of OAM, there is a reduction in computational overhead while the approximation ratio becomes less optimal.
- Set Cover Solution: This method always selects the orientation angle that maximizes the coverage of sensor nodes.

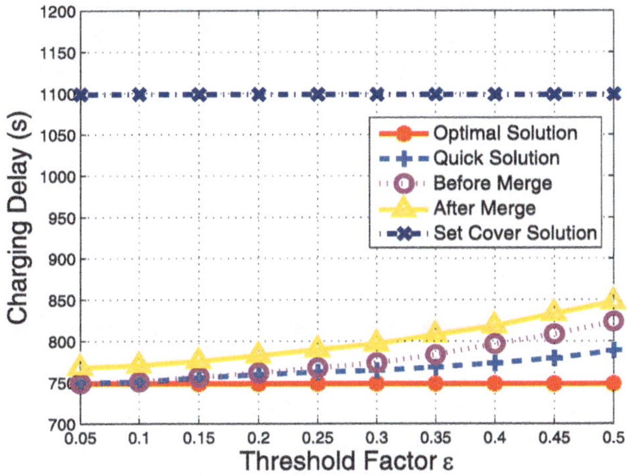

Fig. 6.20 Charging delay of different solutions with varying discretization threshold ϵ

6.1.4.5 Experiment Results

Threshold Factor ϵ As illustrated in Fig. 6.20, we evaluate the charging delay across four different solutions. The threshold factor ϵ is set between 0.1 and 0.5, with the cluster count k fixed at 5 and the charging threshold δ for sensor nodes at the intersection established at 50%.

The charging delay achieved by the discretization and merging solutions is at least 49% lower compared to the Set Cover solution. Additionally, for $\epsilon = 0.1$, the minimal charging delay is 314.14 s, while the maximum possible charging delay is given by $\frac{1}{1-0.1^2} \times 314$.

Threshold Factor δ Figure 6.21 illustrates the influence of the sensor nodes' charging threshold at the intersection. The charging threshold δ ranges between 50 and 90%, with the threshold factor ϵ fixed at 0.2, and the K-means clustering algorithm's cluster count k set to 5.

By modifying the charging threshold δ of sensor nodes at various intersections, the overall charging delay can be impacted. Moreover, the QS algorithm delivers comparable outcomes and substantially reduces computation costs compared to the optimal solution. In WRSNs with differing setups, the charging threshold δ influences the overall charging delay in varying ways. Hence, the charging threshold δ should be customized for the specific application. Experimental results show that the charging threshold δ affects the total delay. In real-world applications, it should be adjusted to fit the actual conditions.

Upon verifying that the proposed scheme is appropriate for small-scale WRSNs, we will perform comprehensive simulations to showcase its effectiveness in large-scale networks.

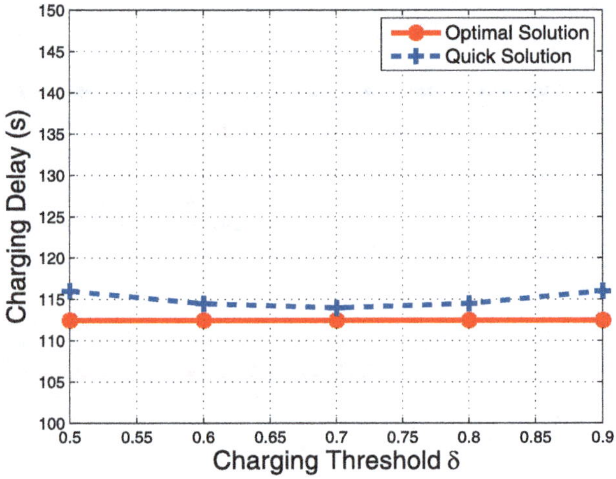

Fig. 6.21 Charging delay with varying δ

6.2 Robust Charging Model

In this section, we employed a mobile robot fitted with a Powercast TX91501 wireless charger, serving as the mobile charger (MC), with an energy reserve of 50 J. To replicate omnidirectional charging, the TX91501 charger utilized a rotating charging direction. The energy usage rate for the MC's movement was 0.1 J/m, while the charging energy usage rate was 0.4 J/s. We deployed 11 rechargeable smoke sensors throughout a building, each having a battery capacity of 5 J, and introduced various obstacles in the environment. To assess the reliability of our approach, a large quantity of smoke was released at location (4,−3), causing it to rapidly reach all sensors and mimic a fire monitoring situation. We measured the packet loss rate for each node in challenging conditions and documented the location and packet loss rate data for each node. The base station was positioned at (0,0). The experiment contrasted the reliability of different techniques, confirming the effectiveness of our method.

6.2.1 Problem Statement

6.2.1.1 Network Model

In this study, we utilize the standard omnidirectional wireless charging technology [8]. To measure the impact of obstacles on wireless signal strength in a complex environment, we compute the Fresnel diffraction coefficient F_d based on the

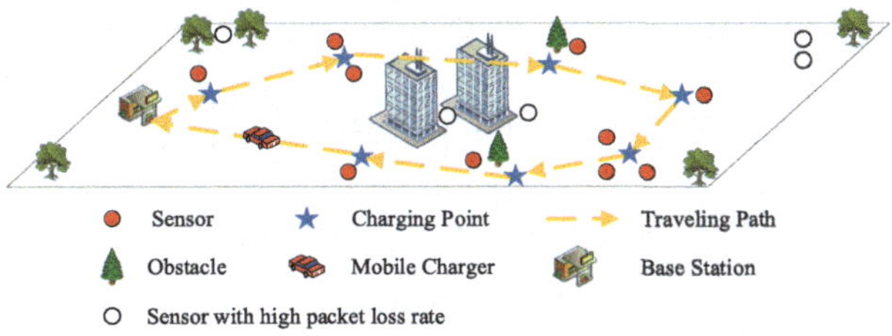

Fig. 6.22 A diagram of charging service in a WRSN

position of the charging spot c_j [9]. Assuming the MC is positioned at the charging spot c_j and recharges sensor s_n, the charging power $P(d)$ can be represented as

$$P(d) = \begin{cases} \dfrac{\alpha_c F_d}{(d+\beta_c)^2}, & d \le \sqrt{\dfrac{\alpha_c F_d}{P_{\min}}} - \beta_c \\ 0, & d > \sqrt{\dfrac{\alpha_c F_d}{P_{\min}}} - \beta_c \end{cases}. \tag{6.42}$$

In this context, α_c and β_c are two fixed parameters influenced by the surrounding conditions [10, 11]. The Fresnel diffraction coefficient is represented by F_d [9]. The Euclidean distance between the charging point c_j and the sensor s_n is denoted by d, and P_{min} symbolizes the minimum power that the sensor can receive from the MC. If $P\,(d) < P_{min}$, the energy received by the sensor s_n can be disregarded (Fig. 6.22).

Within the omnidirectional charging mode, as indicated by [8], the charger is capable of delivering power to several sensors at once without notably diminishing the power received by any individual sensor. We denote the charging period when the MC is positioned at c_j as t_j. Subsequently, the overall energy obtained by sensor s_n can be expressed as:

$$E_{s_n} = \sum_j P(d_j)t_j$$

where $P(d_j)$ denotes the power acquired by the sensor s_n from the charging location c_j, and t_j represents the duration for which the MC remains at c_j.

$$u_{C'}(s_n) = \sum_{c_j \in C'} P(d)t_j, \tag{6.43}$$

where C' represents the set of charging spots that correspond to all potential locations C of MC.

Every sensor possesses a finite energy capacity denoted as U_n^{th}. If the transmitted energy surpasses this capacity, the surplus energy will be lost. Consequently, the actual energy received by sensor s_n can be described as

$$U_{tot}(s_n) = \min\left\{u_{C'}(s_n), U_n^{th}\right\}. \tag{6.44}$$

Afterwards, the overall charging utility of the whole network can be expressed as

$$U_{tot}\left(C'\right) = \sum_{n=1}^{N} U_{tot}(s_n). \tag{6.45}$$

Typically, the energy expenditure of MCs is composed of two elements: the energy needed for travel and the energy required for recharging.

Regarding travel expenses, let $R\left(C'\right)$ represent the length of the travel path and ν the energy expenditure per unit length. Consequently, the travel expenditure is given by $\nu R\left(C'\right)$. For charging expenses, let ρ signify the cost per unit time. Therefore, the charging expenses can be calculated as $\rho \sum_{c_j \in C'} t_j$.

Thus, the total energy expenditure for MC can be formulated as

$$F\left(C'\right) = \nu R\left(C'\right) + \rho \sum_{c_j \in C} t_j. \tag{6.46}$$

6.2.1.2 Risk-Averse Model

To enhance network robustness, our strategy prioritizes replenishing sensors with minimal risks (i.e., a low packet loss rate) because sensors with lower risk correspond to higher robustness [12]. Consequently, we introduce the CVaR (Conditional Value at Risk) model [13] to assess the risk associated with charging a node. CVaR signifies the anticipated loss in the worst-case scenario. This model is widely acknowledged across various fields for managing different risks. For example, in finance, CVaR aids in avoiding investment risks [14]. In the energy sector, CVaR models assist in protecting against power system failures due to the unpredictability of renewable energy resources [15, 16]. Furthermore, in the IoT field, the CVaR model mitigates risks arising from device failures and uncertainties in energy consumption [17, 18]. We will also investigate the potential of measuring robustness using the CVaR model.

To begin, we define the Value at Risk (VaR) at a risk level $\alpha \in (0, 1]$ as

$$\mathrm{VaR}_\alpha\left(C'\right) = \inf\left\{\tau \in R, \Pr\left[U\left(C', y\right) \le \tau\right] \ge \alpha\right\}. \tag{6.47}$$

Here, τ is the value of VaR. VaR is the α-quantile of the random function $U\left(C', y\right)$'s value [19]. Based on VaR, we define the CVaR as

$$\mathrm{CVaR}_\alpha\left(C'\right) = E_y\left[U\left(C', y\right) \mid U\left(C', y\right) \le \mathrm{VaR}_\alpha\left(C'\right)\right]. \tag{6.48}$$

Here $U\left(C', y\right)$ represents a statistical utility function defined by the sample value y, where C' denotes the set of designated charging spots, y serves as a sample parameter indicating the effectiveness of a node, and α is a parameter used to adjust the degree of risk aversion. This study concentrates on maximizing the utility value in the worst cases referenced by α. A smaller α value corresponds to a more severe worst case. VaR denotes the highest utility value in the α-worst cases [20], while CVaR represents the expected utility of all samples y that meet the condition $U\left(C', y\right) \leq \text{VaR}_\alpha\left(C'\right)$ [13]. Figure 6.23 displays the connection between VaR and CVaR.

Observe that CVaR outperforms VaR [13] in risk evaluation, as it captures the impact of the entire utility distribution in the α-worst scenarios. CVaR is thus effective in risk assessment and mitigation [13]. Furthermore, its ability to measure expected utility gains in α-worst scenarios is a significant benefit. Essentially, both *risk* and *charging utility* can be expressed together through the single metric *CVaR*, making it ideal for addressing the network robustness challenge.

According to [13], we define an auxiliary function $H\left(C', \tau\right)$ to describe CVaR. $H\left(C', \tau\right)$ can be defined as follows:

$$H\left(C', \tau\right) = \tau - \frac{1}{\alpha} E\left[\max\left\{\tau - U\left(C', y\right), 0\right\}\right]. \tag{6.49}$$

In this context, $E\left[\max\left\{\tau - U\left(C', y\right), 0\right\}\right]$ represents the expected value of the discrepancy between VaR and CVaR, given that the optimal value of τ is VaR. Consequently, $H\left(C', \tau\right)$ serves as a measure for quantifying CVaR.

Observe that the challenge of solving $\max_{C' \subseteq C} \text{CVaR}_\alpha\left(C'\right)$ corresponds to the task of solving $\max_{<C', \tau>} H\left(C', \tau\right)$ [13]. Furthermore, $H\left(C', \tau\right)$ presents several beneficial properties. For instance, $H\left(C', \tau\right)$ is concave with respect to *au* for any given set C', and the gradient of $H\left(C', \tau\right)$ is bounded, as mentioned in [17].

In real-world scenarios, we prioritize system performance (e.g., efficient charging utility) under worst-case conditions rather than average situations to enhance system robustness [13]. Hence, in this section, our goal is to *optimize* $H\left(C', \tau\right)$ *(i.e., maximize the effective charging utility in* α*-worst cases)*. This will *improve network robustness (reliability) by refilling nodes with minimal risks (i.e., low packet loss rate)*.

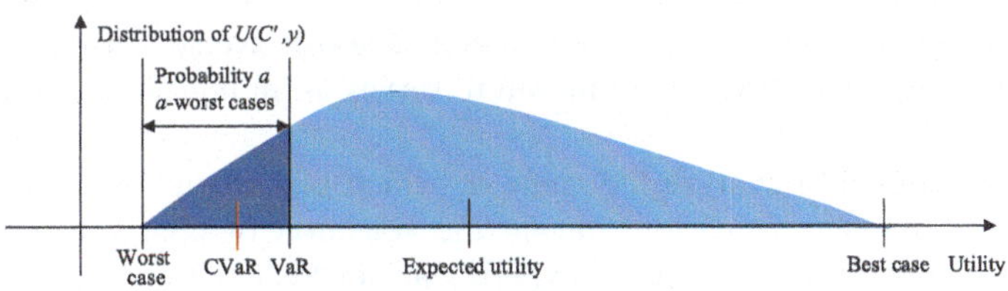

Fig. 6.23 An illustration of risk measures: VaR and CVaR

In the event of an incident (such as a fire, typically spanning an extended period), if a sensor node functions correctly and there is no packet loss (enabling it to transmit fire alerts to the base station within a single transmission cycle), the sensor node is termed an *effective sensor node*. The energy received by this effective sensor is referred to as *effective energy (i.e., effective charging utility)*. The effective energy $U(s_n)$ acquired from MC follows a Bernoulli distribution with a packet loss rate of p_n. We label $U(s_n)$ as the effective energy. For an effective node s_n, we get $U(s_n) = U_{tot}(s_n)$; otherwise, $U(s_n) = 0$.

Let $ildey$ represent a particular value from the sample y, and the overall effective charging utility of the complete network can be described as follows:

$$U\left(C', \tilde{y}\right) = \sum_{n=1}^{N} \widetilde{U}\left(s_n\right). \tag{6.50}$$

In this context, $\widetilde{U}(s_n)$ represents the effective energy in sample $\widetilde{y}$. Referencing Eqs. (6.49) and (6.50), the auxiliary function of CVaR, $H(C', \tau)$, can be approximated as

$$H\left(C', \tau\right) \approx \tau - \frac{1}{n_y \alpha} \sum_{\tilde{y}} \left[\max\left\{\tau - U\left(C', \tilde{y}\right), 0\right\}\right]. \tag{6.51}$$

In this equation, the sample size n_y is given by $O\left(\frac{1}{\tilde{\epsilon}^2} \log \frac{1}{\tilde{\delta}}\right)$, where $\tilde{\epsilon}$ and $\tilde{\delta}$ are within the interval (0,1).

Based on the Dvoretzky-Kiefer-Wolfowitz inequality and its derivation process as detailed in [21], when using the mean of n_y samples as the expected value in Eq. (6.49), there is at least a $1 - 2\exp(-2n_y\tilde{\epsilon}^2)$ probability that the CVaR value approximation error (i.e., the approximation error between the two sides of Eq. (6.51)) is less than $\tilde{\epsilon}$. Consequently, if the number of samples is $n_y = O\left(\frac{1}{\tilde{\epsilon}^2} \log \frac{1}{\tilde{\delta}}\right)$, then with at least $1 - \widetilde{\delta}$ probability, the CVaR approximation error will be less than $\tilde{\epsilon}$.

We define $H\left(C', \tau\right)$ as the *risk-averse charging utility value*, which represents the anticipated value of the effective charging utility under α-worst scenarios. It is important to note that we approximate this anticipated value by averaging all sample values y, and hence, the effective charge utility's distribution does not need to match any specified mathematical distribution model. The risk-averse charging utility acts as an approximation to CVaR, and therefore serves as an indicator of the system's robustness [12].

We now thoroughly analyze the value α, which is a crucial factor in assessing risks (i.e., in α-worst scenarios) during the selection of charging targets. This attribute will be validated through experiments in Sect. 6.2.4. When $\alpha = 1$, it signifies that risks are disregarded, leading the MC to favor nodes with higher expected utility values. On the other hand, when $\alpha = 0.4$, meaning attention is given to the charging utility in the 40%-worst scenarios, the MC will prioritize sensors

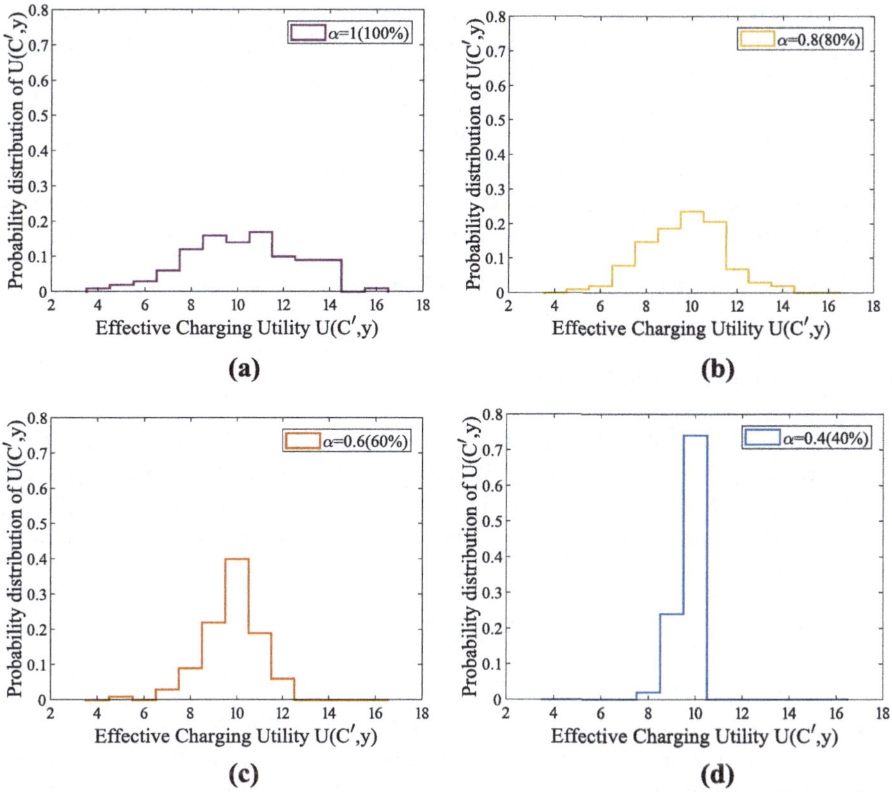

Fig. 6.24 Distribution of $U(C', y)$. (**a**) $\alpha = 1(100\%)$. (**b**) $\alpha = 0.8(80\%)$. (**c**) $\alpha = 0.6(60\%)$. (**d**) $\alpha = 0.4(40\%)$

with lower risk. Charging these low-risk sensors helps stabilize the distribution of effective charging utility, thus enhancing robustness.

Figure 6.24 demonstrates how the charging utility value $U(C', y)$ distribution varies with different α levels. As α decreases from 1 to 0.4, the concentration of effective charge utility increases. This suggests that lower α values reduce the impact of packet loss on the effective charging utility. When $\alpha = 1$, representing a risk-neutral position, the distribution is dispersed, leading to significant variations in effective charge utility, which can impede timely event detection.

There are three key reasons that make the CVaR model optimal for guaranteeing network resilience with mobile charging:

1. The objective is to enhance network robustness under worst-case conditions with constrained energy resources (i.e., the limited energy budget of the MC). CVaR symbolizes the expected worst-case utility, thereby its maximization also maximizes loading utility for robustness.

2. The CVaR model necessitates the utility function to be influenced by sample values y. In a WRSN, the utility function $U(C', y)$ is a statistically characterized random quantity function. Different sample values y result in diverse utility values, aligning with the CVaR model requirements.
3. Packet loss rates among nodes follow binomial distributions with varying probabilities. The effective load utility distribution is intricate and discrete, posing modeling challenges. However, the CVaR model imposes no restrictions on this distribution, rendering it suitable for addressing the RACO problem.

Therefore, the CVaR model is designed to measure robustness.

6.2.1.3 Problem Formalization

While maintaining a WRSN, an MC visits each charging location sequentially to power the sensors. However, the MC's energy reserve, indicated by B, is typically finite. As a result, the MC needs to go back to the base station (BS) to recharge, ensuring it does not exhaust its energy. Thus, the subsequent routing constraint must be adhered to:

$$\nu R\left(C'\right) + \rho \sum_{c_j \in C} t_j \leq B.$$

Considering this limitation, our task is to determine: Which charging spots and corresponding charging times maximize the efficient charging benefit in the α-worst case scenarios within an intricate environment? We describe this problem as follows:

$$\begin{aligned} &(\boldsymbol{P1}) \ \max H\left(C', \tau\right), \\ &\text{s.t. } \nu R\left(C'\right) + \rho \sum_{c_j \in C'} t_j \leq B. \end{aligned}$$

To tackle problem P1, we face several technical challenges: (1) Measuring the Impact of Obstacles: Quantifying how obstacles affect the efficiency of charging in complex environments is challenging. (2) Nonlinear Risk-Averse Utility Function: The utility function for risk aversion is nonlinear. (3) Intricate Auxiliary Function: The auxiliary function, which is a complicated two-parameter function, cannot achieve its optimal value by neglecting either parameter. (4) Unbounded and Continuous Search Domain: The search domain for determining the optimal charging location is unbounded and continuous. (5) NP-Hard Problems: Problem P1 consists of multiple NP-hard problems, making it very hard to solve.

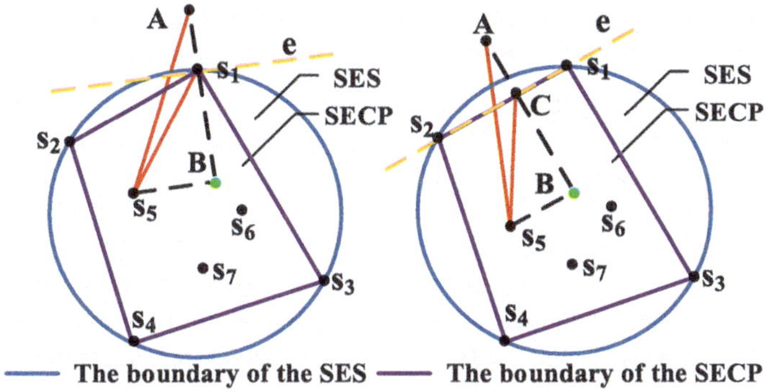

Fig. 6.25 MC must stop within the smallest enclosing convex polygon (SECP)

6.2.2 Schematic Design

To enhance the charging utility in the α-worst scenarios, we start by introducing discretization models to measure the risk-averse charging utility. Subsequently, we create a near-optimal algorithm with a defined performance assurance to address the RACO problem. Lastly, to additionally boost the loading utility, we devise a path optimization strategy to minimize the travelling expenses of MC.

6.2.2.1 Smallest Enclosing Convex Polygon

In order to address the problem of finding optimal charging locations in a boundless 2D plane, we initially build the Smallest Enclosing Space (SES) [22] to minimize the area under consideration. The SES represents the smallest circle that contains all the sensor nodes [22]. Nonetheless, we found that this circular area can be enhanced further.

To further reduce the search space, we convert the SES into the Smallest Enclosing Convex Polygon (SECP), which basically serves as the convex hull for the set of sensor nodes. This SECP is smaller in comparison to the SES and connects the sensor nodes (as depicted in Fig. 6.25), encompassing all sensors and potential locations where an MC can reside and charge. Unlike past research [22, 23], which used the smallest enclosing space/disk (SES) for designing mobile charging schemes, the proposed SECP is more compact. As a result, our method decreases the search space and computational as well as memory requirements compared to earlier approaches.

This alteration considerably reduces the region under consideration, enhancing the efficiency and feasibility of identifying charging locations within the limitations of the WRSN.

Lemma 6.1 *To maximise the total risk-averse loading utility of all sensors the MC must stop within the SECP covering all nodes in the network.*

Proof As shown in Fig. 6.25, assume a point A exists outside the Smallest Enclosing Convex Polygon (SECP). We denote the nearest point (or sensor) within the SECP to A as s_1 or C. For the purpose of proving Lemma 6.1, we will use s_1 as an instance.

Draw an edge e such that it is perpendicular to $|As_1|$. Given that the SECP is a convex polygon, every sensor node s_n within the SECP will be positioned on the opposite side of edge e relative to point A. As an example, consider an arbitrary sensor, named s_5. Draw a line $|s_5 B|$, parallel to e, which intersects the line $|As_1|$ at point B.

This gives us the following relationships:

$$|As_5|^2 = |Bs_5|^2 + |AB|^2$$

$$|s_1 s_5|^2 = |Bs_5|^2 + |s_1 B|^2$$

If $|AB| > |s_1 B|$, it can be deduced that $|As_5| > |s_1 s_5|$. Thus, for any point A outside the SECP, there exists a point A' within the SECP that is closest to A, assuring that for any sensor s_n, $|A' s_n| < |As_n|$. As per Eq. (6.42), $P(|A' s_n|) > P(|As_n|)$. Consequently, for any point A outside the SECP, one can always find a point A' inside the SECP that performs better than A. This indicates that the best location for the Mobile Charger (MC) to recharge must be inside the SECP.

After narrowing down MC's search space from an unbounded 2D plane to SECP, we focus on identifying the charging location. Since the charging power function (i.e., Eq. (6.42)) is continuous, there are countless potential charging points within the SECP, each with a distinct charging power. Hence, we initially discretize the infinite continuous charging into finite values. Subsequently, we partition the continuous 2D charge plane into finite segments with varying discretized power levels. □

6.2.2.2 Charging Power Discretization

As indicated by Eq. (6.42), the charging power function is nonlinear and continuous, posing challenges in solving problem **P1**. To mitigate this difficulty, the power function is approximated using a piecewise constant function, thereby converting the continuous and infinite search space into a finite one (Fig. 6.26).

Definition 6.1 Suppose $l(0) = 0$ and $l(R) = \sqrt{\frac{\alpha_c F_d}{P_{\min}}} - \beta_c$. Consequently, the piecewise constant function may be written as:

$$\tilde{P}(d) = \begin{cases} P(l(1)), \ d = l(0) \\ P(l(r)), \ l(r-1) < d \leq l(r) (r = 1, \ldots, R) \\ 0. \qquad d > l(R) \end{cases} \tag{6.52}$$

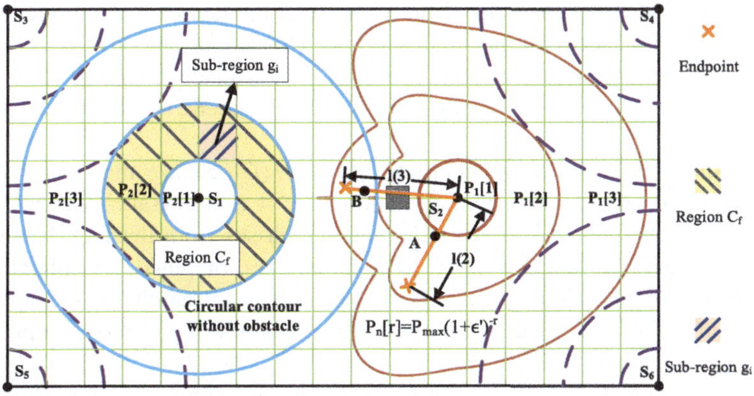

Fig. 6.26 An example of discretized charging regions

In this context, d denotes the Euclidean distance between the charging point c_j and the sensor s_n, and F_d refers to the Fresnel diffraction coefficient for the MC located at c_j. Within our piecewise function, $l(r)$ signifies the discrete version of d. We express $l(r) = \beta_c\left(\left(1+\epsilon'\right)^{\frac{r}{2}}\sqrt{F_d}-1\right)$ for $r = 1, 2, \ldots, R-1$, indicating that $l(r)$ relies on c_i's coordinates because F_d depends on c_i's position. Consequently, we can ascertain r's value for any specified point in the area. Accordingly, the equivalent discrete power is given by:

$$P(l(r)) = \frac{\alpha_c F_d}{\beta_c^2 F_d \left(1+\epsilon'\right)^r} = \frac{\alpha_c}{\beta_c^2}\left(1+\epsilon'\right)^{-r} = P_{\max}\left(1+\epsilon'\right)^{-r}$$

Where $P_{\max}$ represents the peak charging power. We define $P_n[r]$ as the discretized form of the charging power, thus obtaining:

$$P_n[r] = P_{\max}\left(1+\epsilon'\right)^{-r} \tag{6.53}$$

Remark Keep in mind that the discrete rate ϵ' serves as a variable to manage the granularity of charging power discretization. As per Eq. (6.53), reducing ϵ' will decrease the granularity. Consequently, the gap between consecutive discretized charges will be narrower, resulting in an increased number of discretized charges (R).

6.2.2.3 Approximation Greedy Algorithm

In the described discretization method, the infinite and continuous two-dimensional plane is partitioned into M small sections, each acting as the charge point C for the MC. It is important to note that we consider all points within the same section to have identical discretized power. Given that the MC has a limited energy capacity, it cannot access all the small sections. Hence, our objective is to choose a subset of the recharging points to maximize the risk-averse recharging utility of the network. To achieve this, we propose a Risk-Averse Greedy (RAG) algorithm (i.e., Algorithm 23).

To optimize the risk-averse charging utility $H(C', \tau)$, we must find the best values for τ and C'. To ascertain the optimal τ, it is necessary to construct the optimal charging spot set C^*. A main challenge arises from the fact that without a fixed τ value, the function $H\left(C', \tau_i\right)$ cannot be computed, complicating the determination of C^*. Hence, a practical approach is to search for the optimal τ within the interval $[0, \Gamma]$ with a granularity of σ, where Γ represents the upper limit of τ.

When ignoring packet loss and risk aversion, and applying solely the greedy method to maximize $U_{tot}(C')$, the resultant value of $U_{tot}(C')$ can be seen as the value of Γ here. Following the determination of the near-optimal τ, the subsequent step is to ascertain the near-optimal C'.

To identify the optimal set of charging spots C', we devise a near-optimal algorithm based on a greedy approach. At each iteration, we consistently select the charging spot c^* that maximizes the risk-averse charging utility value rate, specifically

$$c^* = \arg \max_{c \in C \setminus C'} \frac{H\left(C_i' \cup \{c\}, \tau_i\right) - H\left(C_i', \tau_i\right)}{F\left(C_i' \cup \{c\}\right) - F\left(C_i'\right)}. \tag{6.54}$$

The numerator, $H\left(C_i' \cup \{c\}, \tau_i\right) - H\left(C_i', \tau_i\right)$, indicates the increase in the risk-averse charging utility value following the choice of a new charging position c. The denominator, $F\left(C_i' \cup \{c\}\right) - F\left(C_i'\right)$, defines the rise in energy cost, which incorporates both the traveling and charging expenses.

For each given value τ_i, the corresponding set of charging spots C_i' can be determined using Eq. (6.54). For each pair $\left\langle C_i', \tau_i\right\rangle$, the risk-averse utility value $H\left(C_i', \tau_i\right)$ is computed. Subsequently, the pair $\left\langle C_i', \tau_i\right\rangle$ that provides the highest risk-averse utility value $H\left(C_i', \tau_i\right)$ is chosen as the optimal solution. Further details can be found in the RAG algorithm.

Initially, the RAG algorithm seeks the best τ value with a precision of σ (Lines 2–3). Subsequently, it computes the marginal risk-averse charging utility Δ_H^c and the corresponding marginal energy cost Δ_F^c for each unchosen charging spot c (Lines 6–9). Then, the RAG algorithm selects the charging spot c^* that maximizes the ratio Δ_H^c / Δ_F^c (Line 10). If the total energy cost, including c^*, remains within the limit B, c^* is added to the set of charging spots C_i' (Lines 11–13).

Once all pairs of $\left\langle C_i', \tau_i\right\rangle$ are obtained, the RAG algorithm picks the pair $\left\langle C', \tau'\right\rangle$ that has the highest $H\left(C_i', \tau_i\right)$ value and outputs C' and $H\left(C', \tau'\right)$ as the results (Lines 19–20).

Algorithm 23 Risk-Averse Greedy (RAG) Algorithm

Require: Charging positions set C, user-customized risk level $\alpha \in [0, 1]$ with default value 1, range of the parameter $\tau \in [0, \Gamma]$ and searching granularity $\sigma \in [0, \Gamma]$, the number of sensors N, energy constraint B, and coefficients ν, ρ.

Ensure: The selected charging set C' and risk-averse charging utility $H\left(C', \tau\right)$.

```
Initial: 𝓜 ← ∅;
for i = {1, 2, 3, ..., ⌈Γ/σ⌉} do
    Re-initial: C;
    C'_i ← ∅;
    𝓑 = arg max {H(c, τ_i) | c ∈ C, F(c) ≤ B};
    while Not all sensors s_n have been fully charged do
        for Each c ∈ C do
            Calculate marginal risk-averse charging utility Δ^c_H ← H(C'_i ∪ c, τ_i) − H(C'_i, τ_i).
            Calculate marginal energy cost Δ^c_F ← F(C'_i ∪ {c}) − F(C'_i) by applying ESP algorithm.
        end for
        c* = arg max {Δ^c_H / Δ^c_F | c ∈ C};
        if F(C'_i ∪ {c*}) ≤ B then
            C'_i ← C'_i ∪ {c*};
            C ← C \ c*;
        else
            Break;
        end if
    end while
    C'_i = arg max_{C' ∈ {𝓑, C'_i}} H(C', τ_i);
    𝓜 ← 𝓜 ∪ {(C'_i, τ_i)};
end for
(C', τ') = arg max_{(C'_i, τ_i) ∈ 𝓜} H(C'_i, τ_i);
return The selected charging set C' and risk-averse charging utility H(C', τ').
```

6.2.2.4 Ellipse-Based Shorten Path Algorithm

After constructing an initial charging path, the Ellipse-based Shorten Path (ESP) algorithm (i.e., Algorithm 24) is proposed to further shorten the path.

Assume there are ω grids with the center of each grid g_i represented by v_i. The nearest neighbor algorithm is employed to form a Hamiltonian cycle consisting of ω center points, denoted as $R(C^{CEN}) = \{v_0, v_1, \ldots, v_\omega, v_0\}$. This cycle, $R(C^{CEN})$, serves as the initial path in our approach. Subsequently, the ESP algorithm is applied to further optimize the charging path.

The ESP algorithm operates in the following manner. For each grid g_i, our goal is to identify the optimal point v_i' within grid g_i to substitute the original point v_i. An ellipse is constructed to find the tangential point, which serves as the optimal point v_i'. Specifically, v_{i-1} and v_{i+1} act as the focal points of the ellipse. If the line $|v_{i-1}v_{i+1}|$ formed by v_{i-1} and v_{i+1} intersects g_i, we select the point on $|v_{i-1}v_{i+1}|$ that is closest to v_i as v_i' (i.e., point v_3' in Fig. 6.27(4)).

For every edge e of g_i, as illustrated in Fig. 6.28, we begin by selecting an endpoint ep from edge e. The ellipse that passes through this endpoint is considered

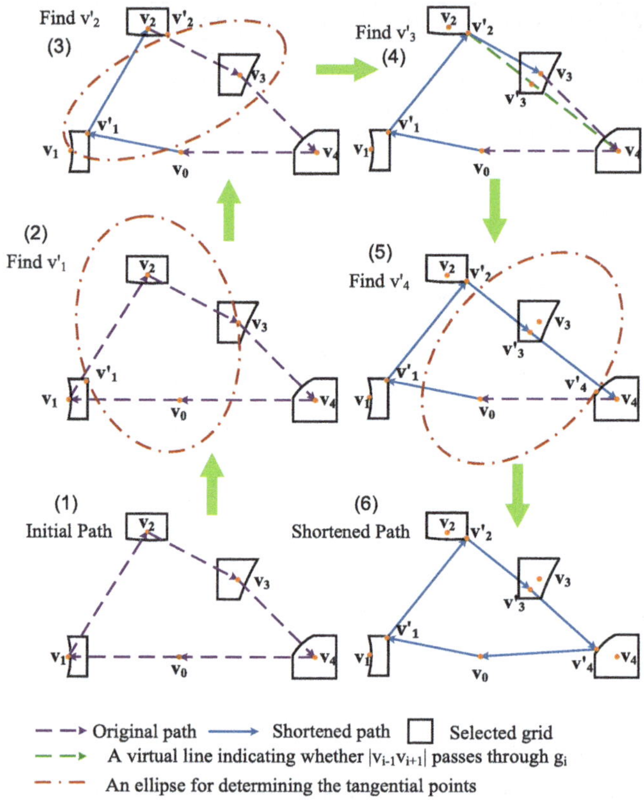

Fig. 6.27 An example of ellipse-based shorten path algorithm

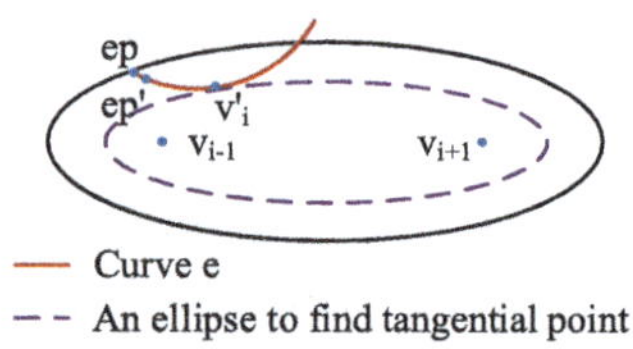

Fig. 6.28 Case 1: e represents a line segment or an arc, and both focal points of the ellipse are on the outside of the corresponding circle

'smaller' than the one that passes through the other endpoint. Here, 'smaller' indicates that the sum of the distances from this point to the two foci is less than that from the other point. Subsequently, we employ the *tangential point determination method* to verify if a tangential point exists on e. If it does, we attempt to locate the tangential point, denoted as v_i' in Fig. 6.28, and identify it as the optimal point on edge e. After identifying all optimal points for all edges in grid g_i, we choose the point with the minimal $R(C')$ as the optimal point v_i' for grid g_i.

In order to determine the tangential point, we take into account different positional relationships between the ellipse and the arc. The tangential point is

Algorithm 24 Ellipse-based Shorten Path (ESP) Algorithm

Require: The grid list obtained by the nearest neighbor rule $G = \{g_1, g_2, g_3, \ldots, g_\omega\}$, an initial path created by center points of grids $R(C^{CEN}) = \{v_0, v_1, \ldots, v_i, \ldots, v_\omega\}$.
Ensure: An optimized path.

for Each $g_i (i = 1, 2, 3, \ldots, \omega)$ **do**
  $V \leftarrow \emptyset$;
  for Each edge e in g_i **do**
    Obtain the endpoint ep in edge e and the ellipse going through ep is smaller than the ellipse going through the other endpoint.
    if there is a tangential point on edge e **then**
      $V \leftarrow$ the tangential point of the ellipse and e;
    else
      $V \leftarrow ep$;
    end if
  end for
  $v_i = argmin_{v \in V} |R(C')|$;
end for
return An optimized path $R(C')$.

identified using the Ferrari method [24]. If a tangential point cannot be determined, ep is used as the value of v_i' to achieve the best local solution.

A demonstration of path shortening can be seen in Fig. 6.27. To clarify the concept, even though v_i is overridden in the ESP algorithm, we describe the regional center path connected through the center of grid g_i as $R\left(C^{CEN}\right) = \{v_0, v_1, \ldots, v_i, \ldots, v_\omega, v_0\}$, and the results derived from the ESP algorithm as $R\left(C'\right) = \left\{v_0, v_1', \ldots, v_i', \ldots, v_\omega', v_0\right\}$. The thorough procedure of the ESP algorithm is depicted in Fig. 6.27 with an example. Initially, the original path (i.e., $R\left(C^{CEN}\right)$) is displayed in Fig. 6.27(1). Next, as illustrated in Fig. 6.27(2), an ellipse is formed using v_0 and v_2 as foci, and we determine the optimal point v_1' (end or tangential point) on the ellipse and each edge of g_1. Subsequently, v_1 is replaced with v_1'. Following this, as shown in Fig. 6.27(3), v_1' and v_3 are chosen as the foci to repeat the process until the near-optimal path $R\left(C'\right)$ is formed (i.e., Fig. 6.27(4) (5) (6)).

Notice that once the ESP algorithm replans the locations of the charging points, the distances between these points will alter. Thus, with the nearest neighbour method, the sequence of traversal derived from the original centre points might not correspond to that from the charging points provided by the ESP algorithm. Nevertheless, we adhere to the traversal order based on the original centre points without making any further modifications. Generally, there are three main considerations outlined below.

- First, using the ESP Algorithm does not affect the overall approximation ratio of Algorithm 1. This is because in Algorithm 1, the ESP algorithm is employed solely for computing $F\left(C_i' \cup \{c\}\right) - F\left(C_i'\right)$. In this step, we typically select the optimal charging point c within the grid based on the point set C_i' and compute the value of $F(C_i' \cup \{c\}) - F(C_i')$.[1] Nonetheless, re-optimizing the placements of charging points in the point set C_i' using the ESP algorithm (i.e., the optimization process depicted in Fig. 6.27) will yield significantly better results than simply determining the charging point within a grid. Consequently, our ESP algorithm, which optimizes all charging points collectively, surpasses the error-free single charging point optimization method and remains a pure optimization strategy free from new errors.

- Second, altering the traversal order might not result in an improvement. For instance, in Fig. 6.27(6), v_3 becomes the nearest neighbor of v_0 instead of v_1. This observation suggests that the difference between $|v_0v_1|$ and $|v_0v_3|$ is minimal. Consequently, selecting the charging point v_3 using the nearest neighbor heuristic does not offer a significant benefit over v_1. Thus, even if the nearest neighbor relationships among charging points are altered, it remains uncertain whether the traversal order adjustment shortens or lengthens the charging path. Hence, we cannot ensure that adjusting the traversal order will yield a better outcome.
- Ultimately, it may be unnecessary to re-schedule the traversal sequence. The ESP algorithm optimises the locations of charging points based on a predefined traversal sequence. Consequently, the optimised characteristics of the charging points determined by the ESP algorithm will remain valid only if the initial traversal sequence is preserved. Altering the traversal sequence of the MC will cause the "optimised" charging points to lose their benefits compared to the original network centre points. Hence, modifying the traversal sequence of the MC for the "optimised" charging points will negate their optimised attributes. If the charging points lose their optimised nature, the re-scheduled traversal sequence based on these charging points will be redundant (i.e., the re-scheduled traversal path will offer no advantage over the original path, as depicted in Fig. 6.27(1)).

Considering the three arguments mentioned earlier, we conclude that re-planning the traversal order is unnecessary. As a result, no further changes to the traversal order are made.

6.2.2.5 Tangential Point Determination Method

Although the ESP algorithm faces significant computational overhead due to the difficulty in determining the tangential point from the edge function e and the ellipse equation using the Ferrari method [24], we address this complexity by introducing a

[1] The greedy algorithm aims to determine an optimal charging point c^* for the current condition in each greedy iteration. Thus, C_i' obtained after multiple iterations represents the set of charging points rather than merely grids. If we compute the optimal charging point in one grid only, while other points are predetermined, the ESP algorithm will clearly find the optimal solution. Therefore, the ESP algorithm does not introduce errors when used to identify the charging point in a single grid within Algorithm 1.

method for determining tangential points. For each edge, we choose the endpoint that can generate a smaller ellipse. If additional intersections exist on edge e, we compute the tangent point; otherwise, no tangent point is identified.

The **tangential point determination method** is composed of the following two rules:

- As depicted in Fig. 6.28, when e represents a line segment or an arc, and both focal points of the ellipse lie outside of the associated circle, a point ep' will be taken near ep on e. The proximity between ep' and ep must be very small, after which it will be assessed if ep' is within the ellipse. If it is, we will determine a tangential point v_i' as the optimal choice. Otherwise, ep will be chosen.
- As illustrated in Fig. 6.29, when either focal point v_{i-1} or v_{i+1} of the ellipse falls inside the circle to which the arc e pertains, we first determine the intersection points using the ellipse's equation and the function defining edge e. If there is only a single intersection point ep, it will be selected as the optimal point. For cases where there are multiple intersection points, the tangential point will be identified as the best option. Figure 6.29 demonstrates a scenario with four intersection points.

According to the outlined rules, only line segments and arcs are considered. Nevertheless, obstacles can lead to numerous irregular closed curves (illustrated as red curves in Fig. 6.26). Thus, we consider an irregular closed curve equivalent to a circle, making the rules applicable.

6.2.2.6 Quadratic Path Optimization

By employing the aforementioned methods, we can minimize the path error. Additionally, to mitigate the error caused by the greedy approach, a **quadratic path optimisation (QPO)** method has been developed.

To demonstrate our quadratic path optimization method, we begin by defining the concept of region C_f. As depicted in Figs. 6.26 and 6.30, C_f, where $f = 1, 2, 3, \ldots$, represents multiple equivalent regions possessing the same discrete power achieved prior to grid discretization. Corresponding to each grid region g_i, there exists a region C_f. This leads us to Lemma 1 effortlessly.

Lemma 6.2 *At most one sub-region g_i in the region C_f can be selected by RAG algorithm, and C_f corresponds to g_i.*

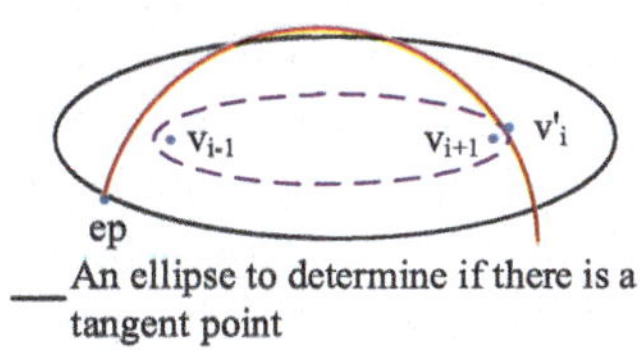

Fig. 6.29 Case 2: any point of the elliptic focus v_{i-1} or v_{i+1} is inside the circle corresponding to the arc

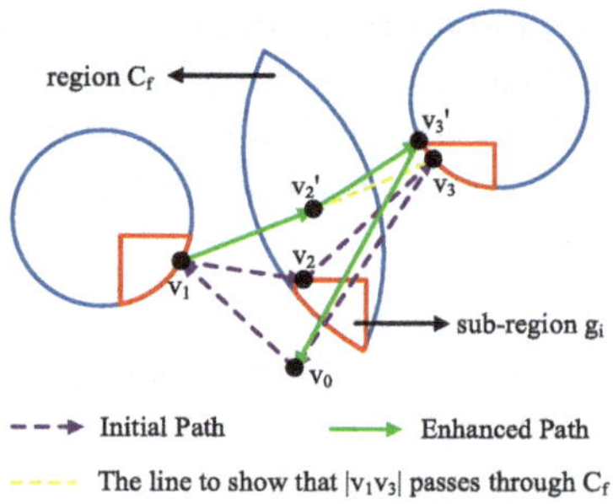

Fig. 6.30 An example of Quadratic Path Optimization (QPO)

Proof Assume that the sub-region g_i within C_f is chosen using Algorithm 23. If g_i is chosen again in a subsequent step, implying that the MC remains stationary and continues charging there, then no travel cost will be incurred. If a different sub-region in C_f is chosen, the additional travel cost will be positive, while the charging utility will be the same as in g_i. Thus, by applying the greedy strategy outlined in Sect. 6.2.2.3, Lemma 6.2 is validated. □

Based on Lemma 6.2, we introduce a **quadratic path optimization (QPO)** scheme to enhance path optimization further. Utilizing the ESP algorithm, we can optimize the charging spot locations within sub-region g_i. Subsequently, after acquiring the charging spot set C' using the RAG algorithm, the ESP algorithm is applied again for a secondary optimization over region C_f (i.e., the ESP algorithm is executed with C_f as input instead of the initial input g_i). This approach minimizes the error caused by the greedy strategy. The reason is that the greedy approach (i.e., the RAG algorithm) focuses on points within the grids (i.e., sub-region g_i), whereas the QPO scheme;s optimization considers points beyond these constraints (i.e., region C_f), thus reducing the error from the greedy approach. Unlike the path optimization procedure in Sect. 6.2.2.4 (i.e., ESP), this optimization strategy is implemented only in the final iteration. Figure 6.30 illustrates an example of QPO, showing the search for optimal points (e.g., v_2') within region C_f, significantly reducing the path length.

6.2.3 *Theoretical Analysis*

For ease of our analysis, we represent the function $U(C', y)$ for any specific y on the set C' as $U(C')$ when it does not cause ambiguity. It is crucial to recognize that modifications in C' lead to alterations in the sensors charged by the MC and the total charging energy $U_{tot}(C')$, thereby the sample variable y cannot stay the same. If we consider the sample variable y to signify the total successful sending rate s_{tot}, then $U(C') = s_{tot}U_{tot}(C')$. As the constant coefficient s_{tot} does not influence the characteristics of $U(C')$, we exclude s_{tot} in our subsequent analysis, thus $U(C') = U_{tot}(C')$.

6.2.3.1 Discrete Approximation Analysis

Lemma 6.3 *Suppose a charging spot is selected at random, with its practical charging power represented as $P(d)$, and the Fresnel diffraction coefficient for this spot is denoted as F_d. Let*

$$l(0) = 0, \quad l(R) = \sqrt{\frac{\alpha_c F_d}{P_{\min}}} - \beta_c,$$

$$l(k) = \beta_c \left((1+\epsilon')^{\frac{k}{2}} \sqrt{F_d} - 1 \right) \quad \textit{for } k = 1, 2, \ldots, R-1.$$

Using the discrete strategy and the definition of piecewise constant function, the approximate error of power discretization can be given as

$$1 \le \frac{P(d)}{\tilde{P}(d)} \le 1 + \epsilon'.$$

Proof When $d = l(0) = 0$, we have

$$\frac{P(d)}{\tilde{P}(d)} = \frac{P(0)}{P(l(1))} = \frac{\alpha_c / \beta_c^2}{\alpha_c F_d / \beta_c^2 F_d (1+\epsilon')} = 1 + \epsilon'.$$

For $l(r-1) < d \le l(r)$, we get

$$\frac{P(d)}{\tilde{P}(d)} = \frac{P(d)}{P(l(r))} \le \frac{P(l(r-1))}{P(l(r))} = \frac{\frac{\alpha_c F_d}{\beta_c^2 F_d^{l(r-1)} (1+\epsilon')^{r-1}}}{\frac{\alpha_c F_d}{\beta_c^2 F_d (1+\epsilon')^r}} = 1 + \epsilon',$$

$$\frac{P(d)}{\tilde{P}(d)} = \frac{P(d)}{P(l(r))} \ge 1.$$

When $d > l(R)$, we have $P(d) = \tilde{P}(d) = 0$. Hence, Lemma 6.3 is proved. □

Theorem 6.4 *Let $\epsilon = \frac{2\epsilon'}{1+\epsilon'}$. The optimal value H after discretization has an approximation ratio of $1 - \frac{\epsilon}{2}$ compared with the optimal value H^* of problem P1.*

Proof Let U represent the optimal charging utility post discretization of charging power, U^* signify the optimal charging utility of problem P1, $C_1'^*$ be the original problem's optimal solution, and $C_2'^*$ be the optimal solution following the discretization of charging power. With the discretization, the original problem can be reformulated as $\max U(C') = \sum_{n=1}^{N} U(s_n) = \sum_{n=1}^{N} \sum_{c_j \in C'} \tilde{P}_n(d) t_j$, subject to

$$\mu R(C') + \rho \sum_{c_j \in C'} t_j \le B.$$

By Lemma 6.3, $\tilde{P}_n(d) \geq \frac{1}{1+\epsilon} P_n(d)$, and thus, we have $U = \sum_{n=1}^{N} \sum_{c_j \in C'^*_2} \tilde{P}_n(d) t_j \geq \sum_{n=1}^{N} \sum_{c_j \in C'^*_1} \tilde{P}_n(d) t_j \geq \sum_{n=1}^{N} \sum_{c_j \in C'^*_1} \frac{1}{1+\epsilon'} P_n(d) t_j \geq \frac{1}{1+\epsilon'} \sum_{n=1}^{N} \sum_{c_j \in C'^*_1} P_n(d) t_j = \frac{1}{1+\epsilon'} U^*$.

Keep in mind that C'^*_1 and C'^*_2 may not be connected, so Theorem 6.4 cannot be directly established using Lemma 6.3 and summation properties. Therefore, proving the above equation is required.

Therefore, when $\epsilon = \frac{2\epsilon'}{1+\epsilon'}$, the approximate rate of $1 - \frac{\epsilon}{2}$ can be obtained, namely

$$U \geq \left(1 - \frac{\epsilon}{2}\right) U^*.$$

Then, we have $H = \tau - \frac{1}{\alpha} \mathrm{E}[\max(\tau - U, 0)] \geq \tau - \frac{1}{\alpha} \mathrm{E}\left[\max\left(\tau - \left(1 - \frac{\epsilon}{2}\right) U^*, 0\right)\right] \geq \left(1 - \frac{\epsilon}{2}\right) \left[\tau - \frac{1}{\alpha} \mathrm{E}\left[\max\left(\tau - U^*, 0\right)\right]\right] = \left(1 - \frac{\epsilon}{2}\right) H^*$. □

6.2.3.2 Submodular Function Analysis

Definition 6.2 (Normalization, Monotonicity, and Submodularity) Given a non-empty finite set V, for the set function $f : 2^V \rightarrow \mathbb{R}_+$, we have the following rules:

- If $f(\emptyset) = 0$, the function f is normalized.
- f is called a monotone function if $f(S) \leq f(T)$ for all $S \subseteq T \subseteq V$.
- If $f(S \cup \{e\}) - f(S) \geq f(T \cup \{e\}) - f(T)$ for all $S \subseteq T \subseteq V, e \in V \setminus T$, the function f is submodular.

Lemma 6.4 *The utility function $U(C', y)$ on the set C' is a normalized, monotone, and submodular function for arbitrary y.*

Proof Based on the definition of the function, $U(\emptyset) = 0$, which means that $U(C')$ acts as the normalized function. For any $C'' \subseteq C' \subseteq C$, we get

$$U(C'') = \sum_{n=1}^{N} U_{C''}(s_n) \leq \sum_{n=1}^{N} U_{C'}(s_n) = U(C').$$

Therefore, $U(C')$ is a monotonically increasing function.

Our next step is to demonstrate the submodularity of $U(C')$. Given that $U(C')$ represents the aggregate utility of N sensors, it suffices to show that for each sensor s_n within the range $1 \leq n \leq N$.

$$U(C'' \cup \{c\})(s_n) - U(C'')(s_n) \geq U(C' \cup \{c\})(s_n) - U(C')(s_n).$$

Considering the utility threshold U_n^{th} for each sensor, we derive:

$$U(C')(s_n) = \min\left\{u(C')(s_n), U_n^{th}\right\}.$$

According to Lemma 6.4, we get Theorem 6.5. □

Theorem 6.5 *The auxiliary function $H(C', \tau)$ is monotone, submodular, but not necessarily normalized on set C' for any given τ.*

Proof Based on Lemma 6.4, the function $U(C', y)$ is characterized as normalized, monotone, and submodular. Following [17], if $U(C', y)$ maintains these properties on the set C' for any y, then the auxiliary function $H(C', \tau)$ will also be monotone and submodular, although it may not be normalized on C' for any given τ. Consequently, Theorem 6.5 is established. The detailed proof is omitted here for brevity. □

The characteristics of $H(C', \tau)$ allow for additional approximation ratio analysis of the algorithm in subsequent sections.

6.2.3.3 Computational and Memory Complexity

Theorem 6.6 *The computational complexity of the RAG algorithm is $(O\left(\left\lceil\frac{\Gamma}{\sigma}\right\rceil N^3 \epsilon^{-2}\left(n_y + \mathcal{R}\right)\right))$, where $\mathcal{R}$ is the total number of grids.*

Proof First, to search for the optimal value of τ, the RAG algorithm carries out $\left\lceil\frac{\Gamma}{\sigma}\right\rceil$ cycles. In each cycle, we ensure a pair (C_i', τ_i) to select the optimal τ_i and corresponding C_i'. Then, our algorithm is carried out for at most $O(N)$ iterations, and in each iteration an element c^* is added to the optimal set C_i'. The number of elements in C_i' will not exceed N. This is because only when a sensor in the charging range of the MC is fully charged, the MC will try to find the next c^* by adopting the GCPS algorithm [25]. In other words, when the MC is locating at any charging spot in C_i', it will fully charge at least one node (i.e., $|C_i'| \leq N$).

To determine the value of c^*, we need to calculate ΔH and ΔF of each unselected charging spot c separately.

For ΔH, the RAG algorithm needs to calculate the utility increment for $O(N^2\epsilon^{-2})$ (number of region C_f) regions. This is because different sub-regions g_i in the same region C_f have the same value of ΔH. Hence, we calculate ΔH based on region C_f instead of g_i. To obtain $E[\max\{\tau - U, 0\}]$, we need to calculate n_y sample values of $U(C', y)$ on average. Therefore, calculating ΔH has a time complexity of $O(N^2\epsilon^{-2}n_y)$. For ΔF, the RAG algorithm needs to calculate the energy cost increment for $M = O(\mathcal{R}N^2\epsilon^{-2})$ regions, because different regions of

g_i have different values of ΔF. Therefore, the overall computational complexity of the RAG algorithm is

$$O\left(\left\lceil\frac{\Gamma}{\sigma}\right\rceil N\left(N^2\epsilon^{-2}n_y + \mathcal{R}N^2\epsilon^{-2}\right)\right) = O\left(\left\lceil\frac{\Gamma}{\sigma}\right\rceil N^3\epsilon^{-2}\left(n_y + \mathcal{R}\right)\right).$$

□

Theorem 6.7 *The memory complexity of the RAG algorithm is* $O(N(\mathcal{R}N\epsilon^{-2} + \lceil\frac{\Gamma}{\sigma}\rceil + 1))$, *where* $\mathcal{R}$ *is the total number of grids.*

Proof The RAG algorithm we're proposing is a straightforward iterative process. During each iteration, four variables are tracked: Δ_H^c, Δ_F^c, the highest Δ_H^c/Δ_F^c, and the associated c. Only these four variables need to be updated in every iteration. Consequently, the iteration procedure itself requires $O(1)$ memory. It's essential to examine the sizes of the lists that log different details throughout the RAG algorithm's execution. Typically, three major steps need to be considered concerning memory complexity.

(1) The total count of regions following spatial discretization is $O(\mathcal{R}N^2\epsilon^{-2})$. Consequently, we must reserve $O(\mathcal{R}N^2\epsilon^{-2})$ space for C to store all regional data.
(2) We need to allocate space for recording $\lceil\frac{\Gamma}{\sigma}\rceil$ C_i'. As proved in Theorem 6.6, we have $|C_i'| < N$. Therefore, we need $O(N\lceil\frac{\Gamma}{\sigma}\rceil)$ memory space.
(3) We need N space to record the information of all sensor nodes.

Therefore, the overall memory complexity of the RAG algorithm is

$$O(\mathcal{R}N^2\epsilon^{-2} + N\left\lceil\frac{\Gamma}{\sigma}\right\rceil + N) = O(N(\mathcal{R}N\epsilon^{-2} + \left\lceil\frac{\Gamma}{\sigma}\right\rceil + 1)).$$

□

It is important to mention that the RAG algorithm operates offline, with the base station performing its tasks before the mobile charger attends to the nodes. Based on our simulation findings, when the sensor node count is $N = 50$, a typical computer (CPU: i7-9700, GPU: GTX 1660, memory: 8G) can calculate the algorithm in a matter of minutes. This duration is minimal compared to the sensor's operational period (several days). Furthermore, the RAG algorithm's memory usage is merely about 1MB, which is very low. Consequently, the RAG algorithm is suitable for large-scale systems.

6.2.4 Simulation and Experiments

6.2.4.1 Experimental Setup

As illustrated in Fig. 6.32, a mobile robot equipped with Powercast's TX91501 wireless charger (Powercast, http://www.powercastco.com) is employed as an MC, boasting an energy capacity of $B = 50\,\text{J}$. Since the Tx91501 is a directional charger, it continuously rotates its charging direction to emulate an omnidirectional charger. The MC incurs a traveling cost rate of $v = 0.1\,\text{J/m}$ and a charging cost rate of $\rho = 0.4\,\text{J/s}$. Eleven rechargeable smoke sensors, each with a battery capacity of 5 J, are placed within the building depicted in Fig. 6.31 to detect fire. Concurrently, various obstacles with different shapes are situated in this area. Each node's packet loss rate is gauged in the challenging environment. The information regarding their positions and packet loss rates is: A : $(14, -3)$, 0.52; B : $(13, -2)$, 0.48; C : $(13, -4)$, 0.49; D : $(11, -2)$, 0.45; E : $(0, -2)$, 0.05; F : $(-4.5, -2)$, 0.24; G : $(-4.5, -4)$, 0.26; H : $(5.5, 1)$, 0.02; I : $(-3, -8)$, 0.51; J : $(6, -8)$, 0.56; K : $(13, -8)$, 0.59. The base station is located at $(0, 0)$.

In order to simulate fire monitoring scenarios, we introduce a substantial amount of smoke at the coordinates $(4, -3)$. The smoke will quickly disperse throughout the area, allowing all sensors to detect it. Subsequently, we assess the reliability of each method to evaluate the features of our approach (Fig. 6.32).

We then provide detailed descriptions of the implementation of our experiments, covering the algorithm execution platform, mobile robot setups, power measurement methods, navigation approaches, obstacle avoidance techniques, and movement strategies for the robots.

To emulate fire surveillance scenarios, we introduce a substantial quantity of smoke at the coordinates $(4, -3)$. The smoke disperses rapidly throughout the vicinity, enabling all sensors to detect it. Subsequently, we assess the reliability of each method to analyze the features of our approach.

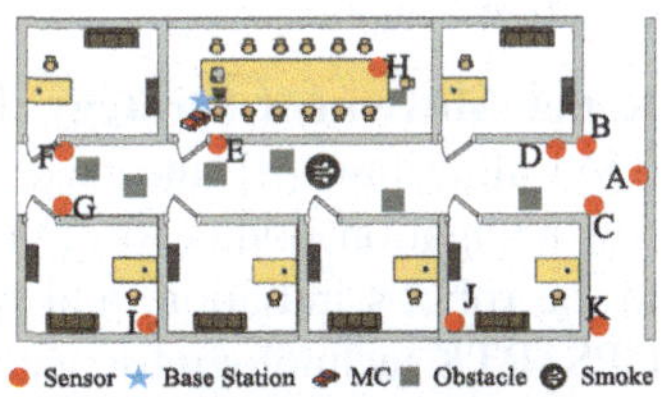

Fig. 6.31 A diagram of experiment scene

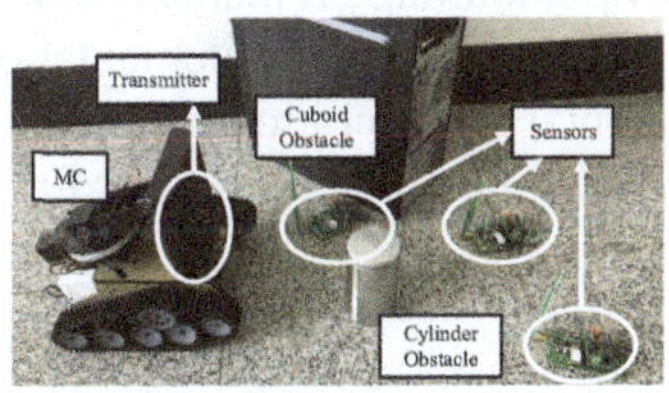

Fig. 6.32 Test-bed devices: an MC, several sensors, and various types of obstacles

Provided are the detailed implementation aspects of our experiments, concentrating on the platform for algorithm execution, configurations of mobile robots, techniques for power monitoring, methods of navigation, obstacle avoidance strategies, and the movement tactics of robots.

Algorithm Execution Platform The RAG algorithm is executed on a computer featuring an i7-9700 CPU, a GTX 1660 GPU, and 8GB of RAM. The algorithm finishes in just a few minutes, consuming around 1MB of memory, which ensures the platform meets both the computational and memory demands of the algorithm.

Mobile Robot Configurations The mobile robot operates using a quad-core ARM A57 CPU and is equipped with a 128-core NVIDIA Maxwell GPU, along with 4GB of 64-bit LPDDR4 memory (25.6 GB/s). As the RAG algorithm is executed on the PC at the base station, the robot's responsibilities are limited to fixed-point navigation and automatic obstacle avoidance, both of which are easily managed by its microprocessor.

Power Monitoring Technology An ADC circuit is employed for digital-to-analogue conversion to continuously observe the voltage at the sensor node's battery end, thereby assessing the remaining energy from the voltage readings. Nonetheless, the CC2530 sensor chip introduces an error margin of approximately 7.5%, and future enhancements might involve substituting this chip to minimize the error.

Navigation Technology The mobile robot navigates using GPS integrated with RTK (Real-Time Kinematic) technology. GPS by itself has considerable positioning inaccuracies, but RTK carrier phase differential technology enhances precision to the centimetre level. This is accomplished by setting up an RTK base station at a stationary location and utilizing the real-time differential data between the base station and the robot.

Obstacle Avoidance Technology The mobile robot navigates around obstacles by utilizing infrared sensors. Upon detecting an obstacle within the sensor's proximity, the robot discerns its path utilizing the reflected infrared light, thereby facilitating effective evasion.

Robot Movement Strategy By implementing the RAG and obstacle avoidance (OA) algorithm [9], the base station establishes a sequence of loading locations and navigation points to circumvent obstacles. These paths are designated prior to the robot's initiation, and infrared sensors additionally secure safety. Utilizing GPS+RTK technology for accurate waypoint localization, the robot traverses point-to-point along preplanned routes.

The provided implementation specifics offer a thorough summary of the experimental configuration, guaranteeing that every component is cohesively integrated to assess the efficiency of our fire monitoring system.

6.2.4.2 Baseline Setup

As there are no prior studies examining the influence of both risk aversion and obstacles on charging utility in a WRSN, we compare several well-known and comparable algorithms: the greedy algorithm (GA), the Charging Utility Maximization with Obstacles (NICE) algorithm [9], the Obstacle Boundary Partitioning (OBP) algorithm [26], and the random algorithm (RAN).

GA is essentially equivalent to the RAG, but it does not incorporate the risk-averse model. GA substitutes $H(C', \tau)$ in RAG with $U_{tot}(C')$ and eliminates the iterative process of finding the value of τ in the RAG algorithm. Therefore, the GA algorithm is designed for a system without failures (i.e., no packet loss).

In our earlier research, the NICE algorithm [9] aims to optimize loading utility when obstacles are present. Nonetheless, it lacks a risk-averse feature, and its discretisation and path planning methods can still be improved.

The concept of OBP involves segmenting the entire region into areas where power remains constant and areas where power is zero, defined by the boundaries of obstacles, as outlined in [26]. The positions for loading that are not obstructed are chosen at random by RAN.

6.2.4.3 Experimental Results

Initially, we examine the risk-averse utility among the theoretical, simulation, and experimental outcomes depicted in Fig. 6.33, taking into account various capacities of the MC's rechargeable battery. The theoretical analysis neglects the energy expenditure due to the MC's rotation, resulting in a 4.9–5.4% discrepancy between

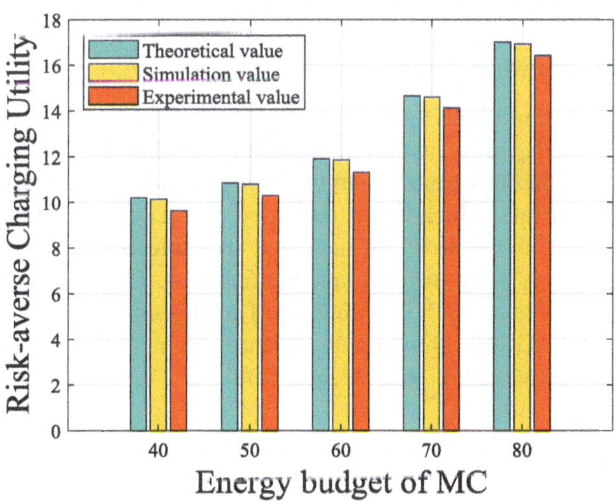

Fig. 6.33 Comparison of theoretical, simulation, and experimental results

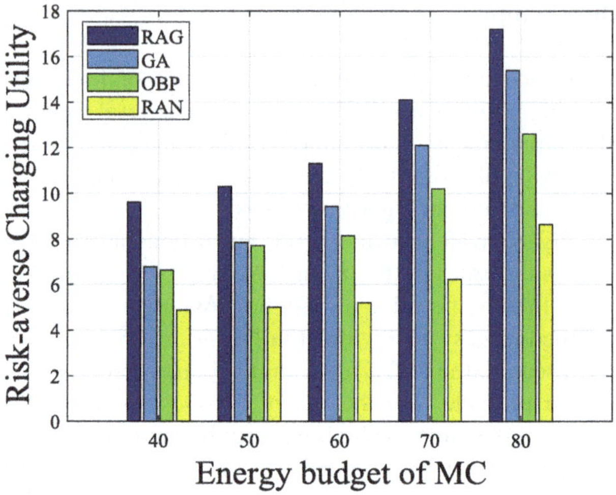

Fig. 6.34 Risk-averse charging utility vs. Energy budget of MC

the theoretical and simulation/experimental outcomes. Nonetheless, the simulation and experimental findings closely match the theoretical predictions, verifying that the proposed method is practical for real-world implementation (Fig. 6.34).

Subsequently, we assign $\alpha = 0.4$ and assess the efficiency of four different algorithms across various energy budgets allocated for the MC. Our RAG algorithm uniformly surpasses the performance of the other algorithms. The main reasons for this are:

1. GA lacks risk-averse measures.
2. NICE does not have an effective discretization scheme or efficient path planning method.
3. OBP is inefficient when dealing with obstacles.

The RAG algorithm outperforms the other algorithms by a minimum of 21.3% in terms of risk-averse utility, within the budget interval of 40–80 J.

We also assess the network's reliability across various algorithms, specifically examining the error rate, which is the likelihood of not detecting a fire once smoke has fully dispersed in the area. As indicated in Table 6.1, with $B = 50$ J, the system's error rate is 5.5% when implementing GA. Conversely, the error rate reduces dramatically to just 0.01% with RAG. This demonstrates that the substantial robustness of the RAG algorithm greatly enhances the network's reliability through thorough testing (Figs. 6.35, 6.36, 6.37, and 6.38).

Table 6.1 Comparison between RAG algorithm, GA, NICE, OBP and RAN in the error rate of the system

	$B = 40\,\mathrm{J}$	$B = 50\,\mathrm{J}$	$B = 60\,\mathrm{J}$	$B = 70\,\mathrm{J}$
RAN	11.4%	10.4%	9.7%	8.5%
OBP	8.4%	7.6%	7.4%	6.9%
NICE	7.1%	6.4%	6.1%	5.8%
GA	6.2%	5.5%	5.1%	4.8%
RAG	0.011%	0.01%	0.0098%	0.0092%

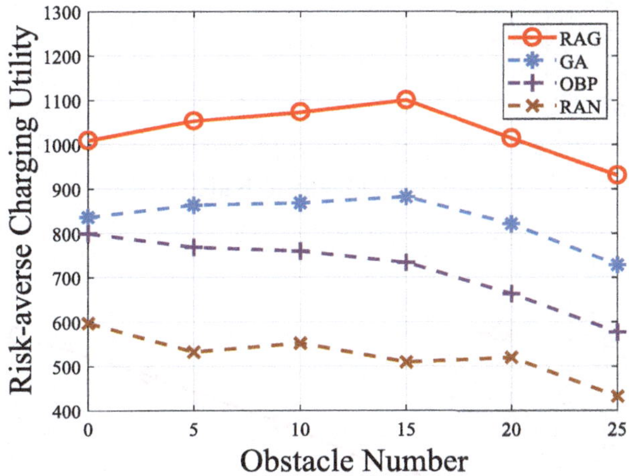

Fig. 6.35 Risk-averse charging utility vs. Obstacle number θ

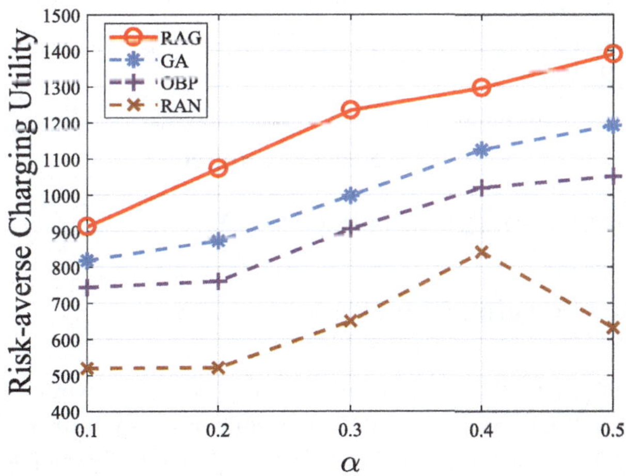

Fig. 6.36 Risk-averse charging utility vs. Risk-level α

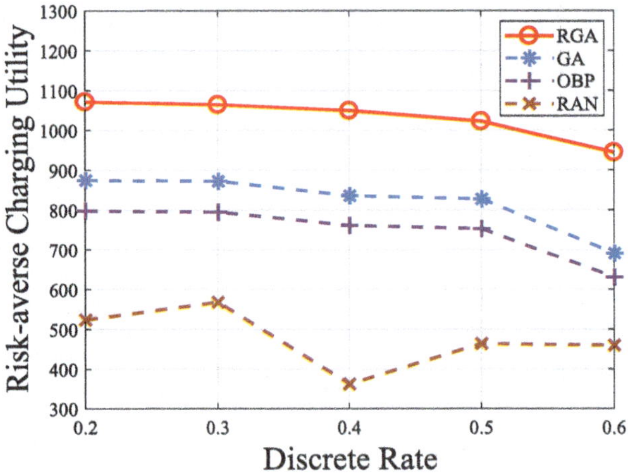

Fig. 6.37 Risk-averse charging utility vs. Discrete rate ϵ'

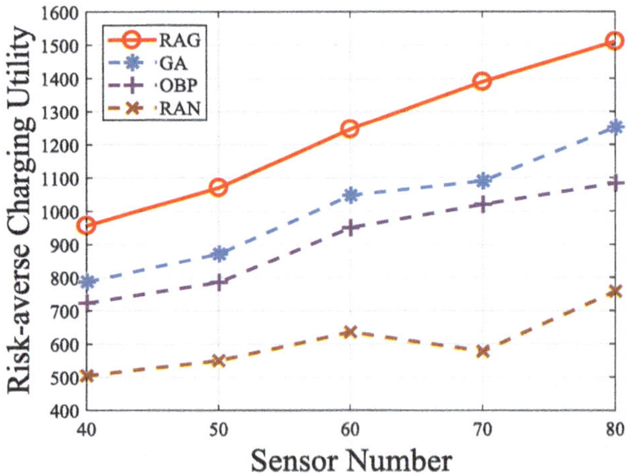

Fig. 6.38 Risk-averse charging utility vs. sensor number N

6.3 Precise Charging Model

To tackle the energy bottleneck in wireless sensor networks, wireless rechargeable sensor networks (WRSNs) have become a prominent research focus. Nevertheless, the use of inaccurate discretization methods and erroneous charging models creates a significant disparity between theoretical findings and practical applications, impeding widespread use. This section aims to develop an accurate charging approach to optimize charging utility in complex environments, including both line-of-sight (LOS) and non-line-of-sight (NLOS) scenarios. Initially, we create discretization techniques for the charging area and orientation to precisely build the charging model. To take into account signal propagation in the presence of obstacles, we introduce an innovative electromagnetic wave reflection model. We frame the mobile charging issue as a submodular function maximization problem, which our proposed algorithm can solve with an approximation guarantee. Lastly, extensive experiments and simulations show that our methods surpass comparative algorithms by an average of 31.45% regarding charging utility in complex environments.

6.3.1 Problem Statement

6.3.1.1 Network Model

Typically, within a complex environment, O static obstacles denoted by $O = \{o_1, o_2, \ldots, o_O\}$ are randomly placed on a 2-D plane Ω. In this region, a WRSN is employed to track events. The WRSN is comprised of three elements: a base station (BS), a mobile charger (MC), and several rechargeable sensors.

The BS is tasked with gathering data from sensors. Additionally, it can offer power services to the MC, including battery replacement and recharging.

An MC is employed to power sensors using WPT technology. It leverages a transmission antenna to deliver energy. The MC's energy storage is usually constrained, allowing it to cater to only a limited number of nodes. When its energy is depleted, it must return to the BS for recharging. We design a crawler track featuring a *two-rows M-elements half-wavelength dipole antenna array* as an MC. By modifying the number of elements in the antenna array, the MC can utilize either omnidirectional or directional antennas to power sensors.

N rechargeable sensors, denoted as $S = \{s_1, s_2, \ldots, s_N\}$, are positioned at fixed locations within a 2-dimensional plane Ω for the purpose of event monitoring. These sensors are equipped with omnidirectional antennas to receive energy from the MC. It is important to note that sensors must not be placed within obstructions and the MC is also unable to traverse through obstructions.

6.3.1.2 Charging Model

When MC is serving a sensor s_n at a charging spot p_i, according to the *Friis Transmission Formula* [27], the charging power can be expressed as

$$P(p_i, s_n) = \frac{P_T G_T G_R \lambda^2}{[4\pi d(p_i, s_n)]^2}. \tag{6.55}$$

In this context, $d(p_i, s_n)$ denotes the Euclidean distance between points p_i and s_n. The variable λ stands for the wavelength of electromagnetic radiation. P_T indicates the power output of the transmitting antenna. G_T and G_R signify the gains of the transmitting and receiving antennas, respectively.

Subsequently, to enhance the charging model, the transmitting antenna gain is described by [27] as

$$G_T = \varepsilon_T D(\Theta, \varphi), \tag{6.56}$$

with ε_T denoting the transmitting antenna efficiency and $D(\Theta, \varphi)$ indicating the directivity of the transmitting antenna, which can be formulated as

$$D(\Theta, \varphi) = \frac{4\pi F(\Theta, \varphi)^2}{\int_0^{2\pi} d\varphi \int_0^{\pi} F(\Theta, \varphi)^2 \sin\Theta d\Theta}. \tag{6.57}$$

In this context, $F(\Theta, \varphi)$ represents the direction function of the transmitting antenna. Since the sensors and the MC are positioned on the same horizontal plane in this study, the elevation angle is given by $\Theta = \frac{\pi}{2}$ [27] (which is the angle with the z-axis). Consequently, the direction function of the antenna array depends solely on the azimuth angle φ in the horizontal plane. Hence, we can simplify $D(\Theta, \varphi)$ and $F(\Theta, \varphi)$ to $D(\varphi)$ and $F(\varphi)$, respectively.

Based on [28], if the phase of the current in the first row is $\frac{\pi}{2}$ behind that of the second row, the directional function of our antenna (a two-row, M-element, half-wavelength dipole antenna array) can be represented as:

$$F(\varphi) = 2\cos[\frac{\pi}{4}(\cos\varphi - 1)] \prod_{i=1}^{\log M} 2\cos(2^{i-2}\sin\varphi). \tag{6.58}$$

The spacing between adjacent rows and antenna elements is determined as $\lambda/4$. Modifying the value of M will influence the antenna array's directivity (i.e., the extent of signal concentration, or the beam pattern's width). Assume there are $\mathcal{M}$ strategies for adjusting the antenna array; consequently, there will be $\mathcal{M}$ distinct directivities $D_m(\varphi)$ ($m \in \{1, 2, \ldots, \mathcal{M}\}$).

We then incorporate the signal diffraction effect into our model. Based on the WRSNs charging model from [2], the Fresnel diffraction model in [29], and Eq. (6.56), the charging power $P(p_i, s_n)$ can be reformulated as

$$P(c_i, s_n) = \begin{cases} \frac{\alpha F_d D_{m_i}(\varphi)}{[d(p_i, s_n)+\beta]^2}, & \frac{\alpha F_d D_{m_i}(\varphi)}{[d(p_i, s_n)+\beta]^2} \geq P_{min} \\ 0. & \frac{\alpha F_d D_{m_i}(\varphi)}{[d(p_i, s_n)+\beta]^2} < P_{min} \end{cases} \tag{6.59}$$

In this context, $c_i = \langle p_i, \theta_i, m_i \rangle$ represents a *charging strategy*. Here, p_i denotes the location of the charging spot, θ_i is the orientation angle of the mobile charger, and m_i indicates the antenna array adjustment strategy chosen at this time. Moreover, $\varphi = \arccos \frac{\overrightarrow{r_{\theta_i}} \cdot \overrightarrow{p_i s_n}}{d(p_i, s_n)}$ defines the azimuth angle of the sensor relative to the mobile charger, where $\overrightarrow{r_{\theta_i}}$ is a unit vector at angle θ_i.

Parameters α and β are constants determined by the environmental conditions [2]. The Fresnel diffraction coefficient F_d [29] measures the effect of diffraction on the wireless charging signal when obstacles are present. P_{min} represents the minimum power that the MC needs to supply to charge the sensors effectively. If $P(c_i, s_n) < P_{min}$, the sensor receives negligible energy [30].

In the many-to-one charging framework,[2] as noted in [30], the charger is capable of delivering energy to several sensors at once without significantly diminishing the power each sensor receives. We define the time dedicated to charging strategy c_i as t_i, and therefore, the total energy (or utility) received by sensor s_n can be described by:

$$\text{Utility} = \sum_i t_i P(c_i, s_n)$$

This model successfully represents the charging dynamics in environments containing multiple sensors and obstructions, guaranteeing efficient energy transfer by taking environmental factors into account.

$$u_{C'}(s_n) = \sum_{c_i \in C'} P(c_i, s_n) t_l, \tag{6.60}$$

where C' is the set of selected charging strategies.

A sensor typically stores energy in a battery or supercapacitor, thus its capacity E^c is finite. Prior to recharging by MC, sensor s_n must retain a specific amount of residual energy E_n^r for continued operation. Next, we concentrate on the amount of energy sensors can obtain from MC. We define $U_n^{th} = E^c - E_n^r$ as the utmost energy a sensor can receive. If the amount of incoming energy surpasses this limit, the excess energy (i.e., $u'_C(s_n) - U_n^{th}$) will be lost. Consequently, the effective energy/utility acquired by sensor s_n is expressed as

$$U_{C'}(s_n) = \min\left\{u_{C'}(s_n), U_n^{th}\right\}. \tag{6.61}$$

Afterward, the overall charging utility of the whole network can be expressed as

$$U\left(C'\right) = \sum_{n=1}^{N} U_{C'}(s_n). \tag{6.62}$$

In this section, we address the energy expenditure of the MC, which generally comprises two components: travel cost and charging cost. The travel cost pertains to the energy used while navigating the WRSN for recharging the sensors. We represent the path length as $R\left(C'\right)$ and the energy cost per unit distance as ν. Consequently, the travel cost is calculated as $\nu R\left(C'\right)$. The charging cost can be

[2] The many-to-one charging framework has been extensively researched in [29–34] and finds its use in various application domains.

denoted by $P_T \sum_{c_i \in C'} t_i$, with P_T representing the power output of the transmitting antenna.

Hence, the total energy expenditure for MC can be represented as

$$F\left(C'\right) = \nu R\left(C'\right) + P_T \sum_{c_i \in C'} t_i. \tag{6.63}$$

6.3.1.3 Problem Formalization

In this paper, we address a mobile recharging issue in which a MC visits each recharging point sequentially to recharge sensors, ensuring their continuous operation. The MC has a restricted energy capacity/budget B, necessitating a return to the BS for refueling before depletion. Accordingly, the following routing constraint must be met:

$$\nu R(C') + P_T \sum_{p_i \in C'} t_i \leq B. \tag{6.64}$$

Our problem here is: *In a complex environment with obstacles placed randomly, our challenge is to identify optimal charging strategies and durations that will enhance the charging utility of the entire network, taking into account both LOS and NLOS scenarios.* We describe this Directional chArging uTility mAximisation (DATA) problem in complex environments as follows:

$$\begin{aligned} &\textbf{(DATA)} \quad max \quad U(C'), \\ &s.t. \;\; \nu R(C') + P_T \sum_{p_i \in C'} t_i \leq B. \end{aligned} \tag{6.65}$$

Within the DATA issue, it has been demonstrated that the utility maximization problem is a sophisticated variant of the *set cover problem* as discussed in [31], which is categorized as NP-hard. Moreover, when routing limitations are taken into account, determining the shortest Hamiltonian cycle is required. This bears resemblance to the famous Traveling Salesman Problem (TSP), which is likewise NP-hard.

To sum up, the DATA problem is classified as an NP-hard problem, which poses a considerable difficulty.

6.3.2 Schematic Design

In this part, we tackle the errors in discretization and the inaccurate charging model by presenting two discretization methods that turn the charging area and

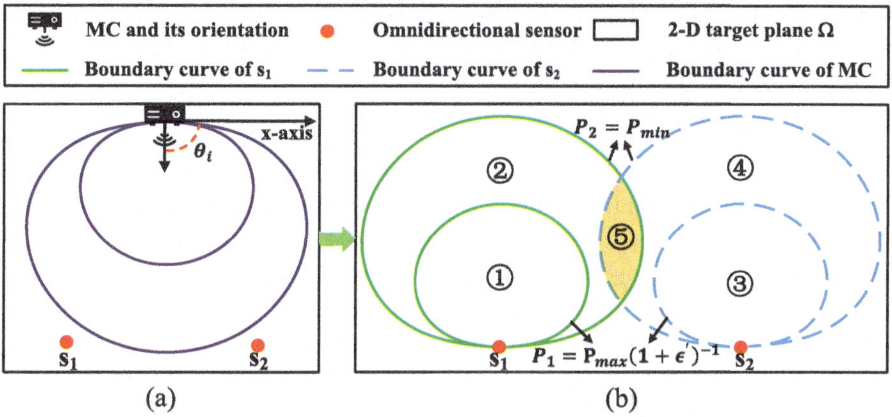

Fig. 6.39 An example of area discretization

orientation angle from infinite to finite. Furthermore, we create an electromagnetic wave reflection model applicable for both LOS and NLOS charging scenarios to enhance wireless charging in intricate environments. Lastly, we introduce a near-optimal greedy scheduling algorithm to address the DATA issue.

6.3.2.1 Area Discretization

Given that the region Ω for the MC is both continuous and unbounded, our main objective is to divide this region into a finite series of sub-regions. Contrary to conventional studies that emphasize discretizing areas for signal transmitters (refer to Fig. 6.39a for the MC), our attention is on discretizing regions for receivers (i.e., sensors), illustrated in Fig. 6.39b.

Our discretization approach relies on treating charging spots with akin power levels as if they have the same power. Hence, the entire charging zone can be subdivided into a limited number of sub-areas. Subsequently, we calculate the suitable discretized power for each sub-area using the following formula:

$$P_k = \begin{cases} P_{max}(1+\epsilon')^{-k}, & 1 \le k < K \\ P_{min}. & k = K \end{cases} \tag{6.66}$$

ϵ' is the discretized threshold, representing the gap between neighboring discretized power levels. P_{max} is the maximum charging power, calculated as $P_{max} = \frac{\alpha D_{m_i}(\varphi) F_d}{(d(p_i, s_n)+\beta)^2}$. P_{max} is obtained when three conditions are satisfied: (1) the distance between the MC and sensor s_n is $d(p_i, s_n) = 0$, (2) the azimuth angle $\varphi = 0$, i.e., the maximum radiation direction, and (3) $F_d = 1$ for Eq. (6.59). $K = \lceil \frac{\ln(P_{max}/P_{min})}{\ln(1+\epsilon')} \rceil$

represents the number of discretized power values. After determining K discretized power values and P_{max}, we assign the discretized power P_k for each region.

Whenever the charging power of a spot satisfies $P_k \leq P(p_i, s_n) < P_{k-1}(P_0 = P_{max})$, its charging power can be approximated as P_k. Using this method, all charging spots with the same discretized power can be aggregated into the same sub-region. As shown in Fig. 6.39b, the discretization results for two sensors s_1 and s_2 are depicted, with five sub-regions marked ① ~ ⑤ constructed. We select three representative areas ①, ④, and ⑤ to calculate their discretized power: $P(①) = P_1 = P_{max}(1+\epsilon')^{-1}$, $P(④) = P_2 = P_{min}$, and $P(⑤) = 2P_2 = 2P_{min}$.

In the process of area discretization, another objective is to determine the boundaries of discretization for each node. In this study, the points on the *boundary curve* (contour) meet the condition

$$P(p_i, s_n) = \frac{\alpha F_d D_{m_i}(\varphi)}{[d(p_i, s_n) + \beta]^2} = P_k. \tag{6.67}$$

Upon creating the boundary contours (as shown in Eq. (6.67)) for all sensors, we can derive all sub-regions for MC. Within each sub-region, the charging position can be identified based on the method described in [32]. Next, we examine the characteristics of the suggested discretization approach.

Theorem 6.8 *Let* $\epsilon = \frac{\epsilon'}{1+\epsilon'}$*; thus, the ratio of the approximated optimal charging utility* U^* *post area discretization to the globally optimal utility* U^{OPT} *is* $1-\epsilon$.

Proof This proof follows the same methodology as those presented in [29] and [35]; therefore, we will not include the details here to conserve space. □

6.3.2.2 Orientation Angle Discretization

As indicated by Eq. (6.67), even a minor alteration in the azimuth angle φ of the MC (an angle represented by the orientation angle θ_i) will lead to considerable changes in the boundary curves, potentially affecting the area discretization outcome. Figure 6.40a–d illustrates this with orientations θ_i^1 to θ_i^3 of the MC. When the MC's orientation shifts from θ_i^1 to θ_i^3, the boundary curves of all nodes are modified accordingly.

Hence, for precise wireless charging, it is essential to account for orientation discretization. Nonetheless, like area discretization, the possible orientation angles of the MC are continuous and unlimited. To tackle this, we propose a new scheme for discretizing orientation angles.

To discretize the orientation angles, we start by scanning all possible angles for the MC to determine the number of sub-regions and calculate the charge for each region. Next, to minimize the search space, the angles are merged. When two

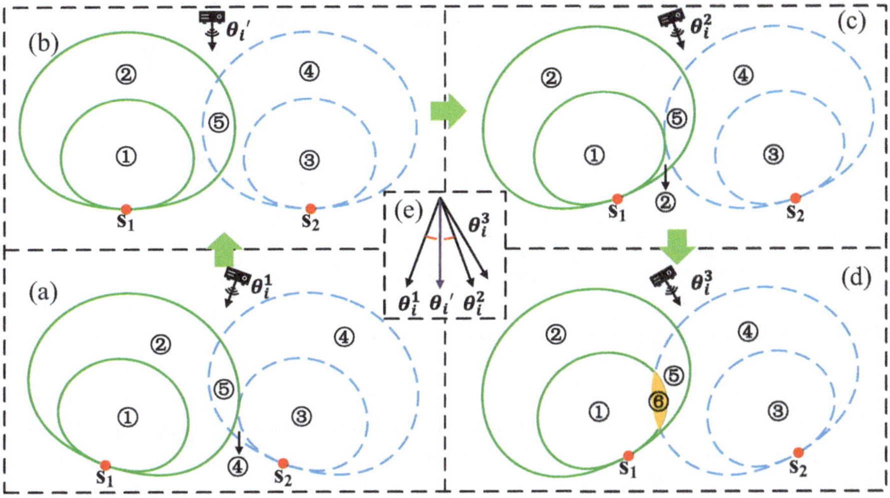

Fig. 6.40 An example of orientation angle discretization

distinct orientation angles (e.g., θ_i^1 and θ_i^2) exhibit the same sub-region counts and power for each sub-region, they can be combined.

As depicted in Fig. 6.40, an illustration demonstrates the merging of two angles. We begin with an arbitrary orientation angle for the MC, such as θ_i^1 in Fig. 6.40a, where five sub-regions ① ~ ⑤ are outlined. We then rotate the orientation angle to θ_i^2 in Fig. 6.40c, during which the five sub-regions consistently maintain the same power as in Fig. 6.40a. This implies that all angles within the range $[\theta_i^1, \theta_i^2]$ can be combined into a single angle. If we continue rotating to angle θ_i^3 in Fig. 6.40d, an additional region (i.e., ⑥ in yellow) emerges, resulting in a different number of sub-regions. Therefore, angle θ_i^3 cannot be merged into $[\theta_i^1, \theta_i^2]$.

Finding the values of θ_i^1 and θ_i^2 is simple. We look for all instances where more than two curves converge at a single point to ascertain the upper and lower limits of discrete intervals (e.g., θ_i^1 and θ_i^2 for $[\theta_i^1, \theta_i^2]$).

Ultimately, once all the upper and lower limits of the discrete intervals are established, we compute the mean value, i.e., $\theta_i' = (\theta_i^1 + \theta_i^2)/2$, as the discretized angle. This value will be utilized to substitute all angles within the range $[\theta_i^1, \theta_i^2]$.

A fundamental issue with discretizing orientation angles is illustrated in Fig. 6.40a–c. Even a minor alteration in the MC's orientation angle can lead to changes in the positions of sub-regions, thereby impacting the length of the MC's travel path [32].

An example is presented in Fig. 6.41a, where the previous and next charging spots of the MC are p and n. Here, the purple circle corresponds to region ① in Fig. 6.40b with a selected/discretized orientation angle θ_i'. Consequently, the charging spot s will be selected, forming a charging path $p \rightarrow s \rightarrow n$. However, suppose the MC selects angle θ_i^1 in Fig. 6.40a, creating the blue dotted sub-region

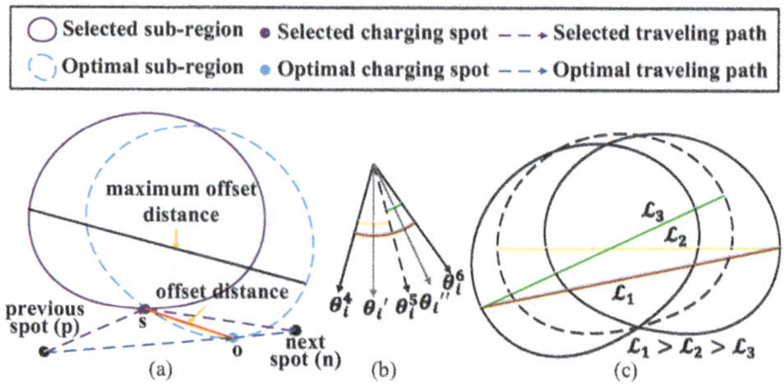

Fig. 6.41 A diagram of discretized angle interval restriction

(i.e., region ① in Fig. 6.40a), the corresponding charging spot and charging path will be o and $p \rightarrow o \rightarrow n$, respectively. Obviously, $p \rightarrow s \rightarrow n$ and $p \rightarrow o \rightarrow n$ have different lengths, indicating that different orientation angles will induce different paths, which may yield calculation errors in the path.

The deviation in path is associated with the *offset distance* (i.e., the separation between the chosen spot and the ideal spot) [32]. As illustrated in Fig. 6.41a, the chosen and ideal spots are indicated by s and o, respectively, and the offset distance is shown as the red line. Clearly, a greater offset leads to a larger error.

For analyzing the maximum path error, this offset value cannot be utilized directly. This is due to the fact that the value is derived under specific conditions when the previous and following points are known. Hence, to express the maximum path error induced by area and orientation angle discretization, given the unpredictability of the positions of the previous and subsequent spots, we define the *maximum offset distance* $\mathcal{L}$ (depicted as the black line in Fig. 6.41a). Regardless of the locations of the preceding and succeeding spots, the offset distance will never surpass this value. A greater maximum offset distance suggests a larger error and potentially results in increased travel costs.

The maximum offset distance relates to the relative rotation angle of the two sub-regions in Fig. 6.41a (i.e., the size of the discretized angle interval, e.g., $[\theta_i^1, \theta_i^2]$). Thus, if the discretized angle interval (e.g., $[\theta_i^1, \theta_i^2]$ in Fig. 6.40e) is set too large, the offset distance and error will also be large. Hence, a compulsory task is to limit the range of the orientation angle, which thus guarantees the charging performance bound (i.e., charging path error).

To limit the value range of the angle, we define a *maximum discretized angle interval threshold* θ^{max} to constrain and reduce the gap between the optimal charging spot and the selected one. By this means, we can bound the path error.

We present an example to demonstrate the necessity of setting an appropriate angle interval restriction in Fig. 6.41b–c. After orientation angle discretization, as shown in Fig. 6.41b, an angle interval $[\theta_i^4, \theta_i^6]$ with an included angle of $\frac{5\pi}{18}$ and an offset $\mathcal{L}_1$ is obtained.

Unexpectedly, by partitioning the angle interval $[\theta_i^4, \theta_i^6]$ into two segments, namely $[\theta_i^4, \theta_i^5]$ with an angle of $\frac{\pi}{6}$ (θ^{max}) and $[\theta_i^5, \theta_i^6]$ with $\frac{\pi}{9}$, two smaller offsets $\mathcal{L}_2$ and $\mathcal{L}_3$ are obtained (refer to Fig. 6.41c). This implies that the value of $\mathcal{L}$ (e.g., $\mathcal{L}_{max} = \mathcal{L}_2$) can be effectively constrained by suitably choosing the angle interval, thereby minimizing the path error.

Theorem 6.9 *The approximate path denoted as $R(C')$ using γ charging points adheres to the inequality $|R(C')| \leq |R^*(C')| + 2\gamma \mathcal{L}_{max}(\theta^{max})$, where $\mathcal{L}_{max}(\theta^{max})$ represents the highest deviation between the chosen charging point and the optimal charging point.*

Proof As illustrated in Fig. 6.41, even if the change in the MC's orientation angle alters the sub-region's location, the sub-region will remain within the maximum boundary curve (i.e., $P(p_i, s_n) = P_{min}$). Utilizing the Lagrange multiplier method [36], the value of $\mathcal{L}_{max}(\theta^{max})$ can be determined. Subsequently, this theorem can be demonstrated as per [32]. The detailed proofs are omitted to conserve space. □

The aforementioned techniques are capable of transforming the continuous charge area and the orientation angle from an infinite scope to a finite one, thereby addressing the issue of imprecise discretization.

Through a thorough investigation, we find that a potential problem that remains unaddressed by almost all previous literature is the *influence of reflection on electromagnetic waves caused by obstacles*. Henceforth, we embark on our initial effort to construct a model for the reflection of electromagnetic waves in complex settings.

6.3.2.3 Electromagnetic Wave Reflection Model

The phenomenon of signal reflection, previously overlooked in existing works, is prevalent in complex environments. To address this issue, we have developed a model for electromagnetic wave reflection.

- **Reflection Surface Determination.** Reflection primarily takes place when electromagnetic waves strike the surfaces of obstacles. In this context, we are focusing on the reflection on each individual surface (plane) of these obstacles. The challenge arises from the irregular and complex shapes of obstacles, which often comprise multiple surfaces, thereby increasing computational complexity. Consequently, it is essential to identify which surface(s) of the obstacle will influence wireless charging (Fig. 6.42).

  We put forward the concept of the *maximum effective charging area* (see examples in Fig. 6.42a) for sensor, which refers to an area that sensor can get replenished by reflection. The boundary curve of such an area can be obtained as

$$\frac{\alpha F_d D_{m_i}(0)}{[d(p_i, s_n) + \beta]^2} = P_{min}. \tag{6.68}$$

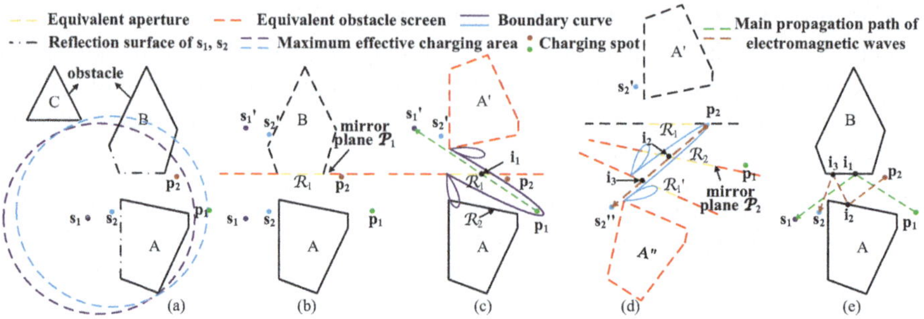

Fig. 6.42 A diagram for electromagnetic wave reflection model. (**a**) Reflection of electromagnetic waves between obstacles. (**b**) Mirror plane reflection. (**c**) Reflected obstacles. (**d**) Multiple reflections. (**e**) The propagation path of an electromagnetic wave reflected between two obstacles

If the source of the electromagnetic waves (i.e., MC) is positioned outside the designated area, the power received by sensor s_n will fall below P_{min} and can be disregarded. Likewise, the reflections of electromagnetic waves that occur outside this area can also be neglected. Therefore, we only need to consider the *reflective surface* of obstacles that are either fully or partially within this area. Figure 6.42a illustrates the reflective surfaces of obstacles A and B. In this context, solely these reflective surfaces are capable of reflecting signals; other surfaces have no impact on the charging process and are subsequently disregarded. We will focus on the initial reflection when identifying the reflection surface, deferring the discussion of multiple reflections for later.

- **Mirror Transformation Scheme.** To model the detailed reflection process, a *mirror transformation scheme* is proposed.

  The occurrence of signal reflections, frequently neglected in earlier studies, is prevalent in complex environments. To tackle this issue, we develop a model for electromagnetic wave reflection.

Reflection Surface Determination Reflection primarily happens when electromagnetic waves encounter obstacle surfaces. Our study centers on the reflection from each plane of obstacles. A major issue is that obstacles are typically irregular and comprised of numerous surfaces, resulting in high computational demands. Consequently, it's necessary to identify which surfaces of the obstacle will influence wireless charging.

We introduce the concept of the *maximum effective charging area* (see examples in Fig. 6.42a) for sensors, which denotes a region where the sensor can be recharged through reflection. The outline of this region can be derived as follows:

$$\frac{\alpha F_d D_{m_i}(0)}{[d(p_i, s_n) + \beta]^2} = P_{min}.$$

If the electromagnetic wave source (such as MC) is positioned outside this region, the sensor s_n will detect a power level lower than P_{min}, which can be disregarded. Likewise, electromagnetic waves reflected from outside this region can be overlooked. Hence, we should only consider the reflection surface of the obstacle that lies fully or partially within this area.

Figure 6.42a illustrates the reflective surfaces of obstacles A and B. Only surfaces capable of reflecting signals are taken into account; any other surfaces are disregarded as they do not influence the charging process. Initially, we will focus on charging a node through a single reflection to determine the reflection surface, with multiple reflections addressed subsequently.

Mirror Transformation Scheme To model the detailed reflection process, we propose a *mirror transformation scheme*.

As illustrated in Fig. 6.42a, there are three obstacles labeled as A, B, and C. The highest effective charging zones for the two sensors s_1 and s_2 are shown as purple and blue circles. The MC is employed to recharge sensors s_1 and s_2, with potential charging positions indicated at p_1 and p_2. Because of the obstruction caused by the obstacles, s_1 and s_2 cannot receive direct charging via the LOS path when the MC is located at p_1 and p_2, making them NLOS nodes.

Taking s_1 as an example, when the MC is at p_1 to replenish s_1, electromagnetic waves can be reflected on the surface $\mathcal{R}_1$ (i.e., the yellow dotted line in Fig. 6.42b) first and then transmitted to s_1 (i.e., $p_1 \rightarrow i_1 \rightarrow s_1$ in Fig. 6.42e).

To find such a reflection path, we propose a mirror transformation scheme. The main idea is to *convert the method of charging sensors through reflection (NLOS charging) into directly charging virtual sensors without reflection (LOS charging).*

(1) Single Reflection: First, each reflection surface of obstacles is regarded as a mirror (e.g., $\mathcal{P}_1$). We create *virtual mirror sensors* s_1' and s_2' for s_1 and s_2, which are symmetrical to mirror $\mathcal{P}_1$ as shown in Fig. 6.42b. The reflection surface $\mathcal{R}_1$, part of $\mathcal{P}_1$, is regarded as an aperture where electromagnetic waves can directly propagate. The rest of $\mathcal{P}_1$ is considered a screen that blocks all signals (i.e., the red dotted line).

In complicated environments, electromagnetic waves passing through an aperture (i.e., reflected by $\mathcal{R}_1$) could still be blocked by other obstacles' surfaces. Specifically, the electromagnetic waves reflected by $\mathcal{R}_1$ will no longer be affected by the obstacle above $\mathcal{R}_1$ (i.e., obstacle B) but may be affected by the obstacle below $\mathcal{R}_1$ (i.e., obstacle A). Therefore, as shown in Fig. 6.42c, we omit obstacle B and create a *virtual mirror obstacle* A' with the mirror plane $\mathcal{P}_1$.

Using this method, when the MC is at p_1, it can directly charge s_1'; hence, s_1' is an LOS node. We draw a line connecting p_1 and s_1' that intersects $\mathcal{R}_1$ at i_1. Then we depict the main propagation path from p_1 to s_1 by connecting both to i_1 (see the green dotted line in Fig. 6.42e). As a result, the signal propagation path is $p_1 \rightarrow i_1 \rightarrow s_1$, solving the problem of charging the NLOS node s_1.

(2) Multiple Reflectionstext: Even if we construct the virtual mirror sensor for s_2, we still cannot charge s_2' through the LOS path from spots p_1 or p_2. Therefore, we attempt to replenish it by *multiple reflections*.

As shown in Fig. 6.42d, we construct virtual mirror objects for obstacle A', $\mathcal{R}_1$, and s_2' as A'', $\mathcal{R}_1'$, and s_2'', based on the mirror plane $\mathcal{P}_2$. At this time, we can draw a line from p_2 to s_2'', intersecting with $\mathcal{R}_2$ and $\mathcal{R}_1'$ at i_2 and i_3. Finally, we can determine the main signal propagation path for charging s_2 (i.e., $p_2 \rightarrow i_2 \rightarrow i_3 \rightarrow s_2$, see the brown dotted line in Fig. 6.42e). The main reflection points are i_2 and i_3 on obstacles A and B, respectively. Therefore, upon encountering obstacles while serving NLOS nodes, we can replicate the aforementioned procedure to determine a charging path from the MC to the intended sensor. By utilizing an antenna array with greater directivity (i.e., a more focused and elongated beam), electromagnetic waves are able to pass through narrow apertures, allowing for efficient one-to-one charging.

(3) Charging Power for Reflection: After determining the signal propagation path, we calculate the charging power using the method in [29], incorporating Fresnel diffraction. Thus, the power function is transformed into

$$P(c_i, s_n') = \frac{\alpha\eta F_d D_{m_i}(\varphi)}{[d(p_i, s_n) + \beta]^2}, \tag{6.69}$$

where $\eta \in (0, 1]$ represents the reflection coefficient of the obstacle.

Afterward, we can apply the discretization scheme described in Sects. 6.3.2.1 and 6.3.2.2 along with Eq. (6.67) to create boundary curves (i.e., $P(c_i, s_n') = P_{min}$, e.g., the purple curve in Fig. 6.42c and the blue one in Fig. 6.42d). When the MC is located on the boundary of the curve, the received power of the virtual sensor s_n' is P_{min} (i.e., $P(c_i, s_n') = P_{min}$). Hence, when the MC is situated inside the curve, the virtual sensor s_n' is able to receive substantial energy. For practical purposes, we disregard charge spots inside the curve that cannot be accessed by the MC, and the accessible charge spots form the candidate spots for the MC.

Next, we select p_1 and p_2 as the charging spots for the MC from the candidate spots identified within the inner region of the purple and blue curves using the greedy method described in Sect. 6.3.2.4. Note that the exact positions of p_1 and p_2 are not predetermined. For clarity, the charging spots chosen by the greedy method are illustrated in advance in Fig. 6.42.

(4) LOS Charging with Reflection: As previously discussed, we have facilitated power delivery to NLOS nodes via electromagnetic wave reflections. Nonetheless, this solution also applies to LOS nodes. For standard LOS nodes (both virtual and actual), by determining the reflective surfaces using the maximum effective charging area, we can create equivalent virtual nodes. This technique enables the formation of a virtual sensor set derived from sensor s_n, designated as s_n^+. All virtual sensors s_n^+ corresponding to sensor s_n are then incorporated into our charging strategy.

It is crucial to understand that virtual nodes s_n^+ are all capable of being served and function independently of s_n. To boost charging efficiency, incorporating virtual nodes into the charging selection process effectively raises the node density.

Another important point to note is that the virtual sensor utilizes the same battery as the physical sensor s_n. Consequently, the charging utility derived from charging a virtual sensor will be attributed to sensor s_n. Hence, the utility function for sensor s_n (referring to Eq. (6.60)) can be modified to

$$u_{C'}(s_n) = \sum_{s'_n \in s_n^+ \cup \{s_n\}} \sum_{c_i \in C'} P(c_i, s'_n) t_i. \tag{6.70}$$

Electromagnetic wave transmission (penetration) has not been addressed. The reason is that the wave's intensity is greatly reduced after passing through obstacle surfaces. Moreover, assuming the obstacles are metallic (conductors), they will block all transmission. Consequently, most existing research typically disregards the impact of transmission [29, 37].

6.3.2.4 Approximation Greedy Algorithm

As stated in Sect. 6.3.2.1, based on the MC's orientation angle and antenna strategy, we partition the endless candidate region into a limited number of sub-regions. By discretizing the orientation angles (refer to Sect. 6.3.2.2), a finite set of orientation angles is produced. Consequently, the search space for our charging strategy is reduced to a finite tally. In Sect. 6.3.2.3, several virtual sensors are established for each actual sensor to quantitatively assess the effects of electromagnetic wave reflection caused by obstacles.

Consider S^+ as the set that includes both sensors and virtual sensors, and let C be the set encompassing all possible discretized charging strategies. Due to the MC's restricted energy capacity, it cannot adopt every charging strategy in C. Hence, our goal is to select a subset of charging strategies that optimize the charging benefit. To accomplish this, we introduce a Precise Directional Charging (PDC) algorithm.

To find the best charging strategy, we use a greedy approximation algorithm. At each step, the MC chooses the charging strategy c^* with the maximum ratio of charging utility to energy usage.

$$c^* = \arg\max_{c \in C \setminus C'} \frac{U(c, S^+)}{E(c)}$$

where $U(c, S^+)$ represents the benefit of charging with strategy c applied to the sensor set S^+, and $E(c)$ stands for the energy used by strategy c. This procedure continues until the energy budget is depleted or no additional charging strategies are available to choose.

Using this method, the PDC algorithm is capable of determining the best charging strategies in intricate settings to optimize charging utility, all while keeping energy consumption within the defined budget.

$$c^* = \arg\max_{c \in C \setminus C'} \frac{U(C' \cup \{c\}) - U(C')}{F(C' \cup \{c\}) - F(C')}, \tag{6.71}$$

where the numerator $U(C' \cup \{c\}) - U(C')$ indicates the rise in charging utility when a new charging strategy c is introduced to the current charging strategy set C'. Similarly, the denominator $F(C' \cup \{c\}) - F(C')$ signifies the escalation in energy consumption.

Algorithm 25 Precise Directional Charging (PDC) algorithm

Require: N rechargeable sensors $S = \{s_1, s_2, \ldots, s_N\}$, energy constraint B of MC, and coefficients ν, P_T.
Ensure: The selected charging set $C' \subseteq C$ and total charging utility $U(C')$.
1: Construct virtual sensors by using the electromagnetic reflection model (i.e., Sect. 6.3.2.3) and form the set S^+ containing the sensor and the virtual sensor;
2: Execute area and orientation angle discretization (i.e., Sects. 6.3.2.1 and 6.3.2.2) and form Charging Strategy Set C based on S^+;
3: Initial: $C' \leftarrow \emptyset$, $F(C') \leftarrow 0$;
4: **while** Not all sensors s_n have been fully charged **do**
5:     **for** each $c \in C$ **do**
6:         Calculate marginal charging utility $\Delta_U^c \leftarrow U(C' \cup \{c\}) - U(C')$;
7:         Calculate marginal energy cost $\Delta_F^c \leftarrow F(C' \cup \{c\}) - F(C')$ by using path planning method in [32];
8:     **end for**
9:     $c^* \leftarrow arg\ max\{\Delta_U^c / \Delta_F^c | c \in C \setminus C'\}$;
10:     **if** $F(C' \cup \{c^*\}) \leq B$ **then**
11:         $C' \leftarrow C' \cup \{c^*\}$;
12:         $C \leftarrow C \backslash \{c^*\}$;
13:     **else**
14:         **Break;**
15:     **end if**
16: **end while**
17: Return C', $U(C')$.

The PDC process starts by building the sensor node set S^+, which consists of both real and virtual sensors, utilizing the electromagnetic reflection model (see Sect. 6.3.2.3). Following this, the candidate charging strategies set C is generated through the techniques of area discretization and orientation angle discretization (refer to Sects. 6.3.2.1 and 6.3.2.2).

During each cycle, we determine the additional charging utility Δ_U^c and the related additional energy consumption Δ_F^c for each unchosen charging strategy c (see Lines 5–8).

Next, PDC determines the charging strategy c^* with the largest Δ_U^c / Δ_F^c value. If the total energy consumption after adding c^* does not exceed B, c^* is added to the selected charging strategy set C' (i.e., Lines 9–13). Finally, the subset C' and the overall charging utility $U(C')$ are returned.

6.3.3 Theoretical Analysis

Remark 6.1 It is essential to be aware of the charging duration t_c assigned to strategy c in order to compute Δ_U^c and Δ_F^c. For this purpose, we utilize the concept of temporal discretization [38, 39] to further break down c into several virtual charging strategies, each with a uniform minimum time slice t_{min}. Consequently, we can compute Δ_U^c and Δ_F^c and greedily select c.

Lemma 6.5 *The function $U(C')$, which represents utility, is characterized by being non-negative, monotonic, and submodular.*

Proof The proof follows the same reasoning as demonstrated in [29] and [35], thus we are leaving it out to conserve space. □

Theorem 6.10 *The Precise Directional Charging procedure achieves an approximation ratio of $\frac{1}{4}(1-\frac{1}{e})(1-\epsilon)$.*

Proof According to Theorem 6.8, after area discretization, our solution has an approximation ratio of $1-\epsilon$. According to [32, 38], the solution after time discretization has the approximation ratio of $\frac{1}{2}$. Further, we have shown that our objective is a submodular maximization problem with routing constraints. Thus, according to [40], the greedy algorithm we adopted has an approximation ratio of $\frac{1}{2}(1-\frac{1}{e})$ with a slightly relaxed budget constraint. By multiplying the three approximation ratios, we can prove this theorem. □

Theorem 6.11 *The time complexity of our Precise Directional Charging algorithm is $O(\mathcal{M}N^5\mathcal{O}^4\epsilon^{-4})$.*

Proof We omit the proof here to save space. □

It is important to note that in our method, the count of discretized time slices [38, 39] remains fixed; therefore, the time complexity of Algorithm 25 remains unchanged by the number of time slices. Should the number of time slices be adjustable, the time complexity of Algorithm 25 would have to be scaled accordingly. We exclude the detailed proof for brevity.

6.3.4 Simulation and Experiments

6.3.4.1 Experimental Setup

As depicted in Fig. 6.43, the system utilizes a crawler track that incorporates a Universal Software Radio Peripheral (USRP), set up with a two-row, 2-element antenna array, serving as an MC and possessing an energy capacity of $B = 50\,\text{kJ}$. This setup supports three antenna configurations: a single half-wave dipole antenna (omnidirectional antenna), a two-row 1-element antenna array (directional antenna

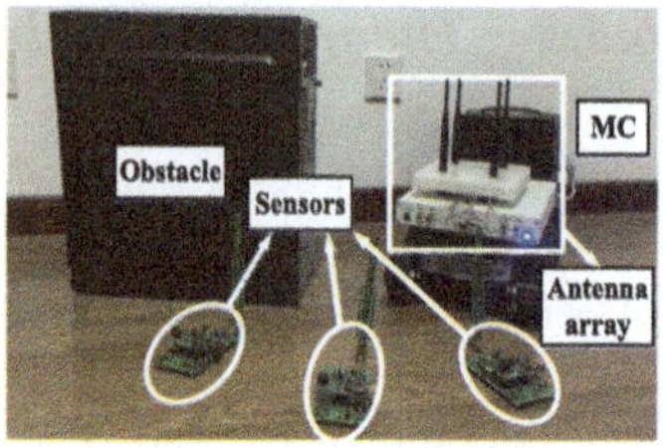

Fig. 6.43 Test-bed devices: an MC, several sensors, and obstacle

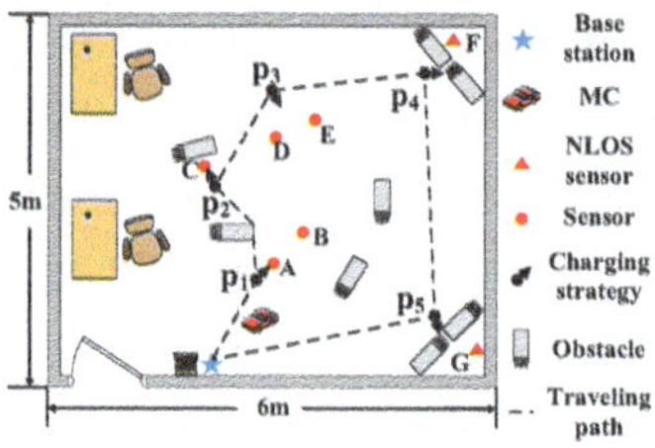

Fig. 6.44 A diagram of experiment scenario

with lesser directivity), and a two-row 2-element antenna array (directional antenna with enhanced directivity).

Moreover, the energy expenditure for the MC per unit length is $\nu = 0.1$ kJ/m, and the energy consumption of the antenna array per unit time is $P_T = 0.4$ kJ/s. The study employs seven sensors (i.e., $A \sim G$ in Fig. 6.44) outfitted with P2110 power receivers (Powercast, http://www.powercastco.com), each with a battery capacity of 2.5 kJ. The upper energy limits U_n^{th} for the sensors are 1, 1.25, 1.5, 1.75, 2, 2.25, and 2.5 kJ. The experiments are performed in a 6×5 m room shown in Fig. 6.44.

6.3.4.2 Baseline Setup

As previous research has not addressed accurate charging in complex scenarios, we propose three baseline methods for evaluation: Charging Utility Maximization with Obstacles algorithm (NICE) [29], Obstacles Boundary Partition algorithm (OBP) [41], and Random Algorithm (RAN).

Within NICE, a low-gain omnidirectional antenna is utilized. It accounts solely for the diffraction of electromagnetic waves caused by barriers, while disregarding the reflection [29].

OBP utilizes directional antennas to segment the entire area into regions with constant power and regions with no power, according to the boundaries formed by obstacles [41].

RAN randomly selects the charging spots that are not covered by obstacles.

6.3.4.3 Experimental Results

Firstly, to verify the experimental and simulation outcomes, we examine the discrepancies between theoretical, simulation, and experimental results as depicted in Fig. 6.45. In the theoretical and simulation results, the energy consumption due to the MC's directional rotation is neglected, causing a 4.4–5.1% difference between the theoretical/simulation results and the experimental data. Our simulation and experimental outcomes correspond well with the theoretical predictions, showing the practicality and advantage of our scheme in real-world applications.

We then analyze the charging dynamics of PDC in a complex setting. The MC is allocated an energy budget of 80 kJ. Initially, the MC charges nodes A and B at location p_1. Subsequently, it pauses at point p_2, utilizing reflected electromagnetic waves to boost the charging efficiency for node C. Afterwards, it refuels nodes D and E at p_3. Finally, it remains at p_4 and p_5, employing reflected electromagnetic waves to power two NLOS sensor nodes F and G. This scenario illustrates that the MC can deploy versatile charging strategies to address both LOS and NLOS situations through directed charging or energy reflection for multiple sensors simultaneously.

We subsequently evaluated the charging efficiencies of four algorithms under varying energy budgets through experiments. As illustrated in Fig. 6.46, PDC excels beyond other algorithms by an average utility margin of 30.5%. There are two main factors contributing to these outcomes:

1. NICE solely accounts for the diffraction of electromagnetic waves, disregarding their reflection.
2. The directional charging discretization technique in OBP lacks sufficient accuracy.

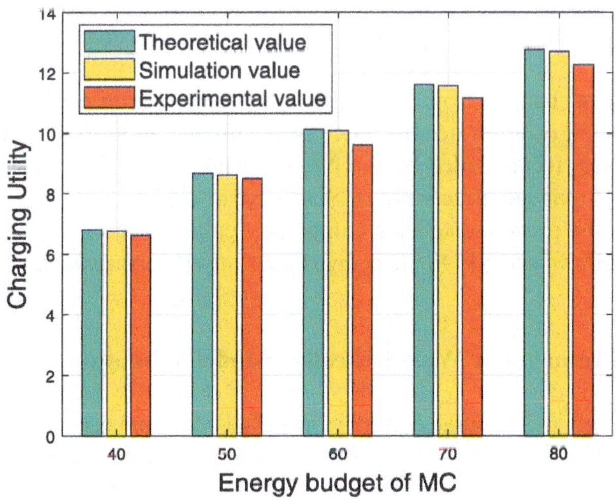

Fig. 6.45 Comparison of theoretical, simulation, and experimental results

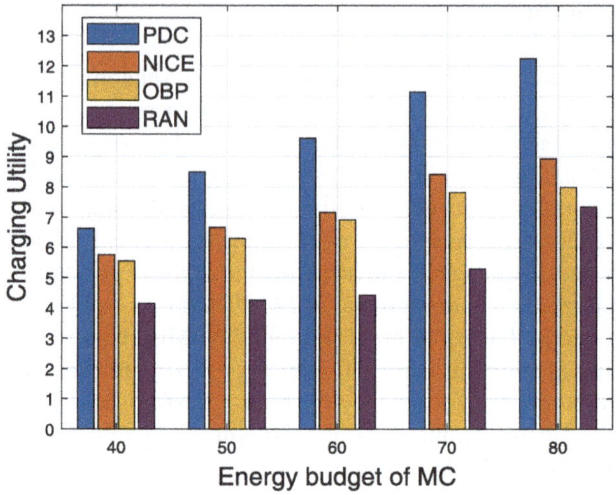

Fig. 6.46 Charging utility vs. Energy budget of MC

Fig. 6.47 The charging power heatmap in our practical experiment

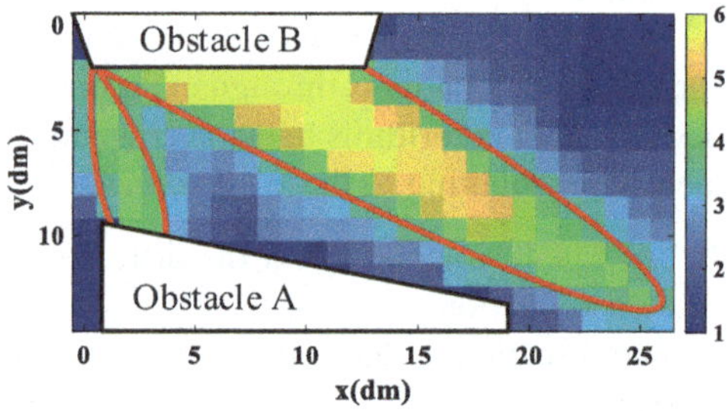

Consequently, the designed model for electromagnetic wave reflection along with a precise discretization approach can significantly enhance the efficiency of charging.

As the budget changes from 50 to 80 kJ, the difference in performance between PDC and other algorithms steadily increases. This is due to PDC's ability to serve two NLOS nodes (represented by the two red triangles in Fig. 6.44), which NICE and OBP fail to manage effectively in NLOS conditions.

To sum up, the proposed scheme can greatly enhance energy efficiency, particularly in scenarios where NLOS charging occurs amidst obstructions.

6.3.4.4 Electromagnetic Wave Reflection Model Validation

We have verified the accuracy of the proposed electromagnetic wave reflection model. Figure 6.42a and b illustrate two obstacles, A and B, with a sensor placed at s_1. The power received at various points is shown in Fig. 6.47. Theoretical values derived from our reflection model are represented by the red curve in

Fig. 6.47, which matches the purple curve in Fig. 6.42c. Our observation reveals that the experimental outcomes are consistent with the theoretical predictions (i.e., Eq. (6.69)), confirming the accuracy and validity of our reflection model.

In this part, extensive simulations are conducted to evaluate the performance of our scheme in terms of discretized threshold ϵ', discretized angle interval threshold θ^{max}, number of antenna strategies $\mathcal{M}$ (determined by the number of the half-wavelength dipole antennas), and number of NLOS sensors $\mathcal{N}$ on the charging utility. Note that all simulation results presented here are the average values of the charging utility, which have been simulated for 200 times in different random network topologies.

6.3.4.5 Simulation Configurations

In our simulation setup, 100 sensors and 20 obstacles are randomly distributed within a 100×100 m square region. Consistent with [29], $\alpha = 130$ and $\beta = 13$. Additionally, the energy capacities of the sensors and the MC are 50 and 10,000 J respectively. The MC has a movement energy consumption rate $u = 3$ J/m and a charging energy consumption rate $P_T = 6$ J/s. Furthermore, we have set the discretized threshold $\epsilon' = 0.2$ and incorporated $\mathcal{M} = 6$ antenna strategies (i.e., the transmitting antenna array supports six distinct beam patterns).

6.3.4.6 Performance Comparison

As shown in Fig. 6.48, when the discretized threshold ϵ' varies from 0.1 to 0.5, PDC shows a higher utility improvement of at least 32.9% compared to other

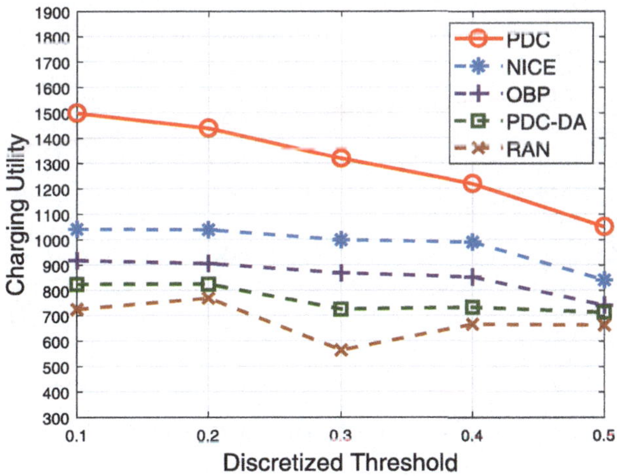

Fig. 6.48 Charging utility vs. Discretized threshold ϵ'

algorithms. Apart from RAN, all algorithms display a decreasing trend. This is because, according to Theorem 6.8, a larger ϵ' leads to a bigger approximation error, thereby reducing the charging utility.

As shown in Fig. 6.49, our scheme outperforms other algorithms by 21.1% on average in utility. The performance of PDC gradually decreases as θ^{max} changes from 10° to 60°. This is due to Theorem 6.9 in Sect. 6.3.2.2, which states that a larger θ^{max} results in a larger path error, ultimately reducing the charging utility.

As illustrated in Fig. 6.50, when the variety of antenna strategies ranges from 2 to 10, PDC consistently outperforms other algorithms by an average of 35.6%. Since NICE and OBP do not employ antenna arrays, their charging efficiency does not vary with the antenna strategy. The effectiveness of PDC increases as the number of antenna strategies grows. This is due to the fact that more strategies provide the MC with greater flexibility, enabling it to adapt its approach to different scenarios (such as LOS and NLOS). Moreover, a higher directivity antenna increases the received power for NLOS nodes.

As shown in Fig. 6.51, the charging utility of PDC is 38.4% higher than other algorithms on average. When the number of NLOS sensors N increases from 0 to 50, all algorithms except RAN show a significant decreasing trend.

As NICE and OBP are unable to accommodate NLOS nodes, an upsurge in NLOS nodes lowers the density of nodes that can be served, consequently diminishing the charging utility.

Moreover, the decrease in PDC is considerably less pronounced than in NICE and OBP since NLOS nodes, though less effective, can still be catered to. Serving NLOS nodes with the MC makes one-to-many charging more difficult, lowering the charging efficiency. Nonetheless, with a high directivity antenna approach, the MC is capable of performing efficient one-to-one charging.

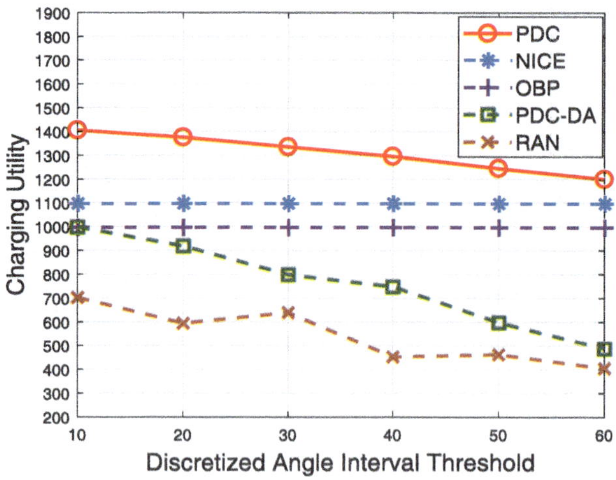

Fig. 6.49 Charging utility vs. Discretized interval threshold θ^{max}

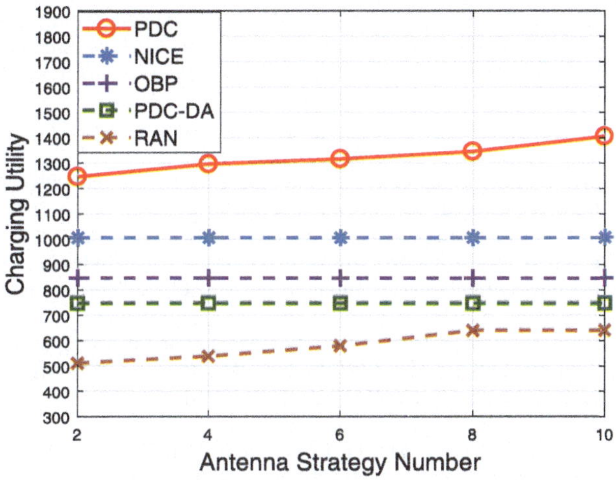

Fig. 6.50 Charging utility vs. Antenna strategy number $\mathcal{M}$

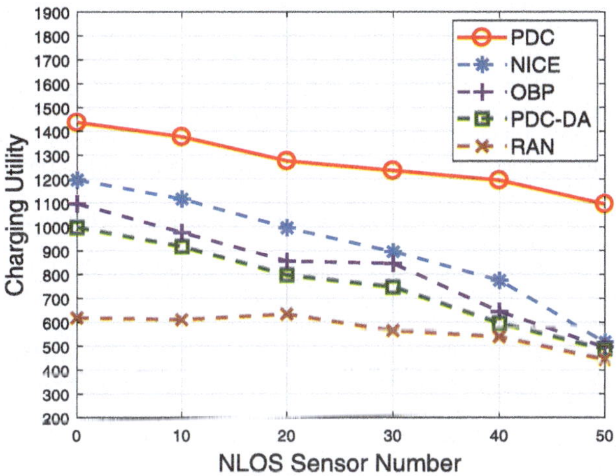

Fig. 6.51 Charging utility vs. NLOS sensor number N

References

1. K.-F. Ssu, C.-H. Ou, H.C. Jiau, Localization with mobile anchor points in wireless sensor networks. IEEE Trans. Veh. Technol. **54**(3), 1187–1197 (2005)
2. S. He, J. Chen, F. Jiang, D.K. Yau, G. Xing, Y. Sun, Energy provisioning in wireless rechargeable sensor networks. IEEE Trans. Mobile Comput. **12**(10), 1931–1942 (2013)
3. E.G. Farr, A power wave theory of antennas, in *2014 United States National Committee of URSI National Radio Science Meeting* (2014), pp. 1–1
4. G. Dantzig, *Linear Programming and Extensions*, vol. 48 (Princeton University Press, Princeton, 2016)

5. R. Baruri, A. Ghosh, R. Banerjee, A. Das, A. Mandal, T. Halder, An improved k-means text clustering algorithm by optimizing initial cluster centers, in *2019 International Conference on Machine Learning, Big Data, Cloud and Parallel Computing (COMITCon)* (2019), pp. 470–475
6. H. Dai, X. Wang, A.X. Liu, H. Ma, G. Chen, Optimizing wireless charger placement for directional charging, in *IEEE INFOCOM* (2017), pp. 1–9
7. S. Zhang, J. Wu, S. Lu, Collaborative mobile charging for sensor networks, in *9th IEEE International Conference on Mobile Ad-Hoc and Sensor Systems, MASS 2012, Las Vegas, NV, USA, October 8-11, 2012* (IEEE Computer Society, 2012), pp. 84–92
8. Y. Ma, W. Liang, W. Xu, Charging utility maximization in wireless rechargeable sensor networks by charging multiple sensors simultaneously. IEEE/ACM Trans. Netw. **26**(4), 1591–1604 (2018)
9. C. Lin, F. Gao, H. Dai, J. Ren, L. Wang, G. Wu, Maximizing charging utility with obstacles through fresnel diffraction model, in *IEEE INFOCOM* (2020), pp. 2046–2055
10. H. Dai, Y. Liu, A.X. Liu, L. Kong, G. Chen, T. He, Radiation constrained wireless charger placement, in *IEEE INFOCOM* (2016), pp. 1–9
11. H. Dai, X. Wang, A.X. Liu, H. Ma, G. Chen, Optimizing wireless charger placement for directional charging, in *IEEE INFOCOM* (2017), pp. 1–9
12. Y. Chow, A. Tamar, S. Mannor, M. Pavone, Risk-sensitive and robust decision-making: a CVaR optimization approach, in *NIPS* (2015), pp. 1522–1530
13. R.T. Rockafellar, S. Uryasev, Optimization of conditional value-at-risk. J. Risk **2**, 21–42 (2020)
14. Q. Liang, M. Zhu, X. Zheng, Y. Wang, An adaptive news-driven method for cvar-sensitive online portfolio selection in non-stationary financial markets, in *IJCAI* (2021), pp. 2708–2715
15. M. Asensio, J. Contreras, Stochastic unit commitment in isolated systems with renewable penetration under cvar assessment. IEEE Trans. Smart Grid **7**(3), 1356–1367 (2016)
16. H. Yang, S. Zhang, J. Qiu, D. Qiu, M. Lai, Z. Dong, Cvar-constrained optimal bidding of electric vehicle aggregators in day-ahead and real-time markets. IEEE Trans. Ind. Inf. **13**(5), 2555–2565 (2017)
17. L. Zhou, P. Tokekar, An approximation algorithm for risk-averse submodular optimization, in *WAFR* (2018), pp. 101–110
18. A. Choudhry, B. Moon, J. Patrikar, C. Samaras, S. Scherer, Cvar-based flight energy risk assessment for multirotor uavs using a deep energy model, in *IEEE ICRA* (2021), pp. 262–268
19. B. Wilder, Risk-sensitive submodular optimization, in *AAAI* (2018), pp. 6451–6458
20. K. Juselius, *The Cointegrated VAR Model: Methodology and Applications* (Oxford University Press, Oxford, 2006)
21. N. Ohsaka, Y. Yoshida, Portfolio optimization for influence spread, in *WWW* (2017), pp. 977–985
22. L. Fu, P. Cheng, Y. Gu, J. Chen, T. He, Optimal charging in wireless rechargeable sensor networks. IEEE Trans. Veh. Technol. **65**(1), 278–291 (2016)
23. C. Lin, C. Guo, H. Dai, L. Wang, G. Wu, Near optimal charging scheduling for 3-d wireless rechargeable sensor networks with energy constraints, in *IEEE ICDCS* (2019), pp. 624–633
24. W.S. Anglin, J. Lambek, *The Cubic and Quartic Equations* (Springer, New York, 1995)
25. C. Lin, F. Gao, H. Dai, L. Wang, G. Wu, When wireless charging meets fresnel zones: even obstacles can enhance charging efficiency, in *IEEE SECON* (2019), pp. 1–9
26. X. Wang, H. Dai, W. Wang, J. Zheng, N. Yu, G. Chen, W. Dou, X. Wu, Practical heterogeneous wireless charger placement with obstacles. IEEE Trans. Mobile Comput. **19**(8), 1–10 (2019)
27. C.A. Balanis, *Antenna Theory: Analysis and Design*, 4th edn. (Wiley, New York, 2016)
28. R.L. Haupt, *Antenna Arrays: A Computational Approach* (Wiley-IEEE Press, New York, 2010)
29. C. Lin, F. Gao, H. Dai, J. Ren, L. Wang, G. Wu, Maximizing charging utility with obstacles through fresnel diffraction model, in *IEEE INFOCOM* (2020), pp. 2046–2055
30. H. Dai, X. Wang, A.X. Liu, H. Ma, G. Chen, Optimizing wireless charger placement for directional charging, in *IEEE INFOCOM* (2017), pp. 1–9

31. S. Zhang, Z. Qian, J. Wu, F. Kong, S. Lu, Wireless charger placement and power allocation for maximizing charging quality. IEEE Trans. Mobile Comput. **17**(6), 1483–1496 (2018)
32. T. Wu, P. Yang, H. Dai, W. Xu, M. Xu, Charging oriented sensor placement and flexible scheduling in rechargeable wsns, in *IEEE INFOCOM* (2019), pp. 73–81
33. H. Dai, C. Wu, X. Wang, W. Dou, Y. Liu, Placing wireless chargers with limited mobility, in *IEEE INFOCOM* (2020), pp. 2056–2065
34. C. Lin, Y. Zhou, F. Ma, J. Deng, L. Wang, G. Wu, Minimizing charging delay for directional charging in wireless rechargeable sensor networks, in *IEEE INFOCOM* (2019), pp. 1819–1827
35. C. Lin, F. Gao, H. Dai, L. Wang, G. Wu, When wireless charging meets fresnel zones: even obstacles can enhance charging efficiency, in *IEEE SECON* (2019)
36. D.P. Bertsekas, *Constrained Optimization and Lagrange Multiplier Methods* (Academic Press, Cambridge, 1982)
37. J. Liu, Y. Zeng, T. Gu, L. Wang, D. Zhang, Wiphone: smartphone-based respiration monitoring using ambient reflected wifi signals. Proc. ACM Interact. Mobile Wearable Ubiquitous Technol. **5**(1), 23:1–23:19 (2021)
38. C. Lin, C. Guo, H. Dai, L. Wang, G. Wu, Near optimal charging scheduling for 3-d wireless rechargeable sensor networks with energy constraints, in *IEEE ICDCS* (2019), pp. 624–633
39. P. Yang, T. Wu, H. Dai, X. Rao, X. Wang, P. Wan, X. He, MORE: multi-node mobile charging scheduling for deadline constraints. ACM Trans. Sensor Netw. **17**(1), 7:1–7:21 (2020)
40. C. Lin, F. Gao, H. Dai, L. Wang, G. Wu, When wireless charging meets fresnel zones: even obstacles can enhance charging efficiency, in *IEEE SECON* (2019)
41. X. Wang, H. Dai, W. Wang, J. Zheng, N. Yu, G. Chen, W. Dou, X. Wu, Practical heterogeneous wireless charger placement with obstacles. IEEE Trans. Mobile Comput. **19**(8), 1910–1927 (2020)

Chapter 7
Novel Theory and Method in WRSNs

7.1 Wireless Charging with Fresnel Zones

With the advent of Wireless Power Transfer (WPT) technology, Wireless Rechargeable Sensor Networks (WRSNs) have emerged as a promising solution for prolonging the lifespan of wireless sensor networks. However, in practical scenarios, obstacles are pervasive within WRSNs. Previous studies often assume that obstacles invariably weaken signal strength and therefore disregard their impact for the sake of computational ease. This presumption contradicts fundamental signal propagation principles, rendering these methods impractical for real-world applications. In this section, we explore the wireless signal propagation process and present a theoretical charging model designed to enhance charging efficiency by leveraging obstacles. By applying the concept of Fresnel Zones (FZs), we reformulate the wireless charging model and discretize the charging power to pinpoint optimal charging locations and times. We frame the problem of maximizing charging efficiency (EMO) in the presence of obstacles as a submodular function maximization problem and propose a cost effective algorithm to address it. Ultimately, test-bed experiments and simulations show that our approaches outperform comparison algorithms by at least 10% in terms of improved charging efficiency.

7.1.1 Problem Statement

7.1.1.1 Network Model

A WRSN generally comprises three primary elements: several rechargeable sensors, a mobile charger (MC), and a base station (BS).

As shown in Fig. 7.1, a collection of rechargeable sensors $S = \{s_1, s_2, \ldots, s_N\}$ is randomly deployed across a 2D plane to monitor events. Each sensor is

C. Lin et al., *Wireless Rechargeable Sensor Networks for Internet of Things*,
Wireless Networks, https://doi.org/10.1007/978-981-97-9543-7_7

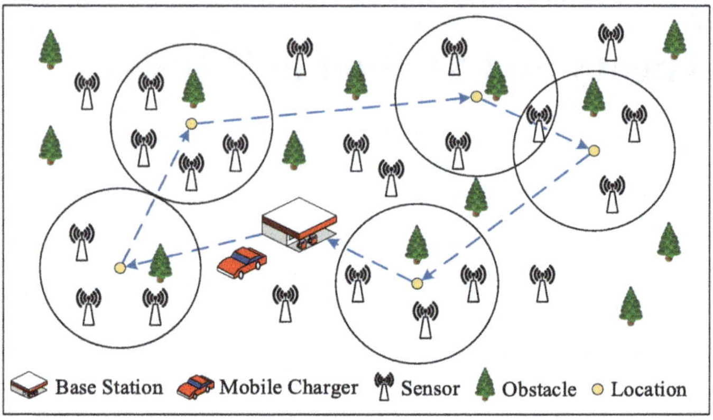

Fig. 7.1 A typical wireless rechargeable sensor network

equipped with a receiving coil that can absorb RF energy (Powercast, http://www.powercastco.com) from a transmitting coil using WPT technology. The MC, equipped with the transmitting coil, is tasked with recharging the sensors, ensuring their continued operation. The MC establishes a charging schedule that logs the charging duration t_j at each corresponding charging location c_j within the selected candidate set C_{sel}. The BS gathers sensory data from the sensors and offers rapid energy replenishment services to the MCs, such as energy supply or battery replacement. The BS is generally considered the starting and ending point of the MC's charging route.

7.1.1.2 Signal Propagation Model with Obstacles

To extend the lifespan of a WRSN, the essential issue is how to optimize the energy charged to the sensors. Thus, we introduce a signal propagation model for wireless power transfer.

In real-world situations, obstacles are common and generally influence charging efficiency. Particularly, throughout the wireless signal transmission process, encountering obstacles causes some signals to be reflected or scattered, hindering their ability to pass through.

Accurately modeling signal propagation with obstacles is complicated. For simplicity, we initially disregard these effects. The wireless energy transmission model can thus be treated as a free-space transmission model described by Friis's free space equation, i.e.,

$$P_r = P_t \frac{G_t G_r \lambda^2}{(4\pi d)^2}$$

where: P_r is the power received by the sensor, P_t is the transmitted power, G_t and G_r are the gains of the transmitting and receiving antennas, respectively, λ is the wavelength of the signal, d is the distance between the transmitting and receiving antennas.

$$P_r = P_t G_s G_r (\frac{\lambda}{4\pi d^2}). \tag{7.1}$$

Equation (7.1) illustrates the received power P_r at a distance d from the power transmitter with a source power P_t. The terms G_s and G_r denote the gains of the source and receiver antennas, respectively. The symbol λ stands for the wavelength of the electromagnetic wave in free space. As per [1], an empirical model for wireless recharging in WRSNs is described as follows:

$$P_r = \frac{G_s G_r \eta}{L_p} \left(\frac{\lambda}{4\pi (d + \beta)} \right)^2 P_t,$$

where η stands for rectifier efficiency, L_p symbolizes polarization loss, and β is a constant used to modify Friis's free space equation for short-distance transmissions. We represent C as the collection of all possible charging locations c_j of the MC.

The power $p(s_i, c_j)$ that sensor s_i obtains from the MC situated at location c_j (i.e., $c_j \in C$) can be represented by the subsequent empirical model:

$$p(s_i, c_j) = \frac{G_s G_r \eta}{L_p} \left(\frac{\lambda}{4\pi (d_{ij} + \beta)} \right)^2 P_t,$$

where d_{ij} denotes the distance between sensor s_i and charging location c_j. This model assists in identifying the optimal charging positions and times to enhance the energy delivered to the sensors in a WRSN.

$$p(s_i, c_j) = \begin{cases} \frac{\alpha}{(d(s_i,c_j)+\beta)^2}, & d(s_i, c_j) \le D \\ 0, & d(s_i, c_j) > D \end{cases}, \tag{7.2}$$

The function $p(s_i, c_j)$ decreases monotonically as the distance $d(s_i, c_j)$ increases. The constants α and β are both non-negative, determined by hardware configurations and the environmental context [1, 2]. We represent the Euclidean distance between sensor s_i and position c_j as $d(s_i, c_j)$. D represents the maximum effective range of a charger at the MC's rated power. It is clear that if a sensor is placed at a distance D from a charger, the power it receives will be minimal and hence can be disregarded. Therefore, we set this energy gain to 0 in this study (Fig. 7.2).

To proceed, we develop a practical charging model incorporating obstacles. The objective is to examine how obstacles influence the energy received. For this, we utilize an off-the-shelf TX91501 wireless charger and wireless sensors with P2110 power receivers, both sourced from Powercast (http://www.powercastco.com). As illustrated in Fig. 7.15, the initial distance between the sensor and the transmitter is

Fig. 7.2 Experimental scene

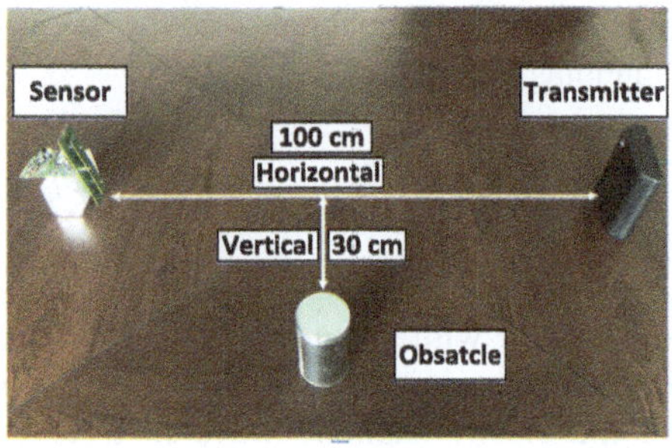

Fig. 7.3 Obstacles with varying shapes and locations

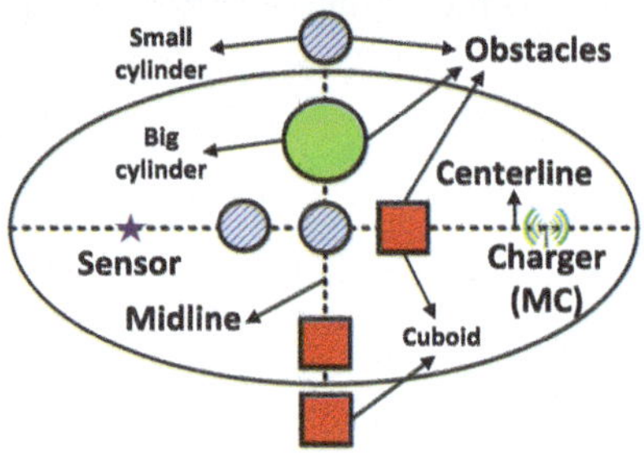

1 m. In our study, we use two obstacles: an iron cylinder and a cuboid object. In Fig. 7.3, the obstacle's position ranges from −30 to 30 cm along both the horizontal and vertical axes. The impact of obstacles on the energy received at each position is shown in Fig. 7.16.

Figure 7.16 shows an intriguing discovery: placing the obstacle 30 cm from the centerline results in a 10% energy increase for the sensor compared to the absence of obstacles (noted by the purple line). Additionally, there is a significant drop in energy efficiency, nearly 47%, when the obstacle is positioned closer to the midline. Similar outcomes were observed with a cylindrical obstacle. These findings suggest that obstacles can both positively and negatively affect signal propagation, an aspect that cannot be overlooked, particularly regarding wireless charging [3].

The primary takeaway from this experiment is that *obstacles do not necessarily weaken signal strength; in some cases, they can improve it*. This observation indicates that *carefully selecting charging locations can further boost signal strength (i.e., charging efficiency f discussed in Sect. 7.2.1.4) by effectively leveraging obstacles*. These findings highlight our ongoing effort in this section: *strategically using obstacles can further improve charging efficiency* (Fig. 7.4).

Following this, we shall endeavor to provide a theoretical analysis of the outcomes derived from the aforementioned experiments.

7.1.1.3 Energy Model

It is important to highlight that, under the one-to-many charging model, a sensor can be charged one or more times. Consequently, the full or partial charging mode can

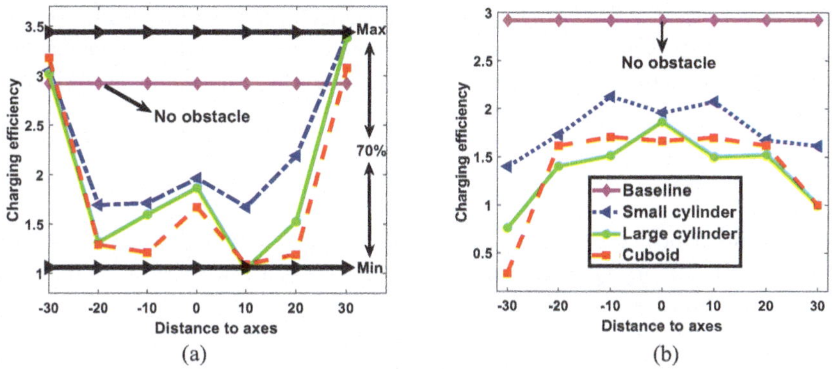

Fig. 7.4 Charging efficiency with obstacles far from $-30\,cm$ to $30\,cm$ on horizontal and vertical views. (**a**) Obstacle in vertical location. (**b**) Obstacle in horizontal location

be employed [4]. The cumulative charging energy of a sensor s_i can be expressed as

$$E_c(s_i) = \sum_{j=1}^{M} p(s_i, c_j)t_j. \tag{7.3}$$

In this context, c_j refers to a charging site within C_{sel} where the MC halts. Set C_{sel} (i.e., $C_{sel} \subseteq C$) includes the chosen candidate charging spots as per Algorithms 1 and 2, and M is the number of elements in C_{sel}. The value $p(s_i, c_j)$ represents the power acquired by sensor s_i, while t_j denotes the respective charging time when the MC remains at c_j.

Assuming no loss of generality, sensors have rechargeable batteries with a capacity of $Q_B(s_i)$. If the charging power $E_c(s_i)$ exceeds $Q_B(s_i) - Q_l(s_i)$, the sensor will be unable to receive energy.

Let $Q_l(s_i)$ represent the remaining energy of sensor s_i. Therefore, the energy received by sensor s_i can be calculated as

$$Q(s_i, C_{sel}) = \min\{E_c(s_i), Q_B(s_i) - Q_l(s_i)\}. \tag{7.4}$$

Our attention then shifts to the MC's energy consumption, encompassing both the charging and traveling expenses. In line with [5], we presume the MC is equipped with a single energy storage/supply and evaluate the charging and traveling costs together.

The charging cost E_C can be derived by Eqs. (7.31) and (7.34):

$$E_C = P_t \sum_{j=1}^{M} t_j, \tag{7.5}$$

where P_t represents the constant transmission power of MC.

The travel expense E_M is defined by the distance of the charging path, forming a closed circuit that begins at the BS, goes through every selected candidate charging point in C_{sel} exactly once, and ends back at the BS. The value of E_M can be determined as

$$E_M = g \cdot L(C_{sel}), \tag{7.6}$$

where g is the energy used by MC for each unit of path length, and $L(C_{sel})$ signifies the length of the charging path. Using Eqs. (7.5) and (7.6), we determine the overall energy expenditure E_{tot} of MC as

$$E_{tot} = E_M + E_C. \tag{7.7}$$

Certainly, the overall energy usage of the MC comprises both the travel expenses and the charging expenses.

7.1.1.4 Problem Formulation

Prior to defining the problem, it is necessary to verify that MC possesses sufficient energy to return to BS. We have

$$E_{tot} \leq E_B, \tag{7.8}$$

where E_B represents the energy budget or capacity of MC.

Definition 7.1 (Charging Efficiency f) indicates the total energy eventually obtained by all sensors. According to Eq. (7.4), we have

$$f(C_{sel}) = \sum_{i=1}^{N} Q(s_i, C_{sel}) = \sum_{i=1}^{N} \min\{E_c(s_i), Q_B(s_i) - Q_l(s_i)\}, \tag{7.9}$$

where C_{sel} is the selected charging location set.

Based on Eqs. (7.8) and (7.9), our goal is to maximize the total received energy under the limited energy budget. Hence, we address the charging Efficiency Maximization problem with Obstacles (EMO):

$$\textbf{(P1)} \quad max \quad f(C_{sel}). \tag{7.10}$$

$$s.t.\ E_{tot} \leq E_B. \tag{7.11}$$

Our problem here is *how to accurately identify the optimal charging locations and times for the MC in order to utilise obstacles and maximise charging efficiency?*

7.1.2 *Schematic Design*

To start, we transform the infinite array of loading locations into a finite set by discretizing the loading zone. Then, we introduce a simplified model that incorporates both the amplified and diminished impacts of obstacles. Additionally, we divide the charging duration into multiple time segments to discretize it, leading to a redefinition of the EMO problem. We subsequently prove that the EMO problem represents a submodular function maximization issue and propose an approximation algorithm to address it. Finally, we illustrate how to ascertain the optimal charging path amidst obstacles.

7.1.2.1 Charging Area Discretization

To address the EMO problem, it is necessary to identify the best charging locations. The infinite number of potential charging sites presents a major challenge. By implementing charging power discretization, the entire charging area is segmented into several discrete regions, assuming uniform charging efficiency within each region. This approach simplifies the search space and reduces computational complexity while providing an approximate solution [6, 7] (refer to our proofs in Sect. 7.1.3.1).

First, we provide an example of charging area discretization for a single sensor. As shown in Fig. 7.5, we set sensor s_i as the center of $\mathcal{K}$ concentric circles with different radii R_k $(1 \leq k \leq \mathcal{K})$, where the largest radius $R_{\mathcal{K}}$ is equal to the maximum effective coverage distance D.

When the MC is located in the region between the k-th and $(k-1)$-th concentric circles, the charging power $p(s_i, c_j)$ can be approximated to a constant $p^{[k]} = \frac{\alpha}{(R_k+\beta)^2}$ (see our example in Fig. 7.6). Based on Eq. (7.31), the approximated

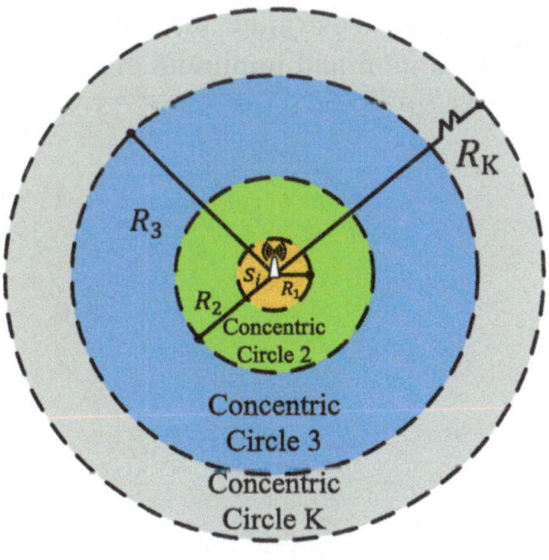

Fig. 7.5 $\mathcal{K}$ concentric circles with the same center s_i

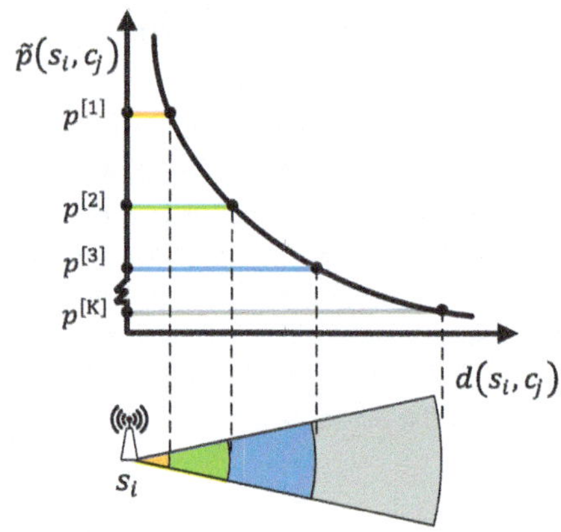

Fig. 7.6 The approximated charging power after discretization

charging power $\widetilde{p}(s_i, c_j)$ is defined as:

$$\widetilde{p}(s_i, c_j) = \begin{cases} p_{max}, & d(s_i, c_j) = 0, (k = 0), \\ p^{[k]}, & R_{k-1} < d(s_i, c_j) \leq R_k, (1 \leq k \leq \mathcal{K}), \\ 0, & d(s_i, c_j) > R_{\mathcal{K}}. \end{cases}$$

By setting a constant threshold ϵ ($\epsilon > 0$), the approximated charging power $\widetilde{p}(s_i, c_j)$ can be readily obtained after discretization. The radius difference between any two neighboring concentric circles is less than the threshold ϵ:

$$\frac{p^{[k-1]}}{p^{[k]}} = 1 + \epsilon, \frac{p^{[\mathcal{K}-1]}}{p^{[\mathcal{K}]}} \leq 1 + \epsilon, \quad (0 \leq k \leq \mathcal{K}). \tag{7.12}$$

With this design, the maximum approximation error in such a discretization method is less than ϵ.

Next, we determine the values of $\mathcal{K}$, $p^{[k]}$, and R_k. According to Eq. (7.31), the maximum and minimum charging power p_{max} and p_{min} can be calculated as follows:

$$p_{max} = \frac{\alpha}{\beta^2},$$

$$p_{min} = \frac{\alpha}{(R_{\mathcal{K}} + \beta)^2}.$$

Using these values, we can derive R_k and $p^{[k]}$ for each concentric circle:

$$R_k = \sqrt{\frac{\alpha}{p^{[k]}}} - \beta,$$

$$p^{[k]} = \frac{\alpha}{(R_k + \beta)^2}.$$

By ensuring that the radius gap between any neighboring concentric circles is smaller than the threshold ϵ, we guarantee that the maximum approximation error in this discretization technique stays below ϵ.

$$p_{max} = \frac{\alpha}{(0+\beta)^2} = \frac{\alpha}{\beta^2}, \ p_{min} = \frac{\alpha}{(D+\beta)^2}. \tag{7.13}$$

Combining Eqs. (7.12) with (7.49), we derive

$$\frac{p_{max}}{p_{min}} = \frac{(D+\beta)^2}{\beta^2} = (1+\epsilon)^{\mathcal{K}}. \tag{7.14}$$

Based on Eq. (7.14), we can calculate $\mathcal{K}$:

$$\mathcal{K} = \left\lceil \frac{\ln(p_{max}(s_i, c_j))/\ln(p_{min})}{\ln(1+\epsilon)} \right\rceil = 2\left\lceil \frac{ln(1+\frac{D}{\beta})}{\ln(1+\epsilon)} \right\rceil. \tag{7.15}$$

Combining Eqs. (7.31) and (7.12), we have

$$p^{[k]} = \frac{\alpha}{(R_k+\beta)^2} = p_{max} \cdot (1+\epsilon)^{-k}, (0 \leq k \leq \mathcal{K}). \tag{7.16}$$

Consequently, combining Eqs. (7.49) with (7.16), we can obtain R_k:

$$R_k = \beta(1+\epsilon)^{\frac{k}{2}} - \beta, (0 \leq k \leq \mathcal{K}). \tag{7.17}$$

For clearer understanding, Fig. 7.21 illustrates an example of charging area discretization involving multiple sensors. Three concentric circles are centered at $\{s_1,s_2,s_3\}$. Based on Eq. (7.17), the radial intervals between the concentric circles incrementally increase with the distance between the MC and the sensor (Fig. 7.7).

The charging power of the whole region is approximated to the minimum charging power of this region. Moreover, the total charging power received by all sensors is the sum of the charging power of each sensors after discretization. For example, in Fig. 7.21, $\{c_1, c_2, c_3\}$ are charging locations within yellow, purple and green discretization areas respectively. When the charging location c_1 within the yellow area, the total power received by sensors is approximated as $p^{[3]}(s_1, c_1) + p^{[3]}(s_2, c_1) + p^{[3]}(s_3, c_1)$. Similarly, when c_2 locating within the purple area, the

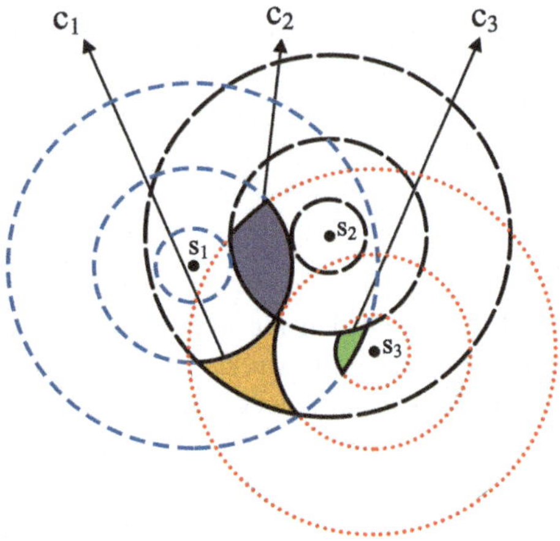

Fig. 7.7 An example of discretization charging areas

total received power is $p^{[2]}(s_1, c_2) + p^{[2]}(s_2, c_2) + p^{[3]}(s_3, c_2)$. The c_3 within green area has an approximated total power of $p^{[3]}(s_1, c_3) + p^{[3]}(s_2, c_3) + p^{[1]}(s_3, c_3)$.

Ultimately, we transform problem $P1$ into problem $P2$:

$$\textbf{(P2)} \quad max \quad f(C_{sel}) = \sum_{i=1}^{N} \min\{\sum_{j=1}^{M} \widetilde{p}(s_i, c_j) \cdot t_j, Q_B(s_i) - Q_l(s_i).\} \tag{7.18}$$

$$s.t.\ E_M + \sum_{i=1}^{N}\sum_{j=1}^{M} \widetilde{p}(s_i, c_j) \cdot t_j \leq E_B. \tag{7.19}$$

While the discretization technique might introduce errors, we shall demonstrate in Sect. 7.1.3 that such errors can be confined within certain limits.

7.1.2.2 Charging Model with Obstacles

In the previously discussed discretization methods (Eqs. (7.31) and (7.16)), the impact of obstacles has been disregarded. Nevertheless, as indicated in Sect. 7.1.1.2, sensors can occasionally generate positive effects (e.g., a 10% increase) or negative effects (e.g., a 47% decrease) [8]. Hence, our findings demonstrate that the charging power is affected by the relative position of both the barrier and the emitter, as well as the distance between them.

Consequently, akin to [9–11], we develop a charging model that considers obstacles. Our objective is to maximize the positive impacts and minimize the negative ones by identifying optimal charging spots.

According to the "Huygens-Fresnel" principle [10], all in-phase Huygens sources within a certain distance can be regarded as secondary waves for the far-field

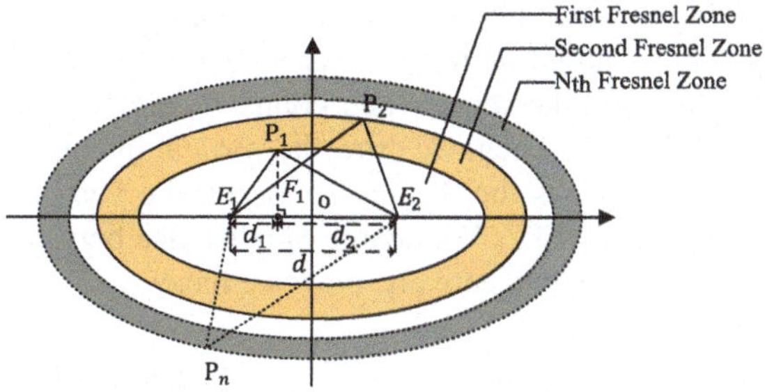

Fig. 7.8 Fresnel Zones: The concentric ellipsoids with transceivers E_1 and E_2 as foci

observation point E. This also explains why a receiver can still receive energy even though the line-of-sight (LOS) path is obstructed by obstacles. If there are obstacles between the transmitter and receiver, the secondary wave can reach the receiver by different paths. These paths can be of different lengths, resulting in a slight difference in signal phase. Depending on the magnitude of the phase shift, the interference between these waves can be constructive or destructive, causing the signal field strength to change. To systematically analyze this change, the concept of Fresnel zones is introduced [12]. In short, Fresnel zones (i.e., concentric ellipsoids) refer to the areas where wireless electromagnetic waves propagate around the line-of-sight path (Fig. 7.8).

As depicted in Fig. 7.17, with E_1 as the transmitter and E_2 as the receiver, the longitudinal section of Fresnel Zones (i.e., the concentric ellipses) is formed with E_1 and E_2 as two focal points. P_n denotes the intersection point between the boundary of the N-th Fresnel zone and the secondary wave charging signal. According to [12], for the N-th ellipse, the difference in path length between the secondary wave charging signal and the original charging signal is:

$$|E_1 P_n| + |P_n E_2| - |E_1 E_2| = \frac{n\lambda}{2},$$

where λ represents the wavelength of the charging signal.

Referring to Eq. (7.38), we note that the path length difference for the First Fresnel Zone (FFZ) spans from 0 to $\frac{\lambda}{2}$. In the same manner, the path length difference for the Second Fresnel Zone (SFZ) extends from $\frac{\lambda}{2}$ to λ, for the Third Fresnel Zone (TFZ) ranges from λ to $\frac{3\lambda}{2}$, and for the N-th Fresnel Zone is from $\frac{(n-1)\lambda}{2}$ to $\frac{n\lambda}{2}$.

Since the path length difference between two adjacent Fresnel Zones is $\frac{\lambda}{2}$, the phase difference is $\frac{2\pi}{\lambda} \cdot \frac{\lambda}{2} = \pi$. Therefore, the electric wave intensity will be enhanced in FFZ by a phase difference of π. Conversely, the SFZ with a phase difference of 2π will reduce the radio strength of FFZ, leading to a decrease in charging efficiency. TFZ will strengthen FFZ because of the phase difference π. In general, the effect of the charging signal in the adjacent Fresnel Zones (i.e., enhance or weaken) is opposite.

In physics, FFZ is the main electromagnetic wave transmission space; hence, we pay close attention to FFZ. As shown in Fig. 7.17, we denote the distance between the MC and the sensor (i.e., points E_1 and E_2 in Fig. 7.17) as d and select a point in FFZ as P_1. Then, we draw the vertical line to the line connecting E_1 and E_2 over point P_1. F_1 is the distance between the vertical foot and point P_1, which is the radius of the FFZ. We denote the distance between the vertical foot and E_1 (or E_2) as d_1 (or d_2), respectively. Now we have:

$$d_1 + d_2 = d.$$

To calculate the radius of the FFZ, we use the formula:

$$F_1 = \sqrt{\frac{\lambda d_1 d_2}{d}}.$$

The width of the FFZ is determined by its radius F_1, which is essential for examining how obstacles affect signal propagation. By strategically positioning the MC and taking the FFZ into account, we can enhance the charging efficiency by leveraging the constructive interference within the FFZ and reducing the impact of destructive interference from other Fresnel zones.

$$\sqrt{F_1^2 + d_1^2} + \sqrt{F_1^2 + d_2^2} = d + \frac{\lambda}{2}. \tag{7.20}$$

Since $d = d_1 + d_2$, according to Eq. (7.39), it can be deduced that:

$$F_1 = \sqrt{\frac{\lambda d_1 d_2}{d}}. \tag{7.21}$$

λ is small and $F_1 \ll d_1, F_2 \ll d_2$, hence, we can derive

$$\sqrt{F_1^2 + d_1^2} \approx d_1 + \frac{F_1^2}{2d_1}, \sqrt{F_1^2 + d_2^2} \approx d_2 + \frac{F_1^2}{2d_2}. \tag{7.22}$$

When $d_1 = d_2 = d/2$, we obtain the maximum value of F_1 as F_{1max}:

$$F_{1max} = \frac{1}{2}\sqrt{\lambda d}. \tag{7.23}$$

In our experiment, we utilize a 915 MHz wireless signal for wireless charging, resulting in $\lambda = 32.7$ cm. The distance between the transceivers is $d = 1$ m. According to Eq. (7.21), we have $F_{1\max} \approx 28.6$ cm, which explains the phenomenon observed when the obstacle is placed 30 cm away, enhancing the charging efficiency (see Figs. 7.15 and 7.3).

Drawing from this observation, we concentrate on enhancing energy efficiency through obstacles. When positioned at the SFZ boundary, an obstacle tends to amplify positive outcomes. As the obstacle is moved further from the boundary (reducing the blocked SFZ area), its effectiveness diminishes. An obstacle that obstructs more than half of the SFZ still demonstrates a positive impact, whereas blocking less than half renders the obstacle mostly ineffective. Given that the SFZ phase difference is 2π and inherently detrimental, placing an obstacle within the SFZ disrupts radio wave propagation, mitigating the SFZ's negative influence. Consequently, the charging effect remains comparable to scenarios without obstacles at similar distances.

Next, we examine the impact of obstacles located at the FFZ boundary. Given that the SFZ has a detrimental effect on the FFZ, obstacles within the SFZ can boost charging efficiency by obstructing harmful radio signals, thus improving overall charging performance (see experimental findings in Sect. 7.1.1.2).

The obstruction also hinders a portion of the region, stopping it from serving as a secondary wave emitter. As the SFZ diminishes the FFZ, the energy within obstacles located in the SFZ will undoubtedly reduce. Based on physical analysis and empirical validation, it is observed that when the obstruction spans over half of the SFZ, the beneficial effect becomes significantly noticeable.

We can therefore reformulate our problem as follows.

Problem Definition Considering a set of sensors and obstacles at predefined positions, identify the optimal charging position of the MC to enhance charging efficiency utilizing the obstacles.

Officially, our issue is described as:

Task Description: Provided with a stationary circle (serving as an obstacle) and one focus of an ellipse, identify the position of the other focus so that the circle is tangent to the ellipse, ensuring compliance with the major and minor axis constraints (Eq. (7.23)).

As shown in Fig. 7.9, a sensor is at $(0, 0)$ and a circular obstacle is at $(0, y)$ with a radius R. The tangent point between the obstacle and the Fresnel Zone is (x_1, y_1). The MC's location (the other focus of the ellipse) is (x_0, y_0). The distance between

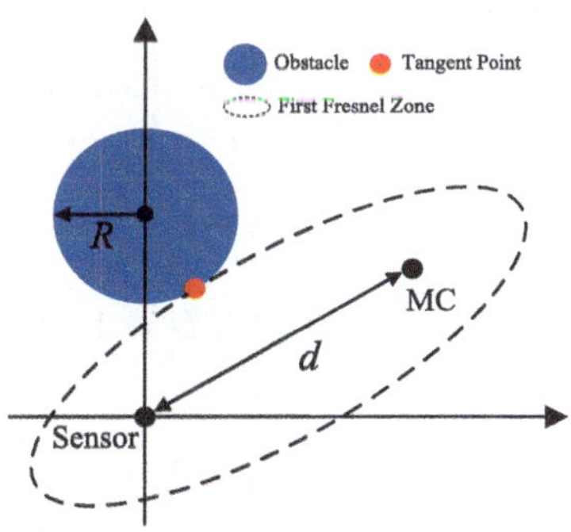

Fig. 7.9 Relationship between obstacle and Fresnel Zone

Fig. 7.10 Various zones separated by Fresnel Zones

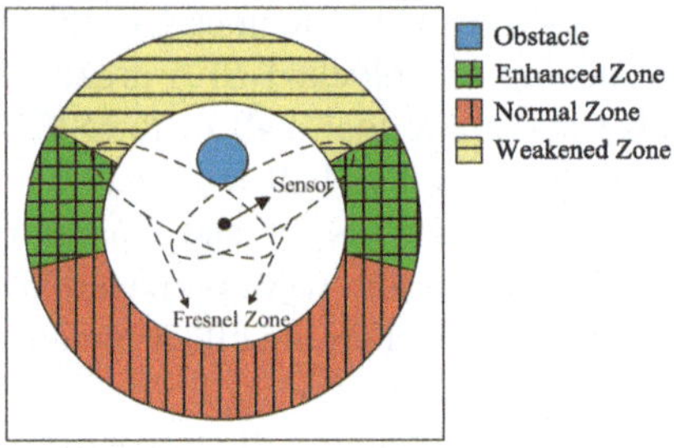

the MC and the tangent point is d. The following equations are derived:

$$\begin{cases} x_0^2 + y_0^2 = d^2; \\ (x_1 - 0)^2 + (y_1 - y)^2 = R^2; \\ \sqrt{{x_1}^2 + {y_1}^2} + \sqrt{(x_1 - x_0)^2 + (y_1 - y_0)^2} = d + \frac{\lambda}{2}. \end{cases} \tag{7.24}$$

The optimal charging location (i.e., (x_0, y_0)) can be determined according to Eq. (7.24). Then we can determine the boundary between enhanced and weakened zones. If an obstacle blocks the FFZ, the charging efficiency will be significantly reduced. The boundary can be obtained by modifying the third formula in Eq. (7.24) to $\sqrt{x_1^2 + y_1^2} + \sqrt{(x_1 - x_0)^2 + (y_1 - y_0)^2} = d + \frac{\lambda}{2} + \frac{\lambda}{4}$ (i.e., an obstacle covers half of the SFZ). In this case, the impact of obstacles becomes progressively weaker.

To express the impact of obstacles on wireless charging, we categorize the candidate locations of the MC into three types: enhanced zones, normal zones, and weakened zones, as shown in Fig. 7.10. Enhanced/weakened zones refer to areas where the MC's charging signals are enhanced/weakened by obstacles. Normal zones indicate areas where signal propagation is unaffected.

Next, we define two constants, ϕ and ω, to express the enhanced and weakened influences of obstacles:

$$p(s_i, c_j) = \begin{cases} \frac{\phi\alpha}{(d(s_i,c_j)+\beta)^2}, \text{Enhanced}, \phi > 1 \\ \frac{\alpha}{(d(s_i,c_j)+\beta)^2}, \text{Normal}, \\ \frac{\omega\alpha}{(d(s_i,c_j)+\beta)^2}, \text{Weakened}, 0 < \omega < 1 \end{cases} \tag{7.25}$$

Here, $d(s_i, c_j) \leq D$. D is the maximum effective charging radius.

7.1.2.3 Charging Scheme Design

In order to address the $P3$ problem, we initially use the discretization method for the charging area, resulting in $N \times \mathcal{K}$ concentric circles. Here, N represents the number of sensors and $\mathcal{K}$ denotes the number of concentric circles centered around each sensor.

Based on the findings in [13], it is possible to calculate the number Z of discretization zones formed by $N \times \mathcal{K}$ concentric circles in a 2D space, where Z satisfies

$$Z \leq (4N \cdot \mathcal{K})^2 - 4N \cdot \mathcal{K} + 2. \tag{7.26}$$

Subsequently, each discretized zone is evaluated using enhanced, normal, and weakened categories as outlined in Sect. 7.1.2.2.

We introduce a set $\theta_z = \{\theta_z(s_1), \theta_z(s_2), \ldots, \theta_z(s_N)\}$ to denote the impact of obstacles on the sensors $\{s_1, s_2, \ldots, s_N\}$ when the MC is situated in a particular discretization area z. The parameter $\theta_z(s_i)$ is assigned values of 1, 0, and -1 to indicate enhanced, normal, and weakened areas, respectively.

Because the discretized areas are numerous, we introduce an algorithm named CCS (Constructing Candidate Set) to streamline the charging candidate set A in the following manner:

This approach allows us to effectively handle the numerous discretized regions and simplify the task of identifying the best charging spots for the MC.

Algorithm 26 Constructing Candidate Set (CCS)

Require: Charging location set C containing Z discretization areas with different charging affects θ.
Ensure: Charging location candidate set A.
$i \leftarrow 0, k \leftarrow 0, A \leftarrow \{c_1\}$;
for each discretization area $c_j \in C$ **do**
  for each candidate location $c_k \in A$ **do**
    if $\theta_k < \theta_j$ **then**
      Remove c_k from A and add c_j into A;
      break;
    else if $\theta_k > \theta_j$ **then**
      c_k is better than c_j and there will be no appropriate position for adding c_j;
      break;
    else if $\theta_k = \theta_j$ **then**
      $A \leftarrow A \cup \{c_j\}$;
      break;
    end if
  end for
end for
return A.

Within the CCS algorithm, our primary focus is to compare elements in A_k against θ_i. For instance, if the MC is capable of delivering charging services to three sensors in two distinct discretization regions, where $\theta_1 = \{0, -1, 1\}$ and $\theta_2 = \{0, 1, -1\}$, we cannot assess the charging efficiency between these two discretization regions. This is due to the fact that we rely on the average power output to determine efficiency while constructing the charging model in the presence of obstacles.

In cases where $\theta_1 = \{0, 1, 1\}$ and $\theta_2 = \{0, 1, -1\}$, the charging efficiency of these discretization regions are similar. This is due to $\theta_1[1] = \theta_2[1]$, $\theta_1[2] = \theta_2[2]$, and $\theta_1[3] > \theta_2[3]$. Therefore, θ_1 can be considered more suitable than θ_2. With CCS, if θ_1 has already been stored in A, we will substitute θ_1 with θ_2.

Once the charging candidate areas A have been identified using the CCS algorithm, we enhance set A by selecting the optimal charging candidate location c^* and mapping out the charging route. We introduce a Greedy Optimal Algorithm (GOA) described in Algorithm 27. The main goal is to maximize the charging efficiency during each iteration when selecting the charging location:

$$c^* = \arg\max \frac{f(C_{sel} \cup \{c_j\}) - f(C_{sel})}{\widetilde{E}_{tot}(C_{sel} \cup \{c_j\}) - \widetilde{E}_{tot}(C_{sel})}, c_j \in C \backslash C_{sel}. \tag{7.27}$$

Here, $\widetilde{E}_{tot}$ represents the total approximated energy cost.

Algorithm 27 Greedy Optimal Algorithm (GOA)

Require: The set A of charging candidate areas, the energy g consumed by MC per unit routes, the Set S of sensors, the energy capacity budget E_B of MC, the coordinates BS of BS.
Ensure: The selected candidate charging location set C_{sel} and corresponding $f(C_{sel})$.
$C_{sel} \leftarrow \varnothing$, $\widetilde{E}_{tot}(C_{sel}) \leftarrow 0$;
while $A \neq \varnothing$ **do**
  for all $c_j \in A$ **do**
    Calculate $\Delta_f^{c_j} \leftarrow f(C_{sel} \cup \{c_j\}) - f(C_{sel})$;
    Calculate the path length from the position to the c_j;
    Calculate $\Delta_{\widetilde{E}_{tot}}^{c_j} \leftarrow \widetilde{E}_{tot}(C_{sel} \cup \{c_j\}) - \widetilde{E}_{tot}(C_{sel})$;
  end for
  $c^* \leftarrow \arg\max\{\Delta_f^{c_j} / \Delta_{\widetilde{E}_{tot}}^{c_j} | c_j \in C \backslash C_{sel}\}$;
  if $(\widetilde{E}_{tot}(C_{sel} \cup \{c^*\}) \leq E_B$ **then**
    $C_{sel} \leftarrow C_{sel} \cup \{c^*\}$;
    $A \leftarrow A \backslash c^*$;
  else
    break;
  end if
end while
return C_{sel}, $f(C_{sel})$.

Another important aspect we must consider is guaranteeing that the MC possesses sufficient energy to get back to the BS (i.e., $\widetilde{E}_{tot}(C_{sel} \cup \{c^*\}) \leq E_B$).

In the event that the sensors at a particular charging candidate spot are fully recharged, we will update A iteratively and choose the suitable charging candidate zone.

While Algorithm 27 is capable of solving $P3$, our charging scheme's design introduces discretization errors, and the GOA algorithm might induce inaccuracies.

In Sect. 7.1.3.1, we demonstrate that these discretization errors can be bounded, indicating that our proposed scheme is promising despite potentially compromising some accuracy.

Having acquired all the charging locations along with their respective charging times, we will now illustrate the process of building the charging route for the MC.

7.1.2.4 Charging Route Planning with Obstacles Avoidance

Given the presence of obstacles, a considerable disparity can emerge between the theoretically optimal results and the actual outcomes when both the charging route and charging efficiency maximization are taken into account simultaneously [14]. Hence, we initially identify all charging locations as outlined in Sect. 7.1.2.3, before delineating the charging route for the MC while considering the obstacles.

Considering the presence of obstacles, the problem of planning a charging route can be seen as a Euclidean Traveling Salesman Problem with Obstacles (ETSPO). To address this problem, we follow these steps:

1. Transform Obstacle Shapes: We convert the obstacles' shapes, whether they are concave polygons or convex multiline shapes, into convex polygons employing the Graham algorithm [15].

2. Calculate Shortest Collision-Free Paths: We determine the shortest collision-free Euclidean routes between every pair of charging locations by forming a visibility graph. The vertices of this graph correspond to the corners of the polygonal obstacles [16]. Each vertex in the set V is traversed and linked by an edge based on the mutual visibility principle. When obstacles are present on the visible path, we identify the shortest collision-free Euclidean routes using an obstacle avoidance algorithm (OA) that is appropriate for the specified network.

3. Construct Complete Graph: We build a complete graph where the weights of the edges represent the distances between vertices that do not collide.

4. Solve TSP: Finally, we solve this Traveling Salesman Problem (TSP) on the obtained complete graph using a TSP-solver [17, 18] to determine the charging tour for the MC. Similar to [19, 20], we employ an A-Star algorithm to optimize the charging path.

As illustrated in Fig. 7.11, in the first step, a starting point (v_S), an ending point (v_E), and two irregularly shaped obstacles (one concave and one convex) are shown, forming the vertex set V. Next, in the second step, the concave obstacle is converted into a convex polygon using the Graham algorithm [15]. In the third step, all vertices are traversed and connected based on the principle of mutual visibility, ensuring no obstacles lie between any pair of vertices. Each connection (edge) represents a potential path for the MC to follow, forming the edge set E. Steps (4)-(6) involve using the A-Star algorithm to develop the charging route. Beginning at the initial point (represented by the blue circle in Fig. 7.11) that has two mutually visible points v_5 and v_6, v_5 is chosen due to its shorter edge weight. The edge weight is defined as the Euclidean distance between the endpoints. This procedure is repeated until

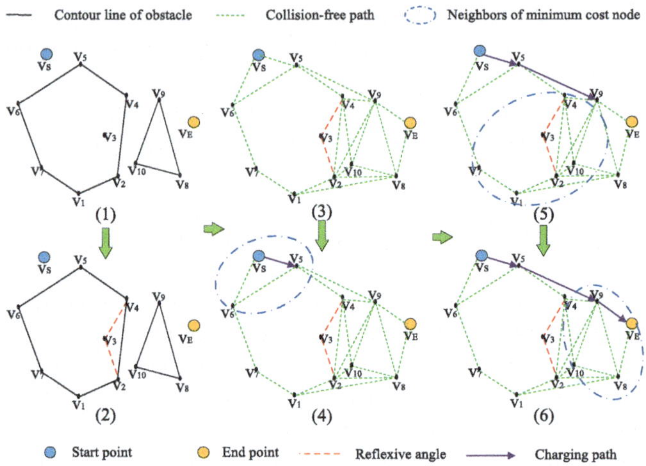

Fig. 7.11 An example of charging route planning

reaching the endpoint. Ultimately, the charging route $v_S \rightarrow v_5 \rightarrow v_9 \rightarrow v_E$ is established.

7.1.3 *Theoretical Analysis*

We analyze the approximation ratio for both charge area discretization and charge time discretization, and then proceed to examine the submodular characteristics. Additionally, we present the approximation ratio of the suggested algorithm.

7.1.3.1 Discretization Approximation Ratio

In earlier sections, we detailed the discretisation processes for both the loading area and the loading time. Consequently, the overall discretisation approximation rate of the solution must account for both aspects.

In order to limit the error in piecewise constant approximation, we introduce a fixed threshold ϵ and establish the subsequent theorem.

Theorem 7.1 *Upon discretizing the charging area, the charging energy achieves an approximation ratio of* $\frac{1}{1+\epsilon}$ *relative to the optimal charging energy.*

Proof Initially, referencing Eq. (7.31), $p(s_i, c_j)$ decreases monotonically as the distance $d(s_i, c_j)$ increases. The discretized charging power is assumed to be the minimum within the discretized charging area. Consequently, we have $1 \leq \frac{p(s_i,c_j)}{\tilde{p}(s_i,c_j)}$.

In conjunction with Eq. (7.12), we derive that $\frac{p(s_i,c_j)}{\widetilde{p}(s_i,c_j)} \le 1+\epsilon$. Thus, we obtain

$$1 \le \frac{p(s_i, c_j)}{\widetilde{p}(s_i, c_j)} \le 1 + \epsilon. \tag{7.28}$$

Prior to discretizing the charging area, as seen in Eq. (7.36), $f(C_{sel})$ is associated with the product of charging power and the respective charging duration. At this point, ignoring the effect of time, we denote C_{sel} as the set of charging candidate locations for the optimal solution of problem $P1$, and C^*_{sel} as the set of charging candidate locations for the approximated solution after the discretization of the charging area. Per Eq. (7.28), we have:

$$f(C^*_{sel}) \le (1+\epsilon) f(C_{sel})$$

This demonstrates that the discretization of the charging area results in an approximation error limited by the factor ϵ. Consequently, the charging energy derived post-discretization is no less than $\frac{1}{1+\epsilon}$ of the optimal charging energy, affirming the reliability of the discretization method.

$$\begin{aligned} &\sum_{c_j \in C^*_{sel}} \widetilde{p}(s_i, c_j) \cdot t_j \ge \sum_{c_j \in C_{sel}} \widetilde{p}(s_i, c_j) \cdot t_j \\ &\ge \sum_{c_j \in C_{sel}} \frac{1}{1+\epsilon} \cdot p(s_i, c_j) \cdot t_j \ge \frac{1}{1+\epsilon} \sum_{c_j \in C_{sel}} p(s_i, c_j) \cdot t_j. \end{aligned} \tag{7.29}$$

Based on Eq. (7.29), it is demonstrated that the charging energy post spatial discretization approximates the optimal charging energy by a factor of $\frac{1}{1+\epsilon}$. ■

Theorem 7.2 *Upon discretizing the charging time, the charging energy for any sensor is approximated to be at least half of the maximum charging energy.*

Proof Referring to Eq. (7.18), let us consider $F^{'}$ as the best solution of problem $P2$ (i.e., the maximum possible energy), where MC can stay for any duration. By discretizing the charging time, and in accordance with the definition of t_{min}, we use $\lfloor \frac{t_j}{t_{min}} \rfloor \cdot t_{min}$ to derive an approximate solution for the optimal charging period. The discrete-time approximate solution for F' is denoted as $F^{'*}$. Therefore, we have

$$\lfloor \frac{t_j}{t_{min}} \rfloor \cdot t_{min} \le t_j. \tag{7.30}$$

We demonstrate that $F^{'*}$ is a viable approximation solution because MC's battery capacity can support the energy usage for any charging candidate within a time slot t_{min}. Referring to Eq. (7.30), another feasible approximation solution $F^{''}$ can be obtained. Clearly, the combined sum of the two approximations $F^{'*}$ and $F^{''}$ surpasses the optimal solution F'. Thus, the following conclusion can be drawn.

$$F'^{*} + F'' \geq F'.$$

Then, we define $F^{\#}$ as the best discretized solution based on the minimum charging time slot t_{min}. It is clear that $F^{\#} \geq F'*$ and $F^{\#} \geq F^{''}$. Hence, we have:

$$2F^{\#} \geq F'* + F^{''} \geq F'.$$

This inequality indicates that the charging energy achieved by any given sensor s_i is at least $\frac{1}{2}$ of the optimal charging energy (i.e., the maximum possible value). ■

Theorem 7.3 *With the discretization of the charging area and time, the aggregate charging energy received by any sensor achieves an approximation ratio of* $\frac{1}{2(1+\epsilon)}$ *compared to the optimal charging energy.*

Proof According to Theorems 7.1 and 7.2, we have verified that the approximation ratio after charging area discretization and charging time discretization is bounded by $\frac{1}{1+\epsilon}$ and $\frac{1}{2}$, respectively. Hence, the overall approximation ratio is $\frac{1}{2(1+\epsilon)}$. ■

7.1.3.2 Complexity Analysis

In our approach, we employ both the CCS and GOA algorithms. Initially, the CCS algorithm is used to determine the optimal candidate charging locations, followed by the GOA algorithm to compute the maximum energy obtained. Consequently, we discuss the complexity of each algorithm below.

To start, we examine the complexity of the CCS algorithm.

In Eq. (7.26), N denotes the total number of sensors, and M can be derived from Eq. (7.15). Consequently, the computational complexity for obtaining M is $T = O(\epsilon^{-1})$. For the CCS algorithm, if the size of the input set is Z, we can determine its complexity as $T = O(\frac{Z(Z-1)}{2}) = O(Z^2) = O(N^4\epsilon^{-4})$. Therefore, the overall computational complexity of the CCS algorithm is $T = O(N^2\epsilon^{-2}) + O(N^4\epsilon^{-4}) = O(N^4\epsilon^{-4})$.

When constructing the weighted graph by the convex hull of obstacles, the Graham Algorithm has a complexity of $T = O(B) = O(1)$, where B indicates the number of obstacles [15]. Then, when applying the principle of mutual visibility, we traverse the weighted graph with all the visible points, and the number of visible points is $B + 2 \approx B$. Hence, we have the corresponding complexity as $T = O(\frac{B(B-1)}{2}) = O(B^2) = O(N^2)$. When planning the charging route, the A-star algorithm has a complexity of $T = O(B^2) = O(N^2)$ [19].

Thus, the overall complexity for conducting the charging route is $T = O(1) + O(N^2) + O(N^2) = O(N^2)$.

Next, we determine the computational complexity of the GOA algorithm.

Within the CCS algorithm, the input set's size is denoted as F. The GOA algorithm must operate F times without modifying F. Thus, its complexity is $T = O(FN^2)$. Therefore, the complexity of the GOA algorithm remains $T = O(FN^2)$.

Thus, by simultaneously accounting for the complexities of CCS and GOA, the total complexity of the suggested scheme is given by $T = O(N^4\epsilon^{-4}) + O(N^2) + O(FN^2) = O(N^4\epsilon^{-4})$.

Theorem 7.4 *EMO encompasses several problems that are classified as NP-hard.*

Proof For the EMO problem, it can be divided into two sub-problems: (i) *how to select the set of charging locations*; and (ii) *how to plan the charging route*. Additionally, it is important to note that these two sub-problems are connected, as finding a solution to the first one lays the foundation for addressing the second one.

To begin with, we transform subproblem into a *Set Cover problem* (SC), whose decision version is recognized as NP-complete, and its optimization version is also acknowledged as NP-hard [21]. The optimization version of the SC problem is described as follows. Consider a set $\mathbb{U}$ (termed as the universe) consisting of m elements ($\mathbb{U} = \{e_1, e_2, \cdots, e_m\}$), an integer k, and a family of subsets $\mathbb{S}$ of $\mathbb{U}$, where $\mathbb{S} = \{\mathbb{S}_1, \mathbb{S}_2, \cdots, \mathbb{S}_k\}$. The objective here is to determine if there is a set covering strategy that employs the minimum number of subsets to cover all elements. We can build an instance of subproblem via an instance of the optimization version of the SC problem. Given a set of sensors S and a set of charging locations C, our problem transforms into finding a subset $C_{sel} \subseteq C$ that maximizes the sensor's received energy $\sum Q(s_i, C_{sel})$ while adhering to budget constraints. Clearly, we can construct an instance of subproblem in polynomial time, establishing that subproblem is NP-hard. Next, we determine the charging route by resolving a traveling salesman problem (TSP), which is known to be NP-hard as well [22]. Therefore, we demonstrate that the EMO problem entails a combination of several NP-hard problems. ■

7.1.4 Simulation and Experiments

In this part, we evaluate our approach against other techniques through test-bed experiments to emphasize its characteristics.

7.1.4.1 Experimental Setup

The test-bed experiments take place in a two-dimensional area containing obstacles. As illustrated in Fig. 7.24, an MC equipped with a TX91501 transmitter (915 MHz) and five rechargeable sensors using Powercast RF-receiving antennas are employed (Powercast, http://www.powercastco.com). The maximum charging range D is 3 meters, which is within the advertised 1 meters (32.8 ft). The sensors have an energy capacity (i.e., $Q_B(s_i)$) of 10.8 KJ. Unlike [9], which uses two different capacity batteries for charging and traveling, our experiment employs an MC with only one battery with a capacity of 2000 KJ.

In our study, we executed the proposed algorithms on the BS instead of the MC. During the experiment, CCS and GOA were able to identify solutions within a few minutes, which is insignificant in comparison to the sensor nodes' lifespan (i.e., over 3 weeks in our setup).

Due to the absence of methods for optimizing charging efficiency in the presence of obstacles in the existing literature, we utilize five algorithms for baseline comparison: Greedy Charging Position Selection algorithm (GCPS) [9], Full Charge algorithm (FC) [23], Full Charge while Disregarding Obstacles' Positive Effects (FCI) [3], Minimum Energy Path algorithm (MEP) [24], and Random Charge algorithm (RAN).

- GCPS algorithm: This algorithm is akin to ours, but it disregards travel expenses when forming potential charging locations, while ours considers both charging efficiency and travel costs.
- FC algorithm: This algorithm utilizes a greedy approach to optimize charging efficiency by having the MC halt at a designated location and charge all sensors within its range to their full energy capacity.
- FCI algorithm [3]: Like the FC algorithm, it considers only the reduction in efficiency due to obstacles and ignores any improvement effects.
- MEP algorithm: For each iteration, it picks the candidate charging locations with the highest energy requirements, and the MC remains at each selected location for one time slot.
- RAN algorithm: It randomly chooses accessible charging spots, and the MC will subsequently charge the sensors one by one until they reach their full energy capacity.

7.1.4.2 Experimental Results

In our experiment, we concentrate on energy efficiency with the deployment of 2–5 sensors for comparative analysis. As illustrated in Fig. 7.27, when $N > 3$, our approach demonstrates the highest charging efficiency, surpassing FC by a minimum of 10%. This improvement is attributed to our algorithm's strategy of selecting the charging position with the highest marginal gains of c as per Eq. (7.54), whereas FC is required to fully charge all sensors within the MC's range, which is comparatively less efficient. Additionally, FCI merely avoids obstacles rather than leveraging them, leading to reduced performance. We validate that our approach can utilize obstacles to further enhance charging efficiency in real-world scenarios (Figs. 7.12 and 7.13).

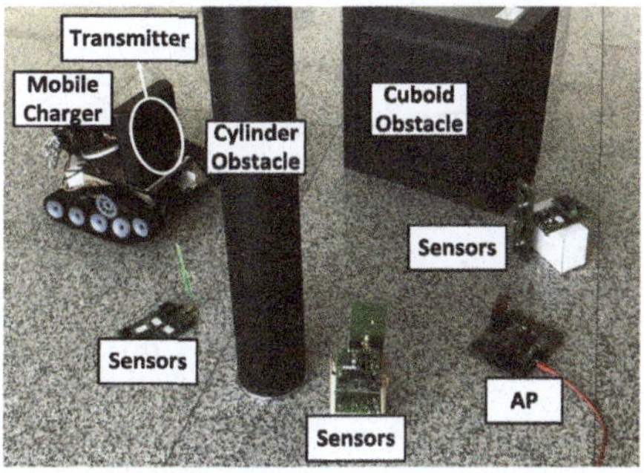

Fig. 7.12 Test-bed prototype: a mobile charger, obstacles, and rechargeable sensors

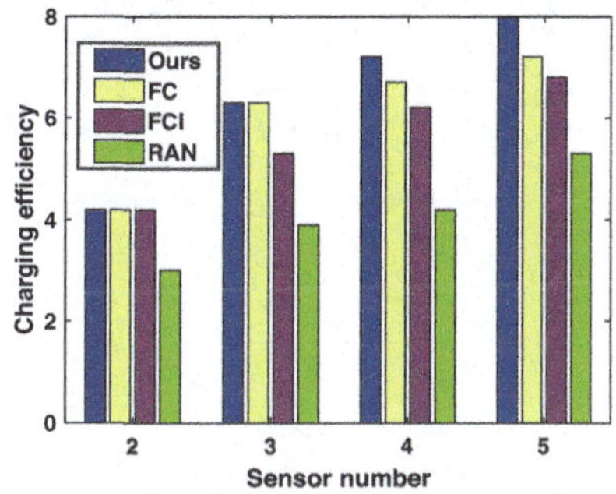

Fig. 7.13 Performance comparison on test-bed experiments

Table 7.1 Simulation configurations

Parameters	Values
System area	100×100 m
Number of sensors	100
Hardware parameter α	100
Hardware parameter β	40
Enhanced influence coefficient ϕ	1.1
Weakened influence coefficient ω	0.7
Minimum charging power p_{min}	0.04
Discretization threshold ϵ	0.25
Obstacle coverage ratio ρ	10%
Energy budget E_B of MC	2500 J
Energy capacity $Q_B(s_i)$ of sensor s_i	50 J

7.1.4.3 Simulation Configurations

In our simulations, related configurations are summarized in Table 7.1.

To provide comprehensive validation of the proposed method, we perform simulations on several parameters: discretization threshold ϵ, MC battery capacity E_B, obstacle coverage ratio ρ, sensor count N, minimum time slot t_{min}, energy consumption g per unit of path length, system area, effective charging distance D, residual charging energy $Q_l(s_i)$ needed by each sensor, and constants α and β in the energy transfer equation.

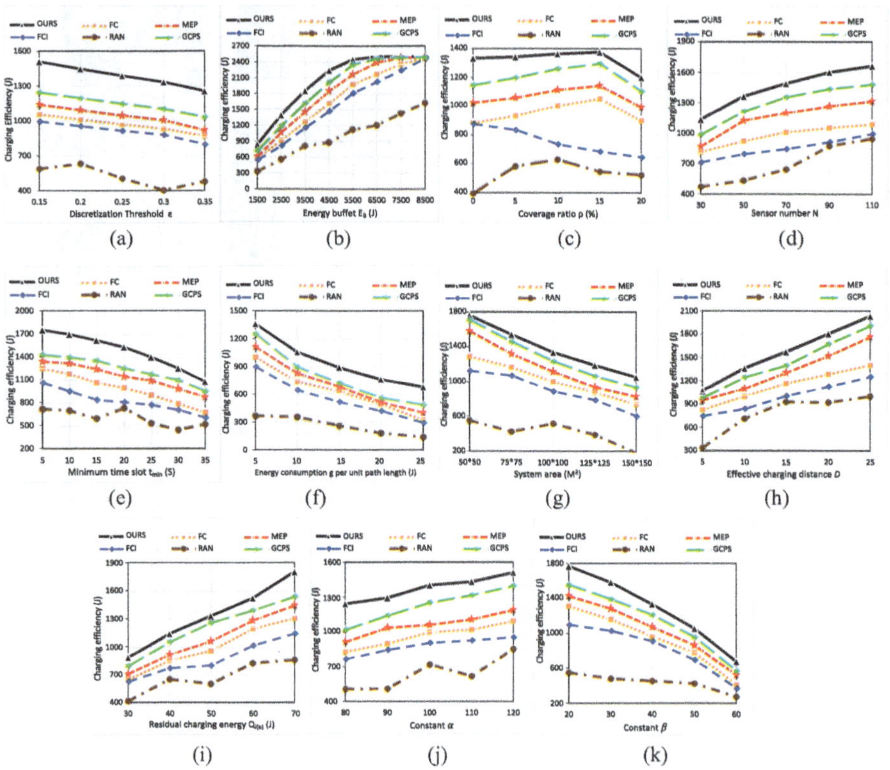

Fig. 7.14 Performance comparison among Ours, GCPS, FC, FCI, MEP, and RAN in charging energy efficiency. (**a**) Efficiency vs. discretization threshold; (**b**) Efficiency vs. energy budget; (**c**) Efficiency vs. coverage ratio; (**d**) Efficiency vs. sensor number; (**e**) Efficiency vs. minimum time slot; (**f**) Efficiency vs. energy consumption per unit path length; (**g**) Efficiency vs. system area; (**h**) Efficiency vs. effective charging distance; (**i**) Efficiency vs. residual charging energy; (**j**) Efficiency vs. constant α; (**k**) Efficiency vs. constant β

7.1.4.4 Performance Comparison

Impact of Charging Discretization Threshold ϵ The error rate for charging area discretization ranges from 0.15 to 0.35 as shown in Fig. 7.14a. Apart from RAN, all algorithms exhibit a decreasing trend as ϵ rises, and our algorithm attains the maximum charged energy compared to the others. Furthermore, as the error rate rises, the charged energy declines.

Our scheme always outperforms other algorithms when the discretization threshold ϵ varies from 0.15 to 0.35. This is because a larger error rate ϵ increases the energy difference between adjacent subregions and causes a longer distance of discretized subregions, leading to a proportional decline in efficiency.

On average, our algorithm is 20.5% better than the GCPS algorithm, 42.4% better than the FC algorithm, 51.9% better than the FCI algorithm, and 32.6% better than the MEP algorithm.

Impact of Energy Budget E_B According to Fig. 7.14b, when the energy budget is increased from 1500 to 5500 J, all algorithms demonstrate a rising trend. Clearly, as the battery capacity grows, the MC has enough energy to offer charging services to a greater number of sensors, thereby improving charging efficiency. However, when the MC's energy capacity goes from 5500 to 8500 J, this rising trend begins to decelerate.

Our proposed method outperforms other algorithms regarding charging efficiency. According to statistics, it is 5% more efficient than the GCPS algorithm, 20.4% more efficient than the FC algorithm, 28.6% more efficient than the FCI algorithm, and 11.1% more efficient than the MEP algorithm.

Impact of Obstacle Coverage Ratio ρ The dimensions of the obstacles will affect the charging efficiency, and we therefore concentrate on the coverage ratio ρ within the plane.

As per the charging model with obstacles discussed in Sect. 7.1.2.2, the coverage ratio ρ influences the dimensions of enhanced, normal, and weakened areas, which consequently impacts the sensors' received power. Illustrated in Fig. 7.14c, as the coverage ratio increases from 0% to 15%, a rising trend is observed in all algorithms except for the RAN and FCI algorithms. This phenomenon is attributed to the enlarged enhanced areas due to the increased coverage ratio.

As the obstacle coverage rate rises from 15 to 20%, there is a significant decline in the performance of all algorithms except for the RAN algorithm. This happens because, under these conditions, obstacles obstruct the line-of-sight transmission power without causing reflection [3]. Additionally, the MC will navigate around the obstacles more often, resulting in higher travel costs.

Moreover, in the absence of obstacles, the charging efficiencies of both FCI and FC are equivalent due to the similarity in their charging schemes. Additionally, the FCI algorithm considers all obstacles as having a negative impact. Consequently, its efficiency significantly decreases as the obstacle coverage ratio increases.

Overall, our algorithm shows an improvement over GCPS, FC, FCI, and MEP by 18.3, 37.6, 74, and 23.2%, respectively, suggesting that our approach leverages obstacles to boost charging efficiency.

Impact of Sensor Number N Considering the charging model with obstacles, the quantity of sensors N affects the sensors located in the effective charging zone, subsequently influencing the charging efficiency and the MC's path planning.

Figure 7.14d demonstrates that every algorithm experiences enhanced performance as the sensor count rises from 30 to 110. With more sensors, MC can extend its charging services to a greater number, resulting in denser charging candidates and thereby improving charging efficiency.

From a statistical perspective, our algorithm outperforms GCPS, FC, FCI, and MEP in charging efficiency by 11.2, 46.9, 68.9, and 24.5% respectively.

Impact of the Minimum Time Slot t_{min} The length of minimum time slot t_{min} will affect the residual time of MC at the charging candidate location.

As illustrated in Fig. 7.14e, all algorithms except the RAN algorithm exhibit a downward trend as the minimum time slot extends from 5 to 30 s. MC necessitates at least one minimum time slot at the candidate location for each iteration. When the minimum time slot is lengthy, the actual charge time is likely to be significantly shorter than the minimum time slot, leading to energy inefficiency. Consequently, the curve declines more rapidly as the time slot increases.

To summarize, our suggested algorithm surpasses GCPS, FC, FCI, and MEP in terms of charging efficiency by 18.2, 49.0, 78.1, and 28.0%, respectively.

Impact of Energy Consumption g Per Unit Path Length The energy usage g per unit of path length influences the traveling cost of the MC because of its limited battery capacity. Therefore, we investigate this aspect in practical situations.

As illustrated in Fig. 7.14f, the performance of all algorithms except for the RAN algorithm diminishes as g rises. This is due to the limited battery capacity of the MC. Evidently, charging efficiency declines significantly as the trip's energy consumption grows. Our approach strikes a balance between effective charging power and travel expenses in the selection of charge candidates. It ensures nearly optimal charge power while also reducing the MC's travel costs.

Taking into account both theoretical analysis and simulation outcomes, our proposed algorithm outperforms other algorithms. Specifically, it shows a 19.8% improvement over the GCPS algorithm, a 47.1% improvement over the FC algorithm, a 69.2% improvement over the FCI algorithm, and a 32.6% improvement over the MEP algorithm.

Impact of System Area As illustrated in Fig. 7.14g, with the expansion of the system area, the charging efficiency of all algorithms except the RAN algorithm declines, demonstrating the superiority of our scheme. This is because the larger the system area, the fewer the number of sensors that can be served.

On average, our scheme is 6.6% better than GCPS algorithm, 34.3% better than FC algorithm, 52.6% better than FCI algorithm, and 18% better than MEP algorithm.

Impact of Effective Charging Distance D In real-world scenarios, the optimal charging range for wireless power transfer can differ between individual MCs. These variations in charging distance impact the number of sensors that can be effectively charged, potentially leading to reduced charging efficiency. Hence, it is crucial to account for the impact of the effective charging distance.

Figure 7.14h illustrates that the efficiency of all algorithms increases with the effective charging distance. With a greater charging effective distance, an MC positioned at the same candidate charging location can serve more sensors. This enhances the MC's charging efficiency and minimizes energy loss during each charge. Additionally, the MC's fixed and limited battery capacity enables it to travel to more candidate charging areas.

In summary, our proposed algorithm surpasses GCPS, FC, FCI, and MEP with improvements of 7.8, 36.6, 56.3, and 17.2%, respectively.

Impact of Residual Charging Energy $Q_l(s_i)$ of Each Sensor The residual power of each sensor in the actual WRSNs is usually different, which will affect the charging performance.

As illustrated in Fig. 7.14i, the charging efficiency of all algorithms, except for the RAN algorithm, improves in relation to $Q_l(s_i)$. After selecting a candidate charging location, the MC must remain longer in other algorithms, except the MEP algorithm, as $Q_l(s_i)$ increases. Consequently, MC uses more energy for charging, and the charging efficiency rises.

Of all algorithms, the core principle of the MEP algorithm is choosing the charging candidate location with the highest energy requirement, and this candidate location is re-evaluated at each interval t_{min}. In our approach, the MC's travel distance using the MEP algorithm could be minimal, yet the charging cost remains significant. Therefore, the MEP algorithm continues to exhibit an upward trend.

Figure 7.14i shows that our proposed algorithm outperforms the GCPS algorithm by 9.8%, the FC algorithm by 33.7%, the FCI algorithm by 52.1%, and the MEP algorithm by 22.5%.

7.2 Wireless Charging with Fresnel Diffraction Model

7.2.1 Problem Statement

7.2.1.1 Network Model

A WRSN consists of three components: several rechargeable sensors, a mobile charger (MC), and a base station (BS).

In our framework, N omnidirectional rechargeable sensors $S = \{s_1, s_2, \ldots, s_N\}$ with fixed locations are deployed on a plane Ω. These sensors are tasked with performing sensing and monitoring activities in the environment. When active, sensors can operate in two modes: work mode and sleep mode. In work mode, they gather and transmit data, whereas in sleep mode, they switch to an energy-saving state, enabling them to last for an extended period (around 10 days in this study). Periodically, the sensors are roused from their sleep to carry out monitoring tasks. After data collection, they revert to sleep mode. For instance, in our experiment described in Sect. 7.1.4, the sensors monitor temperature every hour. After completing the sensing task, they switch to sleep mode. Since the sensors relay data from other nodes only during work mode, we employ a standard energy-saving clock synchronization mechanism, 802.11 PSM [25], to ensure all nodes operate or sleep simultaneously.

Furthermore, the network contains H static three-dimensional obstacles $O = \{o_1, o_2, \ldots, o_H\}$ of various shapes. Sensors are prohibited from being placed within the obstacles, and the mobile charger is unable to traverse these obstacles.

The MC uses WPT technology to recharge the sensors and returns to the BS before depleting its energy, thus only a subset of sensors can be recharged on each charging trip. Additionally, the BS gathers data from the sensors and offers a rapid power supply or battery replacement for the MC.

7.2.1.2 Simplified Charging Model

For the sake of simplicity, we first disregard obstacle impacts and use Friis's free space equation as our energy transfer model. When the mobile charger is located at position c_i, the power received by sensor s_j can be described by the empirical model shown below:

$$p(c_i, s_j) = \begin{cases} \frac{\alpha}{(d(c_i,s_j)+\beta)^2}, & d \leq D \\ 0. & d > D \end{cases} \tag{7.31}$$

In this context, α and β are parameters influenced by both the hardware and the conditions of the environment. The function $d(c_i, s_j)$ represents the direct line-of-sight distance between the sensor s_j and the mobile collector (MC).

It is clear that the strength of the charge diminishes progressively with increasing distance. When the charge drops below a certain threshold p^{th}, the energy detected by the sensors becomes insignificant. Consequently, by defining

$$\frac{\alpha}{(D+\beta)^2} = p^{th}, \tag{7.32}$$

we can obtain

$$D = \sqrt{\frac{\alpha}{p^{th}}} - \beta. \tag{7.33}$$

In this context, D denotes the maximum effective range of a charger. Therefore, if a sensor is positioned at a significant distance from a charger, the power it receives can be disregarded.

It is important to mention that Eq. (7.31) does not account for the influence of obstacles. Nonetheless, in real-world scenarios, obstacles are nearly everywhere and have a substantial effect on wireless signal propagation, which can influence the charging efficiency.

To illustrate this point, we perform a straightforward experiment displayed in Fig. 7.15. We utilize the commercially available TX91501 wireless charger along with wireless rechargeable sensors developed by Powercast (http://www.powercastco.com).

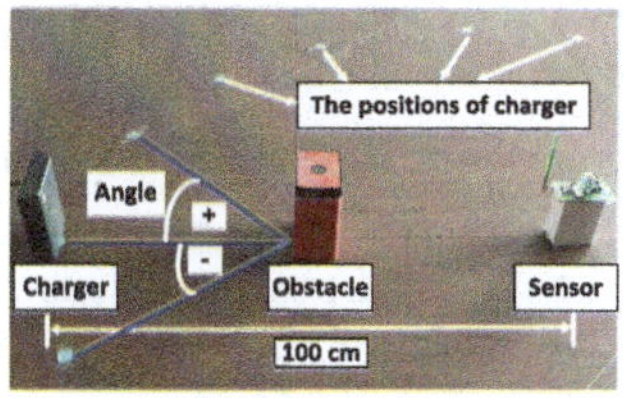

Fig. 7.15 Experimental scene

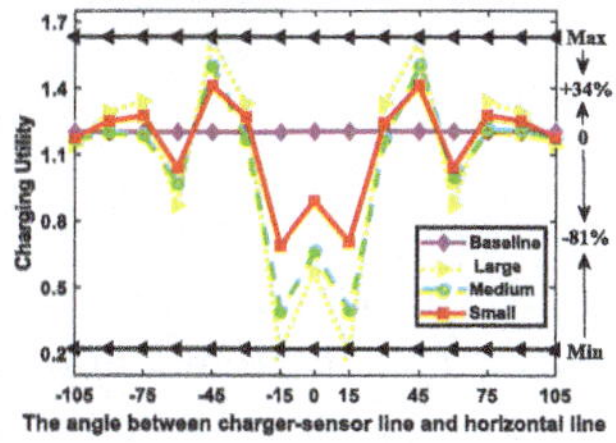

Fig. 7.16 Experimental result

In our study, considering the sensor as the focal point, we construct an arc with a 100 cm radius to represent possible charging positions, ensuring uniform charging power without any obstructions. To reduce angular interference, the sensor is consistently oriented towards the charger in our setup. Furthermore, the sensor and the obstacle positions are stationary, maintaining a fixed distance of 50 cm between them. Subsequently, we position the charger at various points along the arc.

As illustrated in Fig. 7.16, the charging utility (refer to the definition in Sect. 7.2.1.3) is documented against the angle formed between the horizontal line and the line connecting the charger and sensor.

In Fig. 7.16, the impact of obstacles on the charging utility at various angles is illustrated. The large metal obstacle, marked by the yellow dotted line, has dimensions of $12.5 \times 8.5 \times 18.5$ cm. The green dotted line denotes a medium-sized cylindrical metal obstacle with a diameter of 10 cm and a height of 18.5 cm. The red line represents a water cup with a 6.5 cm diameter and a 19.5 cm height. The position of the obstacles is fixed, as depicted in Fig. 7.15. These variously sized obstacles significantly alter the charging efficiency, leading to changes ranging from a −81% decrease to a +34% increase. This shows that the effect is substantial enough to make the free space transfer model invalid in real-world conditions. Additionally, in some instances, obstacles can enhance the charging power by up to 34%.

As a result, some important questions must be considered: (1) What is the approach to developing a new charging model when obstacles are present? (2) How can the charge utility be evaluated using this new model?

7.2.1.3 Energy Cost Model

We define the set of all candidate positions of the MC as C,[1] and the set of charging positions selected for a certain charging schedule as C'.[2] According to Eq. (7.31), the received power of sensor s_j from the charger at c_i is $p(c_i, s_j)$. We define t_i as the corresponding duration of stay when the MC stays at c_i, and therefore the total energy received by the sensor s_j can be formulated as

$$u_{C'}(s_j) = \sum_{c_i \in C'} p(c_i, s_j) t_i. \tag{7.34}$$

The energy received by a sensor is limited, characterized by the capacity of the sensor and the remaining energy. Typically, sensors store energy in a battery or supercapacitor, so their capacity E^c is finite. Before being replenished by the MC, the sensors have a certain amount of remaining energy E_j^r. Therefore, we define $Q_j^{th} = E^c - E_j^r$ as the maximum energy threshold a sensor can receive from the MC.

Since we are ignoring the energy consumed by the node during the charge cycle, E_j^r is the remaining energy of the node when the MC leaves the base station (i.e., a fixed value), which is also the remaining energy when the MC starts to charge the node. Therefore, Q_j^{th} is also a fixed value, and we can develop an offline algorithm to compute a charging strategy based on Q_j^{th}.

Remark 7.1 As we ignore the energy consumed during the charge cycle, if a sensor's maximum energy threshold is less than the energy consumed during the charge cycle, its maximum energy threshold can also be ignored. Therefore, we will no longer arrange charging services for such sensors.

When the received energy of a sensor exceeds this threshold, the extra energy (i.e., $u_{C'}(s_j) - Q_j^{th}$) will be wasted.

We define the charging utility as the effective energy received by the sensor, i.e.,

$$\mathcal{U}_{C'}(s_j) = \min\{u_{C'}(s_j),\ Q_j^{th}\}. \tag{7.35}$$

Definition 7.1 *Charging utility* $\mathcal{U}$ indicates the sum of charging utility of all sensors:

$$\mathcal{U}(C') = \sum_{j=1}^{N} \mathcal{U}_{C'}(s_j). \tag{7.36}$$

[1] C is an infinite set which leads to a high computational overhead. However, by the discretization method introduced in Sect. 7.2.2.2, we can approximate the infinite set as a finite set.

[2] The way to determine C' will be introduced in Sect. 7.2.2.3.

We then focus on the energy consumption of the MC, which consists of two parts: travel cost and charging cost.

The MC travels to all selected positions by path planning to recharge the sensors before they run out of energy. Finding the shortest closed tour is similar to solving an NP-hard traveling salesman problem (TSP) with obstacles [26]. We denote the traveling distance of the MC as $\mathcal{R}(C')$, making the traveling cost $\gamma\mathcal{R}(C')$. Here, γ represents the energy cost per unit length, which depends on the MC's hardware configurations.

Regarding the charging cost, the MC has a fixed rated power σ and transmits electromagnetic waves to provide charging services for sensors at position c_i for a duration of t_i. Thus, the charging cost is $\sigma \sum_{c_i \in C'} t_i$.

Therefore, the total energy cost for C' is

$$F(C') = \gamma\mathcal{R}(C') + \sigma \sum_{c_i \in C'} t_i. \tag{7.37}$$

7.2.1.4 Problem Formulation

The MC supplies sensors with energy using its own battery, which has a finite energy capacity of B. After reaching all chosen charging spots, the MC must conserve sufficient energy to return to the BS for recharging, preventing energy depletion. The equation below must always hold:

$$\gamma\mathcal{R}(C') + \sigma \sum_{c_i \in C'} t_i \le B.$$

With this constraint, our problem is: *What are the optimal charging positions, traversal paths, and dwell times to ensure maximum charging efficiency across the entire network despite obstacles?* We formulate the problem of charging utility maximization with obstacles (NICE) as follows:

$$\begin{aligned} &\textbf{(P1)} \quad max \quad \mathcal{U}(C'), \\ &s.t. \ \gamma\mathcal{R}(C') + \sigma \sum_{c_i \in C'} t_i \le B. \end{aligned}$$

Addressing the NICE problem involves overcoming multiple obstacles: (1) Incorporating the effects of obstacles makes the computation of charging utility much more complex. (2) The infinite number of potential charging positions results from their continuous distribution. (3) NICE combines multiple interrelated NP-hard problems in a non-linear fashion, posing significant challenges.

7.2.2 Schematic Design

In this section, to minimize computational overhead, we begin by discretizing the intricate charge region by outlining contour lines according to energy differences, resulting in multiple candidate positions. Subsequently, we identify positions constrained by energy using a greedy algorithm. Finally, we devise the shortest charging path considering any obstacles.

7.2.2.1 Charging Model with Obstacles

Obstacles have a considerable impact on energy transfer, causing the Friis free space equation to be valid only in perfect conditions, and not in practical situations. Hence, we introduce a new charging model with obstacles grounded on the Fresnel diffraction model. It is important to note that we restrict our analysis to obstacles composed of metals, water, and conductors. For these materials, wave penetration does not happen, and the reflected energy wave behaves as if it is completely blocked.

As stated by the "Huygens-Fresnel" principle [27], every unobstructed wavelet on the wavefront can be considered a source emitting at the same frequency as the incident wave. The vibration of the wave at any given point is a result of the combined effect of all these wavelets.

We introduce the idea of Fresnel zones to describe how barriers influence the energy transfer process. As illustrated in Fig. 7.17, Fresnel zones consist of areas between concentric ellipsoids that are centered on two focal points: a charger and a sensor. Energy traverses these zones, with the first Fresnel zone being the most crucial, while the impact of the outer zones is comparatively insignificant. Prior research has demonstrated that if the first Fresnel zone is clear of obstructions, the Friis free space equation is valid.

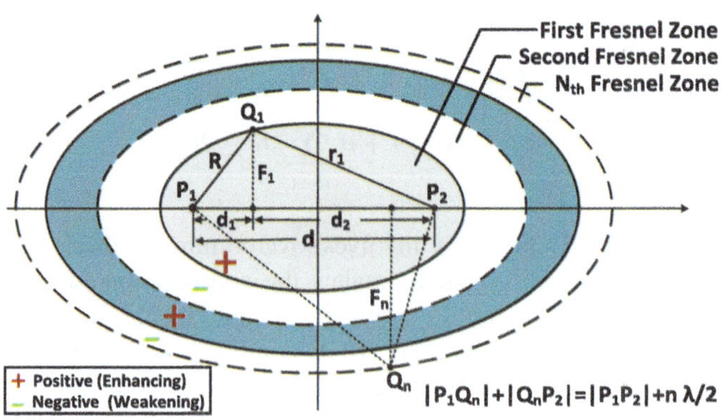

Fig. 7.17 Fresnel Zones: The concentric ellipsoids with charger P_1 and sensor P_2 as foci

In Fig. 7.17, P_1 is the transmitter and P_2 is the receiver. Given the wavelength λ of the charging signal, the n-th ellipse can be expressed as:

$$|P_1 P_n| + |P_n P_2| - |P_1 P_2| = \frac{n\lambda}{2}$$

where P_n represents the point of intersection between the boundary of the n-th Fresnel zone and the charging signal.

$$|P_1 Q_n| + |Q_n P_2| - |P_1 P_2| = n\lambda/2. \tag{7.38}$$

Afterwards, the radius of each Fresnel Zone can be calculated as follows:

$$\sqrt{F_1^2 + d_1^2} + \sqrt{F_1^2 + d_2^2} = d + \lambda/2. \tag{7.39}$$

Given that λ is relatively small (32 cm for powercast) and d is considerably large (e.g., 10 m), the condition $F_1 \ll d_1, d_2$ is satisfied since F_1 is of the same order of magnitude as $\frac{\lambda}{4}$. When the obstacle is very close to the wireless signal source (i.e., d_1 or d_2 is very small), the signal strength will be almost zero, which falls outside the scope of this research.

Hence, we can obtain $F_1 = \sqrt{\lambda d_1 d_2 / d}$. Similarly, the radius of the n-th Fresnel Zone can be obtained as follows:

$$F_n = \sqrt{\frac{n\lambda d_1 d_2}{d_1 + d_2}}. \tag{7.40}$$

From the above illustrations, we observe that the distance difference of the FFZ is $0 \sim \lambda/2$, the Second Fresnel Zone is $\lambda/2 \sim \lambda$, and the Third Fresnel Zone is $\lambda \sim 3\lambda/2$ as shown in Eq. (7.38). Since the phase difference is $\Delta\theta = 2\pi \Delta d/\lambda$, when the distance difference Δd is $\lambda/2$, the phase difference is π.

When the path lengths of two electromagnetic signals differ by $\lambda/2$ and their phase difference is π, the signal strength will be canceled [28]. The wave in the First Fresnel Zone has a phase range of $[0, \pi]$; here, the phase difference 0 represents the energy wave on the LOS path. The Second Fresnel Zone corresponds to a phase range of $(\pi, 2\pi]$, and the Third Fresnel Zone has a $(2\pi, 3\pi]$ range, etc. On average, the contributions of two adjacent zones to the receiver at P_2 are opposite. Hence, the signal strength at P_2 is a composite field, which can be represented by

$$E = E_1 - E_2 + E_3 - E_4 + \ldots, \tag{7.41}$$

where E_n denotes the field or signal strength produced by the individual n-th Fresnel Zone. Equation (7.41) indicates that even-numbered Fresnel Zones exert a weakening or negative effect. Therefore, when obstacles obstruct these even Fresnel Zones, the charging efficiency markedly improves.

Alongside the aforementioned qualitative evaluation, we offer a detailed quantitative analysis for developing an accurate charging model. Our primary concentration is on the impact of obstacles, which differ in shape and placement. In our model, these obstacles are three-dimensional with various shapes. As noted in [29–31], the main influence stems from the vertical surface perpendicular to the line-of-sight (LOS) between the sensor and the charger, while the thickness plays a minor role. This is attributed to the significant impact of the front surface of the obstacle on the rear cross-section, hindering most electromagnetic waves from forming secondary sources.

Materials such as metals and conductors can stop energy waves from passing through them. Even a thin obstacle can prevent these waves, provided there is some sort of barrier. To illustrate this, consider light as an example. When light encounters an obstacle, the surface at the point of contact entirely blocks the light, and the influence of thickness is minimal.

Thus, we can convert the effect of thickness into a problem of multi-screen diffraction. Unfortunately, determining the diffraction due to multiple screens is a highly challenging mathematical issue and no prior research offers precise solutions. Rather, only certain approximation algorithms are currently accessible [29]. Therefore, the impact of the obstacles' shape and size cannot be entirely removed, but the proposed scheme below can enhance accuracy.

The Bullington method, as described in [32, 33], often provides an overly optimistic estimate of received power. Initially, tangential lines are drawn from the transmitter (TX) to the obstacles, choosing the one with the highest elevation angle, ensuring all obstacles either touch or fall beneath this line. This process is similarly applied at the receiver (RX) (i.e., the sensor). The intersection of these lines represents the equivalent screen. As illustrated in Fig. 7.18, for a solitary obstacle, each obstacle can be equated to a single screen using this approach.

It's fascinating to observe that the same obstacle creates different equivalent screens depending on the placement angles. As shown in Fig. 7.18a, when the transceivers are horizontally aligned, the equivalent screen forms a rectangle. In contrast, Fig. 7.18b illustrates that when they are set at an angle, the resulting

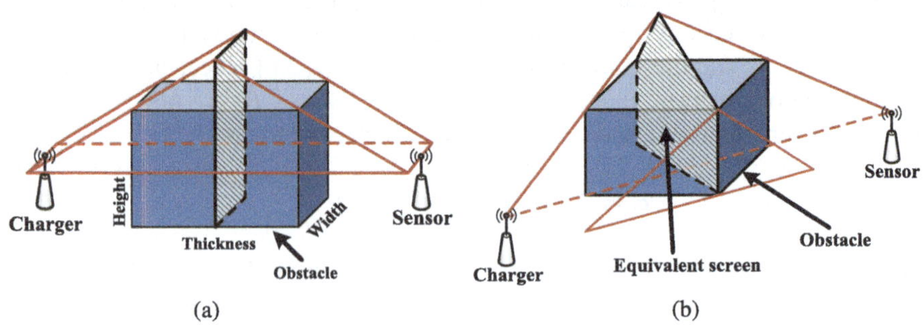

Fig. 7.18 An example for Bullington's method dealing with single obstacle. (**a**) Obstacle in horizontally position. (**b**) Obstacle with a certain angle

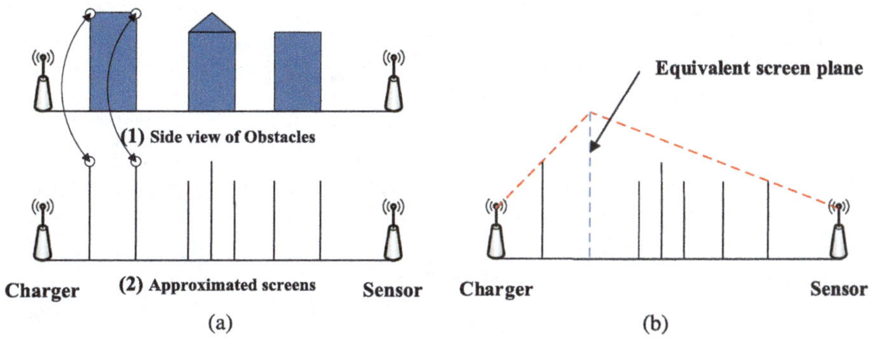

Fig. 7.19 An example for Bullington's method dealing with multiple obstacles. (**a**) Approximation of multiple obstacles by a series of screens. (**b**) Equivalent screen plane after Bullington

equivalent screen becomes an irregular polygon. This difference clearly shows that identical obstacles can produce varied effects when the angles are altered.

Figure 7.19 illustrates that, in the presence of multiple obstacles, two steepest tangential lines (red dotted lines in Fig. 7.19) help define an equivalent screen plane (blue dotted line). Each obstacle is then projected as an equivalent screen on this plane, accounting for various relative angles, as depicted in Fig. 7.18. The final outcome is a collection of irregular polygons on the equivalent screen plane.

After transforming obstacles into a screen, we examine the problem of single-screen diffraction [28, 34] to establish an accurate charging model. As per Babinet's principle [28], defined for scalar optical fields, the total of the fields diffracted by the complementary screens equals the incident wave field when the screens are absent. Using observation point P_2 (i.e., the position of the sensor) to articulate this principle, we have

$$E_0(P_2)F_d^{(a)}(P_2) + E_0(P_2)F_d^{(o)}(P_2) = E_0(P_2), \tag{7.42}$$

with (a) denoting aperture and (o) denoting obstacle. The incident field, $E_0(P_2)$, can be disregarded. Thus, Eq. (7.42) is simplified to

$$F_d^{(o)}(P_2) = 1 - F_d^{(a)}(P_2), \tag{7.43}$$

where $F_d^{(o)}$ and $F_d^{(a)}$ are diffraction coefficients of the obstacle and aperture.

Thus, we can investigate the analogous screen that complements obstacles. Initially, as depicted in Figure 7.20, we begin with a straightforward screen that consists of an irregular opening cut into the infinite screen S.

The spacing between the charger and the infinite screen is d_1, and the spacing between the sensor and the screen is d_2.

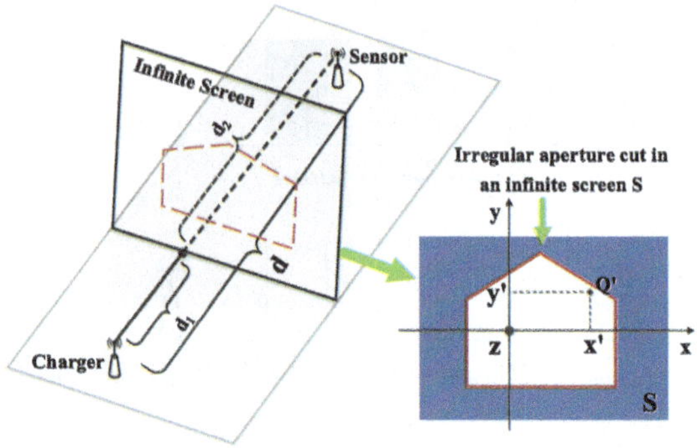

Fig. 7.20 Irregular aperture in infinite screen

In reference to Eq. (7.40), the coordinates x' and y' can be represented using the scale of the First Fresnel Zone radius $F_1 = \sqrt{\lambda d_1 d_2 / d}$ as follows:

$$\begin{cases} x' = \sqrt{n_x \frac{\lambda d_1 d_2}{d_1+d_2}} = \sqrt{n_x}\, F_1, \\ y' = \sqrt{n_y \frac{\lambda d_1 d_2}{d_1+d_2}} = \sqrt{n_y}\, F_1. \end{cases} \tag{7.44}$$

In this context, n_x and n_y represent the number of Fresnel Zones associated with x' and y', respectively. To simplify, the diffraction parameters u and v are defined as

$$\begin{bmatrix} u \\ v \end{bmatrix} = \frac{\sqrt{2}}{F_1}\begin{bmatrix} x' - x_0 \\ y' - y_0 \end{bmatrix} = \begin{bmatrix} \sqrt{2n_x} - \frac{F_1 d_1 x_2 + d_2 x_1}{d_1 d_2} \\ \sqrt{2n_y} - \frac{F_1 d_1 y_2 + d_2 y_1}{d_1 d_2} \end{bmatrix}, \tag{7.45}$$

where (x_0, y_0) represents the equivalent point, derived through mathematical transformations of the source point (x_1, y_1) and the observation point (x_2, y_2). When both the source and observation points (i.e., the charger and sensor positions) lie on the z aperture axis (i.e., $x_1 = x_2 = 0$ and $y_1 = y_2 = 0$), we have $x_0 = y_0 = 0$, simplifying Eq. (7.45) to

$$\begin{bmatrix} u \\ v \end{bmatrix} = \frac{\sqrt{2}}{F_1}\begin{bmatrix} x' \\ y' \end{bmatrix} = \begin{bmatrix} \sqrt{2n_x} \\ \sqrt{2n_y} \end{bmatrix}. \tag{7.46}$$

With these conclusions, the aperture $S_0(x', y')$ is converted into a domain A_0, and subsequently, the diffracted field at point P_2 can be described as

$$E(P_2) = \frac{j}{2} E_0(P_2) \iint_{A_0} e^{-j\frac{\pi}{2}(u^2+v^2)}\, du dv. \tag{7.47}$$

Here,

$$F_d^{(a)}(A_0) = \frac{j}{2} \iint_{A_0} e^{-j\frac{\pi}{2}(u^2+v^2)}\, du dv \tag{7.48}$$

is referred to as the Fresnel diffraction factor. It is important to mention that A_0, u, and v are purely mathematical variables utilized for the sake of representation and derivation, lacking any real physical interpretation. Additionally, A_0 is functionally dependent on c_i and s_j (i.e., $A_0 = A_0(c_i, s_j)$).

7.2.2.2 Spatial Discretization

After developing the new charging model with obstacles, the subsequent task is to choose appropriate charging locations. Because power varies continuously with distance, there are countless potential charging points, demanding substantial computational effort to determine the optimal set. Therefore, we plan to discretize the area to create a finite number of sub-regions, which will ensure near-optimal performance and significantly lower the algorithm's complexity.

The maximum and minimum charging power of sensor s_j are formalized as

$$P_j^{max} = \frac{\alpha}{(0+\beta)^2}, \quad P_j^{min} = p^{th}. \tag{7.49}$$

In this context, 0 represents the smallest charging distance. It should be noted that when the charging distance is 0, the diffraction coefficient becomes $F_d^{(o)}(c_i, s_j) = 1$. To discretize the charging power at sensor s_j, the interval $[P_j^{max}, P_j^{min}]$ is divided into V_j distinct intervals. The power ratio between adjacent discrete charging powers (i.e., the interval boundaries) is kept below the threshold ε^* $(0 < \varepsilon^* < 1)$, meaning,

$$P_j^v = (1+\varepsilon^*)P_j^{v+1}, \tag{7.50}$$

where P_j^v can be represented by

$$P_j^v = P_j^{max}(1+\varepsilon^*)^{-v} \ (1 \le v \le V_j). \tag{7.51}$$

Given that P_j^{max} and P_j^{min} are constant, V_j is fully determined by the threshold ε^*. Specifically, by integrating Eqs. (7.49) and (7.51), V_j is obtained as

$$V_j = \lceil \frac{ln(\frac{P_j^{max}}{P_j^{min}})}{ln(1+\varepsilon^*)} \rceil = \lceil \frac{ln(\frac{\alpha}{\beta^2 p^{th}})}{ln(1+\varepsilon^*)} \rceil. \tag{7.52}$$

As referenced by Eqs. (7.51) and (7.52), once V_j is set, the values for ε^* and each P_j^v $(1 \le v \le V_j)$ can be computed. Subsequently, points with identical values (i.e., P_j^v) are linked to form contours that segment the entire area into various subregions. These contours are concentric circles centered on the sensor in the absence of obstacles, otherwise, they deviate from regular curves. As described by the charging

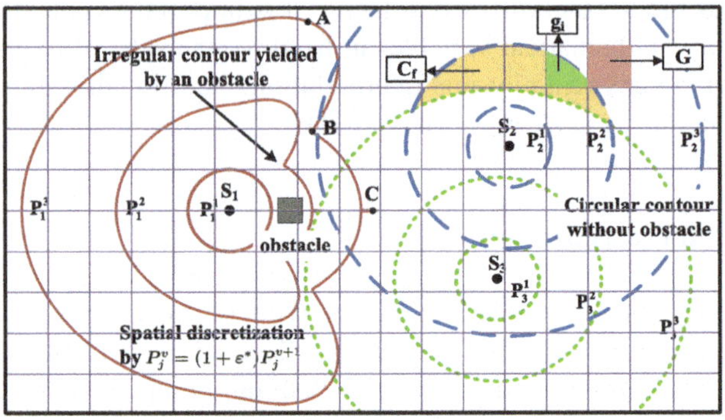

Fig. 7.21 An example of discretized charging regions

model in Sect. 7.2.2.1, if the positions of the sensors and the obstacle are fixed, the charging power at all potential locations around can be accurately determined. Thus, the contour shape delineated by points with the same specific charging power (i.e., P_j^v) can also be faithfully depicted. Specifically, the contour equation is anticipated as follows:

$$c_i : p(c_i, s_j) = \frac{\alpha F_d^{(o)}(c_i, s_j)}{(d(c_i, s_j) + \beta)^2} = P_j^v, \tag{7.53}$$

which can be represented as $B_{s_j}^v$.

Figure 7.21 illustrates the discretization process of charging power using three sensors as an example. Observe that the contour influenced by the obstacle is symmetrical. Additionally, on the outermost isoline of S_1, point A is the most distant point from sensor S_1, point B is the nearest point, point C is farther than point B, and most other points are equidistant. This is because if the charger is located at point A, the charging power will be increased due to obstacles, surpassing most other points that are unaffected by obstacles.

Moreover, these phenomena align with those illustrated in Fig. 7.16.

Once the contours of each sensor are constructed, the entire area is divided into subregions (e.g., region C_f as depicted in Fig. 7.21). Within each subregion C_f, the lowest charging efficiency is estimated as that of the entire subregion C_f. Therefore, all the subregions, which have distinct impacts on the sensors, constitute a collection of potential loading points.

If a point is randomly selected as the MC's dwell position, the loss in performance will rise. Specifically, the sub-regions that are distant from the sensor tend to be quite large, resulting in major inaccuracies in calculating the travel cost. Hence, we partition the whole area into $\Phi = \lceil \frac{|\Omega|}{\Gamma^2} \rceil$ smaller grids G with a side length Γ, as depicted in Fig. 7.21. This approach divides the original charging area into several smaller sub-regions g_i.

A more detailed examination shows that the discretization method introduces errors to the optimal solution. These errors are bounded and will not significantly impact the charging performance.

7.2.2.3 Problem Reformulation and Solution

Upon discretizing the region, we determine all possible positions for the MC to reside. In this scenario, it is assumed that the charging power is uniform across each small sub-region, allowing for the computation of the charging utility at each location. Nonetheless, the MC's limited battery capacity restricts its ability to access all candidate positions. Hence, our objective is to choose a subset of charging positions that optimizes the overall charging utility of the network.

Algorithm 28 Approximation Algorithm for the NICE Problem

Require: The number of sensors N, energy constraint B of MC, and coefficients γ, σ.
Ensure: The selected charging set $C' \subseteq C$ and total charging utility $\mathcal{U}(C')$.

```
Execute spatial discretization and form C subregions;
Initial: C' ← Ø, F(C') ← 0;
while Not all sensors s_j have been fully charged do
    for each c ∈ C do
        Calculate marginal charging utility Δ^c_U ← U(C' ∪ {c}) − U(C');
        Calculate marginal energy cost Δ^c_F ← F(C' ∪ {c}) − F(C') with Algorithm 29;
    end for
    c* ← arg max{Δ^c_U / Δ^c_F | c ∈ C \ C'};
    if F(C' ∪ {c*}) ≤ B then
        C' ← C' ∪ {c*};
        C ← C \ {c*};
    else
        Break;
    end if
end while
Return C', U(C').
```

We present a greedy-based approximation algorithm, which focuses on selecting the loading position c^* in each iteration to maximize the cost-benefit ratio:

$$c^* = \arg \max_{c \in C \setminus C'} \frac{\mathcal{U}(C' \cup \{c\}) - \mathcal{U}(C')}{\mathcal{F}(C' \cup \{c\}) - \mathcal{F}(C')}. \tag{7.54}$$

Here, the numerator $(\mathcal{U}(C' \cup \{c\}) - \mathcal{U}(C'))$ indicates the charging utility gain due to the addition of c. Meanwhile, the denominator $(\mathcal{F}(C' \cup \{c\}) - \mathcal{F}(C'))$ represents the marginal energy consumption, which comprises both charging cost and traveling cost.

7.2.2.4 Routing Problem with Obstacles

After identifying the charging positions, we now concentrate on establishing the MC's charging route. Based on Eq. (7.37) and Algorithm 28, the incremental energy consumption caused by adding location c is

$$\mathcal{F}(C' \cup \{c\}) - \mathcal{F}(C') = \gamma(\mathcal{R}(C' \cup \{c\}) - \mathcal{R}(C')) + \sigma t_{min}. \tag{7.55}$$

It is important to recognize that travel expenses are a crucial element of energy consumption. As indicated by Eq. (7.55), the primary factor influencing marginal energy cost is the distance traveled.

In order to achieve this, it is essential to determine the travel path length of MC. Evidently, identifying the minimum closed tour is akin to resolving a TSP, which is an NP-hard problem [26]. Consequently, we suggest an approximation algorithm that employs the nearest neighbor approach [35] as outlined in Algorithm 29.

Algorithm 29 Nearest Neighbor with Obstacles Algorithm

Require: Charging position set C' and $\mathcal{R}(C')$, newly added charging position $\{c\}$, location of base station c_{bs}, and location of obstacles.
Ensure: The marginal traveling length $\Delta^c_{\mathcal{R}} = \mathcal{R}(C' \cup \{c\}) - \mathcal{R}(C')$.

Initial: $\Delta^c_{\mathcal{R}} \leftarrow 0$, $c_0 \leftarrow c_{bs}$.
while $C' \cup \{c\} \neq \emptyset$ **do**
    for each $c_i \in C' \cup \{c\}$ **do**
        if there are obstacles on the LOS path between c_0 and c_i **then**
            Calculate the shortest Euclidean path (edge (c_0, c_i)) based on obstacle avoidance algorithm (OA) [18];
        else
            Calculate edge (c_0, c_i) (i.e., LOS distance);
        end if
    end for
    Find the edge (c_0, c_i^*) with the minimum length;
    $\Delta^c_{\mathcal{R}} \leftarrow \Delta^c_{\mathcal{R}}$ + edge (c_0, c_i^*);
    $C' \cup \{c\} \leftarrow C' \cup \{c\} - \{c_i^*\}$;
    $c_0 \leftarrow c_i^*$;
end while
$\Delta^c_{\mathcal{R}} \leftarrow \Delta^c_{\mathcal{R}}$ + edge (c_0, c_{bs});
Shorten the path further according to [35].
Return $\Delta^c_{\mathcal{R}}$.

The purpose of Algorithm 29 is to ascertain the marginal travel distance $\Delta^c_{\mathcal{R}} = \mathcal{R}(C' \cup \{c\}) - \mathcal{R}(C')$. Initially, we initialize $\Delta^c_{\mathcal{R}} \leftarrow 0$. Furthermore, since the mobile charger must commence its journey from the base station, we set $c_0 \leftarrow c_{bs}$. If there are obstacles on the LOS path between two charging points, the shortest Euclidean paths can be found using an appropriate obstacle avoidance algorithm (OA) for the network [18]. Otherwise, we directly compute the LOS distance between the two candidate locations.

In each iteration, it is crucial to identify the minimal edge (c_0, c_i^*) and incorporate it into $\Delta_{\mathcal{R}}^c$. This process will proceed until the set $C' \cup \{c\}$ is exhausted.

Upon completing Algorithm 29, and after determining the set of charging positions, a shorter travel path is constructed following the approach in [35]. Assuming the nearest neighbor rule is employed, τ grids $\{g_1, g_2, \ldots, g_\tau\}$ are acquired sequentially, and their respective center points $k_1, k_2, \ldots, k_\tau$ are connected to form the initial closed tour. The powercast dimensions are $10 \times 5 \times 15\,\text{cm}^3$, which is quite small compared to the charging distance, such as 10 m. Therefore, the center of the Powercast can serve as the starting point for our research.

For each point k_i in the set K, we try to link k_{i-1} and k_{i+1} to create the segment $\overline{k_{i-1}k_{i+1}}$ and verify if g_i (the grid of k_i) is covered by the path of $\overline{k_{i-1}k_{i+1}}$. If it is, we determine k_i' within $\overline{k_{i-1}k_{i+1}}$ that is also located in g_i. Otherwise, we perform a binary search along the segment $\overline{k_{i-1}k_{i+1}}$ to find an alternative point k_i' to replace k_i, ensuring that g_i is still path-covered by the segment $\overline{k_{i-1}k_i'}$. The binary search employs the parameter ϱ to regulate the precision.

The initial path (displayed as the red dotted arrow path) is set to $\{k_0k_1k_2k_3k_4k_5k_0\}$. Grid g_1 is path-covered by $\overline{k_0k_2}$; thus, we link k_0 and k_2 with an auxiliary line, and the closest point of k_1 to the auxiliary line is denoted as k_1'. Subsequently, grid g_2 is not path-covered by $\overline{k_1'k_3}$; therefore, a binary search is employed to discover a new path $\overline{k_1'k_2'}$ to replace the segment $\overline{k_1'k_2}$. Specifically, paths 1, 2, 3, 4, and 5 are evaluated, and path 3 is chosen because it path-covers g_2. Hence, we choose node k_2' to substitute k_2. Following the same substitution method, since grid g_5 is not path-covered by $\overline{k_4'k_0}$, k_5' is used to replace k_5. Consequently, the updated traveling path becomes $\{k_0k_1'k_2'k_3'k_4'k_5'k_0\}$. The pertinent theoretical analysis will be detailed in Sect. 7.2.3.2.

7.2.3 *Theoretical Analysis*

7.2.3.1 Submodular Function Theoretical Analysis

Definition 7.2 (Nonnegativity, Monotonicity and Submodularity) For a non-empty finite set V, and an aggregation function $f : 2^V ightarrow R_+$,

- f is called nonnegative if $f(A) \geq 0$ for all $A \subseteq V$;
- f is called monotone if $f(A) \leq f(B)$ for all $A \subseteq B \subseteq V$;
- f is called submodular if $f(\{e\} \bigcup A) - f(A) \geq f(\{e\} \bigcup B) - f(B)$ for all $A \subseteq B, \forall e \in V - B$.

Theorem 7.5 *The function $\mathcal{U}(C')$ is nonnegative, monotonic, and has the property of submodularity.*

Proof According to Definition 7.1, $\mathcal{U}(C')$ is nonnegative, and according to Eq. (7.36), for all $C'' \subseteq C' \subseteq C$, we have

$$\mathcal{U}(C'') = \sum_{j=1}^{N} \mathcal{U}_{C''}(s_j) \leq \sum_{j=1}^{N} \mathcal{U}_{C'}(s_j) = \mathcal{U}(C'), \tag{7.56}$$

which indicates that $\mathcal{U}(C')$ is monotone. Note that, when jointly adopting Algorithm 28 and GCPS algorithm [36], all the charging duration corresponding to each charging position in set C'' is no greater than that in set C', hence we can get Eq. (7.56).

For all $C'' \subseteq C' \subseteq C$, we need to prove $\mathcal{U}(\{e\} \bigcup C'') - \mathcal{U}(C'') \geq \mathcal{U}(\{e\} \bigcup C') - \mathcal{U}(C')$. In [36], it is proved that for any $s_j (0 \leq j \leq N)$, we have

$$\mathcal{U}_{(C'' \cup \{c\})}(s_j) - \mathcal{U}_{C''}(s_j) \geq \mathcal{U}_{(C' \cup \{c\})}(s_j) - \mathcal{U}_{C'}(s_j). \tag{7.57}$$

Based on Eqs. (7.34) and (7.35), we can prove the above inequality in three cases:

Case 1: $Q_j^{th} \leq u_{C''}(s_j)$.

Then we have $\mathcal{U}_{(C')}(s_j) = \mathcal{U}_{(C'')}(s_j) = \mathcal{U}_{(C'' \cup \{c\})}(s_j) = \mathcal{U}_{(C' \cup \{c\}\}}(s_j) = Q_j^{th}$, hence we have

$$\mathcal{U}_{(C'' \cup \{c\})}(s_j) - \mathcal{U}_{C''}(s_j) = 0 = \mathcal{U}_{(C' \cup \{c\})}(s_j) - \mathcal{U}_{C'}(s_j).$$

Case 2: $u_{C''}(s_j) \leq Q_j^{th} \leq u_{C'}(s_j)$.

In this case, $\mathcal{U}_{(C' \cup \{c\})}(s_j) - \mathcal{U}_{C'}(s_j) = 0$, then we get

$$\begin{aligned} &\mathcal{U}_{(C'' \cup \{c\})}(s_j) - \mathcal{U}_{C''}(s_j) \\ &= \min\{Q_j^{th} - u_{C''}(s_j), u_{(C'' \cup \{c\})}(s_j) - u_{C''}(s_j)\} \\ &= \min\{Q_j^{th} - u_{C''}(s_j), p(c, s_j)\Delta t\} \\ &\geq 0 = \mathcal{U}_{(C' \cup \{c\})}(s_j) - \mathcal{U}_{C'}(s_j). \end{aligned}$$

Case 3: $u_{C'}(s_j) \leq Q_j^{th}$.

In this case, we have

$$\mathcal{U}_{(C' \cup \{c\})}(s_j) - \mathcal{U}_{C'}(s_j) = \min\{Q_j^{th} - u_{C'}(s_j), p(c, s_j)\Delta t\},$$

$$\mathcal{U}_{(C'' \cup \{c\})}(s_j) - \mathcal{U}_{C''}(s_j) = \min\{Q_j^{th} - u_{C''}(s_j), p(c, s_j)\Delta t\}.$$

- If $p(c, s_j)\Delta t \leq Q_j^{th} - u_{C'}(s_j)$, then

$$\mathcal{U}_{(C''\cup\{c\})}(s_j) - \mathcal{U}_{C''}(s_j) = p(c, s_j)\Delta t$$
$$= \mathcal{U}_{(C'\cup\{c\})}(s_j) - \mathcal{U}_{C'}(s_j).$$

- If $Q_j^{th} - u_{C'}(s_j) \leq p(c, s_j)\Delta t \leq Q_j^{th} - u_{C''}(s_j)$, then we can get

$$\mathcal{U}_{(C''\cup\{c\})}(s_j) - \mathcal{U}_{C''}(s_j) = p(c, s_j)\Delta t$$
$$\geq Q_j^{th} - u_{C'}(s_j) = \mathcal{U}_{(C'\cup\{c\})}(s_j) - \mathcal{U}_{C'}(s_j).$$

- If $Q_j^{th} - u_{C''}(s_j) \leq p(c, s_j)\Delta t$, then

$$\mathcal{U}_{(C''\cup\{c\})}(s_j) - \mathcal{U}_{C''}(s_j) = Q_j^{th} - u_{C''}(s_j)$$
$$\geq Q_j^{th} - u_{C'}(s_j) = \mathcal{U}_{(C'\cup\{c\})}(s_j) - \mathcal{U}_{C'}(s_j).$$

Then, $\mathcal{U}(C')$ is proved to be submodular.

We can conclude that our optimisation problem is non-negative, monotone and submodular. □

7.2.3.2 Algorithm Approximation Ratio

To bound the performance of our solution in Sect. 7.1.2, we present the approximation ratio analysis of our algorithm and the corresponding proof.

Lemma 7.1 *Having achieved the approximated path $\mathcal{R}(C')$ with τ number of grids, we can obtain $|\mathcal{R}(C')| \leq |\mathcal{R}(C^*)| + 2\sqrt{2}\tau\Gamma$ by path shortening of Algorithm 29 in Sect. 7.2.2.4 with the time complexity $O(\tau^2 \log \frac{\Gamma}{\varrho})$, where ϱ is used to control the granularity of binary search.*

Proof We denote the achieved grids to be path-covered as $G = \{g_1, g_2, \ldots, g_\tau\}$ and the base station k_0 is the start and end point. In addition, we record the optimal stop position, the charging spot obtained by Algorithm 29, and the center location in grid g_i as k_i^*, k_i', and k_i, respectively.

Thereby, we use $\mathcal{R}(C') = \{k_0, k_1^*, \ldots, k_i^*, \ldots, k_\tau^*, k_0\}$ to denote the optimal traveling path. After executing Algorithm 29, we can obtain the traveling path $\mathcal{R}(C^*) = \{k_0, k_1', \ldots, k_i', \ldots, k_\tau', k_0\}$.

We construct an auxiliary detour path containing the optimal path and give the theoretical analysis.

The initial path $\mathcal{R}(C^*)$ obtained by the algorithm includes points $\{k_0, k_1', \ldots, k_i', \ldots, k_\tau', k_0\}$. Each point k_i' is determined through the binary search method within the segment $\overline{k_{i-1}k_{i+1}}$ such that g_i is path-covered.

For each grid g_i, the optimal stop position k_i^* is used to form the optimal path $\mathcal{R}(C')$. The key is to show that the difference between the approximated path and the optimal path is bounded.

Through the path shortening process, each segment $\overline{k_i'k_{i+1}'}$ is adjusted to reduce the overall path length. The adjustments are made such that $|\overline{k_i'k_{i+1}'}| \leq |\overline{k_i^*k_{i+1}^*}| + 2\sqrt{2}\Gamma$. This ensures that the deviation from the optimal path is minimized.

By summing up the deviations for all τ grids, we obtain the total deviation as $2\sqrt{2}\tau\Gamma$. Therefore, the length of the approximated path $|\mathcal{R}(C')|$ is bounded by $|\mathcal{R}(C^*)| + 2\sqrt{2}\tau\Gamma$.

The time complexity of the algorithm is derived from the binary search process used to determine k_i' within each segment $\overline{k_{i-1}k_{i+1}}$. The complexity of each binary search is $O(\log \frac{\Gamma}{\varrho})$, and performing this for τ grids results in an overall complexity of $O(\tau^2 \log \frac{\Gamma}{\varrho})$.

This completes the proof of Lemma 7.1, demonstrating that the path obtained by Algorithm 29 is within a bounded approximation ratio of the optimal path and that the time complexity of the algorithm is polynomial in the number of grids and the granularity parameter ϱ.

As shown in Fig. 7.22, $\{k_0, k_1^*, k_2^*, k_0\}$ is the optimal path, and $\{k_0, k_1', k_2', k_0\}$ is the shortened path by Algorithm 29. Moreover, we construct an auxiliary detour path $\{k_0, k_1^*, k_1', k_1^*, k_2^*, k_2', k_2^*, k_0\}$ by adding $\{k_i^*, k_i', k_i^*\}$ into the optimal path. According to the triangle inequality, we know $|k_0, k_1^*, k_1'| \geq |k_1' k_0|$. Therefore, we have

$$|k_0, k_1^*, k_1', k_1^*, k_2^*, k_2', k_2^*, k_0| \geq |\mathcal{R}(C^{'})|. \tag{7.58}$$

In addition, for the bounded grid, we have

$$|k_i^* k_i' k_i^*| = 2|k_i^* k_i'| \leq 2\sqrt{2}\Gamma.$$

Thus,

$$|k_0, \ldots, k_i^*, k_i', k_i^*, \ldots, k_\tau^*, k_\tau', k_\tau^*, k_0| \leq |\mathcal{R}(C^*)| + 2\sqrt{2}\tau\Gamma. \tag{7.59}$$

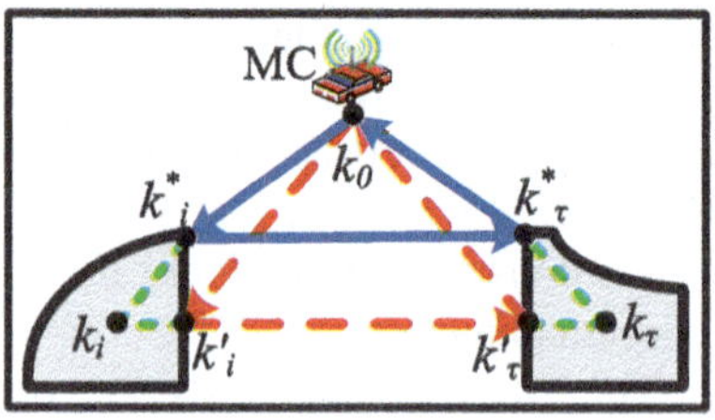

Fig. 7.22 The optimal path and the path obtained by our algorithm

In addition, the existence of obstacles and more fine-grained discretization will not bring in additional errors to the path shorten algorithm. As a result, we obtain $|\mathcal{R}(C')| \leq |\mathcal{R}(C^*)| + 2\sqrt{2}\tau\Gamma$ according to Eqs. (7.58) and (7.59).

Next, we investigate the complexity of path shortening of Algorithm 29, which is composed of the time complexities of iteration and substitution operation. Algorithm 29 executes $O(\tau)$ iterations for constructing the path of τ grids. In each iteration, the binary search consumes $O(\tau log\frac{\Gamma}{\varrho})$ for each substitution operation. Therefore, the time complexity of the algorithm is $O(\tau^2 log\frac{\Gamma}{\varrho})$. □

Theorem 7.6 *Set*

$$\Gamma \leq \frac{\varepsilon \Delta \mathcal{R}(C')}{4\sqrt{2}\tau} \tag{7.60}$$

and regardless of the error in charging model with obstacles, Algorithm 28 has a $\frac{e-1}{4e}(1-\varepsilon)$ *approximation ratio.*

Proof It is initially demonstrated that setting $\varepsilon = \frac{2\varepsilon^*}{1+\varepsilon^*}$ results in the spatial discretization achieving a $1-\frac{\varepsilon}{2}$ approximation ratio relative to the optimum solution. Additionally, Theorem 7.5 confirms that our goal is a problem of maximizing a submodular function with routing constraints. Therefore, per [37], using the greedy approach, Algorithm 28 obtains a $\frac{1}{2}(1-\frac{1}{e})$ approximation ratio given a slightly relaxed budget constraint. Moreover, as stated in [35], the time allocation approach (specifically, the GCPS algorithm [36]) utilized in this study achieves an approximation ratio of $\frac{1}{2}$.

According to Lemma 7.1, we know $|\mathcal{R}(C')| \leq |\mathcal{R}(C^*)| + 2\sqrt{2}\tau\Gamma$. Besides, C' is the result set of our algorithm, and C^* is the optimal solution, thereby we have $|\mathcal{R}(C')| > |\mathcal{R}(C^*)|$. Thus, we can obtain

$$\mathcal{R}(C' \cup \{c'\}) - \mathcal{R}(C') \leq \mathcal{R}(C^* \cup \{c^*\}) - \mathcal{R}(C^*) + 2\sqrt{2}\tau\Gamma,$$

which is reduced to

$$\Delta\mathcal{R}(C') \leq \Delta\mathcal{R}(C^*) + 2\sqrt{2}\tau\Gamma. \tag{7.61}$$

To prove the overall approximation, we calculate

$$\frac{\Delta\mathcal{R}(C^*)}{\Delta\mathcal{R}(C')} \geq \frac{\Delta\mathcal{R}(C') - 2\sqrt{2}\tau\Gamma}{\Delta\mathcal{R}(C')} = 1 - \frac{2\sqrt{2}\tau\Gamma}{\Delta\mathcal{R}(C')}. \tag{7.62}$$

By setting $\Gamma \leq \frac{\varepsilon\Delta\mathcal{R}(C')}{4\sqrt{2}\tau}$, we have

$$\frac{\Delta\mathcal{R}(C^*)}{\Delta\mathcal{R}(C')} \geq (1 - \frac{\varepsilon}{2}). \tag{7.63}$$

Within Eq. (7.60), the variables τ and $\Delta\mathcal{R}(C')$ are determined iteratively. For instance, during the first iteration, where the initial candidate position is chosen, we have $\tau = 1$ and $\Delta\mathcal{R}(C') = \mathcal{R}(\{c\}) - 0$, where $\mathcal{R}(\{c\})$ represents the distance from the base station to the candidate position. Consequently, we obtain the initial Γ and can subsequently determine the final Γ through iterative adjustments based on Eq. (7.60). As a result, the approximation ratio is constrained by $\frac{1}{4}(1-\frac{1}{e})(1-\frac{\varepsilon}{2})^2$.

Consequently, the approximation ratio of the whole algorithm is given below:

$$\frac{1}{4}(1-\frac{1}{e})(1-\frac{\varepsilon}{2})^2 > \frac{1}{4}(1-\frac{1}{e})(1-\varepsilon). \tag{7.64}$$

Therefore, we can conclude that our algorithm has a $\frac{e-1}{4e}(1-\varepsilon)$ approximation ratio. □

7.2.4 *Simulation and Experiments*

7.2.4.1 Experimental Setup

To verify the precision of our spatial discretization technique, we performed an experiment in a practical environment. A sensor node was installed at the location (0, 0), with a nearby obstacle. Following this, we placed the charger sequentially in each grid cell and measured the corresponding charging power, as depicted in Fig. 7.23. The red lines indicate the areas where the charging power remains constant (see Sect. 7.2.2.2). The results corroborate the validity and accuracy of our method, matching the theoretical analysis shown in Fig. 7.21.

In the configuration depicted in Fig. 7.24, a mobile vehicle equipped with the Powercast TX91501 wireless charger (Powercast, http://www.powercastco.com) is used as an MC. The vehicle has a battery capacity of $B = 150$ KJ. The energy consumption per meter for the MC is $\gamma = 100$ J/m. Furthermore, the maximum charging range is set to $D = 2$ meters, and the charger's constant output power is $\sigma = 250$ J/s.

Five rechargeable sensors with light loads, each having a battery capacity of 5 J, are distributed within a 5×5 m office area as shown in Fig. 7.25. Their respective

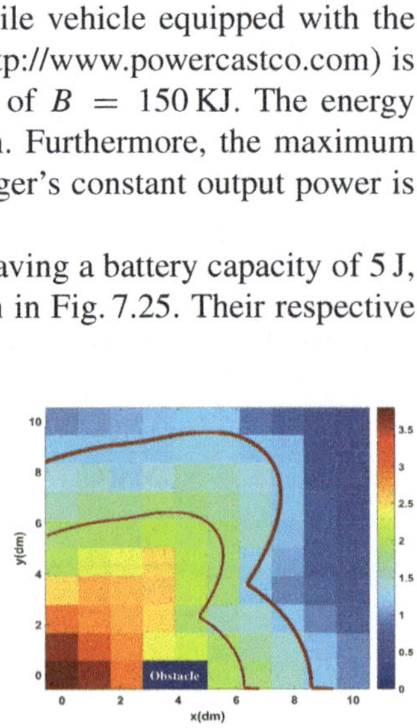

Fig. 7.23 The charging power heatmap in our practical experiment

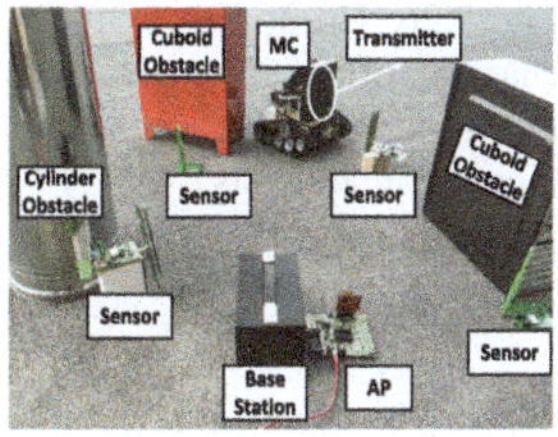

Fig. 7.24 Test-bed scenario

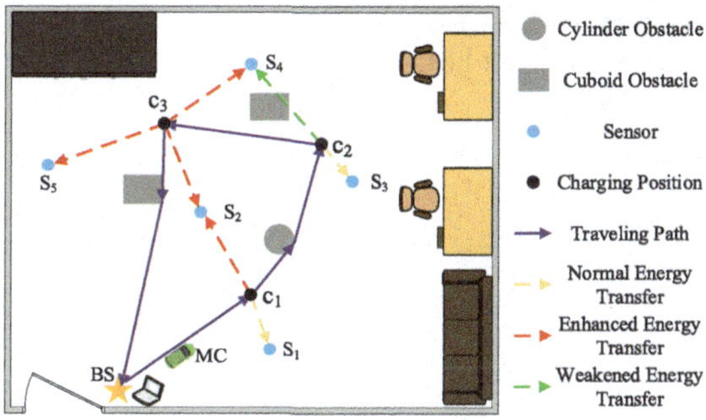

Fig. 7.25 A diagram of experiment scenario

maximum energy thresholds Q_j^{th} are 5, 4.5, 4, 3.5, and 3 KJ. Additionally, a cylindrical obstacle and two cuboid obstacles are present in this space.

7.2.4.2 Baseline Setup

As prior studies have not tackled the challenge of optimizing charging utility amidst obstacles in Wireless Rechargeable Sensor Networks (WRSNs), we present three algorithms for comparative analysis: the Maximum Charging Utility Priority algorithm (MUP), the Obstacles Boundary Partition algorithm (OBP), and the Random algorithm (RAN).

In the MUP algorithm, the spot with the maximum charging utility is selected in each iteration while initially ignoring the routing cost. The path consumption is then evaluated after picking the position [36]. The OBP algorithm functions by splitting the entire area into regions with constant power and regions with no power, based on the obstacles' boundaries [38]. The RAN algorithm selects charging positions randomly that are outside the coverage of obstacles.

7.2.4.3 Experimental Results

Initially, we analyze the theoretical, simulation, and experimental outcomes regarding the energy budget shown in Fig. 7.26. The theoretical outcomes exclude the MC travel time, leading to a difference of $8 \sim 9.5\%$ when compared to the simulation and experimental results. Our simulation and experimental data align well with the

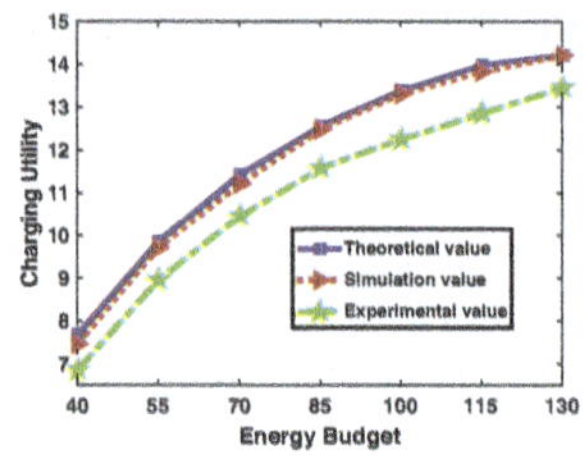

Fig. 7.26 Comparison of charging utility in experiment, simulation, and theoretical analysis

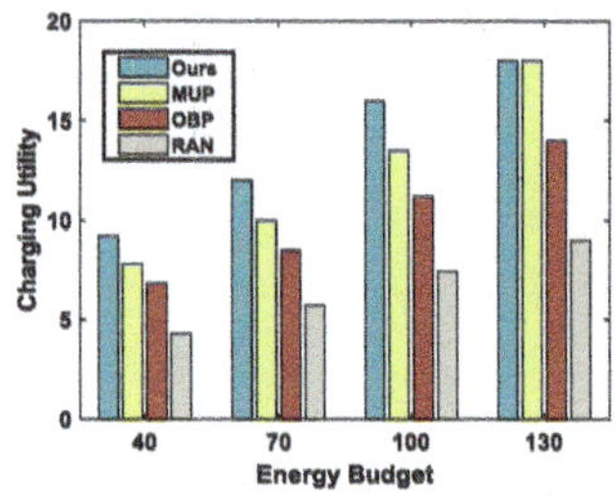

Fig. 7.27 Performance comparison on test-bed experiments

theoretical predictions, confirming the practicality and reliability of our approach in actual applications (Fig. 7.27).

Next, we analyze the overall charging utility of four algorithms as the budget B rises.[3] As shown in Fig. 7.15, our approach achieves the highest utility, surpassing MUP by an average of 11.6%. This is due to MUP consistently opting for the highest charging utility, which may lead to higher travel consumption and lower efficiency. Additionally, OBP does not consider the enhancement effect attributable to obstacles, leading to suboptimal charging positions. As B increases, this effect becomes more pronounced, and the performance disparity between OBP and our approach widens.

Additionally, we present the travel path (i.e., the charging dynamics) derived from Algorithm 1 in Fig. 7.25 with an energy budget of 100 KJ. It becomes clear that by applying Algorithm 1, the MC can use obstacles to boost charging efficiency at points c_1 and c_3 (as depicted by the red arrows showing the improved energy transfer process). Notably, when the MC is located at point c_3, the charging efficiency for S_2, S_4, and S_5 is simultaneously enhanced through obstacles. These experimental outcomes demonstrate that our scheme can efficiently reduce the adverse effects of obstacles on charging efficiency while leveraging them to improve overall efficiency.

[3] In our experiments, the MC's battery capacity (i.e., energy budget) is $B = 130$ KJ. The MC's energy capacity can be set to a value below 130 KJ (i.e., $B = 40 \sim 130$ KJ) by permitting the MC to retain partial energy. We can then determine the charging strategy and corresponding utility using Algorithm 1.

7.3 Wireless Charging under Charging Exclusivity

As a disruptive innovation, wireless power transfer achieves remarkable wireless energy transmission, facilitating dependable power enhancement for wireless rechargeable sensor networks (WRSNs). Previous approaches primarily concentrate on theoretical performance enhancement, overlooking that most Commercial Off-The-Shelf (COTS) rechargeable sensors (e.g., WISP and Powercast) cannot concurrently perform sensing and energy harvesting operations, a condition termed as charging exclusivity. Consequently, their methods are impractical for real-world applications. In this section, we address the issue of charging exclusivity in monitoring stochastic events while optimizing network performance. Specifically, we emphasize the trade-off between charging and sensing tasks and devise a combinatorial optimization problem with routing constraints. We introduce innovative discretization techniques and examine the routing problem to transform the original problem into the maximization of a submodular function. Extensive simulations provide numerical results demonstrating that our algorithm surpasses baseline algorithms by an average of 21.3% in loading utility. Furthermore, we conduct test-bed experiments to validate the practicality of our scheme in real-world scenarios.

7.3.1 *Problem Statement*

7.3.1.1 Model and Problem Statement

The WRSN's network model utilized for stochastic event monitoring is presented in this section. Following this, we provide a comprehensive formulation of the utility optimization problem based on charging exclusivity.

As shown in Fig. 7.28, there are m practical Points of Interest (represented as $O = \{o_1, o_2, \ldots, o_m\}$) within a 2D plane network. Each PoI has a stochastic event arrival rate λ_i, which signifies the event occurrence frequency at that location. We consider n stationary rechargeable sensors (denoted as $S = \{s_1, s_2, \ldots, s_n\}$) randomly deployed throughout the network to monitor these stochastic events at the PoIs. These sensors are equipped with rechargeable batteries of capacity c and utilize the S-MAC [39] and DD [40] protocols. A WCV, having a limited energy budget B, functions as a mobile charger to refill the sensors' energy. The WCV starts from the base station, moves at a constant speed v, halts at several designated sojourn spots (denoted as $X = \{x_1, x_2, \ldots, x_p\}$) to wirelessly charge the nearby sensors, and returns to the base station before exhausting its energy.

7.3.1.2 Event Model and Utility Computation

In this subsection, we introduce our stochastic event framework and the method for calculating event monitoring effectiveness.

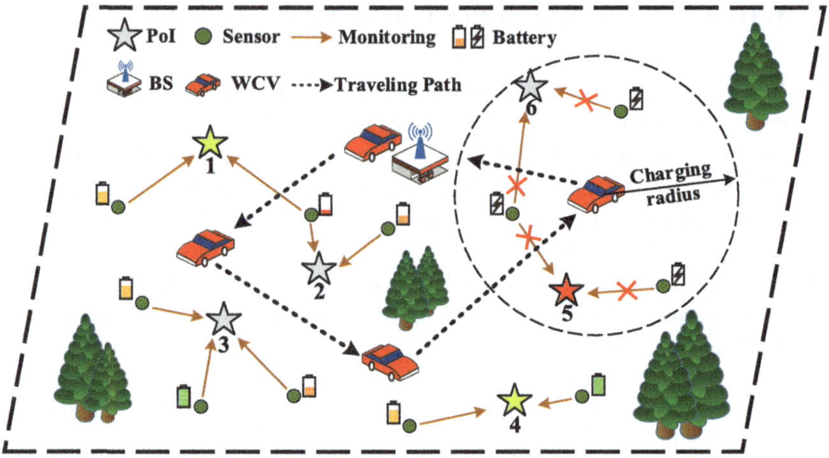

Fig. 7.28 Network status at a certain moment: At PoI 2, 3, and 6, there is no event currently, while stochastic events are occurring at PoI 1, 4, and 5 correspondingly. At PoI 5, the event is missing due to charging exclusivity

In our model, random events at a PoI happen with uniform probability. We presume that events occur independently in both time and space [41, 42]. Based on this assumption, the event generation process at an individual PoI adheres to a Poisson process [43]. Each sensor continuously gathers information from its environment and provides a benefit when an event happens within the sensor's operational area during its lifetime.

The count of events happening at a given point of interest during the time span $[s, s+t]$ adheres to a Poisson distribution.

$$P(N(t) = n) = \frac{(\lambda t)^n e^{-\lambda t}}{n!}, \tag{7.65}$$

where λ denotes the arrival rate, indicating the number of occurrences per unit time.

Furthermore, each event remains for a specific period following its occurrence at a PoI. This period is regarded as a random variable with a probability density function represented by $f(\cdot)$. For instance, if the event duration adheres to an exponential distribution, we have $f(x) = \psi e^{-\psi x}$.

Next, we examine the calculation of monitoring utility for our event surveillance framework. Within the network, sensors independently observe events at Points of Interest (PoIs) with certain probabilities over their operational period. The probability that sensor s_j monitors PoI o_i is represented by P_{ij}. In this investigation, we define P_{ij} as the probability that a data packet produced by sensor s_i while monitoring PoI o_j reaches the base station successfully.

The monitoring probability is expounded upon as follows. When sensor s_i observes or records an event from PoI o_j, it creates a packet and forwards it to

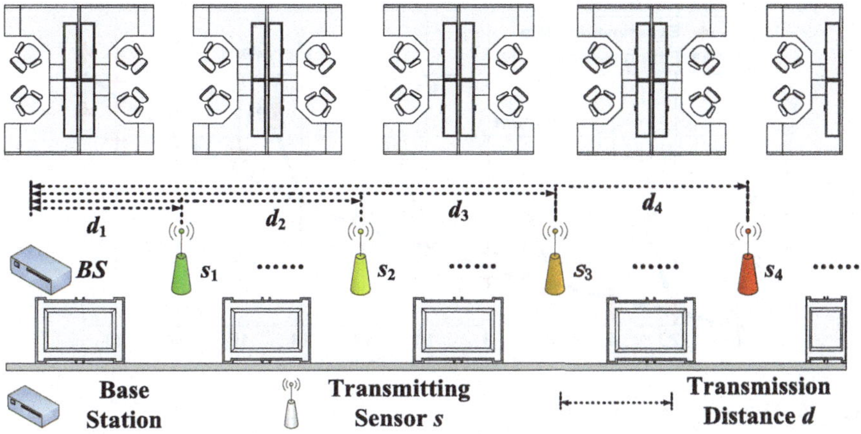

Fig. 7.29 Experiments layout

its subsequent hop node (which could be a relay or the base station) following the network protocol. As a result, the packet usually needs to traverse multiple hops before arriving at the base station. Nevertheless, factors such as transmission range and environmental interferences can degrade packet delivery performance at each hop, causing packet loss. When monitoring data fails to be delivered owing to packet loss during transmission, the monitoring activity of s_i becomes void, leading to a monitoring failure. By evaluating the packet loss rate, we can ascertain the success probability of monitoring.

$$plr(d) = 0.00509d^3 - 0.03071d^2 + 2.253d - 0.4053. \tag{7.66}$$

The issue of packet loss in wireless sensor networks has been widely investigated [44–46]. To determine the relevance of these studies to our research, we carried out practical experiments (refer to the setup in Fig. 7.29). In our experiments, multiple transmitting sensors ($s_1, s_2, s_3, s_4, \ldots$) along with a receiving sensor (or base station) were positioned at varying transmission distances ($d_1, d_2, d_3, d_4, \ldots$) to investigate the correlation between transmission distance (denoted as d) and packet loss rate (denoted as $plr(d)$). The results of these experiments are depicted in Fig. 7.30. The fitting function is described as follows.

$$P_{ij} = \prod_{s_j \in \mathbb{L}(s_i)} \xi(\mathbb{L}, j). \tag{7.67}$$

Furthermore, the charging practices of the WCV can result in a reduced likelihood of monitoring due to charging exclusivity. To underline the critical nature of resolving the charging exclusivity issue, we measured the average charging duration and the rate of event loss throughout a scheduling cycle across several experiments, using the advanced algorithm [47] (refer to Table 7.2). The data reveals

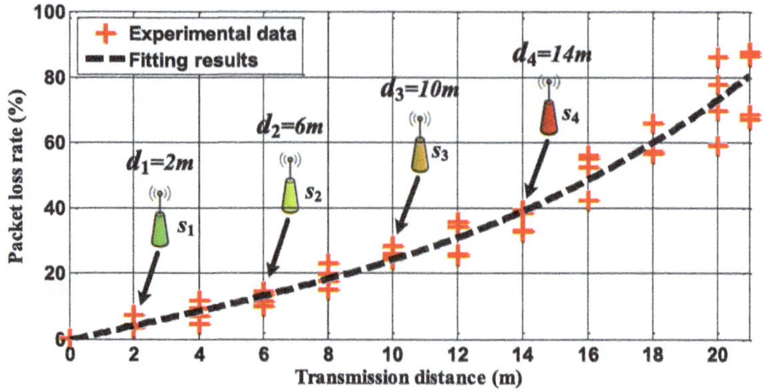

Fig. 7.30 Fitting results of packet loss rate

Table 7.2 Influence of charging exclusivity

Experiment no.	1	2	3	4	5	6
Average charging time (h)	1.80	2.17	2.05	2.13	2.43	1.75
Event loss rate (%)	5.50	6.03	6.43	5.90	6.94	6.52

that the charging duration can extend over several hours, with a longer duration being associated with a higher event loss rate. Nevertheless, crucial events may occur at any time. If the charging exclusivity problem remains unaddressed, these events are likely to be missed during the charging period, which could lead to unforeseen repercussions.

Next, we present the formula for monitoring probability. If a sensor depletes its energy, it ceases to perform sensing activities, and thus the monitoring probability becomes 0. Therefore, we represent the monitoring probability $P_{ij}(t)$ as

$$P_{ij}(t) = \begin{cases} P_{ij}, & working, \\ 0, & exhausted. \end{cases} \tag{7.68}$$

Because of the exclusivity in charging, sensors are unable to execute sensing tasks during their charging period. Hence, the likelihood of monitoring post-charging schedule is

$$P'_{ij}(t) = \begin{cases} P_{ij}, & working, \\ 0, & being\ charged\ or\ exhausted. \end{cases} \tag{7.69}$$

For every PoI, the set of sensors that monitor it is defined as $S_i = \{s_j \mid d(s_j, o_i) \leq D_s\}$, where the sensors are responsible for surveilling PoI o_i. In this context, $d(s_j, o_i)$ denotes the distance between sensor s_j and PoI o_i, while D_s signifies the sensors' detection range.

As sensors operate independently, the likelihood that events at location o_i are detected by the sensors in set S_i is determined by the product of the detection probabilities of the sensors in S_i. Consequently, the probability $P_i(t)$ that events at o_i are detected is indicated as follows:

$$P_i(t) = \prod_{s_j \in S_i} P_{ij}(t)$$

$$P_i(t) = 1 - \prod_{s_j \in S_i} (1 - P_{ij}(t)). \tag{7.70}$$

The likelihood of monitoring is influenced by exclusive charging. Upon the completion of WCV's charging tasks across all dwell points in X, certain nodes in S_i might experience downtime as they are unable to carry out monitoring tasks during charging. Consequently, the probability that S_i monitors o_i is

$$P_i'(X,t) = 1 - \prod_{s_j \in S_i} (1 - P_{ij}'(t)). \tag{7.71}$$

We characterize the lifetime T_i of a point of interest (PoI) o_i as the longest lifetime of any sensor that can observe it. In other words, if every sensor surrounding the PoI is exhausted, the PoI will cease to be monitored, resulting in a missed event. Thus, we get the following:

$$T_i = max\{t_j | s_j \in S_i\}, \tag{7.72}$$

where t_j is the lifetime of sensor s_j.

Be aware that during charging operations, the WCV will fully recharge any sensors located within its coverage area. This enhanced charging capability will, in turn, prolong the operational duration of both the sensors and the Points of Interest (PoIs).

Following [47], in our framework, the monitoring utility of a PoI o_i per unit time is a monotonic concave function of $P_i(t)$, denoted by $u(P_i(t))$. Assume an event begins at time t_s and concludes at t_e. We define $t_b = min\{t_e, T_i\}$ as the point in time when utility ceases to be generated. Thus, its monitoring utility is determined by $\int_{t_s}^{t_b} u(P_i(t))dt$ and the event's duration is $t_e - t_s$, with an associated probability density $f(t_e - t_s)$. Given that the event duration follows the probability function $f(x)$, the expected monitoring utility of an event is $\int_{t_s}^{\infty} \int_{t_s}^{t_b} u(P_i(t))dtf(t_e - t_s)dt_e$. At PoI o_i with an event arrival rate of λ_i, monitoring utility is accumulated for all events within its lifetime T_i. Considering all potential events that occur in $[0, T_i]$, the total monitoring utility of o_i throughout T_i is:

$$U_i = \lambda_i \int_0^{T_i} \int_{t_s}^{\infty} \int_{t_s}^{t_b} u(P_i(t))dtf(t_e - t_s)dt_e dt_s. \tag{7.73}$$

Consequently, after the WCV has finished charging tasks in all sojourn spots in X, the total monitoring utility of o_i is

$$U_i'(X) = \lambda_i \int_0^{T_i'} \int_{t_s}^{\infty} \int_{t_s}^{t_b} u(P_i'(X,t))dtf(t_e - t_s)dt_e dt_s. \tag{7.74}$$

7.3.1.3 Charging Model

We observe that the wireless charging power from the WCV to the sensor diminishes as the distance between them grows [48, 49]. When the power drops below a specific threshold, it becomes unobtainable by the sensors. In particular, the charging model is characterized as

$$e(s_j, x) = \begin{cases} \frac{\varphi}{(\delta + d(s_j,x))^2}, & d(s_j, x) \leq D_c, \\ 0, & d(s_j, x) > D_c. \end{cases} \tag{7.75}$$

In this context, φ and δ are constants determined by hardware and the environment, respectively. The parameter D_c represents the charging radius of the WCV. If the distance between the charger and sensor goes beyond this threshold, the charging power becomes insignificant (essentially zero).

7.3.1.4 Energy Consumption of WCV

The energy cost of the WCV consists of two main components: charging cost and travelling cost. Charging cost is the energy consumed when the WCV charges all the sensors in the vicinity, which can be described as

$$C_k^{(c)} = \beta \cdot \tau_k. \tag{7.76}$$

Here β is the charger's power, and $\tau_k = max_{s_j \in S_k^{(c)}} \frac{c - e_j}{e(s_j, x_k)}$ is the charging time spent at spot x_k, where $S_k^{(c)} = \{s_j | d(s_j, x_k) \leq D_c\}$ and e_j is the residual energy of sensor s_j.

The energy expended by the WCV traveling to chosen destinations is referred to as travel costs, as indicated by

$$C^{(t)}(X) = \alpha \cdot \mathcal{L}(X \cup \{BS\}). \tag{7.77}$$

Here $\mathcal{L}(X \cup \{BS\})$ is the length of the path among base station and spots in X, α is the traveling energy consumption per unit length.

7.3.1.5 Problem Formulation

Let B represent the energy budget of the WCV. During charging and traveling, the overall cost must stay within this budget, hence

$$C^{(t)}(X) + \sum_{x_k \in X} C_k^{(c)} \leq B. \tag{7.78}$$

The issue we address is *determining the optimal set of sojourn spots X for the WCV to charge nearby sensors, ensuring the network's total charging utility is maximized within the budget limitations*. Here, the total charging utility $U(X)$ is described as the aggregate of the charging utility for each PoI. Consequently, we define the Charging Exclusivity-Based Utility Optimization (CEO) problem in this context.

$$\begin{aligned} (\textbf{CEO})\ \max\ & U(X) = \sum_{o_i \in O} (U_i'(X) - U_i) \\ s.t.\ \ & C^{(t)}(X) + \sum_{x_k \in X} C_k^{(c)} \leq B. \end{aligned} \tag{7.79}$$

7.3.2 Schematic Design

7.3.2.1 Area Discretization and Problem Reformulation

To discretize the 2D continuous plane, a straightforward method is to use a piecewise constant function to approximate the charging power (as illustrated in Fig. 7.31a), thereby narrowing down the solution space of the problem.

Our objective is to partition the continuous area into sections. To guarantee the approximation ratio, we first need to establish the number of segments, denoted as Q. We then split the WCV charging range D_c into Q parts with endpoints: $l(0), l(1), \ldots, l(Q)$, arranged in ascending order with $l(0)$ being the closest endpoint and $l(Q)$ being the most distant.

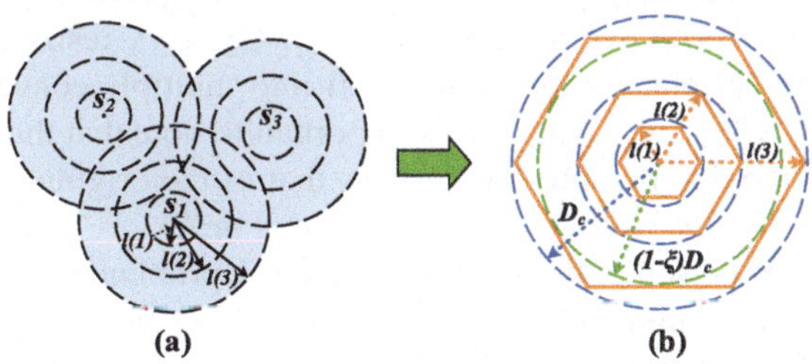

Fig. 7.31 Area discretization: (**a**) Draw concentric circles; (**b**) Replace circles by inscribed regular polygons

To begin with, akin to the approach in [50], we position the sensors at the centers and sketch concentric circles having radii $l(1), \ldots, l(Q)$ around each sensor (refer to Fig. 7.31a). Hence, the estimated charging power of the charger at any spot situated between consecutive circles is assumed to be uniform.

Next, as depicted in Fig. 7.31b, we substitute the concentric circles (blue disks) with a sequence of inscribed regular polygons having σ edges (in this case, $\sigma = 6$) for simplicity, to address the traveling path construction problem (see Sect. 7.3.2.2). In this manner, the 2D plane is partitioned into several polygonal regions. For s_j, these regions are referred to as $H_1^j, H_2^j, \ldots, H_Q^j$. As with the aforementioned concentric circles, the charging power at any location between adjacent polygons is assumed to be consistent.

We establish the subsequent approximation for charging power and constrain the error of this approximation.

Definition 7.3 Letting $l(0) = 0, l(Q) = D_c$, and $l(q) = \delta\frac{\Gamma^q - 1}{\Gamma - 1}((1-\epsilon)^{-1/2} - 1)$, $(q = 1, \ldots, Q-1)$, where $\Gamma = \frac{cos\frac{\pi}{\sigma}}{\sqrt{1-\epsilon}}$, the discrete charging power can be formally expressed by the following piecewise constant function:

$$e_r(s_j, x) = \begin{cases} e(l(1)), & x \in H_1^j, \\ e(l(q)), & x \in H_q^j \backslash H_{q-1}^j \ (q = 1, \ldots, Q), \\ 0, & x \notin H_Q^j. \end{cases} \tag{7.80}$$

Using $e_r(s_j, x)$, the estimated charging power can attain a $(1-\epsilon)$-approximation ratio compared to the true charging power. In this context, ϵ represents a specific error threshold.

It is evident that the $(1-\epsilon)$-approximation ratio is valid for the inner polygon regions $(H_1^j, H_2^j, \ldots, H_{Q-1}^j)$. Regarding the outermost polygon region H_Q^j, when σ is sufficiently large, even though H_Q^j does not entirely cover the charging range (the outermost blue disk in Fig. 7.31b), our method's performance surpasses the scenario in which D_c is slightly decreased to $(1-\xi)D_c$ (the green disk). Here, ξ represents a small positive value.

Without loss of generality, we further subdivide the non-convex polygon regions into smaller convex polygon subregions. For instance, refer to Fig. 7.32a, where non-convex regions A, B, and C are partitioned into convex subregions, i.e., (A_1, A_2), (B_1, B_2, B_3), and (C_1, C_2, C_3), respectively. Following this partition, the 2D plane is finally divided into multiple convex polygon regions, denoted as $Z = \{z_1, z_2, \ldots, z_h\}$. It is important to note that the charging power of each convex subregion remains the same as that of the original region (e.g., the charging power in B_1, B_2, and B_3 is identical to that in B).

By discretizing the area, the CEO problem is converted into choosing subareas from a finite set Z, rather than picking points in a continuous two-dimensional plane, thereby significantly lowering the computational complexity. Consequently,

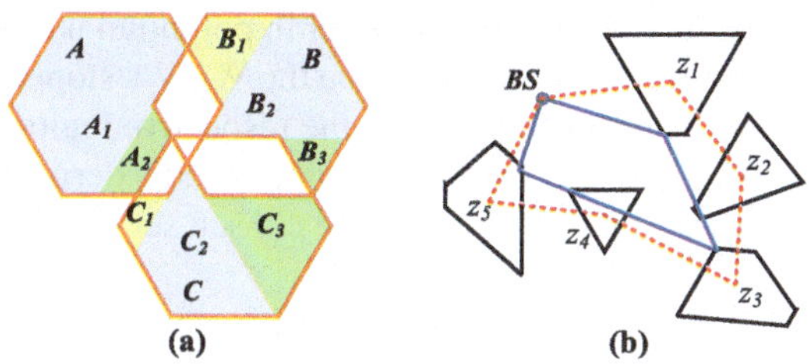

Fig. 7.32 Convex polygon partition: (**a**) Divide areas into convex polygons; (**b**) Touring among disjoint convex polygon areas

our proposed CEO problem can be restated as

$$\textbf{(CEO-R)} \quad \max \; U(Z') = \sum_{o_i \in O} (U_i'(Z') - U_i)$$
$$s.t. \quad C^{(t)}(Z') + \sum_{z_k \in Z'} C_k^{(c)} \leq B. \tag{7.81}$$

Here, Z' is the set of selected subareas.

The CEO-R problem represents a nonlinear combinatorial optimization challenge. It involves maximizing a submodular function subject to general routing constraints and can be approximately addressed by our proposed algorithms.

7.3.2.2 Traveling Path Construction

To tackle the concluding challenge, it is crucial to form the shortest Hamiltonian cycle connecting the chosen locations. This issue resembles the Traveling Salesman Problem (TSP). Nonetheless, post-area discretization, the WCV's travel route has to be planned among selected sojourn areas rather than individual points. To achieve this, we identify the geometric center of each sojourn area (e.g., $z_1, z_2, \ldots, z_5$ as depicted in Fig. 7.32b) to act as surrogate points for these areas. Given that all sojourn areas are segmented into convex polygons following area discretization, the geometric center is located within the subarea itself. Using the identified surrogate points, we employ a nearest neighbor approach [51] to develop an initial route (illustrated by the red dotted line in Fig. 7.32b).

Subsequently, we enhance the initial path by leveraging the characteristics of convex polygons. We map the challenge of constructing the traveling path to the Touring Polygons Problem (TPP) [52, 53]. As illustrated in Fig. 7.32b, our goal is to find a path of the shortest length (represented by the blue path in Fig. 7.32b) that begins at a specific point (i.e., the base station), traverses a sequence of separate convex polygons (i.e., z_1 to z_5), and returns to the starting point.

Assuming that the WCV does not halt at the edges of chosen sojourn regions, these regions can be considered as distinct convex areas with no overlap. We employ the traveling order of the initial path to assist in forming the final travel route. By following the findings in [53], we can identify the optimal route between the selected dwell regions within this order in polynomial time. A point within each dwell region is then randomly picked to be the WCV's stopping point, situated at the intersection of the determined path and the respective region.

The journey cost is determined by the derived travel route. We represent the total expense of the WCV with the chosen set of sojourn areas Z' as:

$$C(Z') = C^{(t)}(Z') + \sum_{z_k \in Z'} C_k^{(c)}. \tag{7.82}$$

7.3.2.3 Approximation Algorithm

Clearly, the two subproblems within our restructured CEO-R challenge, which are the WCV's sojourn area selection problem and the travel path construction problem, are interconnected. Essentially, varying sojourn areas $z_1, z_2, \ldots, z_h$ lead to different travel paths and related travel costs, which in turn affect the selection of sojourn areas. Consequently, these two subproblems should be tackled concurrently.

By discretizing areas in our solution, the CEO-R problem is classified under maximizing a submodular function with general routing constraints. This classification enables us to tackle the problem using an approximation algorithm derived from the method in [54]. Our proposed approximation algorithm addresses the two subproblems concurrently by using a greedy strategy to iteratively choose sojourn areas. During the k-th iteration, a sojourn area z_k is picked and included in the current set to optimize the cost-benefit ratio, i.e.,

$$z_k = \arg\max_{z \in Z \setminus Z'_{k-1}} \frac{U(Z'_{k-1} \cup \{z\}) - U(Z'_{k-1})}{C(Z'_{k-1} \cup \{z\}) - C(Z'_{k-1})}. \tag{7.83}$$

We define $Z'_0 = \varnothing$ as the starting set of sojourn areas and $Z'_k = \{z_1, z_2, \ldots, z_k\}$ as the set chosen in iteration k. The cost $C(Z'_k)$ is computed at each iteration. Whenever a new sojourn area is chosen and added to the current set Z'_{k-1}, a Hamiltonian cycle is generated among the areas, and the corresponding travel cost is evaluated.

The iteration process continues until the energy constraint is exceeded, resulting in the sojourn area set Z'_k, satisfying: $C(Z'_k) \leq B$ and $C(Z'_{k+1}) \geq B$. At the start of the algorithm, we choose a baseline set $\mathcal{Z}$, which contains only the element with the maximum marginal growth. We then compare $U(Z'_k)$ with $U(\mathcal{Z})$ and select the larger one as the result set. The details of the algorithm are outlined in Algorithm 30. This approach addresses all the challenges of the CEO problem, and the performance of our scheme is theoretically verified in the following sections.

Algorithm 30 Approximation Algorithm for CEO-R Problem

Input: The monitoring probability $P_{ij}(t)$ of sensor s_j to PoI o_i, the arrival rate λ_i of PoI o_i, the parameters of charging model φ, δ, energy consumption coefficient α, β, sensors' battery capacity c, residual energy e_j of sensor s_j and energy budget B.
Output: The selected sojourn area set Z', total charging utility $U(Z')$.

Discretize the network plane into subareas by drawing concentric circles with radius $l(1), \ldots, l(Q)$ for each sensor;
Let $Z'_0 \leftarrow \varnothing$, $C(Z') \leftarrow 0$, and $\mathcal{Z} \leftarrow \text{argmax}\{U(z_k)|z_k \in Z, C(Z'_k) \leq B\}$;
while $Z \neq null$ **do**
    for $\forall z \in Z$ **do**
        Compute the charging utility $U(Z'_{k-1} \cup \{z\})$ and $U(Z'_{k-1})$ with corresponding monitoring utility;
        Compute the total cost $C(Z'_{k-1} \cup \{z\})$ and $C(Z'_{k-1})$ with the obtained path among corresponding sojourn areas;
    end for
    $z_k \leftarrow \arg\max_{z \in Z \setminus Z'_{k-1}} \frac{U(Z'_{k-1} \cup \{z\}) - U(Z'_{k-1})}{C(Z'_{k-1} \cup \{z\}) - C(Z'_{k-1})}$;
    if $z_k \leq 0$ **then**
        break;
    end if
    if $C(Z'_k \cup \{z_k\}) \leq B$ **then**
        $Z'_k \leftarrow Z'_k \cup \{z_k\}$;
        $k \leftarrow k + 1$;
    end if
    $Z \leftarrow Z \setminus \{z_k\}$;
end while
$Z' \leftarrow Z'_k$;
if $U(\mathcal{Z}) \geq U(Z')$ **then**
    $Z' \leftarrow \mathcal{Z}$;
end if
Output Z', $U(Z')$;

7.3.3 Theoretical Analysis

In this part, we explain how the act of recharging can improve the monitoring efficiency of Points of Interest (PoIs) by prolonging the sensors' operational lifespan, thus demonstrating the characteristics of the recharging utility function $U(X)$.

When the WCV is engaged in charging activities, it will replenish all sensors within its range to their full capacity. Owing to the charging exclusivity concern, a sensor cannot simultaneously monitor events and gather energy. Consequently, as depicted in Fig. 7.33, the charging activity will result in a temporary suspension of monitoring during the charging period but will prolong the PoI's lifespan and boost the overall monitoring utility. To quantitatively describe the effect of charging exclusivity, we define the charging utility function $U(X)$, which serves as the objective function of the proposed CEO problem. We then investigate the attributes of $U(X)$ that allow us to reformulate the original problem into a submodular function maximization problem with routing constraints.

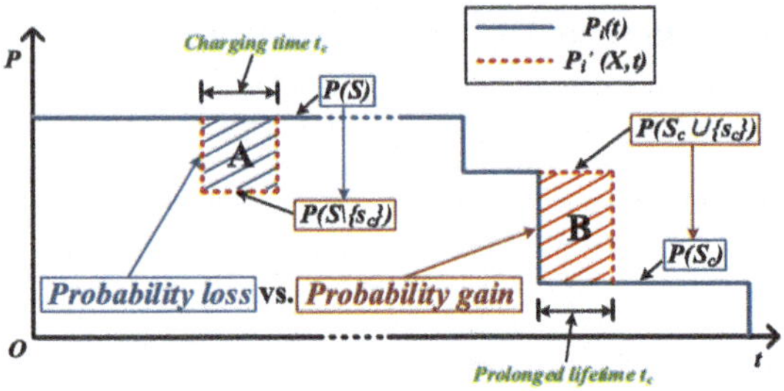

Fig. 7.33 Probability gain and probability loss in different time periods

Definition 7.4 (Nonnegativity, Monotonicity, and Submodularity) Given a finite ground set $\mathcal{V}$, a real-valued set function is defined as $f : 2^{\mathcal{V}} \rightarrow R$, f is called *nonnegative*, *monotone (nondecreasing)*, and *submodular* if and only if it satisfies following conditions, respectively [54].

- $f(\emptyset) = 0$ and $f(A) \geq 0$ for all $A \subseteq \mathcal{V}$ *(nonnegative)*;
- $f(A) \leq f(B)$ for all $A \subseteq B \subseteq \mathcal{V}$ or equivalently: $f(A \cup \{e\}) - f(A) > 0$ for all $A \subseteq \mathcal{V}$ and $e \in \mathcal{V} \backslash A$ *(monotone)*;
- $f(A) + f(B) \geq f(A \cup B) + f(A \cap B)$, for any $A, B \subseteq \mathcal{V}$ or equivalently: $f(A \cup \{e\}) - f(A) \geq f(B \cup \{e\}) - f(B)$, $A \subseteq B \subseteq \mathcal{V}$, $e \in \mathcal{V} \backslash B$ *(submodular)*;

By thoroughly examining the properties of $U(X)$, we derive the following theorem:

Theorem 7.7 *The utility function $U(X)$ related to charging in the CEO problem is nonnegative, monotone, and exhibits submodularity.*

Proof It is evident that $U(\emptyset) = 0$ since no charging implies no charging utility. Given the monotonic nature of $U(X)$, we obtain $U(X) \geq 0$. Hence, the nonnegativity property of $U(X)$ is maintained. □

Given that the overall charging utility of the network is the aggregation of each PoI's utility and that U_i is a constant (refer to Eq. (7.73)), we demonstrate the monotonicity and submodularity of $U_i'(X)$ to account for the total utility $U(X)$.

Without loss of generality, we transform the objective function $U_i'(X)$ into the structure of $h(\mathcal{U}(X))$, where $h(\cdot)$ is a monotone concave function. Subsequently, we demonstrate Theorem 7.2 by showing the nonnegativity, monotonicity, and submodularity of the substitute function $\mathcal{U}(X)$.

In the case of a stochastic event, we treat its duration as a random variable with an expected value given by $E = \int_{t_a}^{\infty} (t_b - t_a) f(t_b - t_a)\, dt_b$, and $U_i'(X)$ can be re-expressed as

$$U_i'(X) \propto \int_0^{T_i'} \int_t^{t+E} u(P_i'(X, x)) dx dt \tag{7.84}$$

$$\propto E \int_0^{T_i'} u(P_i'(X, x)) dx \tag{7.85}$$

$$\propto h(\int_0^{T_i'} P_i'(X, x)dx). \tag{7.86}$$

Given that the arrival rate λ_i is constant for point of interest o_i and the function $u(\cdot)$ is a monotone concave function, we obtain Eq. (7.84). Note that $P_i'(x)$ is a piecewise constant function, hence Eq. (7.85) can be demonstrated. The proof is omitted due to space constraints. From the above derivation, we reach Eq. (7.86), where $\mathcal{U}(X) = \int_0^{T_i'} P_i'(X, x)dx$ and $U_i'(X) = h(\mathcal{U}(X))$.

We demonstrate that the function $\mathcal{U}(X)$ is both monotonic and submodular. For the sake of argument, we assume that all charged nodes possess an equal lifetime since they have the same energy capacity. To keep things straightforward, we focus only on the events occurring within the interval $[0, T_i')$, because E is much shorter than T_i'.

Monotonicity In comparison to the lifespan of a sensor, the charging schedule duration is relatively brief. Thus, we assume that no sensor will deplete its energy during the charging scheduling time frame.

To simplify, we consider that when the WCV charges at the sojourn spot x_k, the charging power is zero, and a sensor s_c is being charged. Under this condition, the charging action is analogous to temporarily turning off the sensor (for a charging duration t_c) and then turning it on again. Essentially, the point in time when the sensor depletes its energy is delayed by t_c, while the overall active period remains the same, as illustrated in Fig. 7.33. The time slot t_c is relocated from the initial charging phase to the end of its operational life, leading to a probability decrease (area A) and a probability increase (area B) during the corresponding intervals.

Let $P(S)$ represent the overall monitoring probability when the sensors in set S are concurrently observing a PoI. Intuitively, $P(S)$ is a submodular function. The probability loss during the charging period can be expressed as $P(S) - P(S \backslash \{s_c\})$ (the height of area A). Once s_c depletes its energy, the remaining active sensors form a subset of $S \backslash \{s_c\}$, referred to as S_c. The probability gain over the extended lifetime t_c is $P(S_c \cup \{s_c\}) - P(S_c)$ (the height of area B). Since S_c is contained within $S \backslash \{s_c\}$, as per Eq. (7.70), it holds that $P(S_c \cup \{s_c\}) - P(S_c) \geq P(S) - P(S \backslash \{s_c\})$ owing to the submodularity of $P(S)$, suggesting that the probability gain surpasses the probability loss. This inequality remains valid when multiple sensors undergo charging. The proof is omitted here due to space constraints. Thus, we conclude the following.

$$\mathcal{U}(X \cup \{x_k\}) - \mathcal{U}(X) \geq 0.$$

Given that the monotonicity property for $\mathcal{U}(X)$ remains valid with zero charging power, it is clear that this property continues to hold when the charging power exceeds zero.

Thus, we demonstrate that $\mathcal{U}(X)$ exhibits monotonicity (Fig. 7.34).

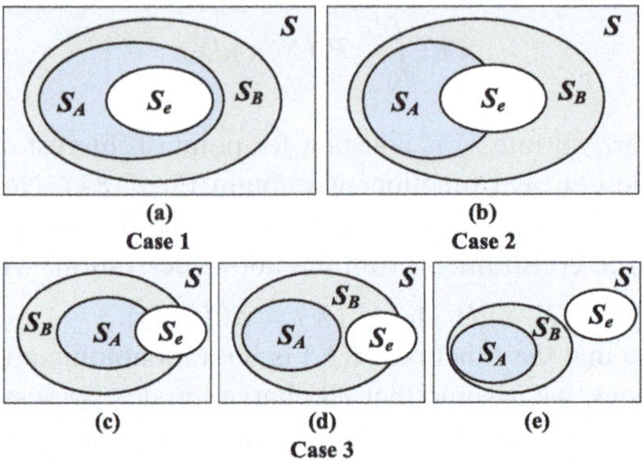

Fig. 7.34 Different relationships of sensor sets S_A, S_B, and S_e in **(Case 1)**, **(Case 2)**, and **(Case 3)**. (**a**) S_B contains S_A, S_A contains S_e. (**b**) S_B contains S_A, S_B contains S_e; S_A and S_e do not have a containment relationship, but there is an intersection. (**c**) S_B contains S_A, S_B and S_e have no containment relationship; S_A and S_e have no containment relationship, but there is a focal intersection of all three sets. (**d**) S_B contains S_A, S_B and S_e have no containment relationship but there is an intersection, and S_A and S_e have no intersection. (**e**) S_B contains S_A, S_B and S_e have no intersection

7.3.4 Simulation and Experiments

7.3.4.1 Simulation Analysis

We conduct thorough simulations to assess the performance of our proposed algorithm from different perspectives. Various baseline algorithms are introduced for comparison.

7.3.4.2 Simulation Setup

Because simulating stochastic events can be challenging and sometimes inconsistent, we incorporate actual statistical data from epilepsy patients as stochastic event inputs in our simulations [55]. In particular, we utilize the frequency and duration of epilepsy patients' pathogenic episodes as the event frequency and duration in our simulations.

In our simulation, we consider 40 Points of Interest (PoIs) that are randomly positioned within a 100×100 m area, with each PoI representing an epilepsy patient. We position 100 rechargeable sensors around these PoIs to detect stochastic events occurring at these locations. A Wireless Charging Vehicle (WCV) moves around the area to recharge the sensors at designated sojourn points. Our goal is to ensure that all stochastic events at the PoIs are detected by the sensors around them and to prevent monitoring failures due to exclusive charging periods. The energy capacities for the sensors and the WCV are $c = 50$ and $B = 10{,}000$, respectively. The parameters are set as follows: $\varphi = 15$, $\delta = 10$, $\alpha = 4$, $\beta = 0.5$, $\sigma = 10$, $D_c = 10$ m, $v = 1.5$ m/s, and $f(x) = e^{-x}$.

In our simulations, we create virtual patients to enhance the practicality of our simulation and stochastic event data. However, we disregard the physical aspects of the scenario (e.g., obstacles and the vertical positioning of devices) and concentrate mainly on the scheduling and effectiveness of charging, considering the exclusivity issue associated with charging.

7.3.4.3 Baseline Setup

We contrast our algorithm (abbreviated as CEO) with four standard algorithms: ME, CCO, CHASE, and CHASE-C. ME (Maximum Energy Algorithm) identifies the dwell areas where the WCV can deliver the maximum energy to adjacent sensors, notwithstanding the incidental utility loss because of charging exclusivity. CCO (Charging Compatibility Optimization) utilizes the same scheduling approach as CEO; however, the distinction is that CCO disregards the charging exclusivity issue (i.e., charging and sensing can occur at the same time) while CEO accounts for it. CHASE [47] is a cutting-edge algorithm, and CHASE-C is its optimal version. In the CHASE algorithm, charging and sensing cannot be done simultaneously (resulting in utility loss), whereas in CHASE-C, we assume that charging and sensing can happen simultaneously.

7.3.4.4 Simulation Results and Analysis

Overall, the numerical data (refer to Figs. 7.35, 7.36, 7.37, 7.38, 7.39, 7.40, 7.41 and 7.42) illustrate through extensive simulations that simultaneous charging and sensing enable CHASE-C and CCO to achieve superior charging utilities compared to the other three algorithms. Conversely, under the condition of charging exclusivity, the outcomes of CHASE and CEO are inferior to those of CHASE-C and CCO. Despite the performance decline due to charging exclusivity, CEO's charging utility outperforms CHASE and ME by an average of 21.3%.

We begin by examining the impact of the event arrival rate λ. As illustrated in Fig. 7.35, when λ rises from 0.5 to 3, the charging utilities of the five algorithms rapidly escalate due to the increased monitoring utility from more frequent events.

Fig. 7.35 Utility vs. λ

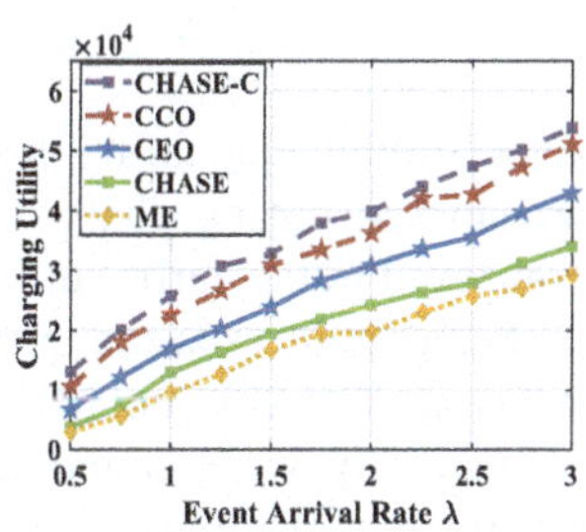

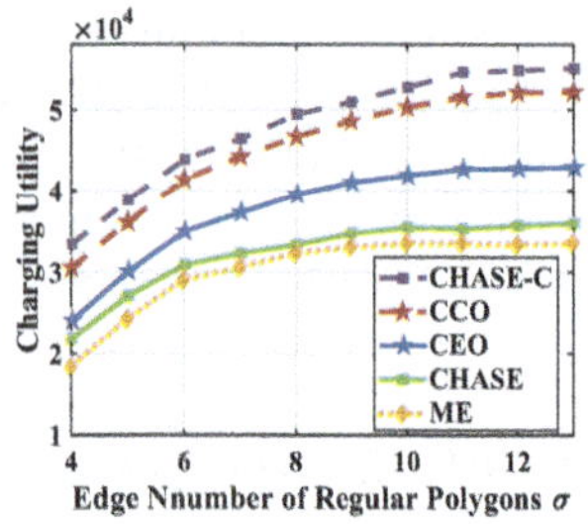

Fig. 7.36 Utility vs. σ

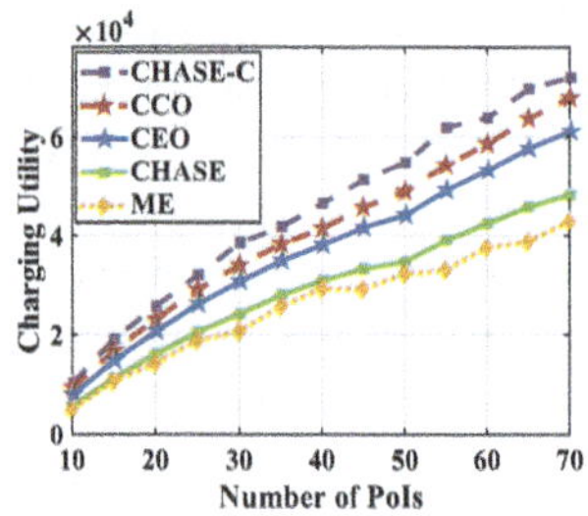

Fig. 7.37 Utility vs. m

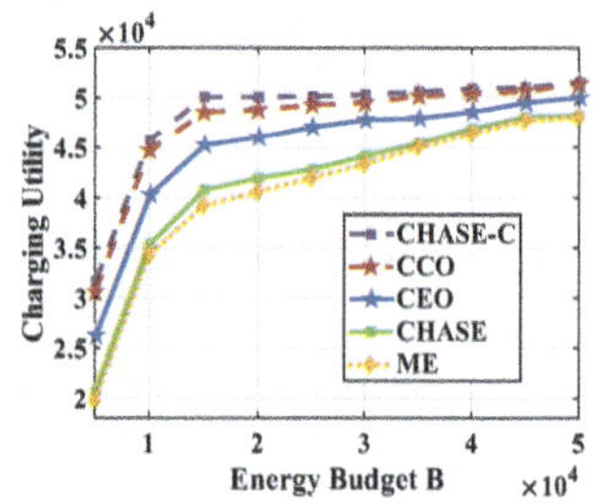

Fig. 7.38 Utility vs. B

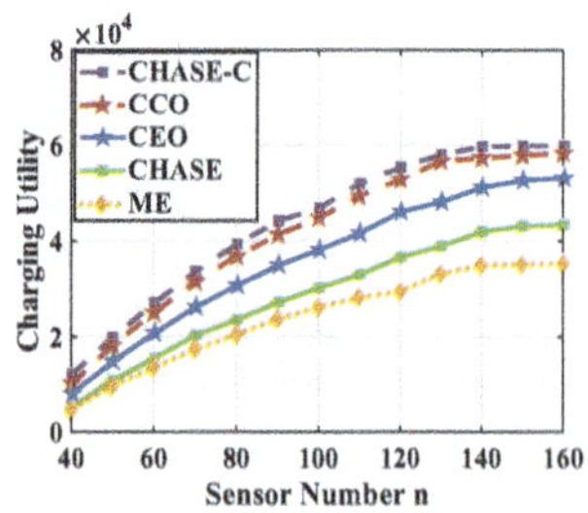

Fig. 7.39 Utility vs. n

Even though the utility loss due to charging exclusivity climbs as more events are missed during charging, the sensors eventually achieve a higher utility gain compared to the earlier utility loss over their prolonged lifespan. This enhancement in the overall charging utility is notable. In this scenario, the CEO algorithm surpasses CHASE and ME by at least 22.9% in charging utility.

Secondly, we examine how the number of edges of regular polygons, denoted as σ, affects performance. Figure 7.36 illustrates that as σ increases from 4 to 13, the

Fig. 7.40 Utility vs. D_c

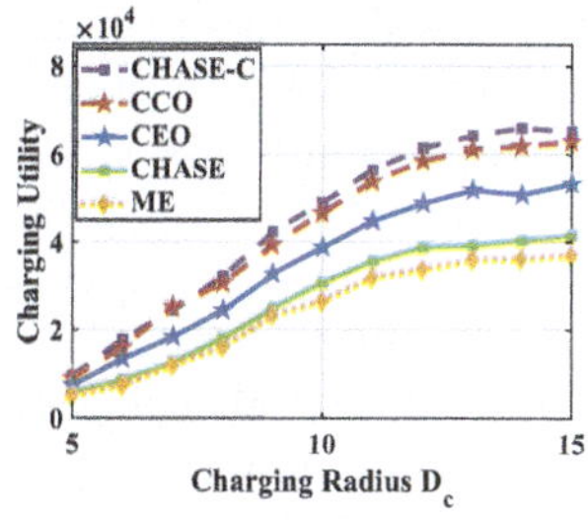

Fig. 7.41 Utility vs. ϵ

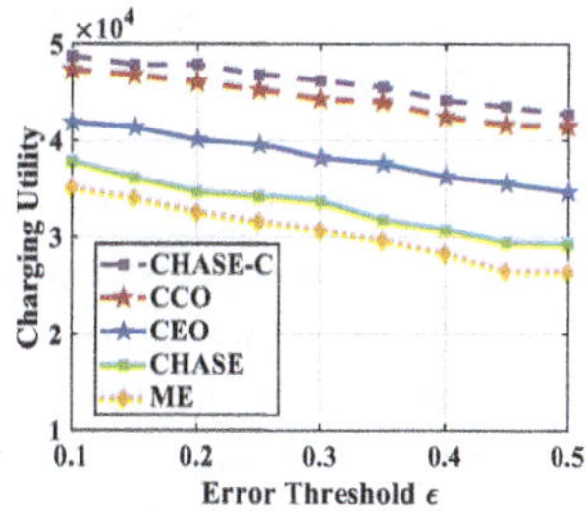

Fig. 7.42 Utility vs. c

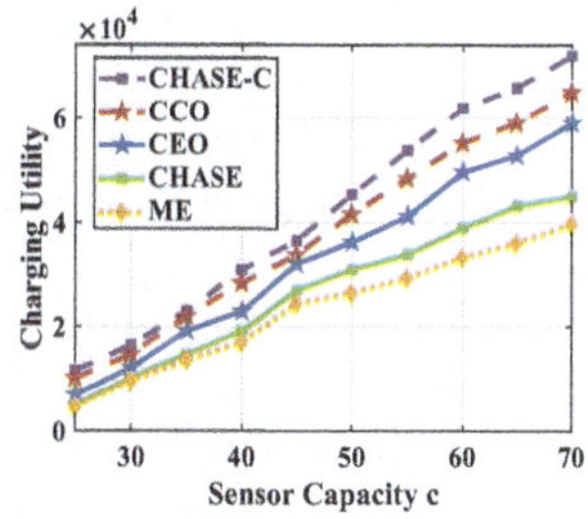

charging performance of the five algorithms initially rises sharply and then levels off. In the discretization of the area, we create concentric regular polygons with σ edges to divide the continuous charge. With a larger σ, the polygon more closely resembles a disc, and the approximate charge model aligns better with the actual model. When the number of edges exceeds 10, the rate of increase diminishes. On average, the CEO algorithm provides a 20.1% higher charging utility compared to CHASE and ME.

Thirdly, we evaluate the effect of varying the number of PoIs m. As illustrated in Fig. 7.37, when m rises from 10 to 70, the charging utilities for the five algorithms increase linearly. Clearly, a greater number of PoIs results in a higher number of events within the network, thus enhancing the monitoring utility. Consequently, this behavior in charging results in higher charging utilities across the five algorithms. However, due to the issue of charging exclusivity, the number of missed events during the charging process may rise, since more PoIs experience reduced monitoring probability, leading to additional monitoring utility loss. Nonetheless, it is important to note that the monitoring utility gained from the extended lifetime of the sensors exceeds the aforementioned utility loss. Our proposed CEO algorithm surpasses CHASE and ME by at least 22.9% in terms of charging utility.

In the fourth place, we explore the effect of the WCV's energy budget B. As demonstrated in Fig. 7.38, when B escalates from 5000 to 50,000, the charging utilities of the five algorithms initially rise quickly and then level off. With a higher energy budget for the WCV, it can choose more sojourn areas and recharge more sensors, thus enhancing the charging utility. Nonetheless, once the budget reaches a threshold, most sensors will be charged, and further budget increments will not yield substantial utility improvements. On average, the CEO algorithm surpasses CHASE and ME by 11.4% in charging utility.

Next, we examine the impact of the number of sensors n. As depicted in Fig. 7.39, an increase in n from 40 to 160 results in a noticeable upward trend in the charging efficiencies of the five algorithms. With a greater sensor density, the WCV is able to charge more sensors simultaneously, leading to higher charging efficiencies. However, once the sensor density reaches a certain level, the monitoring probabilities of the PoIs approach 1, which slows down the growth trend since charging additional sensors does not markedly enhance the monitoring probability or utility. The CEO algorithm surpasses CHASE and ME by a minimum of 21.7% regarding the number of sensors.

We examine the effect of the charging radius D_c. As depicted in Fig. 7.40, as D_c expands from 5 to 15, the charging efficiencies of the five algorithms exhibit nearly linear growth initially because the WCV can charge more sensors within its radius, enhancing the charging efficiency. Nevertheless, the charging power diminishes rapidly with distance. If the charging radius becomes too extensive, charging a distant sensor to full capacity takes a significant amount of time and depletes substantial energy. Thus, the growth trend decelerates when D_c increases beyond a certain threshold. The CEO algorithm surpasses CHASE and ME by a minimum of 24.9% in terms of charging efficiency.

Regarding the impact of the error threshold ϵ, depicted in Fig. 7.41, an increase in ϵ from 0.1 to 0.5 leads to a gradual reduction in load power across the five algorithms. It should be noted that we segment the domain to discretize the charging power. The actual charging amount is approximated to a lower fixed value. As ϵ increases, the discretization becomes less precise, making it more probable for the charging power to be represented by a considerably lower value, hence reducing its utility. On average, the CEO algorithm surpasses CHASE and ME by 20.6% regarding charging utility.

We conclude with an examination of the sensor capacity c. Figure 7.42 illustrates that as c ranges from 25 to 70, the charging utilities of the five algorithms grow swiftly. Sensors with higher capacity have an extended lifespan, leading to greater monitoring utility. Even though a larger capacity can result in a prolonged charging duration, causing an increased utility loss from charging exclusivity, the overall charging utility ascends due to the monotonic nature of the utility function. To summarize, our proposed CEO algorithm surpasses CHASE and ME by a minimum of 16.5%.

References

1. S. He, J. Chen, F. Jiang, D.K. Yau, G. Xing, Y. Sun, Energy provisioning in wireless rechargeable sensor networks. IEEE Trans. Mobile Comput. **12**(10), 1931–1942 (2013)
2. T. Liu, B. Wu, S. Zhang, J. Peng, W. Xu, An effective multi-node charging scheme for wireless rechargeable sensor networks, in *IEEE INFOCOM 2020 - IEEE Conference on Computer Communications* (2020), pp. 2026–2035
3. X. Wang et al., Heterogeneous wireless charger placement with obstacles, in *Proceedings of the 47th International Conference on Parallel Processing* (2018), pp. 16:1–16:10
4. C. Lin, Y. Zhou, H. Dai, J. Deng, G. Wu, MPF: prolonging network lifetime of wireless rechargeable sensor networks by mixing partial charge and full charge, in *IEEE SECON* (2018), pp. 379–387
5. F. Sangare et al., Mobile charging in wireless-powered sensor networks: optimal scheduling and experimental implementation. IEEE Trans. Veh. Technol. **66**(8), 7400–7410 (2017)
6. S. He, J. Chen, F. Jiang, D.K.Y. Yau, G. Xing, Y. Sun, Energy provisioning in wireless rechargeable sensor networks. IEEE Trans. Mobile Comput. **12**(10), 1931–1942 (2013)
7. Y. Shu, H. Yousefi, P. Cheng, J. Chen, Y.J. Gu, T. He, K.G. Shin, Near-optimal velocity control for mobile charging in wireless rechargeable sensor networks. IEEE Trans. Mobile Comput. **15**(7), 1699–1713 (2016)
8. C. Lin, F. Gao, H. Dai, L. Wang, G. Wu, When wireless charging meets fresnel zones: Even obstacles can enhance charging efficiency, in *2019 16th Annual IEEE International Conference on Sensing, Communication, and Networking* (2019), pp. 1–9
9. C. Lin, F. Gao, H. Dai, L. Wang, G. Wu, When wireless charging meets fresnel zones: Even obstacles can enhance charging efficiency, in *2019 16th Annual IEEE International Conference on Sensing, Communication, and Networking* (2019), pp. 1–9
10. F. Depasse, M.A. Paesler, D. Courjon, J.M. Vigoureux, Huygens-fresnel principle in the near field. Opt. Lett. **20**(3), 234–236 (1995)
11. D. Zhang, H. Wang, D. Wu, Toward centimeter-scale human activity sensing with wi-fi signals. Computer **50**(1), 48–57 (2017)
12. H.D. Hristov, *Fresnal Zones in Wireless Links, Zone Plate Lenses and Antennas*, 1st edn. (Artech House, Inc., London, 2000)
13. M. de Berg, O. Cheong, M. van Kreveld, M. Overmars, Computational geometry: algorithms and applications. Math. Gazette **19**(3), 333–334 (2000)
14. C. Lin, F. Gao, H. Dai, L. Wang, G. Wu, When wireless charging meets fresnel zones: even obstacles can enhance charging efficiency, in *IEEE SECON* (2019)
15. M. Gao, T. Cao, T. Tan, Flip to regular triangulation and convex hull. IEEE Trans. Vis. Comput. Graph. **23**(2), 1056–1069 (2017)
16. M.H. Overmars, E. Welzl, New methods for computing visibility graphs, in *Proceedings of the Fourth Annual Symposium on Computational Geometry* (1988), pp. 164–171
17. D. Feillet, P. Dejax, M. Gendreau, Traveling salesman problems with profits. Transp. Sci. **39**(2), 188–205 (2005)
18. L. Babel, Curvature-constrained traveling salesman tours for aerial surveillance in scenarios with obstacles. Eur. J. Oper. Res. **262**(1), 335–346 (2017)
19. K.M. Passino, P.J. Antsaklis, A metric space approach to the specification of the heuristic function for the a* algorithm. IEEE Trans. Syst. Man Cybern. **24**(1), 159–166 (1994)
20. R. Dechter, J. Pearl, Generalized best-first search strategies and the optimality of a*. J. ACM **32**(3), 505–536 (1985)
21. S. Zhang, Z. Qian, J. Wu, F. Kong, S. Lu, Wireless charger placement and power allocation for maximizing charging quality. IEEE Trans. Mobile Comput. **17**(6), 1483–1496 (2018)
22. L. Fu, P. Cheng, Y. Gu, J. Chen, T. He, Optimal charging in wireless rechargeable sensor networks. IEEE Trans. Veh. Technol. **65**(1), 278–291 (2016)

23. C. Lin et al., TSCA: a temporal-spatial real-time charging scheduling algorithm for on-demand architecture in wireless rechargeable sensor networks. IEEE Trans. Mobile Comput. **17**(1), 211–224 (2018)
24. A. Rahman, N. Abu-Ghazaleh, On the expected size of minimum-energy path-preserving topologies for wireless multi-hop networks, in *IEEE INFOCOM 2014 - IEEE Conference on Computer Communications* (2014), pp. 889–897
25. P. Swain, S. Chakraborty, S. Nandi, P. Bhaduri, Performance modeling and analysis of ieee 802.11 ibss psm in different traffic conditions. IEEE Trans. Mobile Comput. **14**(8), 1644–1658 (2015)
26. D. Feillet, P. Dejax, M. Gendreau, Traveling salesman problems with profits. Transp. Sci. **39**(2), 188–205 (2005)
27. F. Depasse, M.A. Paesler, D. Courjon, J.M. Vigoureux, Huygens–Fresnel principle in the near field. Opt. Lett. **20**(3), 234–236 (1995)
28. H.D. Hristov, *Fresnal Zones in Wireless Links, Zone Plate Lenses and Antennas* (Artech House, Inc., London, 2000)
29. A.F. Molisch, *Wireless Communications*, vol. 34 (John Wiley & Sons, New York, 2012)
30. H. Wang, D. Zhang, J. Ma, Y. Wang, Y. Wang, D. Wu, T. Gu, B. Xie, Human respiration detection with commodity wifi devices: do user location and body orientation matter? in *ACM UbiComp* (2016), pp. 25–36
31. F. Zhang, K. Niu, J. Xiong, B. Jin, T. Gu, Y. Jiang, D. Zhang, Towards a diffraction-based sensing approach on human activity recognition. ACM IMWUT **3**(1), 33:1–33:25 (2019)
32. T.S. Rappaport, *Wireless Communications: Principles and Practice* (Prentice Hall, Hoboken, 1996)
33. F. Zhang, D. Zhang, J. Xiong, H. Wang, K. Niu, B. Jin, Y. Wang, From fresnel diffraction model to fine-grained human respiration sensing with commodity wi-fi devices. ACM IMWUT **2**(1), 53:1–53:23 (2018)
34. D. Zhang, H. Wang, D. Wu, Toward centimeter-scale human activity sensing with wi-fi signals. IEEE Comput. **50**(1), 48–57 (2017)
35. T. Wu, P. Yang, H. Dai, W. Xu, M. Xu, Charging oriented sensor placement and flexible scheduling in rechargeable wsns, in *IEEE INFOCOM* (2019), pp. 73–81
36. C. Lin, F. Gao, H. Dai, L. Wang, G. Wu, When wireless charging meets fresnel zones: even obstacles can enhance charging efficiency, in *IEEE SECON* (2019)
37. T. Wu, P. Yang, H. Dai, W. Xu, M. Xu, Collaborated tasks-driven mobile charging and scheduling: A near optimal result, in *IEEE INFOCOM* (2019), pp. 1810–1818
38. X. Wang, H. Dai, W. Wang, J. Zheng, N. Yu, G. Chen, W. Dou, X. Wu, Practical heterogeneous wireless charger placement with obstacles. IEEE Trans. Mobile Comput. **19**(8), 1910–1927 (2020)
39. W. Ye, J.S. Heidemann, D. Estrin, An energy-efficient MAC protocol for wireless sensor networks, in *IEEE INFOCOM* (2002), pp. 1567–1576
40. C. Intanagonwiwat, R. Govindan, D. Estrin, Directed diffusion: a scalable and robust communication paradigm for sensor networks, in *ACM MOBICOM* (2000), pp. 56–67
41. D.K.Y. Yau, N.K. Yip, C.Y.T. Ma, N.S.V. Rao, M. Shankar, Quality of monitoring of stochastic events by periodic and proportional-share scheduling of sensor coverage. ACM Trans. Sensor Netw. **7**(2), 1–49 (2010)
42. S. He, J. Chen, D.K.Y. Yau, H. Shao, Y. Sun, Energy-efficient capture of stochastic events by global- and local-periodic network coverage, in *ACM MobiHoc* (2009), pp. 155–164
43. V. Rai, R.N. Mahapatra, Lifetime modeling of a sensor network, in *DATE* (2005), pp. 202–203
44. J. Zhao, R. Govindan, Understanding packet delivery performance in dense wireless sensor networks, in *ACM SenSys* (2003), pp. 1–13
45. K. Srinivasan, P. Dutta, A. Tavakoli, P. Levis, Understanding the causes of packet delivery success and failure in dense wireless sensor networks, in *ACM SenSys* (2006), pp. 419–420
46. W. Dong, Y. Liu, Y. He, T. Zhu, C. Chen, Measurement and analysis on the packet delivery performance in a large-scale sensor network. IEEE/ACM Trans. Netw. **22**(6), 1952–1963 (2014)

47. H. Dai, Q. Ma, X. Wu, G. Chen, D.K.Y. Yau, S. Tang, X. Li, C. Tian, CHASE: charging and scheduling scheme for stochastic event capture in wireless rechargeable sensor networks. IEEE Trans. Mobile Comput. **19**(1), 44–59 (2020)
48. H. Dai, Y. Zhao, G. Chen, W. Dou, C. Tian, X. Wu, T. He, Robustly safe charging for wireless power transfer, in *IEEE INFOCOM* (2018), pp. 378–386
49. C. Lin, Y. Zhou, F. Ma, J. Deng, L. Wang, G. Wu, Minimizing charging delay for directional charging in wireless rechargeable sensor networks, in *IEEE INFOCOM* (2019), pp. 1819–1827
50. X. Wang, H. Dai, H. Huang, Y. Liu, G. Chen, W. Dou, Robust scheduling for wireless charger networks, in *IEEE INFOCOM* (2019), pp. 2323–2331
51. D.J. Rosenkrantz, R.E. Stearns, P.M. Lewis II, An analysis of several heuristics for the traveling salesman problem. SIAM J. Comput. **6**(3), 563–581 (1977)
52. A. Ahadi, A. Mozafari, A. Zarei, Touring a sequence of disjoint polygons: complexity and extension. Theor. Comput. Sci. **556**, 45–54 (2014)
53. X. Tan, B. Jiang, Efficient algorithms for touring a sequence of convex polygons and related problems, in *TAMC* (2017), pp. 614–627
54. C. Lin, F. Gao, H. Dai, L. Wang, G. Wu, When wireless charging meets fresnel zones: Even obstacles can enhance charging efficiency, in *IEEE SECON* (2019)
55. M. Ihle, H. Feldwisch-Drentrup, C.A. Teixeira, A. Witon, B. Schelter, J. Timmer, A. Schulze-Bonhage, "EPILEPSIAE – A European epilepsy database. Comput. Methods Programs Biomed. **106**(3), 127–138 (2012)

SPRINGER NATURE

GPSR Compliance

The European Union's (EU) General Product Safety Regulation (GPSR) is a set of rules that requires consumer products to be safe and our obligations to ensure this.

If you have any concerns about our products, you can contact us on ProductSafety@springernature.com

In case Publisher is established outside the EU, the EU authorized representative is:

Springer Nature Customer Service Center GmbH
Europaplatz 3
69115 Heidelberg, Germany

The manufacturer's authorised representative in the EU is Springer Nature Customer Service Centre GmbH, Europaplatz 3, 69115 Heidelberg, Germany. If you have any concerns regarding our products, please contact ProductSafety@springernature.com

Printed and bound by CPI Group (UK) Ltd, Croydon, CR0 4YY

30/09/2026

02225297-0016